KAZUKI TAKAHASHI

ZEXAL has a lot of female characters, and the way Mr. Miyoshi draws them is especially cute and awesome!

SHIN YOSHIDA

The manga is different from the anime, and thinking up all the duels by myself makes my head explode. But as long as everyone is having fun, I'm gonna jet!

NAOHITO MIYOSHI

Luna and Yagumo are original manga characters! What? They kinda look like someone? Hah hah hah...Yeah, maybe so.

Volume 4
SHONEN JUMP Manga Edition

Original Concept by **KAZUKI TAKAHASHI**
Production Support: **STUDIO DICE**
Story by **SHIN YOSHIDA**
Art by **NAOHITO MIYOSHI**

Translation & English Adaptation **TAYLOR ENGEL AND IAN REID, HC LANGUAGE SOLUTIONS**
Touch-up Art & Lettering **JOHN HUNT**
Designer **STACIE YAMAKI**
Editor **MIKE MONTESA**

Published by VIZ Media, LLC
P.O. Box 77010
San Francisco, CA 94107

10 9 8 7 6 5 4 3 2 1
First printing, January 2014

www.viz.com

PARENTAL ADVISORY
YU-GI-OH! ZEXAL is rated T for Teen
and is recommended for ages 13 and up.
This volume contains fantasy violence.
ratings.viz.com

www.shonenjump.com

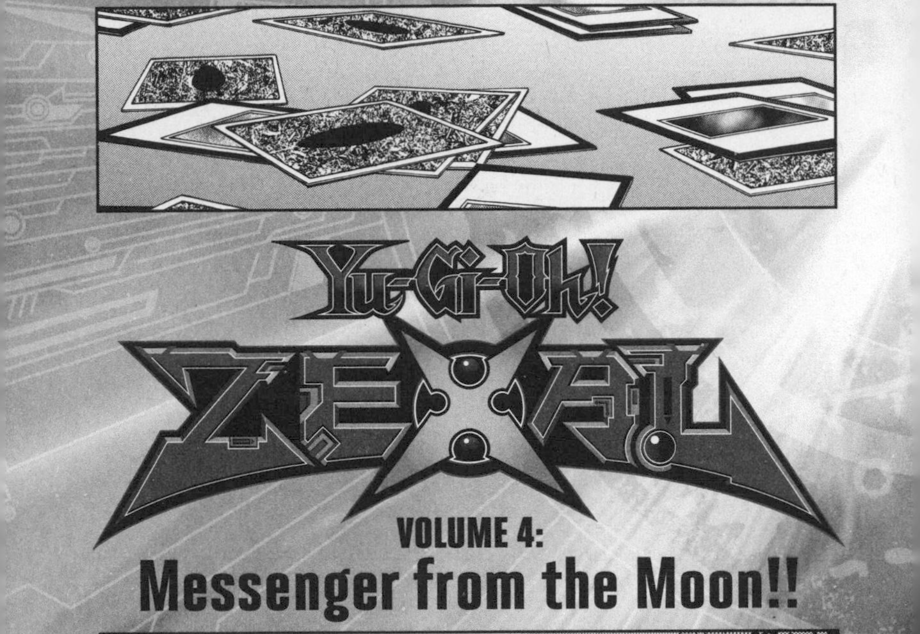

Yu-Gi-Oh! ZEXAL

VOLUME 4:
Messenger from the Moon!!

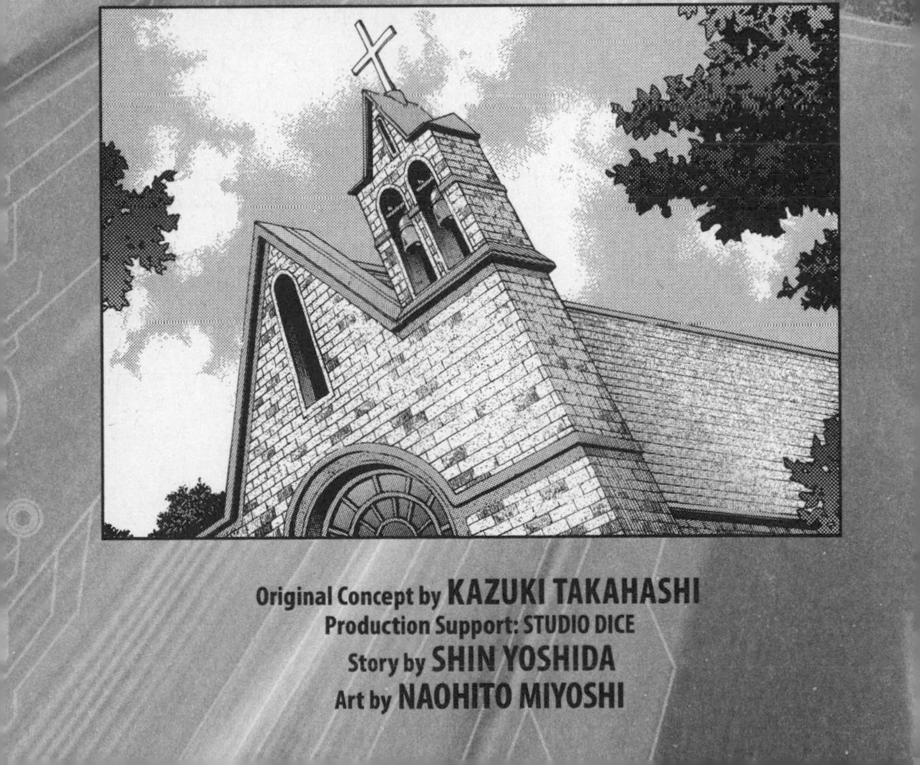

Original Concept by **KAZUKI TAKAHASHI**

Production Support: **STUDIO DICE**

Story by **SHIN YOSHIDA**

Art by **NAOHITO MIYOSHI**

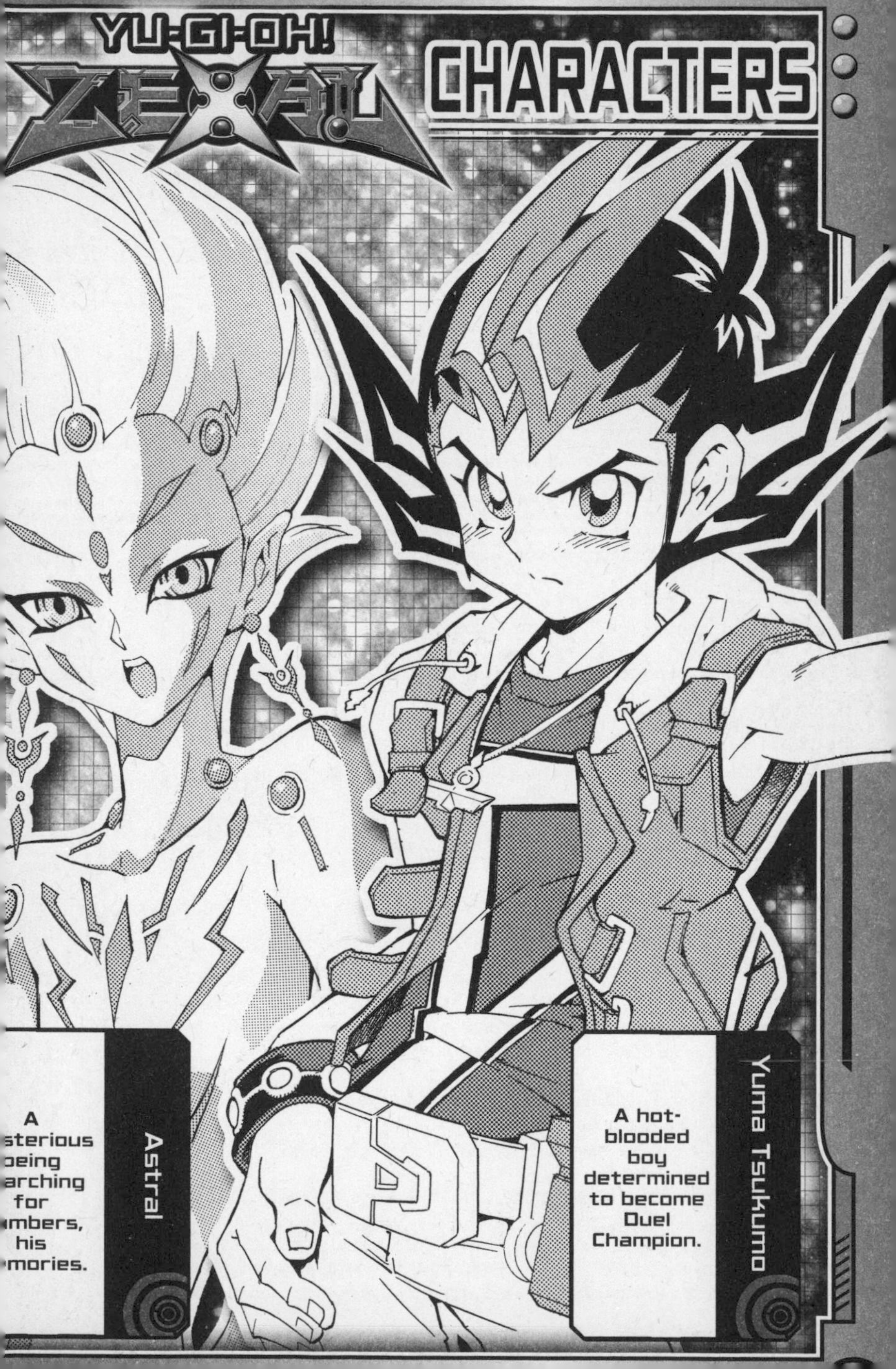
YU-GI-OH! ZEXAL
CHARACTERS
Yuma Tsukumo
A hot-blooded boy determined to become Duel Champion.
Astral
A
sterious
eing
arching
for
mbers,
his
mories.

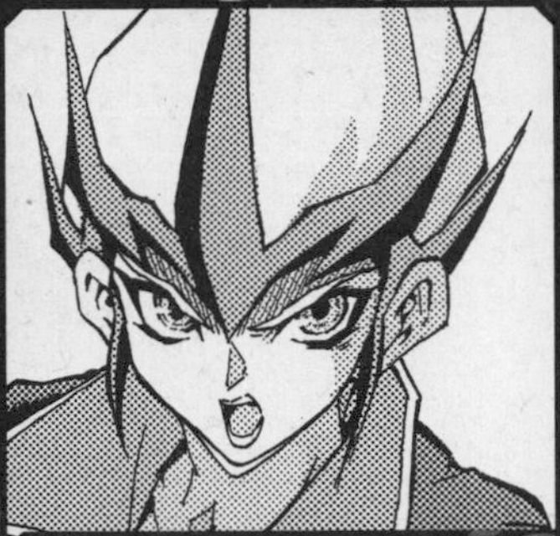

Kaito

A Numbers Hunter who is searching for Numbers to save his little brother.

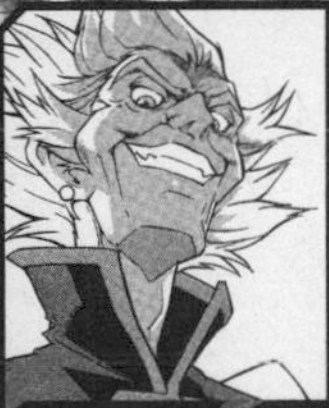

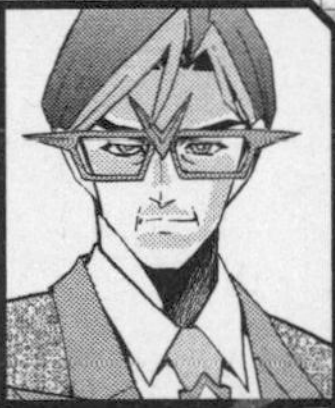

Mr. Heartland | Dr. Faker

These two villains are collecting Numbers to destroy the Astral world.

The Numbers Club

A team Yuma's friends have formed to help him find the Numbers.

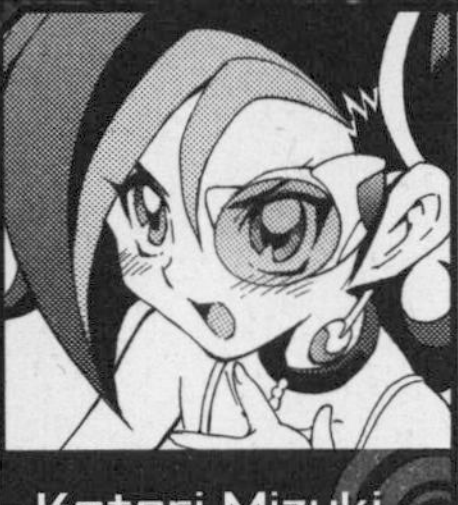

Kotori Mizuki

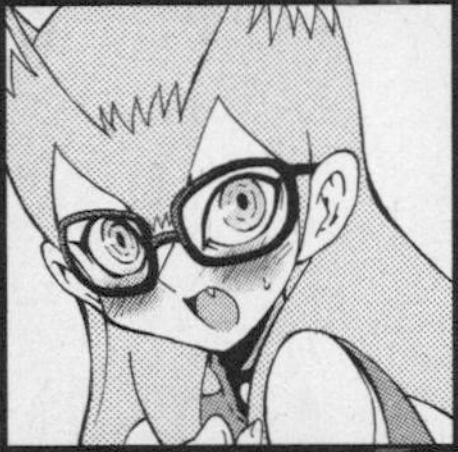

Cathy

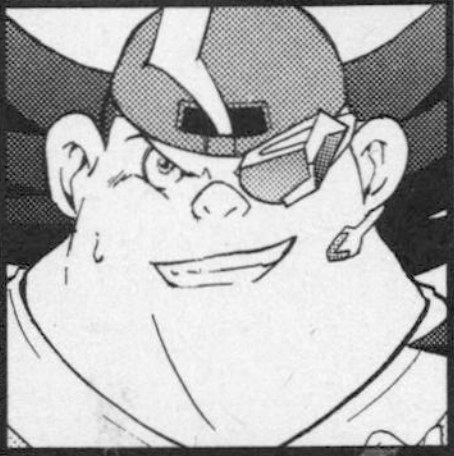

Tetsuo Takeda

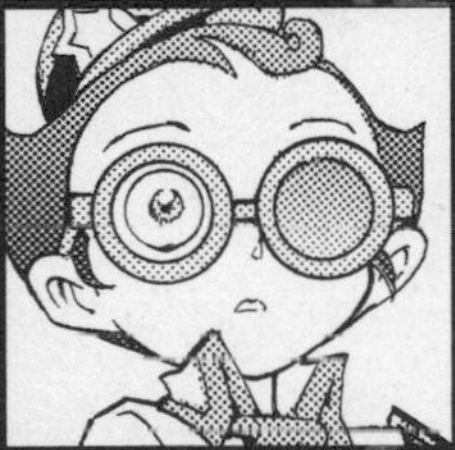

Tokunosuke Hyouri

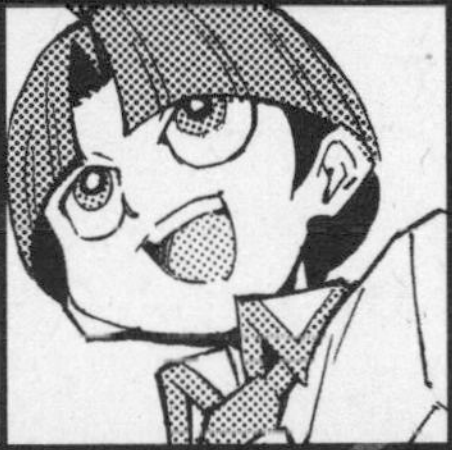

Takashi Todoroki

Previously...

Yuma tackles every challenge that comes his way, and he doesn't give up. Although his skills are suspect, he's crazy about dueling!

One day, Yuma's rival Tetsuo has his deck stolen by Shark, the school's biggest delinquent and duelist, and Yuma ends up dueling Shark. During the duel, the charm Yuma's parents gave him opens a mysterious door, and a strange being called Astral appears!!

Astral is a genius duelist, but only Yuma can see him. Astral's lost memories have become special cards called "Numbers." That begins Yuma and Astral's strange career together.

In order to gather more Numbers, Yuma and his friends infiltrate Heartland and learn that their enemies are bent on destroying the Astral World. To thwart their ambitions, Yuma and the others duel the assassins sent by the enemy and beat them! After defeating the Numbers users, they escape from the amusement park, but then...!!

VOLUME 4
Messenger from the Moon!!

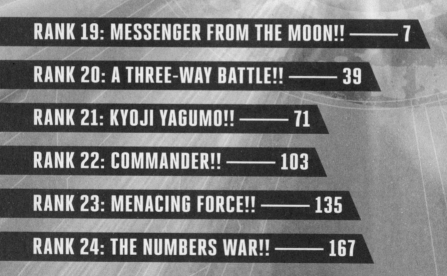

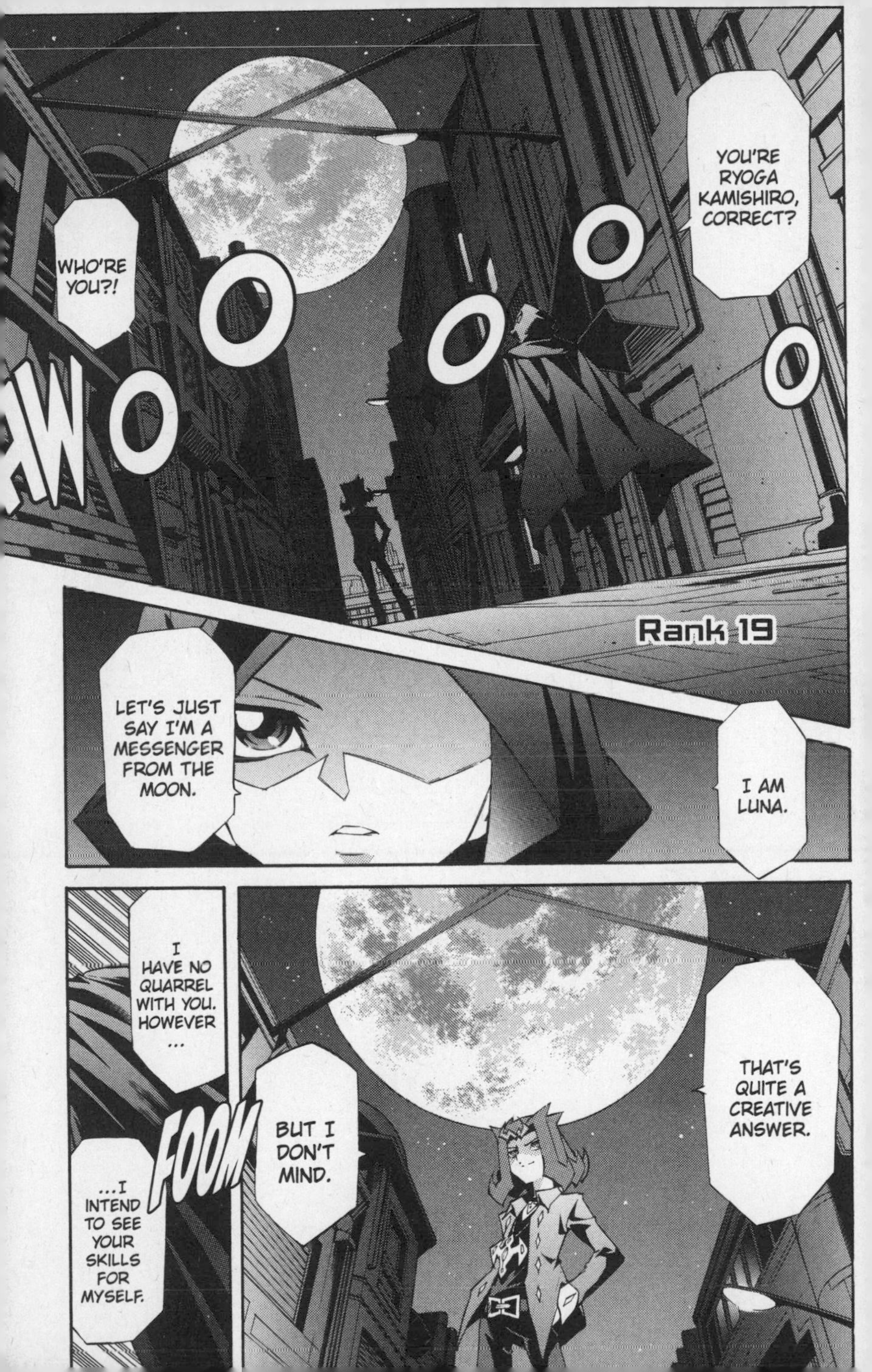
YOU'RE RYOGA KAMISHIRO, CORRECT?
WHO'RE YOU?!
Rank 19
I AM LUNA.
LET'S JUST SAY I'M A MESSENGER FROM THE MOON.
THAT'S QUITE A CREATIVE ANSWER.
BUT I DON'T MIND.
I HAVE NO QUARREL WITH YOU. HOWEVER ...
FOOM
...I INTEND TO SEE YOUR SKILLS FOR MYSELF.

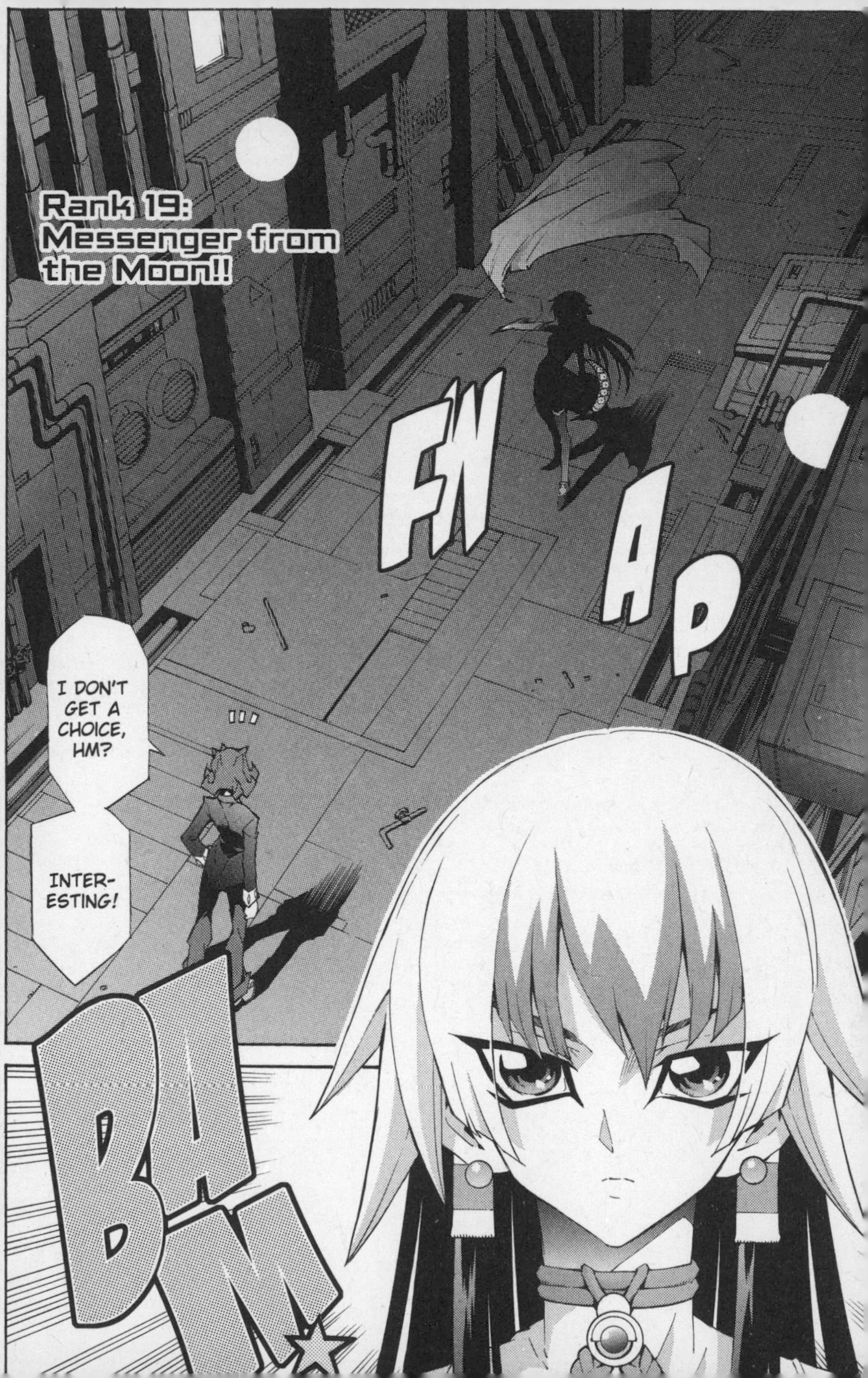
Rank 19:
Messenger from the Moon!!
FWAP
I DON'T GET A CHOICE, HM?
INTER-ESTING!
BAM

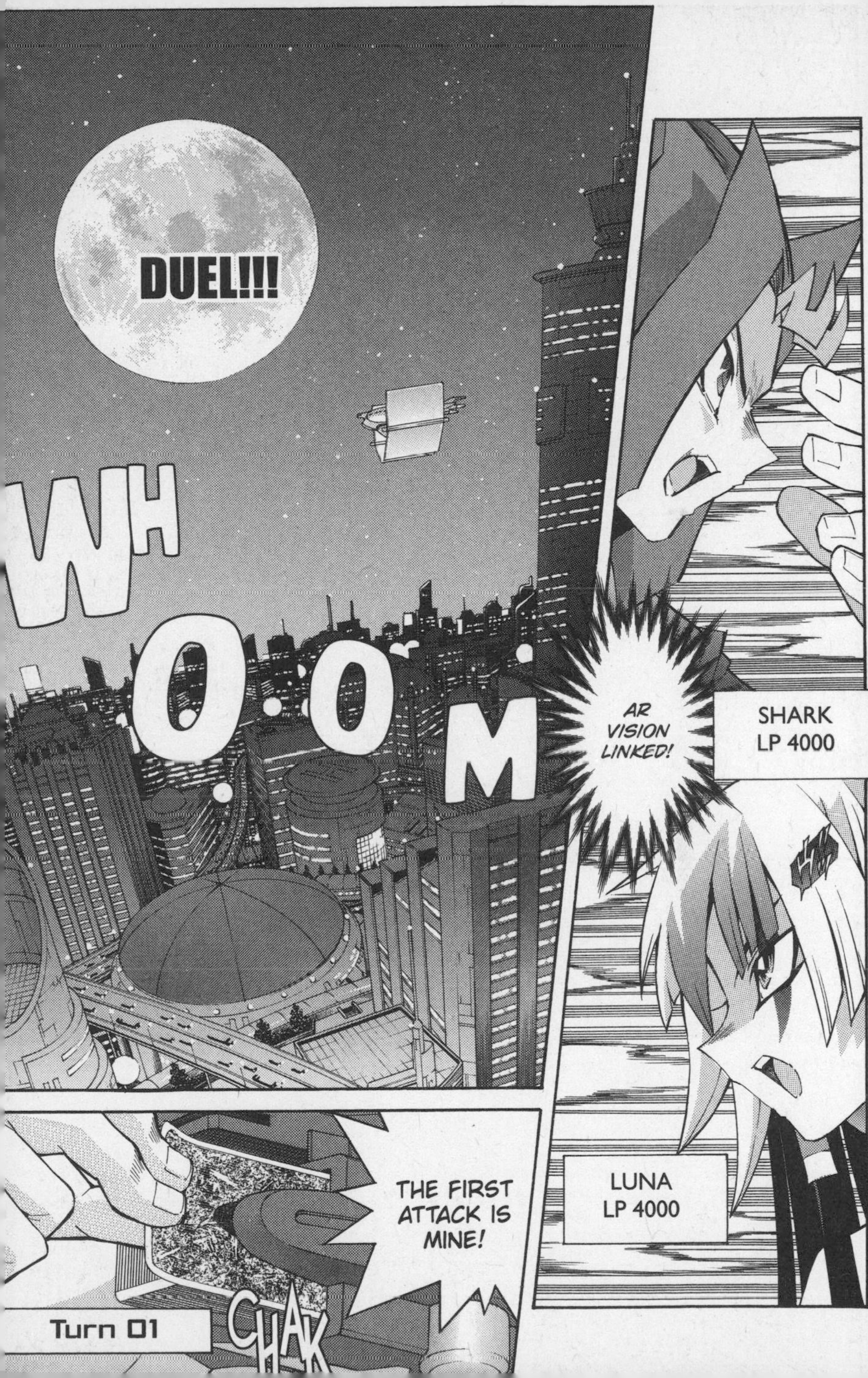
AR VISION LINKED!
SHARK LP 4000
LUNA LP 4000
DUEL!!!
WHOOM
THE FIRST ATTACK IS MINE!
Turn 01
CHAK

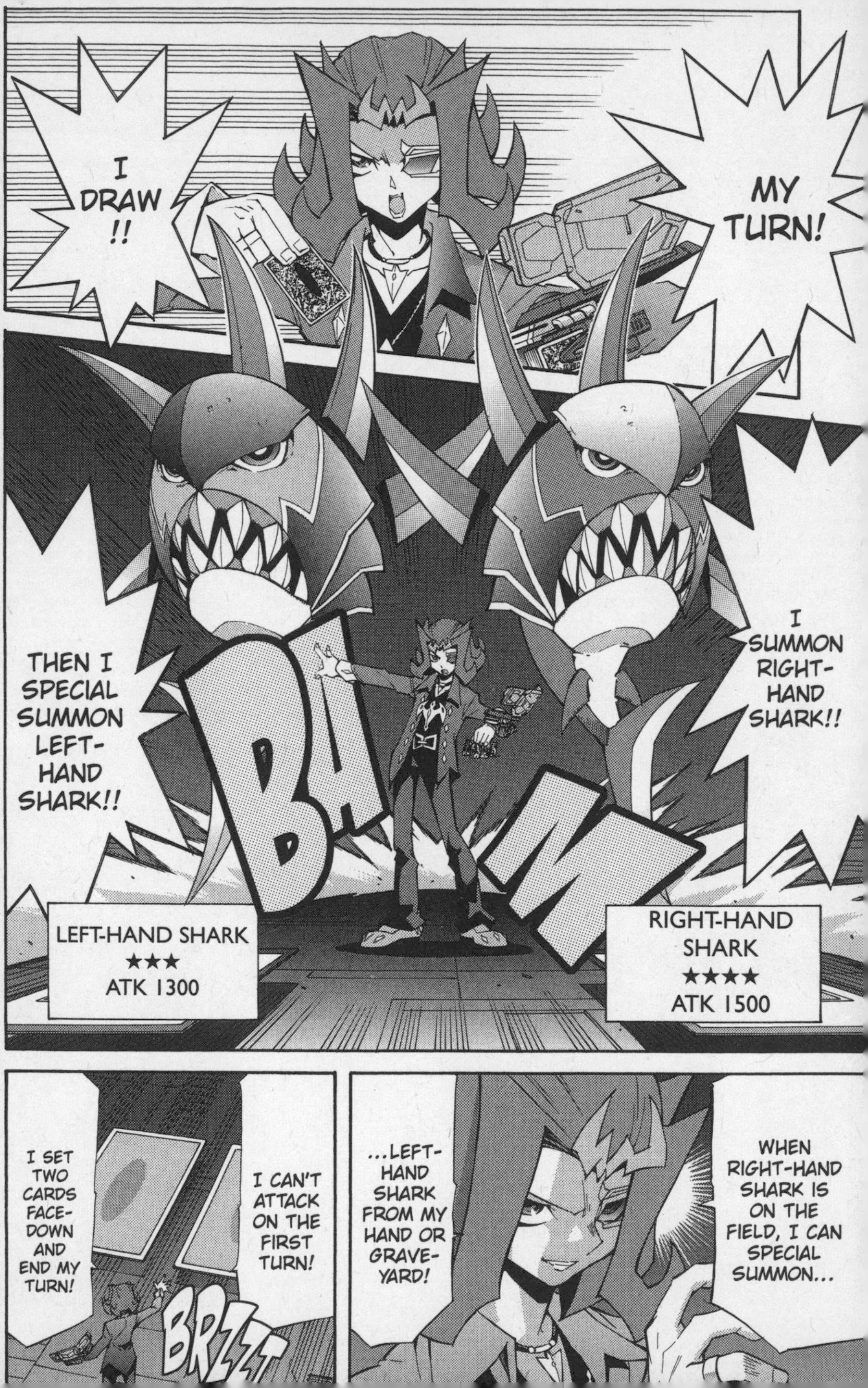
MY TURN!
I DRAW!!
I SUMMON RIGHT-HAND SHARK!!
THEN I SPECIAL SUMMON LEFT-HAND SHARK!!
BAM
RIGHT-HAND SHARK ★★★★ ATK 1500
LEFT-HAND SHARK ★★★ ATK 1300
WHEN RIGHT-HAND SHARK IS ON THE FIELD, I CAN SPECIAL SUMMON...
...LEFT-HAND SHARK FROM MY HAND OR GRAVEYARD!
I CAN'T ATTACK ON THE FIRST TURN!
I SET TWO CARDS FACE-DOWN AND END MY TURN!
BRZZT

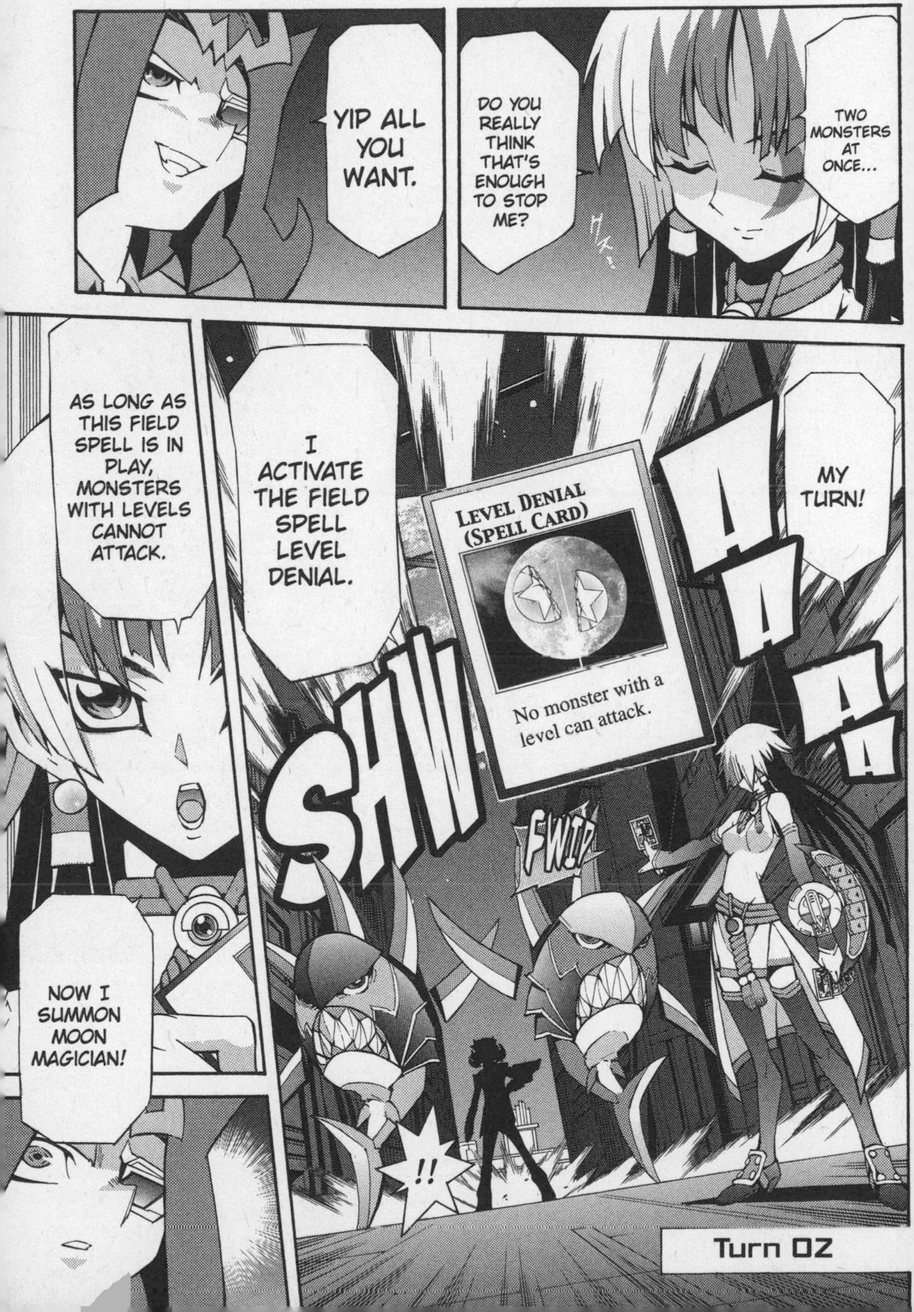
TWO MONSTERS AT ONCE...
DO YOU REALLY THINK THAT'S ENOUGH TO STOP ME?
YIP ALL YOU WANT.
MY TURN!
AAAA
LEVEL DENIAL (SPELL CARD)
No monster with a level can attack.
SHW
FWIP
!!
I ACTIVATE THE FIELD SPELL LEVEL DENIAL.
AS LONG AS THIS FIELD SPELL IS IN PLAY, MONSTERS WITH LEVELS CANNOT ATTACK.
NOW I SUMMON MOON MAGICIAN!
Turn 02

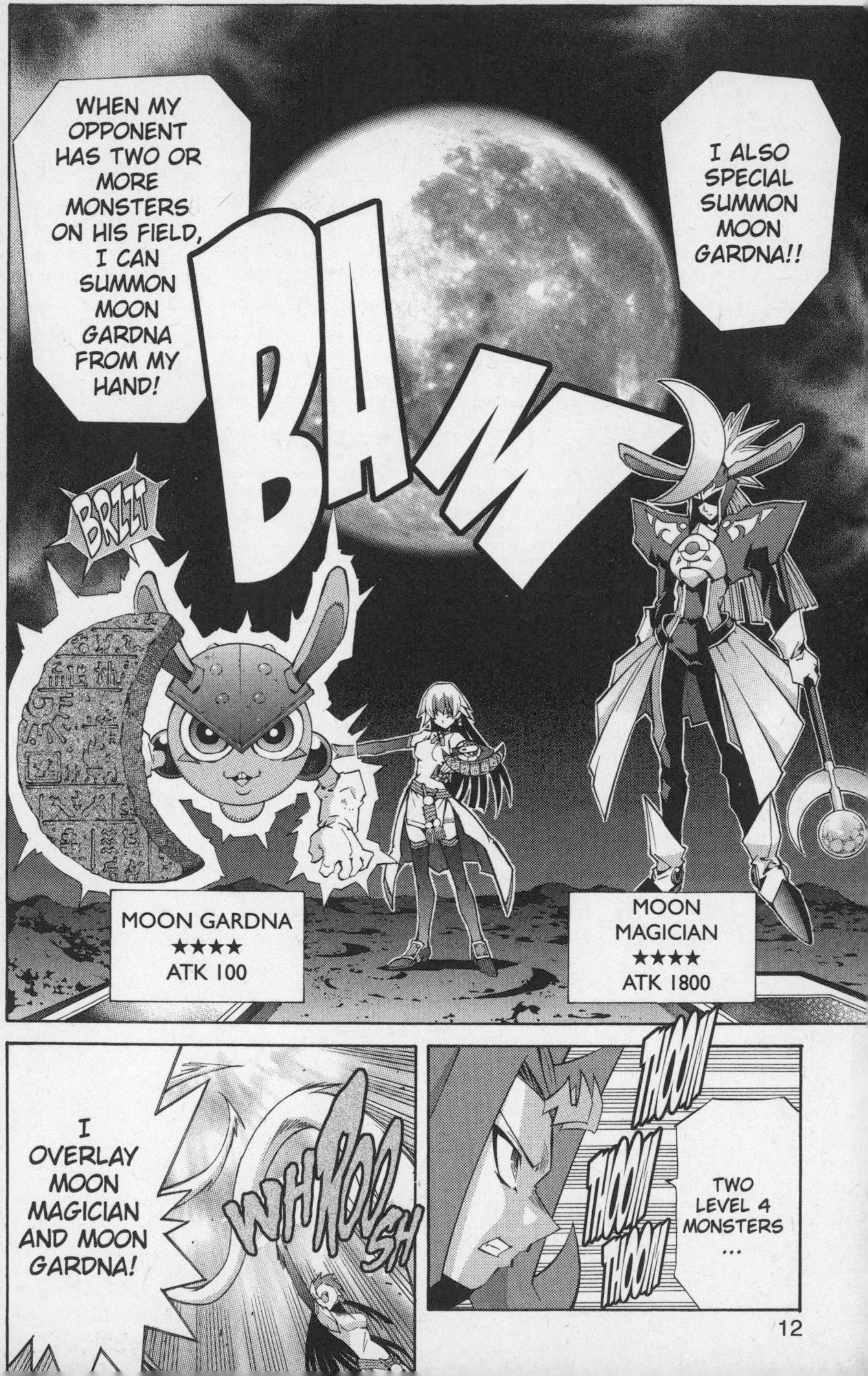
I ALSO SPECIAL SUMMON MOON GARDNA!!
WHEN MY OPPONENT HAS TWO OR MORE MONSTERS ON HIS FIELD, I CAN SUMMON MOON GARDNA FROM MY HAND!
BAM
BRZZT
MOON MAGICIAN ★★★★ ATK 1800
MOON GARDNA ★★★★ ATK 100
THOOM
THOOM
THOOM
TWO LEVEL 4 MONSTERS ...
I OVERLAY MOON MAGICIAN AND MOON GARDNA!
WHOOSH

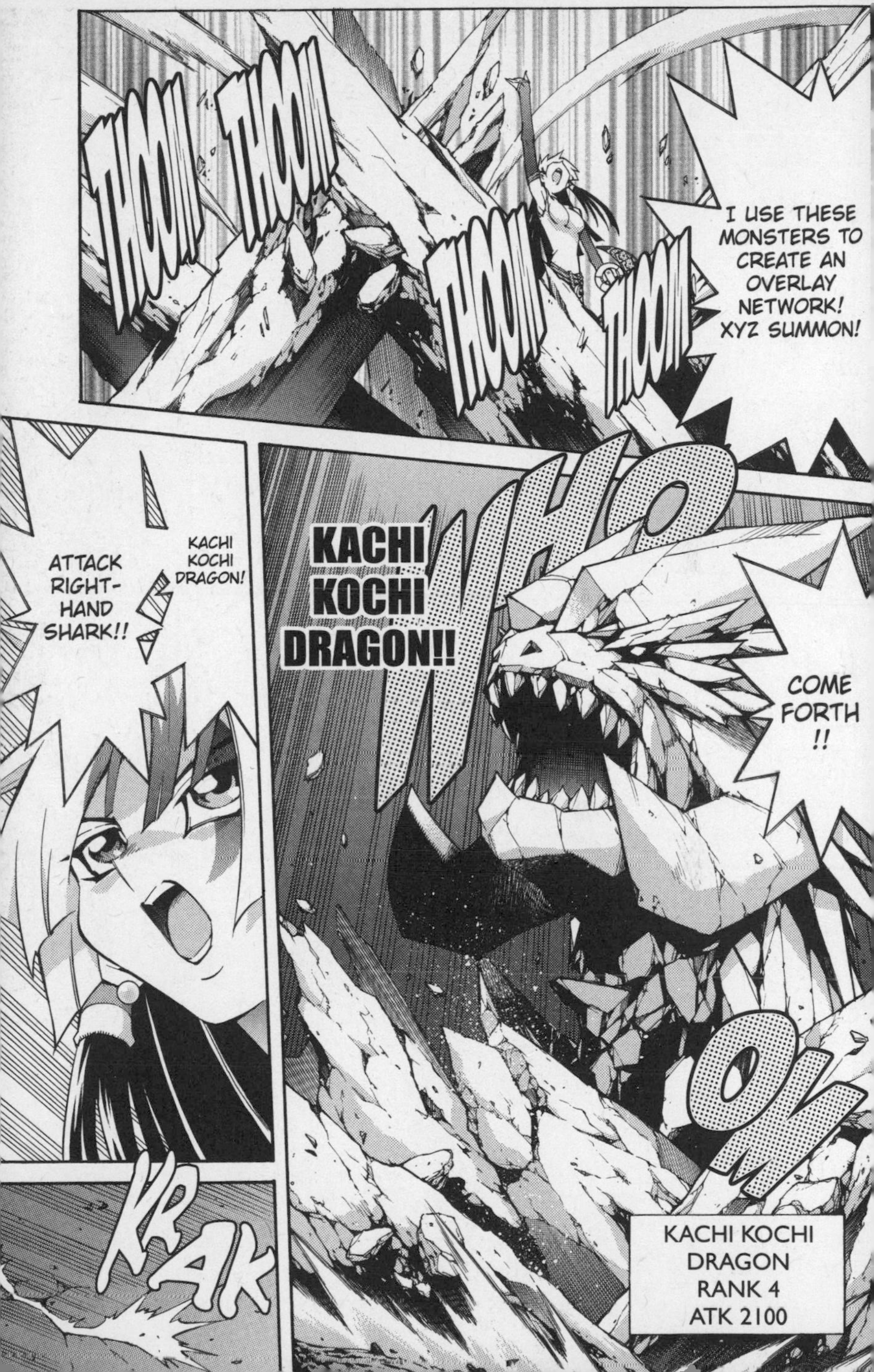
I USE THESE MONSTERS TO CREATE AN OVERLAY NETWORK! XYZ SUMMON!
THOOM
THOOM
THOOM
THOOM
COME FORTH!!
WHOOM
KACHI KOCHI DRAGON!!
KACHI KOCHI DRAGON RANK 4 ATK 2100
KACHI KOCHI DRAGON!
ATTACK RIGHT-HAND SHARK!!
K'RAK

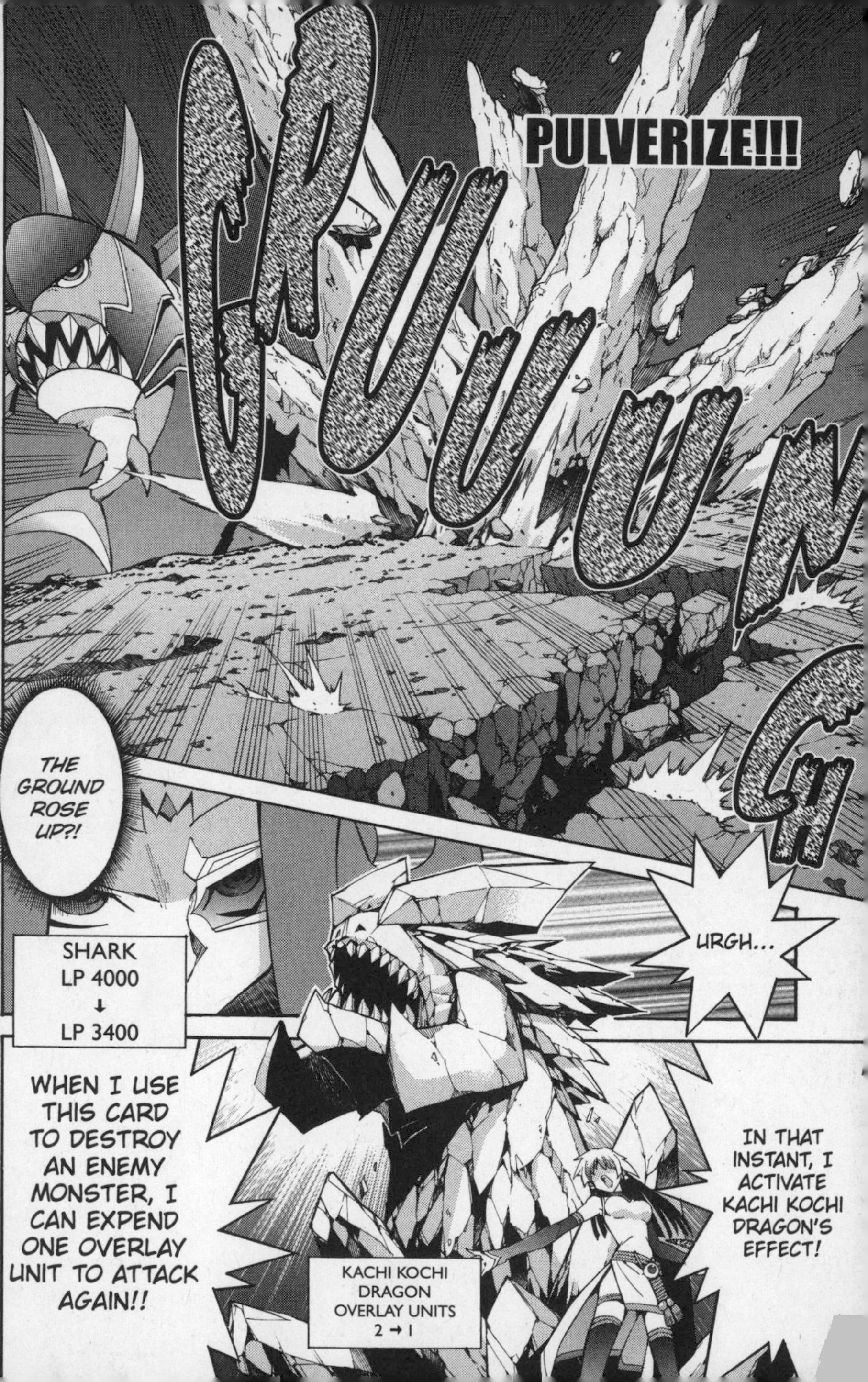
PULVERIZE!!!
CRUUUNCH
THE GROUND ROSE UP?!
URGH...
SHARK LP 4000 ↓ LP 3400
IN THAT INSTANT, I ACTIVATE KACHI KOCHI DRAGON'S EFFECT!
WHEN I USE THIS CARD TO DESTROY AN ENEMY MONSTER, I CAN EXPEND ONE OVERLAY UNIT TO ATTACK AGAIN!!
KACHI KOCHI DRAGON OVERLAY UNITS 2 → 1

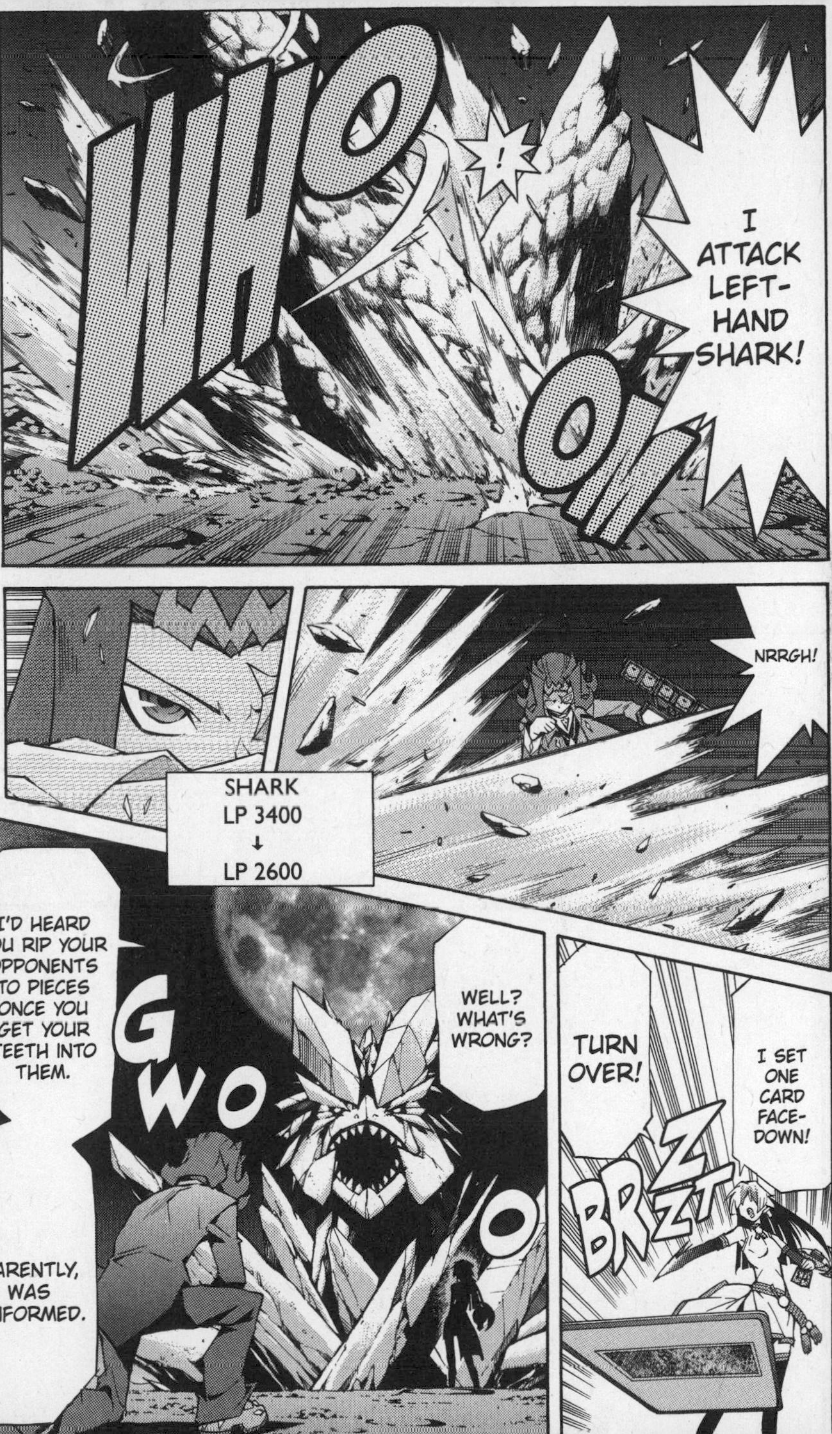
I ATTACK LEFT-HAND SHARK!
!
WHO
NRRGH!
SHARK
LP 3400
↓
LP 2600
I SET ONE CARD FACE-DOWN!
TURN OVER!
BRZZT
WELL? WHAT'S WRONG?
I'D HEARD YOU RIP YOUR OPPONENTS TO PIECES ONCE YOU GET YOUR TEETH INTO THEM.
GWOO
APPARENTLY, I WAS MISINFORMED.

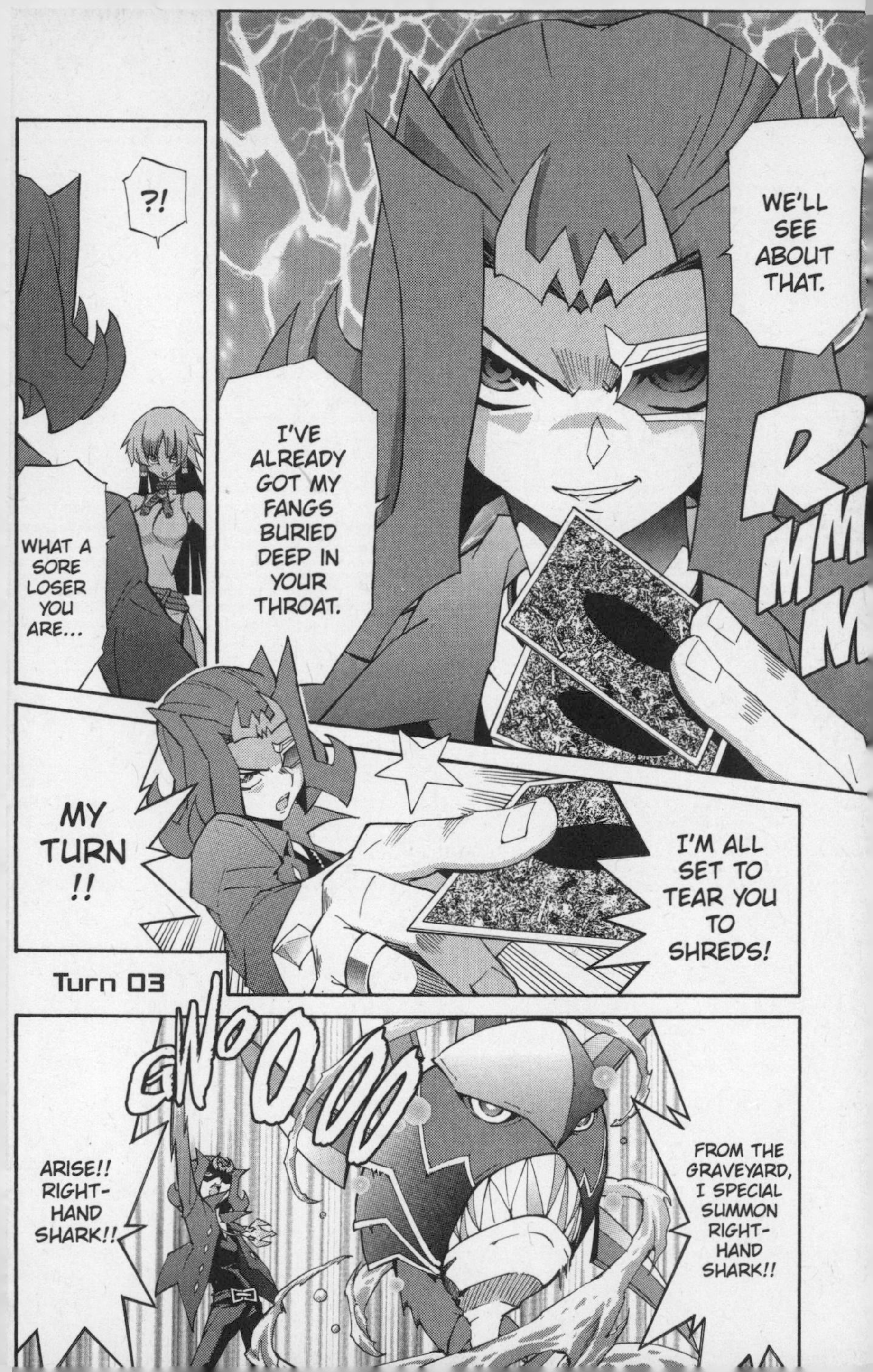
WE'LL SEE ABOUT THAT.
I'VE ALREADY GOT MY FANGS BURIED DEEP IN YOUR THROAT.
RMMMM
?!
WHAT A SORE LOSER YOU ARE...
I'M ALL SET TO TEAR YOU TO SHREDS!
MY TURN!!
Turn 03
FROM THE GRAVEYARD, I SPECIAL SUMMON RIGHT-HAND SHARK!!
GWOOOO
ARISE!! RIGHT-HAND SHARK!!

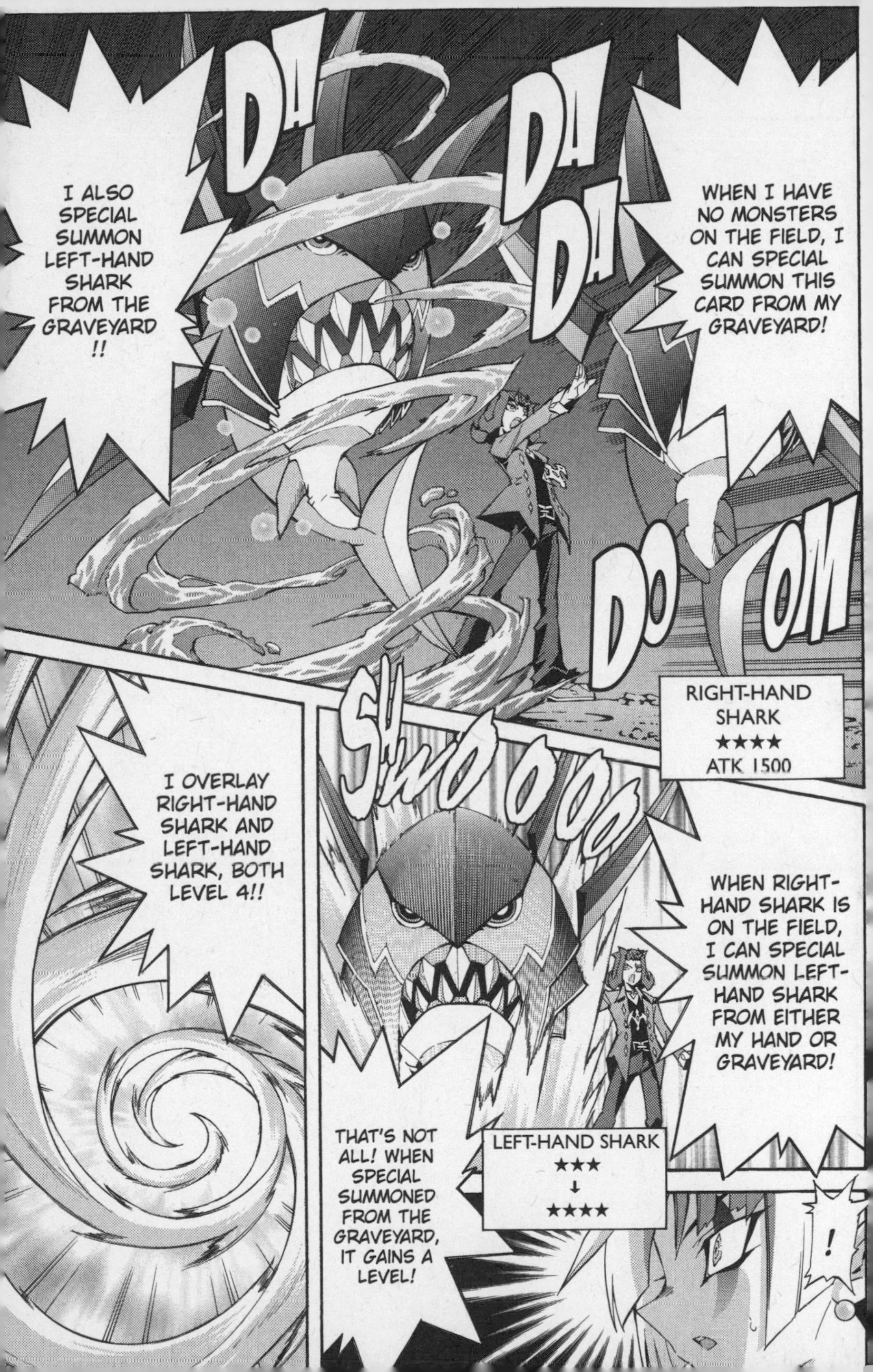
WHEN I HAVE NO MONSTERS ON THE FIELD, I CAN SPECIAL SUMMON THIS CARD FROM MY GRAVEYARD!
DA
DA DA
I ALSO SPECIAL SUMMON LEFT-HAND SHARK FROM THE GRAVEYARD !!
DOOOM
RIGHT-HAND SHARK ★★★★ ATK 1500
SHOOOO
WHEN RIGHT-HAND SHARK IS ON THE FIELD, I CAN SPECIAL SUMMON LEFT-HAND SHARK FROM EITHER MY HAND OR GRAVEYARD!
LEFT-HAND SHARK ★★★ ↓ ★★★★
THAT'S NOT ALL! WHEN SPECIAL SUMMONED FROM THE GRAVEYARD, IT GAINS A LEVEL!
!
I OVERLAY RIGHT-HAND SHARK AND LEFT-HAND SHARK, BOTH LEVEL 4!!

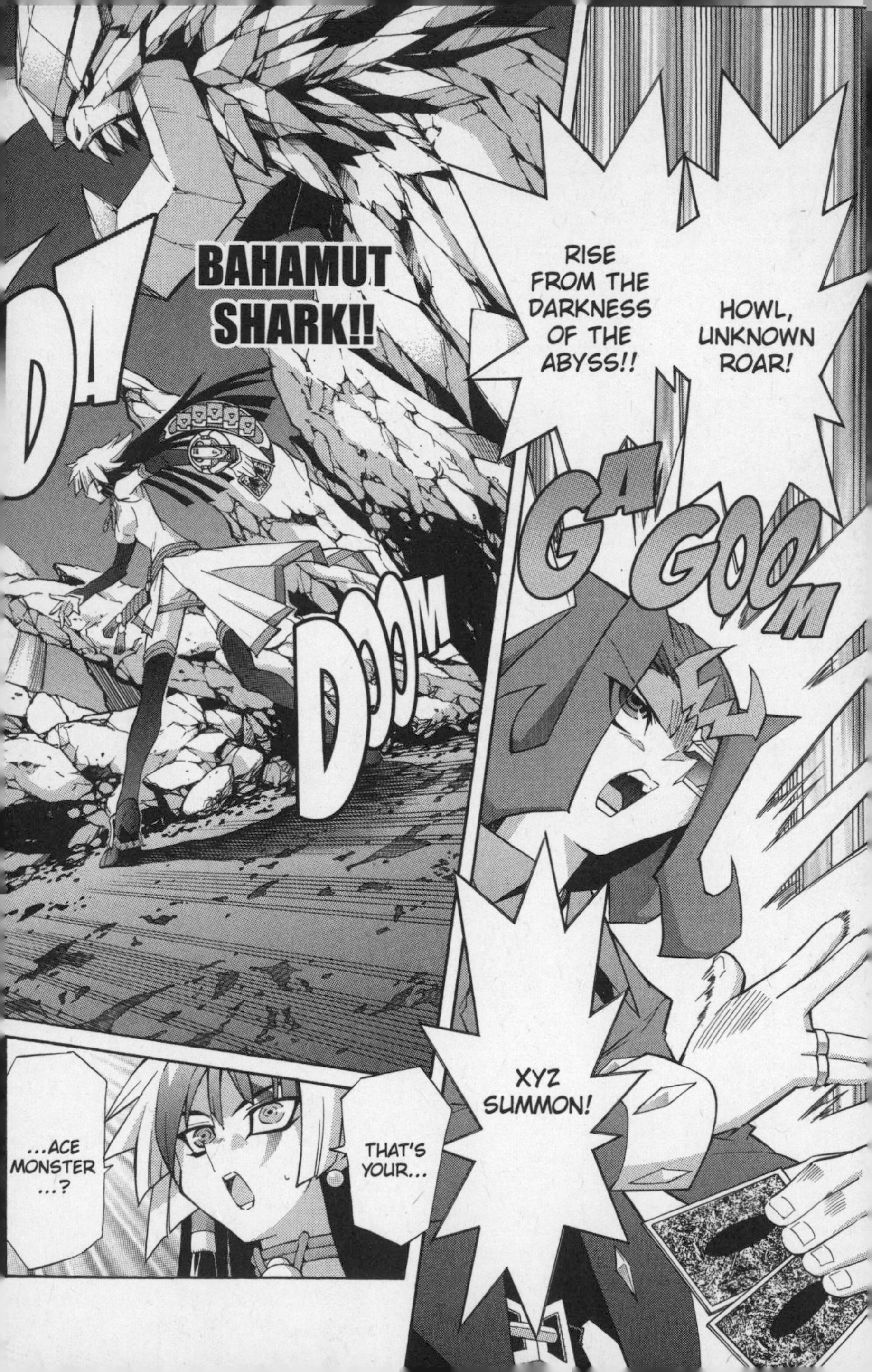

RISE FROM THE DARKNESS OF THE ABYSS!!
HOWL, UNKNOWN ROAR!
GA GOOM
XYZ SUMMON!
BAHAMUT SHARK!!
DA
DOOM
THAT'S YOUR...
...ACE MONSTER...?

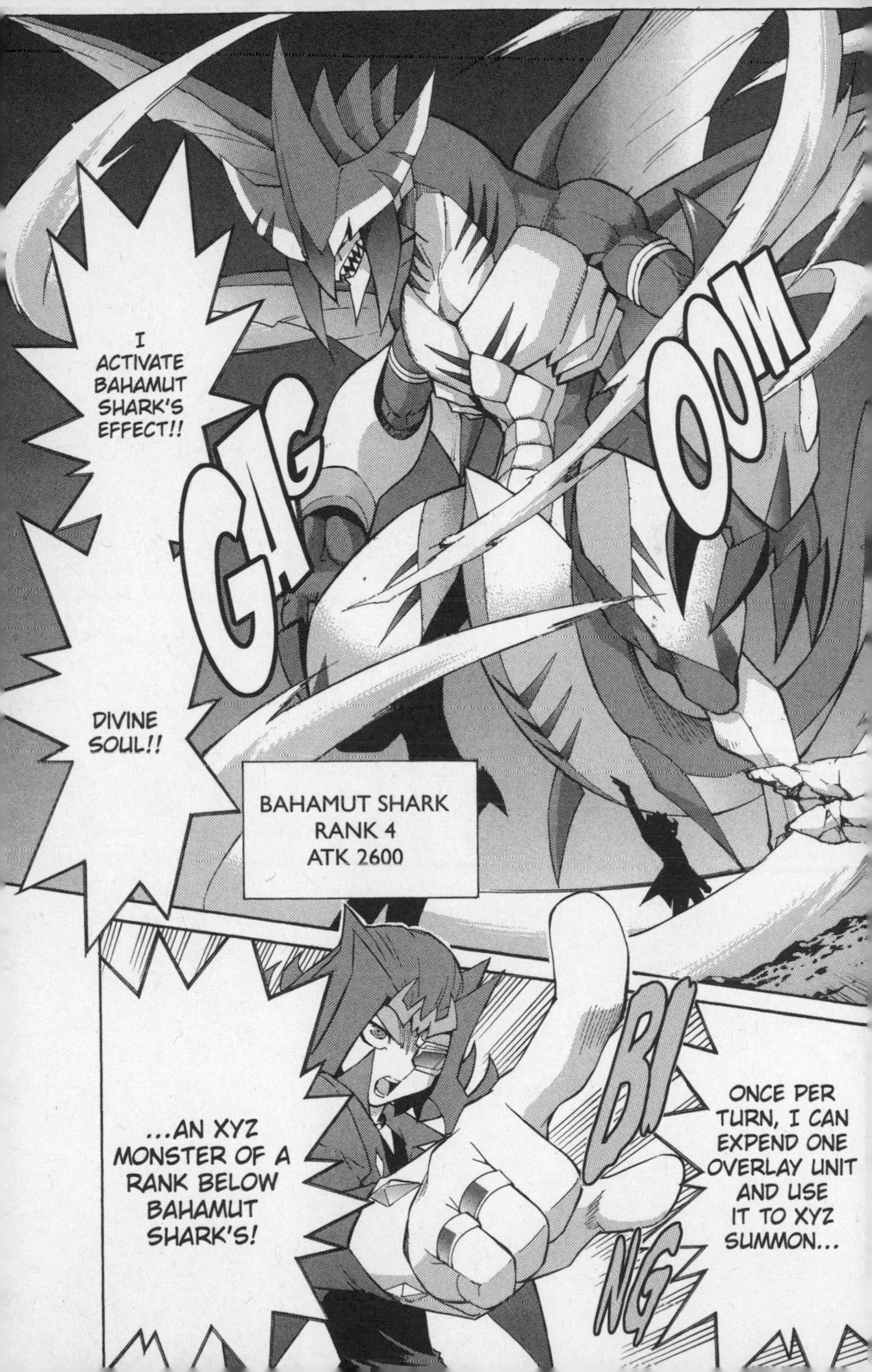
I ACTIVATE BAHAMUT SHARK'S EFFECT!!
GAG
OOOM
DIVINE SOUL!!
BAHAMUT SHARK
RANK 4
ATK 2600
ONCE PER TURN, I CAN EXPEND ONE OVERLAY UNIT AND USE IT TO XYZ SUMMON...
...AN XYZ MONSTER OF A RANK BELOW BAHAMUT SHARK'S!
BI
NG

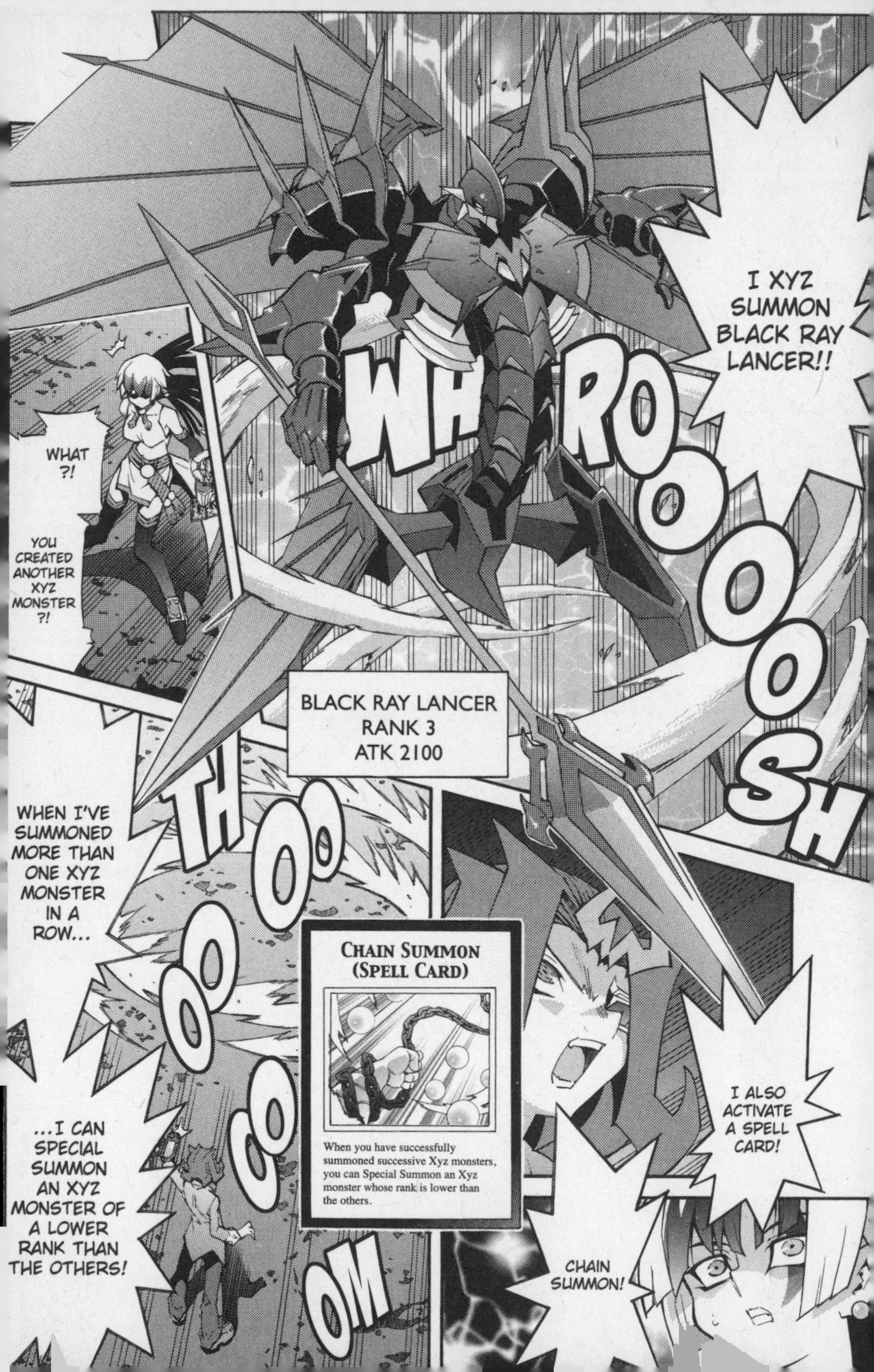
I XYZ SUMMON BLACK RAY LANCER!!
WHROOOOOSH
WHAT?!
YOU CREATED ANOTHER XYZ MONSTER?!
BLACK RAY LANCER RANK 3 ATK 2100
I ALSO ACTIVATE A SPELL CARD!
CHAIN SUMMON!
CHAIN SUMMON (SPELL CARD)
When you have successfully summoned successive Xyz monsters, you can Special Summon an Xyz monster whose rank is lower than the others.
WHEN I'VE SUMMONED MORE THAN ONE XYZ MONSTER IN A ROW...
...I CAN SPECIAL SUMMON AN XYZ MONSTER OF A LOWER RANK THAN THE OTHERS!
THOOOOOOOM

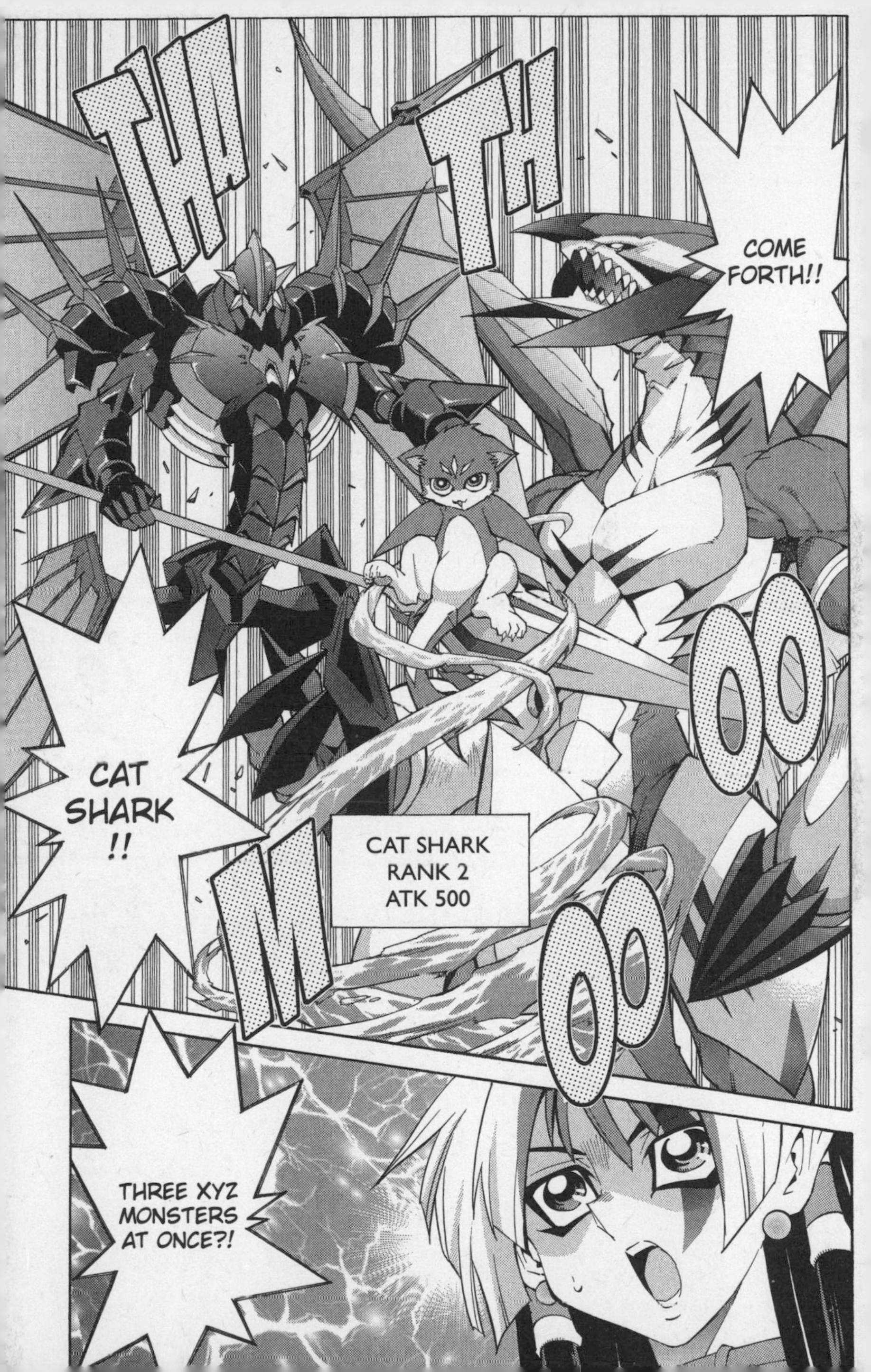
COME FORTH!!
THA TH
CAT SHARK !!
CAT SHARK
RANK 2
ATK 500
MOOOOO
THREE XYZ MONSTERS AT ONCE?!

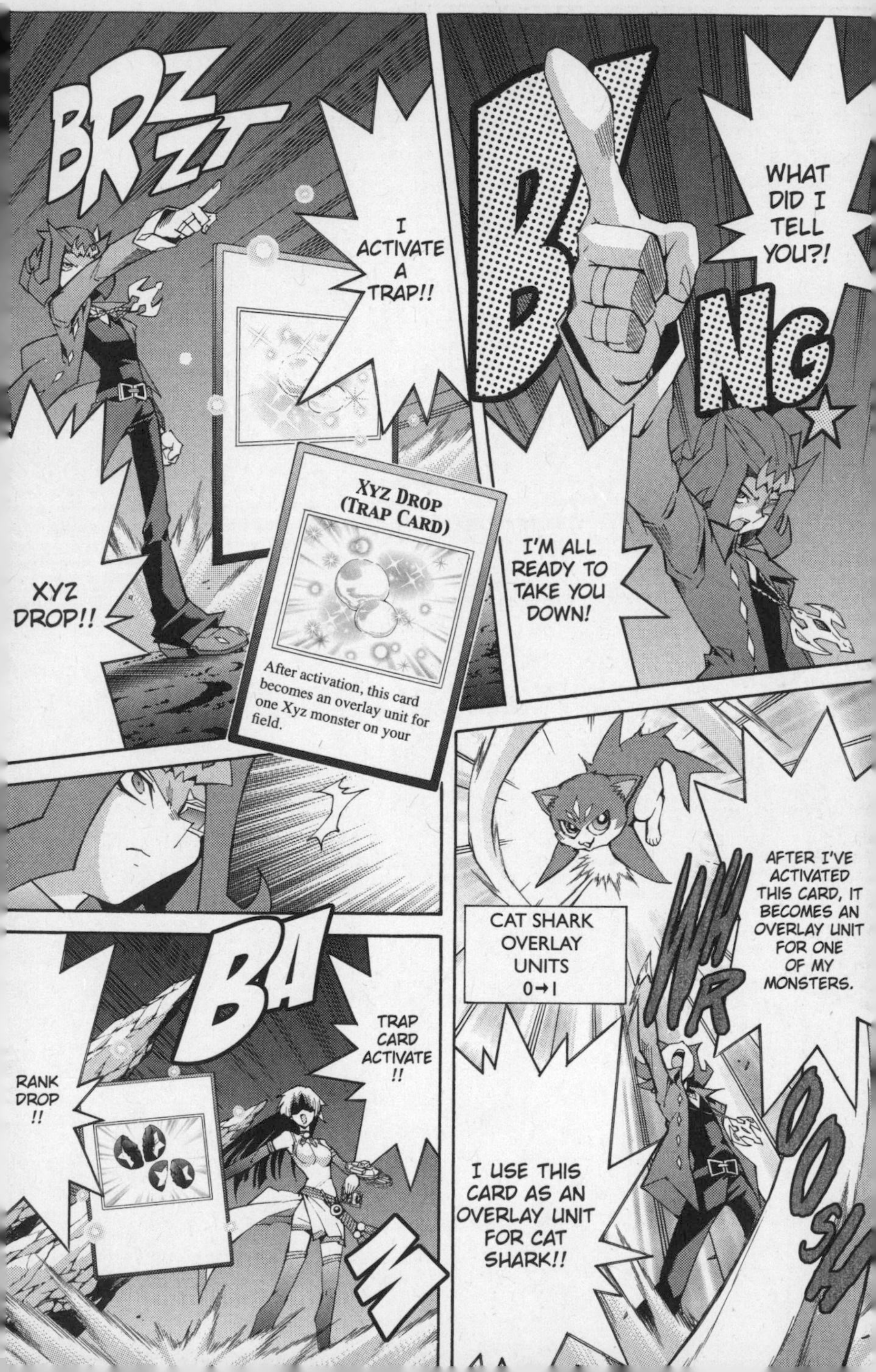
BANG
WHAT DID I TELL YOU?!
I'M ALL READY TO TAKE YOU DOWN!
BRZZT
I ACTIVATE A TRAP!!
XYZ DROP!!
Xyz Drop (Trap Card)
After activation, this card becomes an overlay unit for one Xyz monster on your field.
AFTER I'VE ACTIVATED THIS CARD, IT BECOMES AN OVERLAY UNIT FOR ONE OF MY MONSTERS.
WHIRR
CAT SHARK OVERLAY UNITS 0→1
WHOOSH
I USE THIS CARD AS AN OVERLAY UNIT FOR CAT SHARK!!
BAM
TRAP CARD ACTIVATE!!
RANK DROP!!

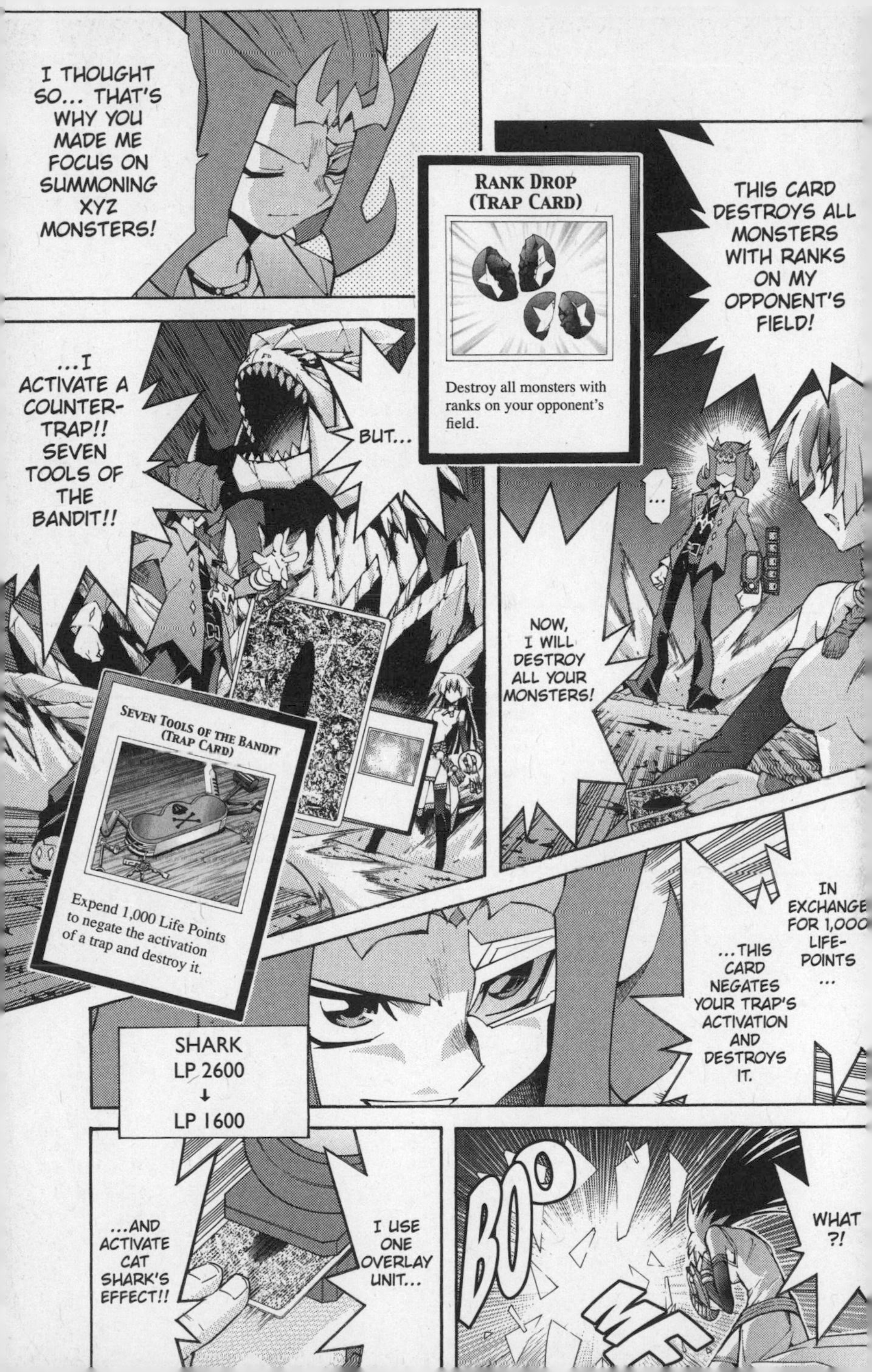
THIS CARD DESTROYS ALL MONSTERS WITH RANKS ON MY OPPONENT'S FIELD!
RANK DROP (TRAP CARD)
Destroy all monsters with ranks on your opponent's field.
...
NOW, I WILL DESTROY ALL YOUR MONSTERS!
I THOUGHT SO... THAT'S WHY YOU MADE ME FOCUS ON SUMMONING XYZ MONSTERS!
BUT...
...I ACTIVATE A COUNTER-TRAP!! SEVEN TOOLS OF THE BANDIT!!
SEVEN TOOLS OF THE BANDIT (TRAP CARD)
Expend 1,000 Life Points to negate the activation of a trap and destroy it.
IN EXCHANGE FOR 1,000 LIFE-POINTS...
...THIS CARD NEGATES YOUR TRAP'S ACTIVATION AND DESTROYS IT.
SHARK LP 2600 ↓ LP 1600
WHAT?!
BOOOM
I USE ONE OVERLAY UNIT...
...AND ACTIVATE CAT SHARK'S EFFECT!!

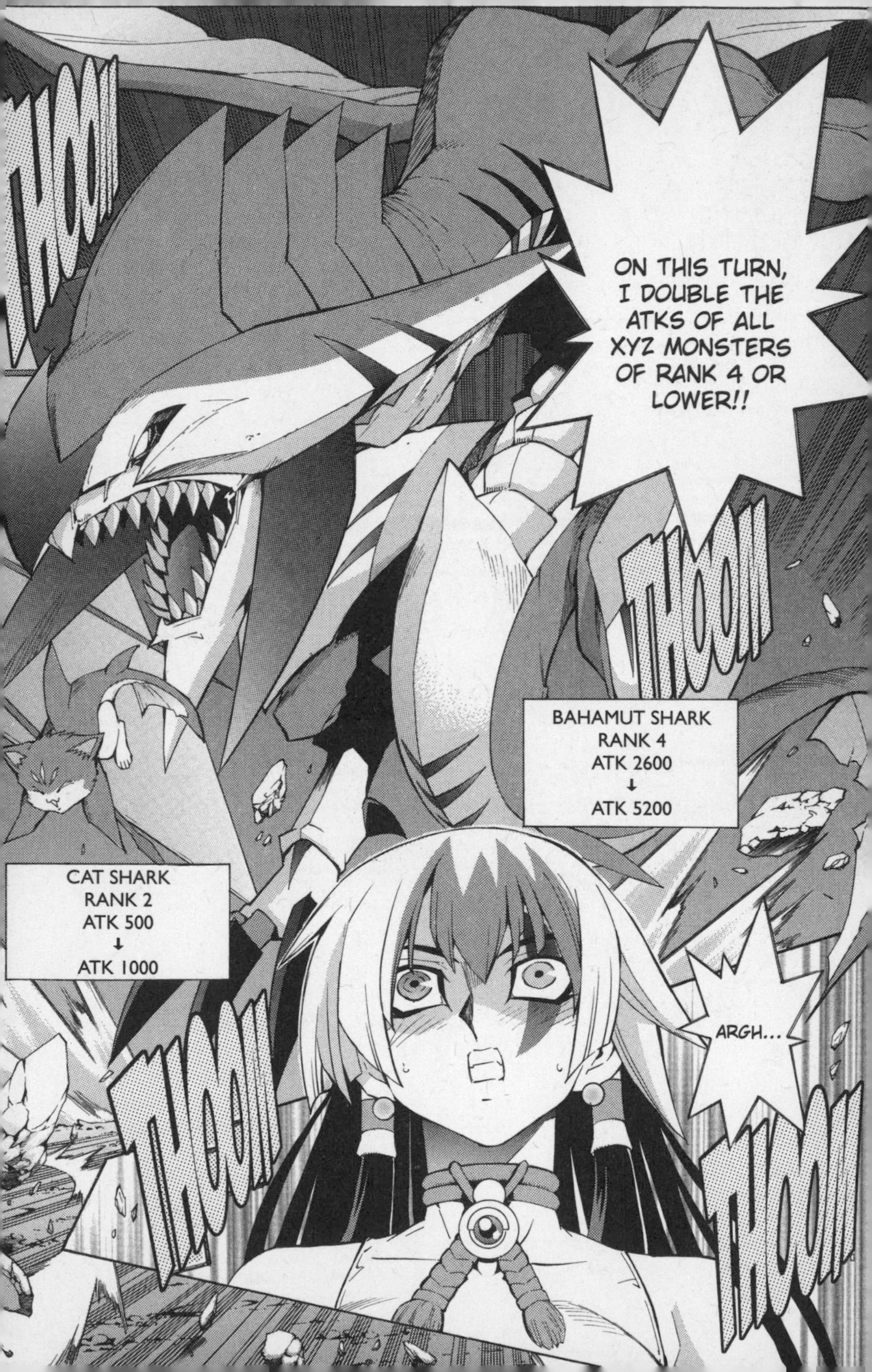
ON THIS TURN, I DOUBLE THE ATKS OF ALL XYZ MONSTERS OF RANK 4 OR LOWER!!
THOOM
THOOM
BAHAMUT SHARK RANK 4 ATK 2600 ↓ ATK 5200
CAT SHARK RANK 2 ATK 500 ↓ ATK 1000
ARGH...
THOOM
THOOM

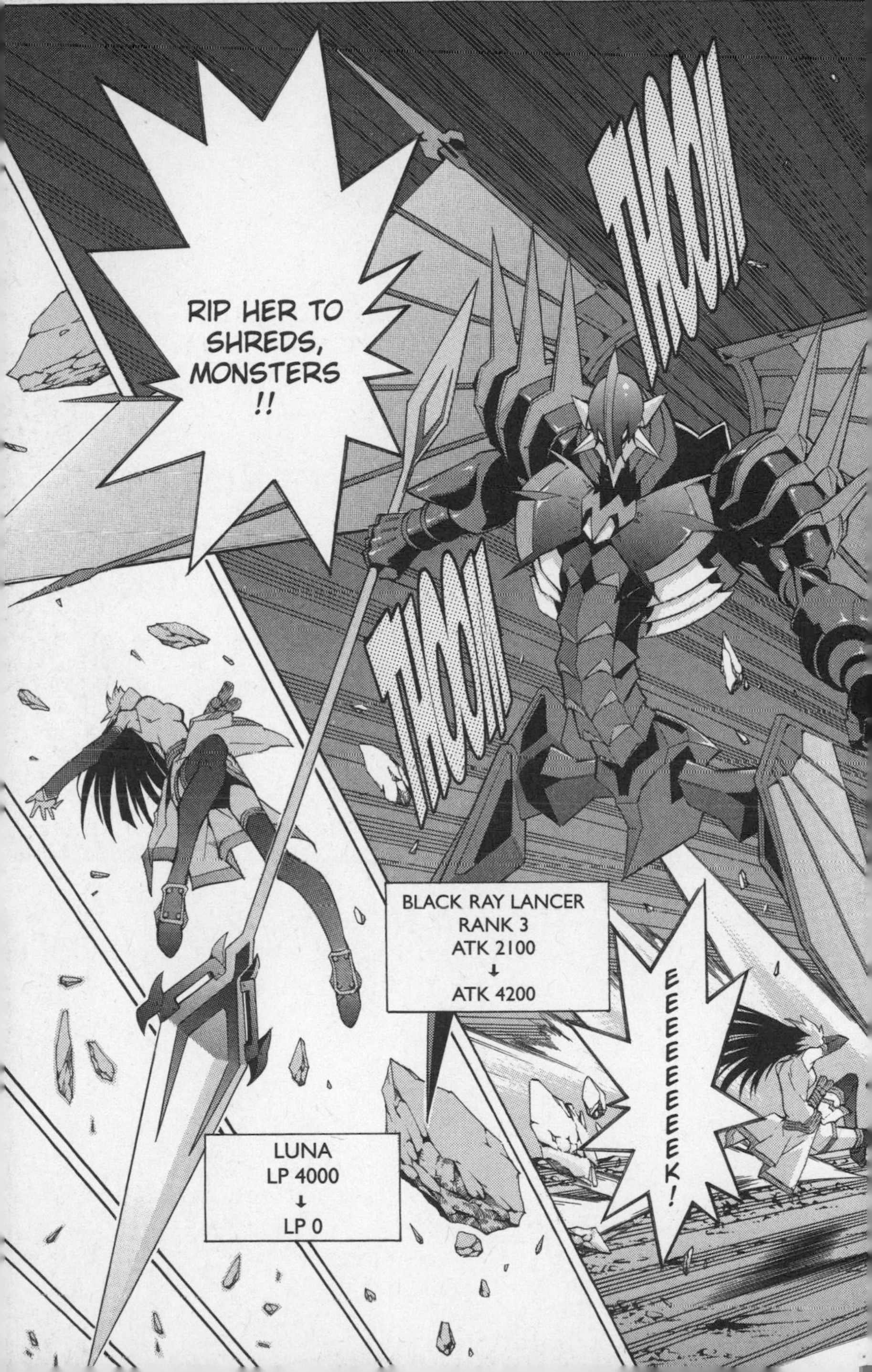
THOOM!!
RIP HER TO SHREDS, MONSTERS !!
THOOM!!
BLACK RAY LANCER
RANK 3
ATK 2100
↓
ATK 4200
EEEEEEEEEK!
LUNA
LP 4000
↓
LP 0

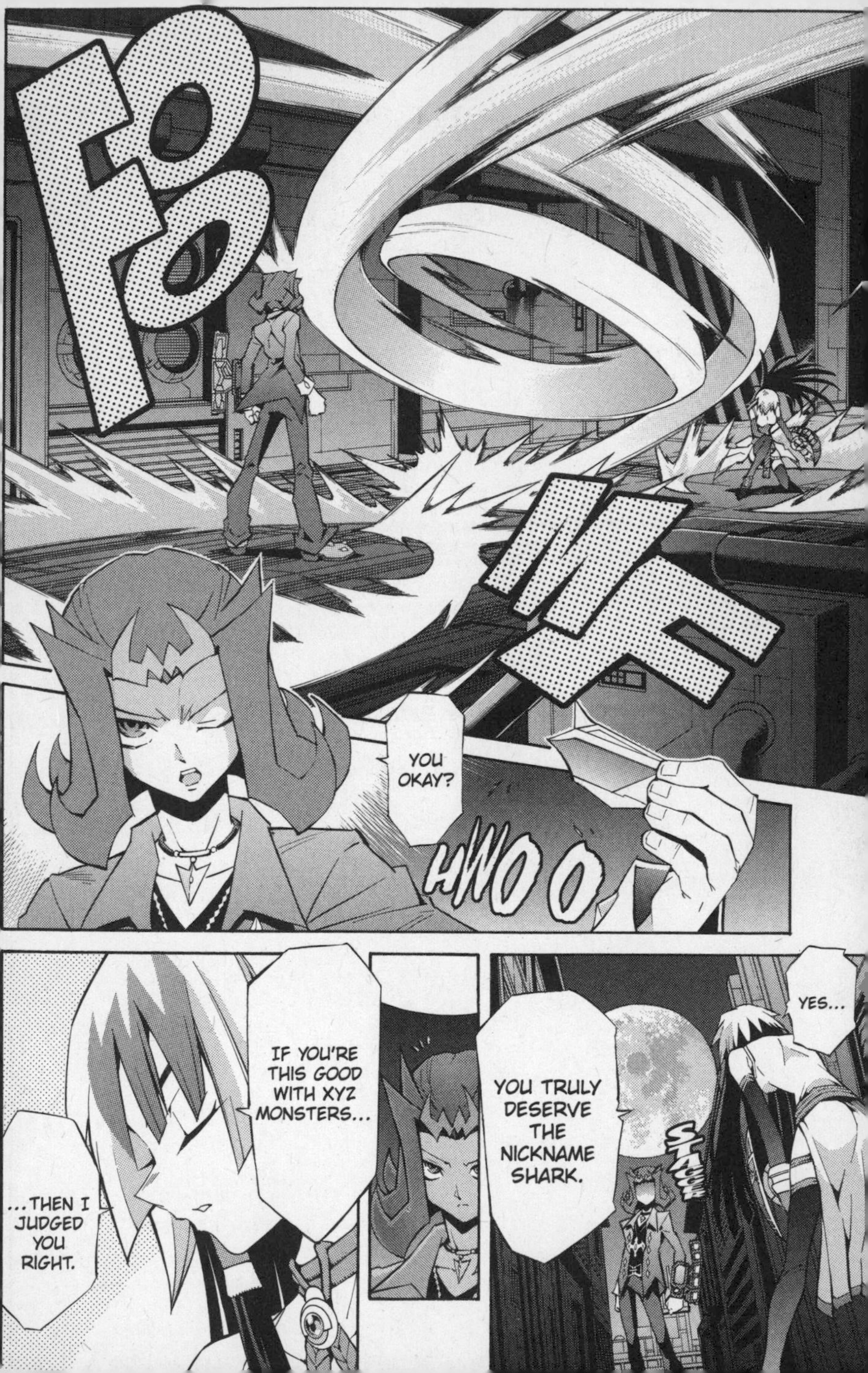
YOU OKAY?
HWOO O
YES...
YOU TRULY DESERVE THE NICKNAME SHARK.
IF YOU'RE THIS GOOD WITH XYZ MONSTERS...
...THEN I JUDGED YOU RIGHT.

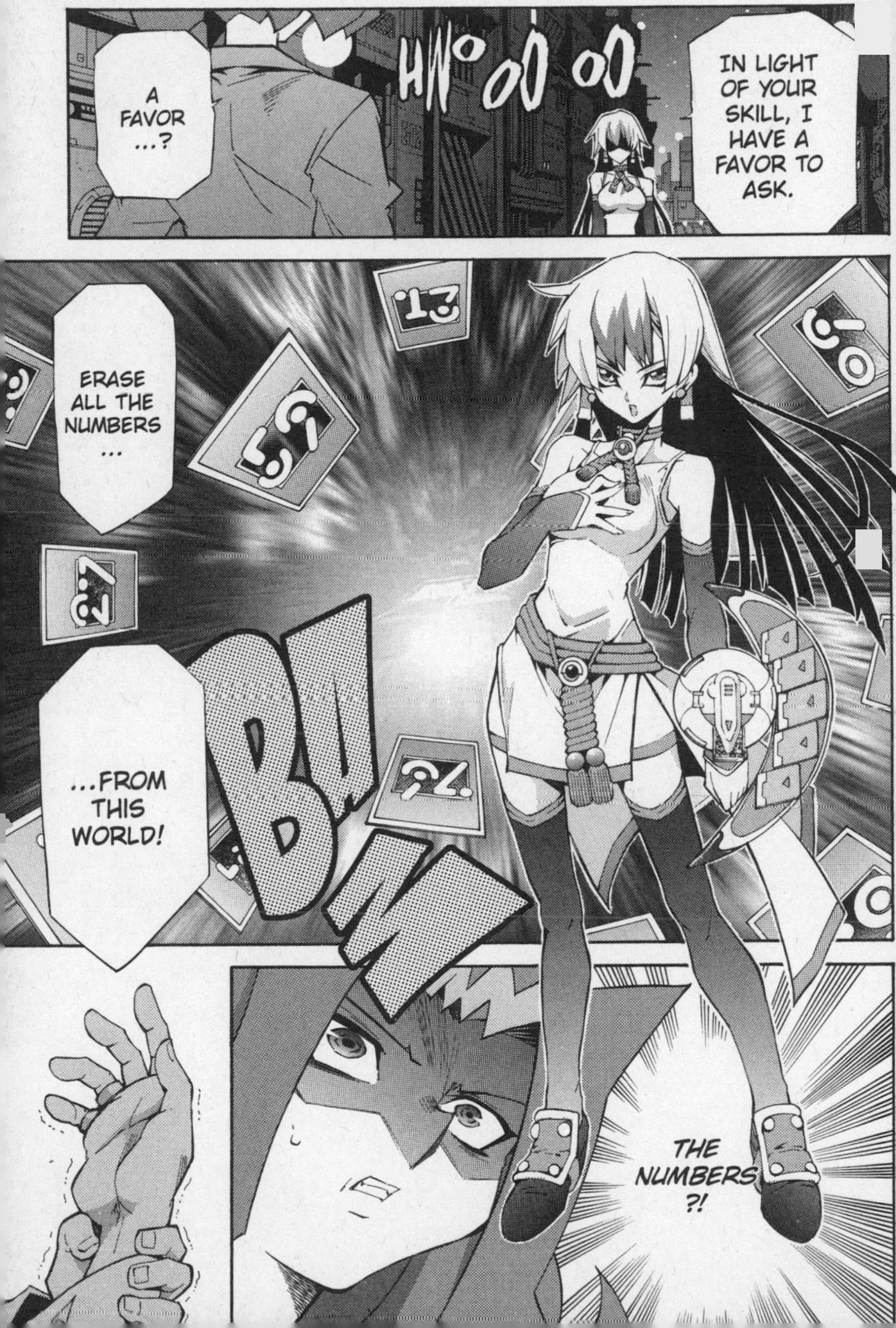
IN LIGHT OF YOUR SKILL, I HAVE A FAVOR TO ASK.
HWOOOOOO
A FAVOR ...?
ERASE ALL THE NUMBERS ...
...FROM THIS WORLD!
BAM
THE NUMBERS ?!

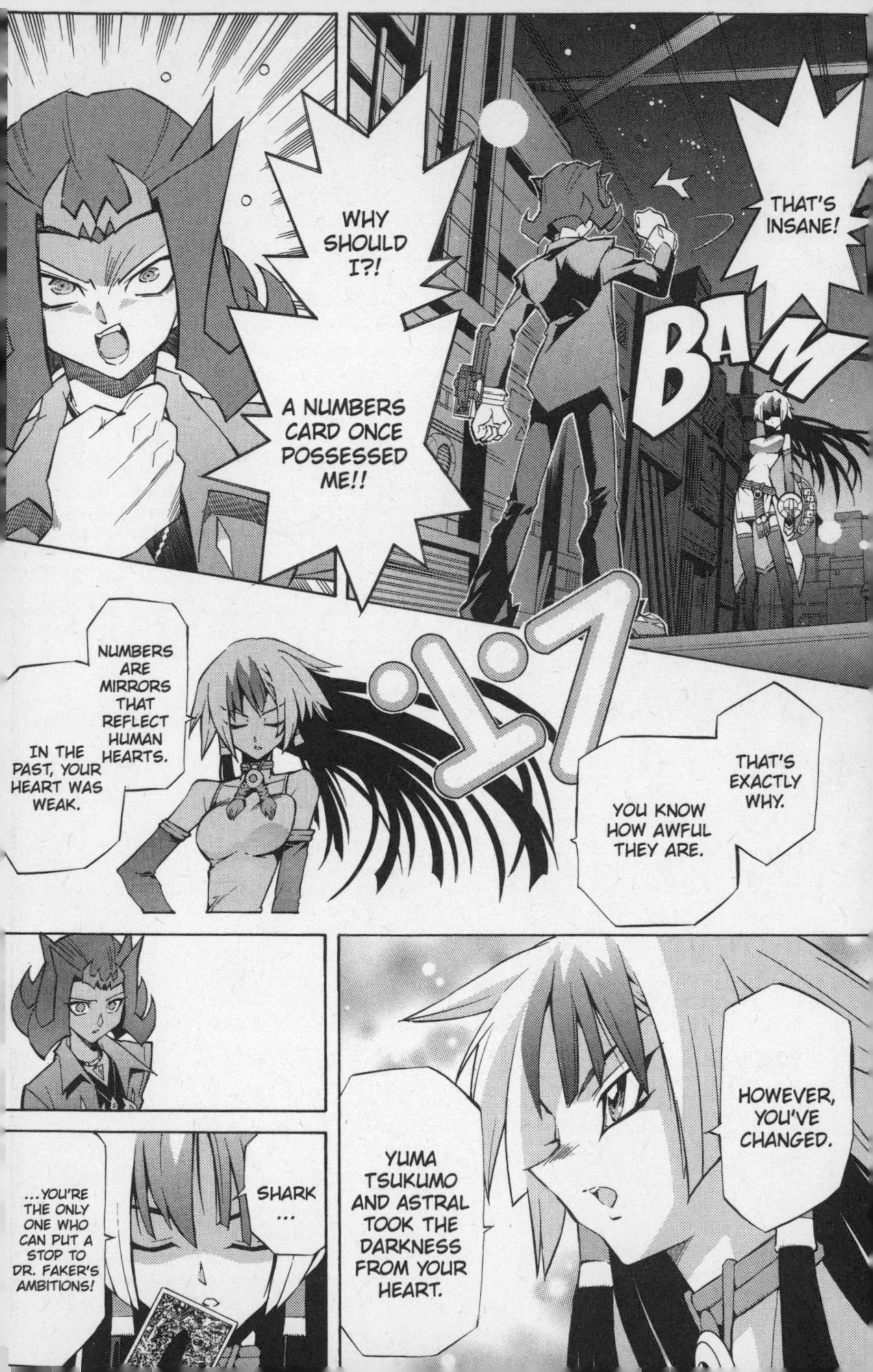
THAT'S INSANE!
BAM
WHY SHOULD I?!
A NUMBERS CARD ONCE POSSESSED ME!!
THAT'S EXACTLY WHY.
YOU KNOW HOW AWFUL THEY ARE.
NUMBERS ARE MIRRORS THAT REFLECT HUMAN HEARTS.
IN THE PAST, YOUR HEART WAS WEAK.
HOWEVER, YOU'VE CHANGED.
YUMA TSUKUMO AND ASTRAL TOOK THE DARKNESS FROM YOUR HEART.
SHARK ...
...YOU'RE THE ONLY ONE WHO CAN PUT A STOP TO DR. FAKER'S AMBITIONS!

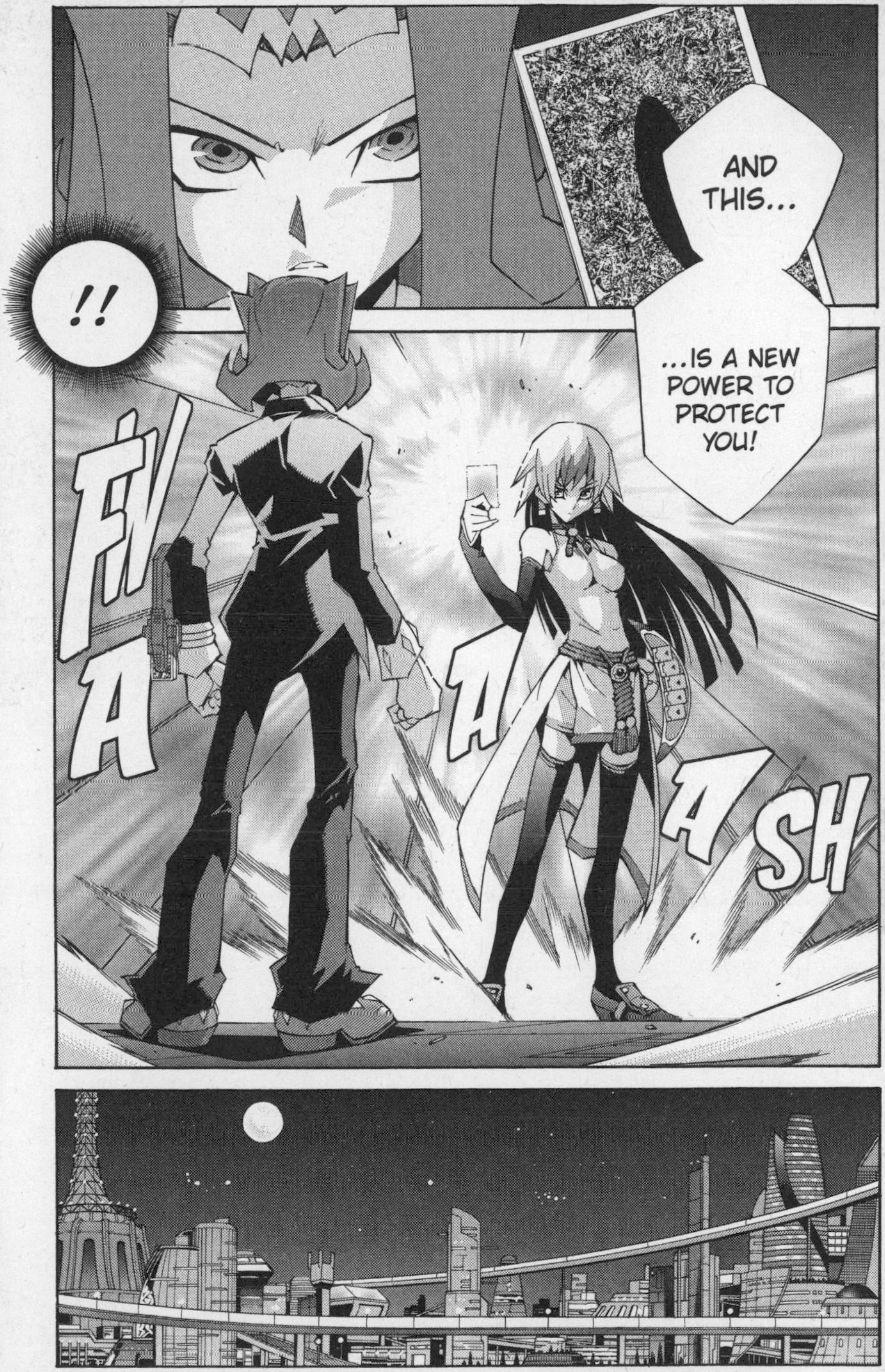
AND THIS...
...IS A NEW POWER TO PROTECT YOU!
!!
FWAAASH

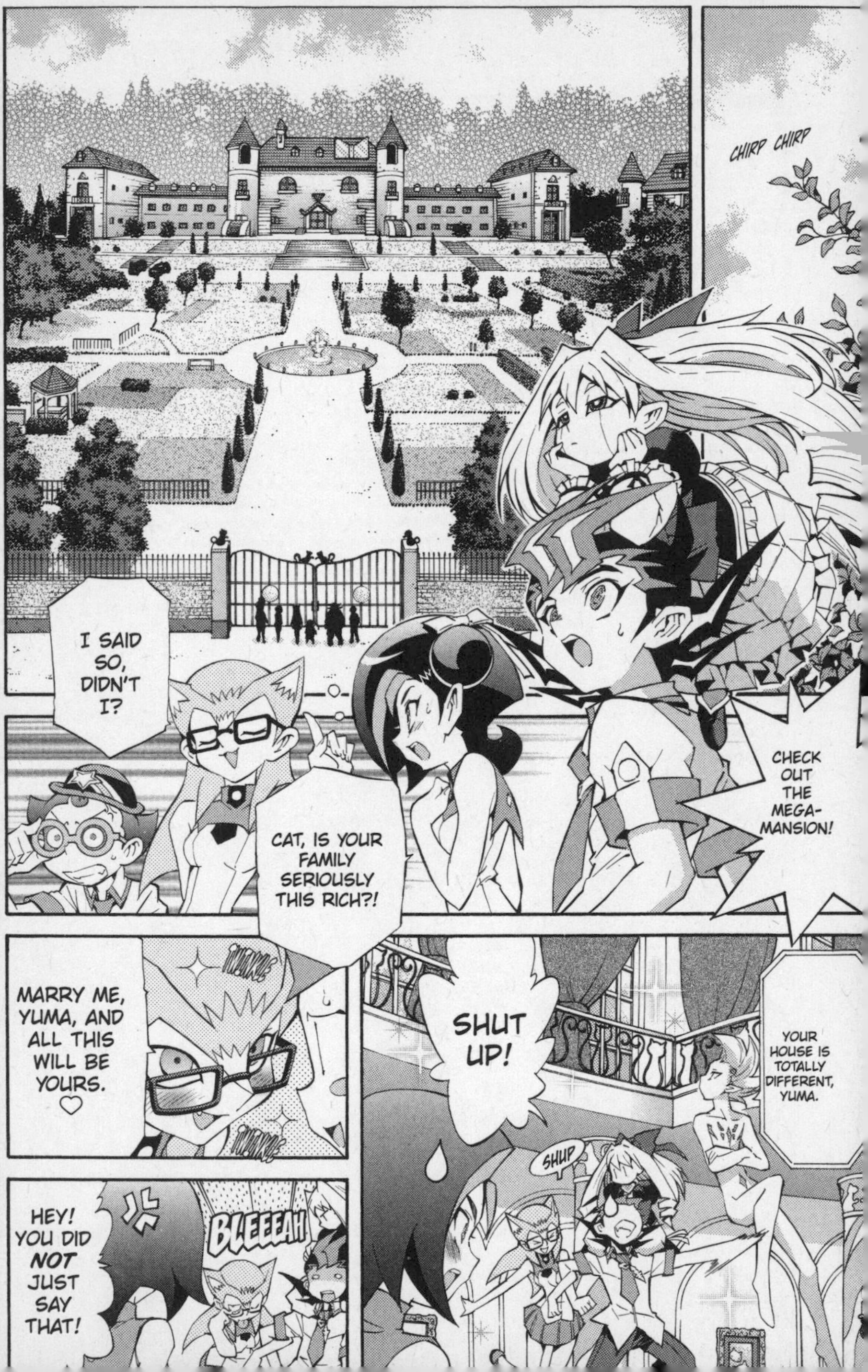
CHIRP CHIRP
CHECK OUT THE MEGA-MANSION!
CAT, IS YOUR FAMILY SERIOUSLY THIS RICH?!
I SAID SO, DIDN'T I?
YOUR HOUSE IS TOTALLY DIFFERENT, YUMA.
SHUT UP!
SHUP
TWINKLE
MARRY ME, YUMA, AND ALL THIS WILL BE YOURS. ♡
TWINKLE
HEY! YOU DID **NOT** JUST SAY THAT!
BLEEEAH

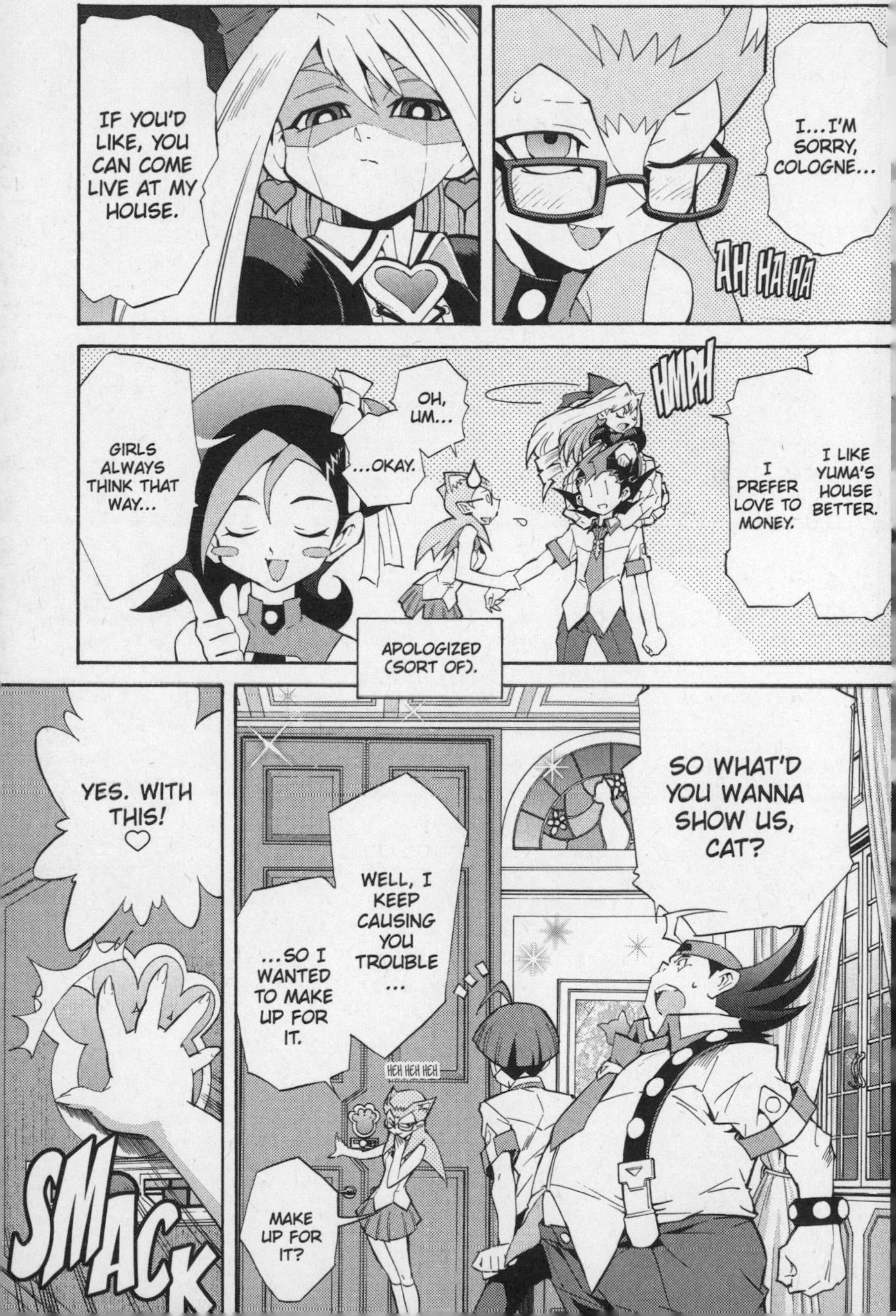
I...I'M SORRY, COLOGNE...
AH HA HA
IF YOU'D LIKE, YOU CAN COME LIVE AT MY HOUSE.
HMPH
I LIKE YUMA'S HOUSE BETTER.
I PREFER LOVE TO MONEY.
OH, UM...
...OKAY.
GIRLS ALWAYS THINK THAT WAY...
APOLOGIZED (SORT OF).
SO WHAT'D YOU WANNA SHOW US, CAT?
WELL, I KEEP CAUSING YOU TROUBLE...
...SO I WANTED TO MAKE UP FOR IT.
HEH HEH HEH
MAKE UP FOR IT?
YES. WITH THIS! ♡
SMACK

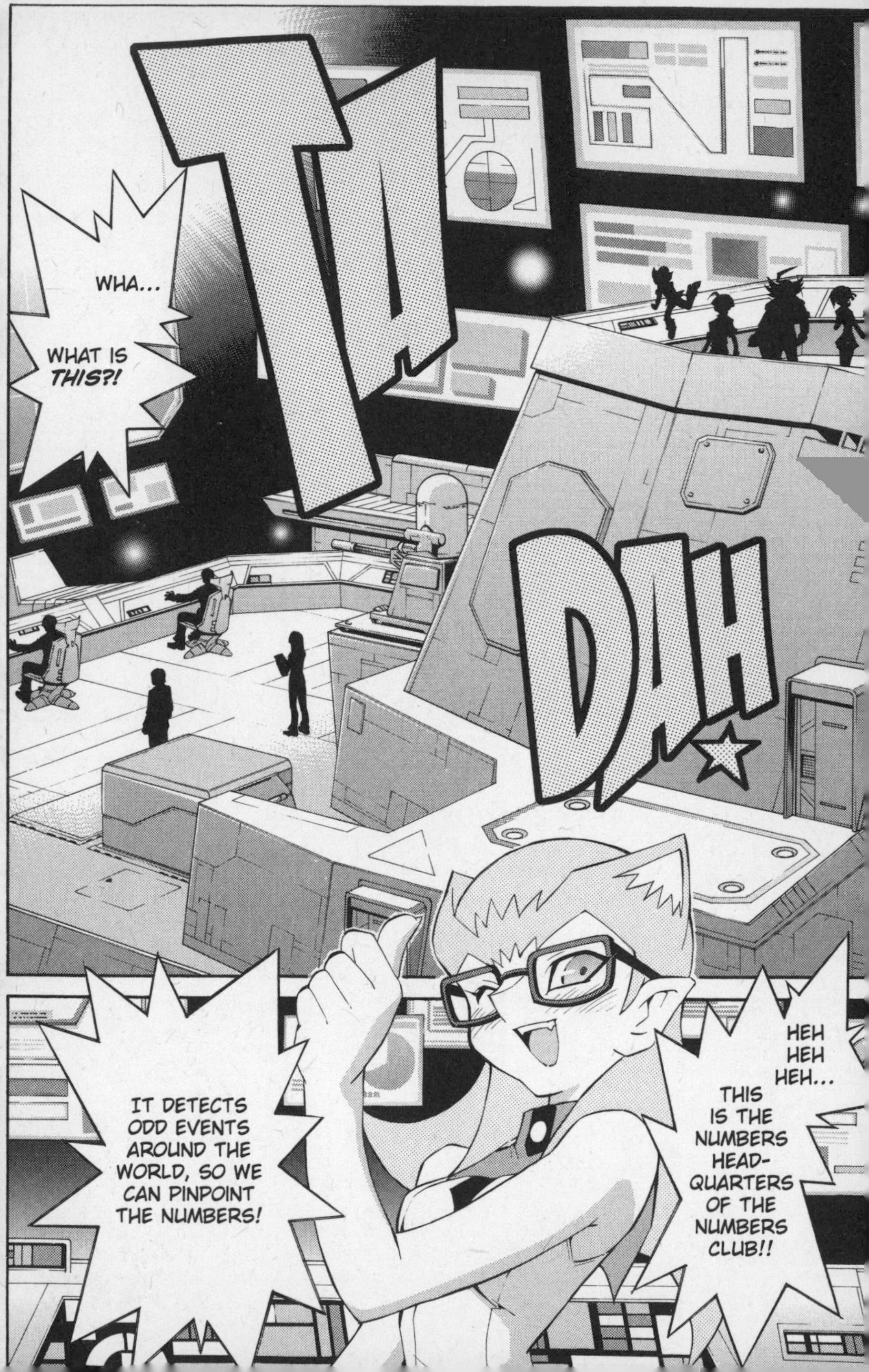
TA
DAH☆
WHA...
WHAT IS THIS?!
HEH HEH HEH... THIS IS THE NUMBERS HEAD-QUARTERS OF THE NUMBERS CLUB!!
IT DETECTS ODD EVENTS AROUND THE WORLD, SO WE CAN PINPOINT THE NUMBERS!

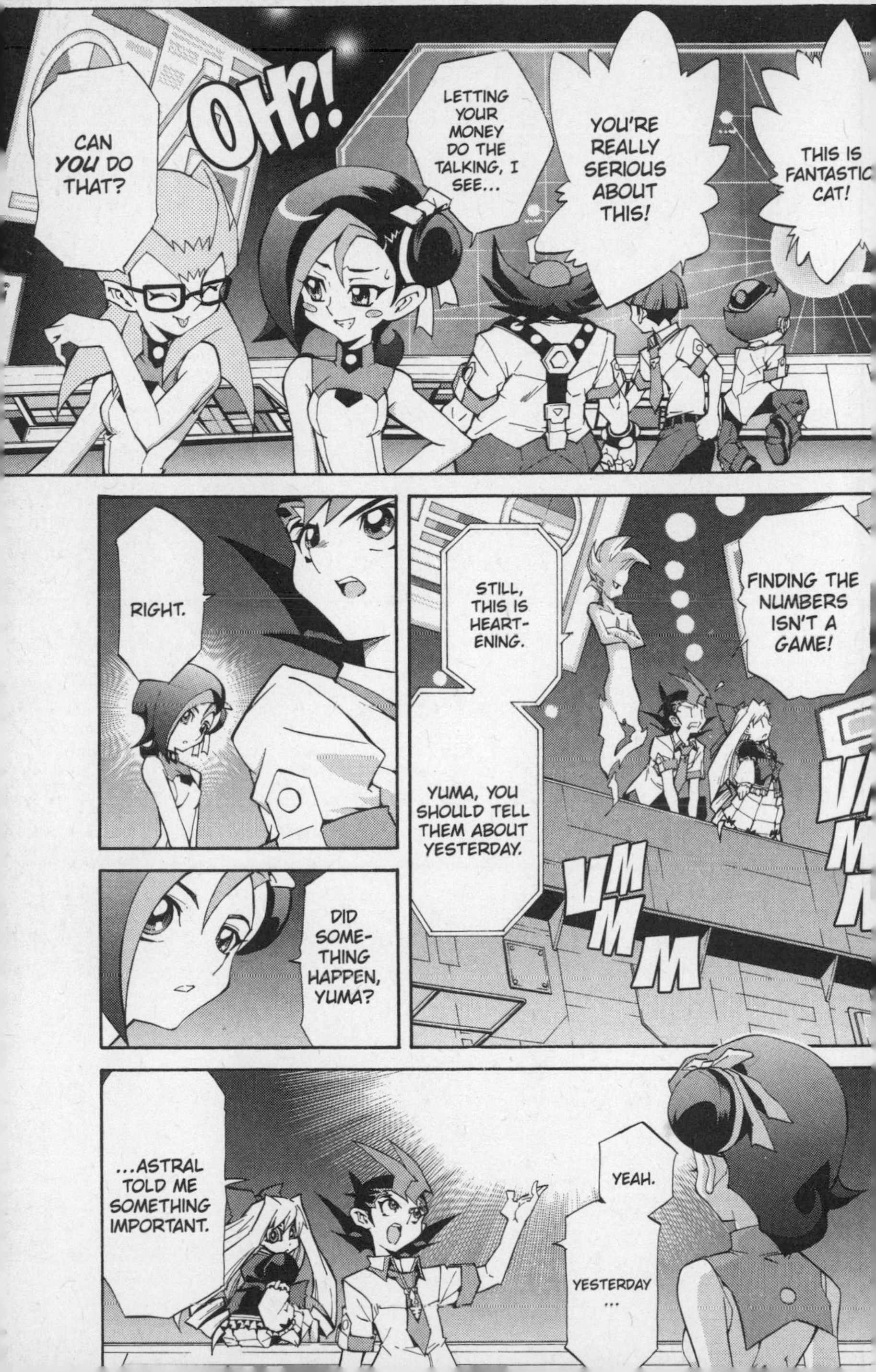
THIS IS FANTASTIC CAT!
YOU'RE REALLY SERIOUS ABOUT THIS!
LETTING YOUR MONEY DO THE TALKING, I SEE...
OH?!
CAN *YOU* DO THAT?
FINDING THE NUMBERS ISN'T A GAME!
STILL, THIS IS HEART-ENING.
YUMA, YOU SHOULD TELL THEM ABOUT YESTERDAY.
VMMM
RIGHT.
DID SOME-THING HAPPEN, YUMA?
YEAH.
YESTERDAY ...
...ASTRAL TOLD ME SOMETHING IMPORTANT.

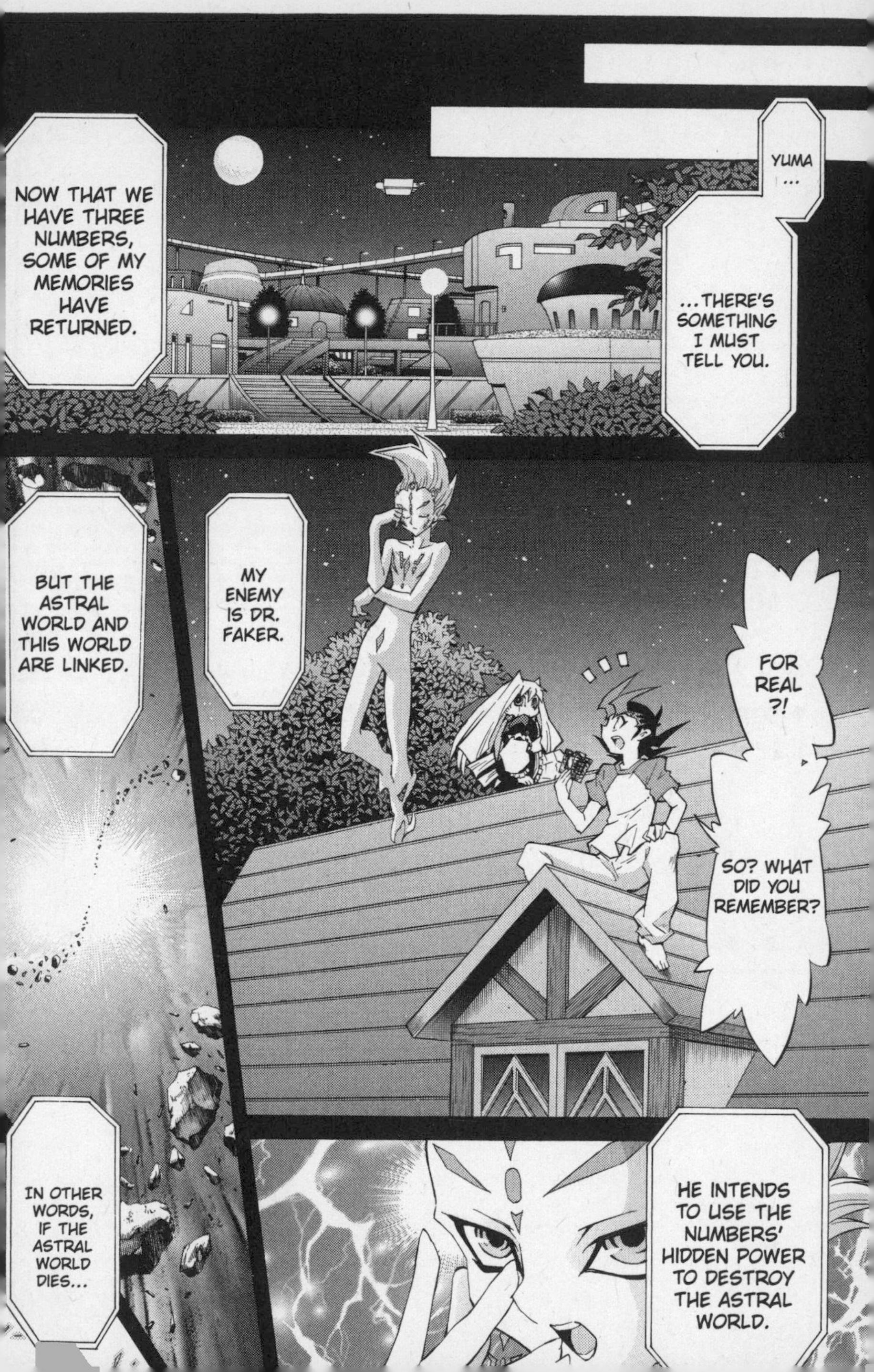
YUMA...
...THERE'S SOMETHING I MUST TELL YOU.
NOW THAT WE HAVE THREE NUMBERS, SOME OF MY MEMORIES HAVE RETURNED.
FOR REAL?!
SO? WHAT DID YOU REMEMBER?
MY ENEMY IS DR. FAKER.
HE INTENDS TO USE THE NUMBERS' HIDDEN POWER TO DESTROY THE ASTRAL WORLD.
BUT THE ASTRAL WORLD AND THIS WORLD ARE LINKED.
IN OTHER WORDS, IF THE ASTRAL WORLD DIES...

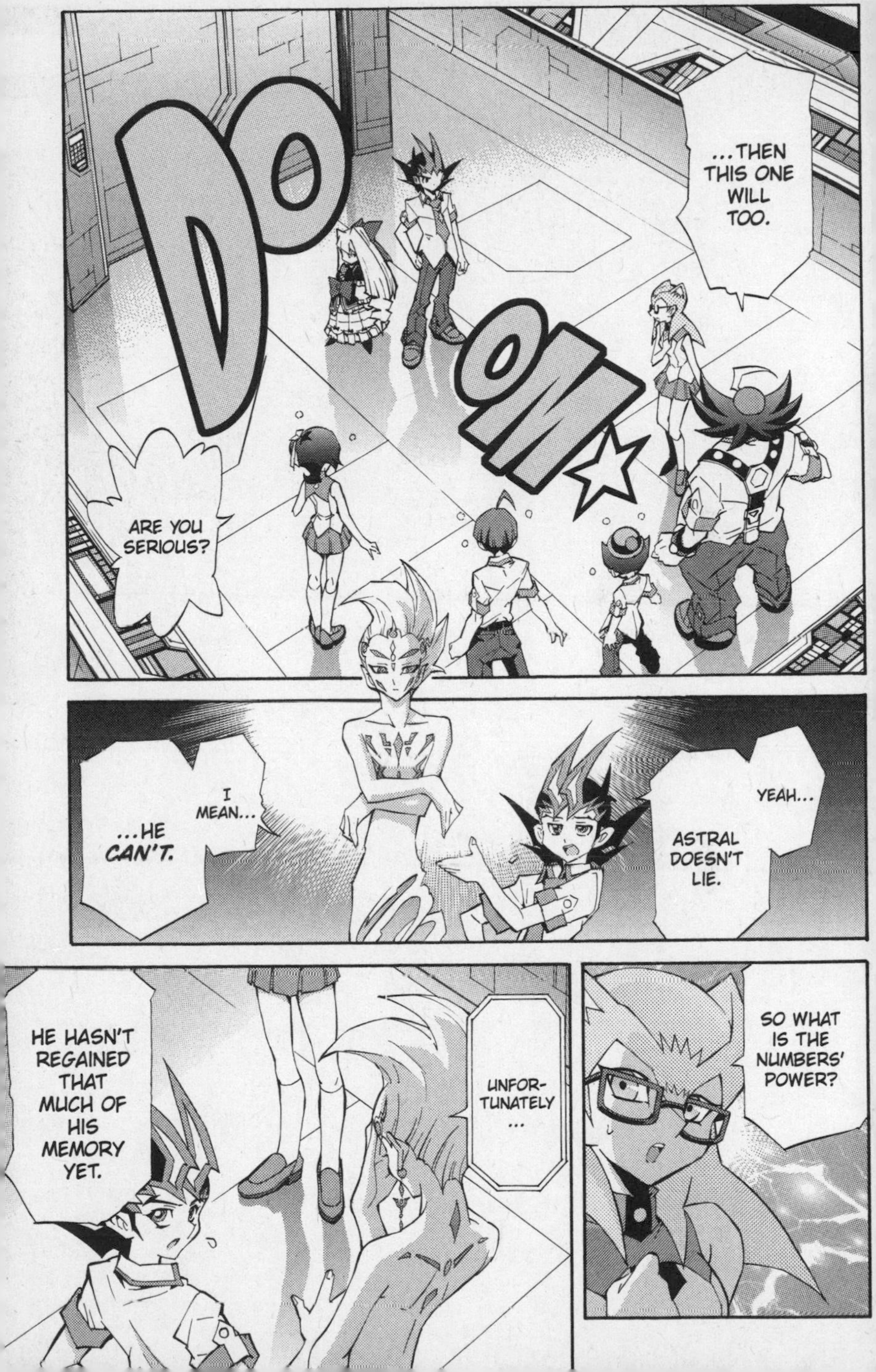
...THEN THIS ONE WILL TOO.
DOON
ARE YOU SERIOUS?
YEAH...
ASTRAL DOESN'T LIE.
I MEAN...
...HE CAN'T.
SO WHAT IS THE NUMBERS' POWER?
UNFORTUNATELY...
HE HASN'T REGAINED THAT MUCH OF HIS MEMORY YET.

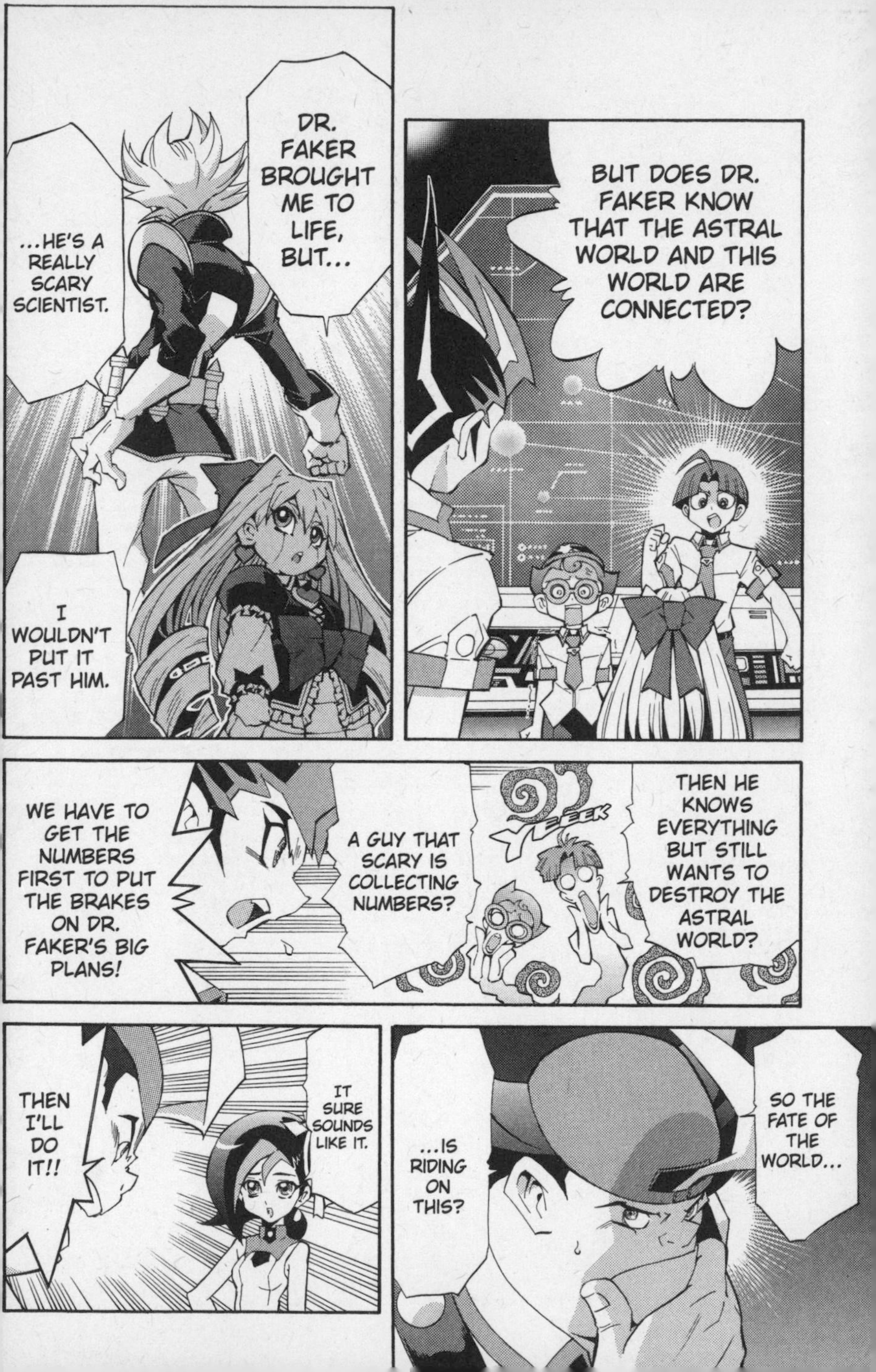
BUT DOES DR. FAKER KNOW THAT THE ASTRAL WORLD AND THIS WORLD ARE CONNECTED?
DR. FAKER BROUGHT ME TO LIFE, BUT...
...HE'S A REALLY SCARY SCIENTIST.
I WOULDN'T PUT IT PAST HIM.
THEN HE KNOWS EVERYTHING BUT STILL WANTS TO DESTROY THE ASTRAL WORLD?
EEEK
A GUY THAT SCARY IS COLLECTING NUMBERS?
WE HAVE TO GET THE NUMBERS FIRST TO PUT THE BRAKES ON DR. FAKER'S BIG PLANS!
SO THE FATE OF THE WORLD...
...IS RIDING ON THIS?
IT SURE SOUNDS LIKE IT.
THEN I'LL DO IT!!

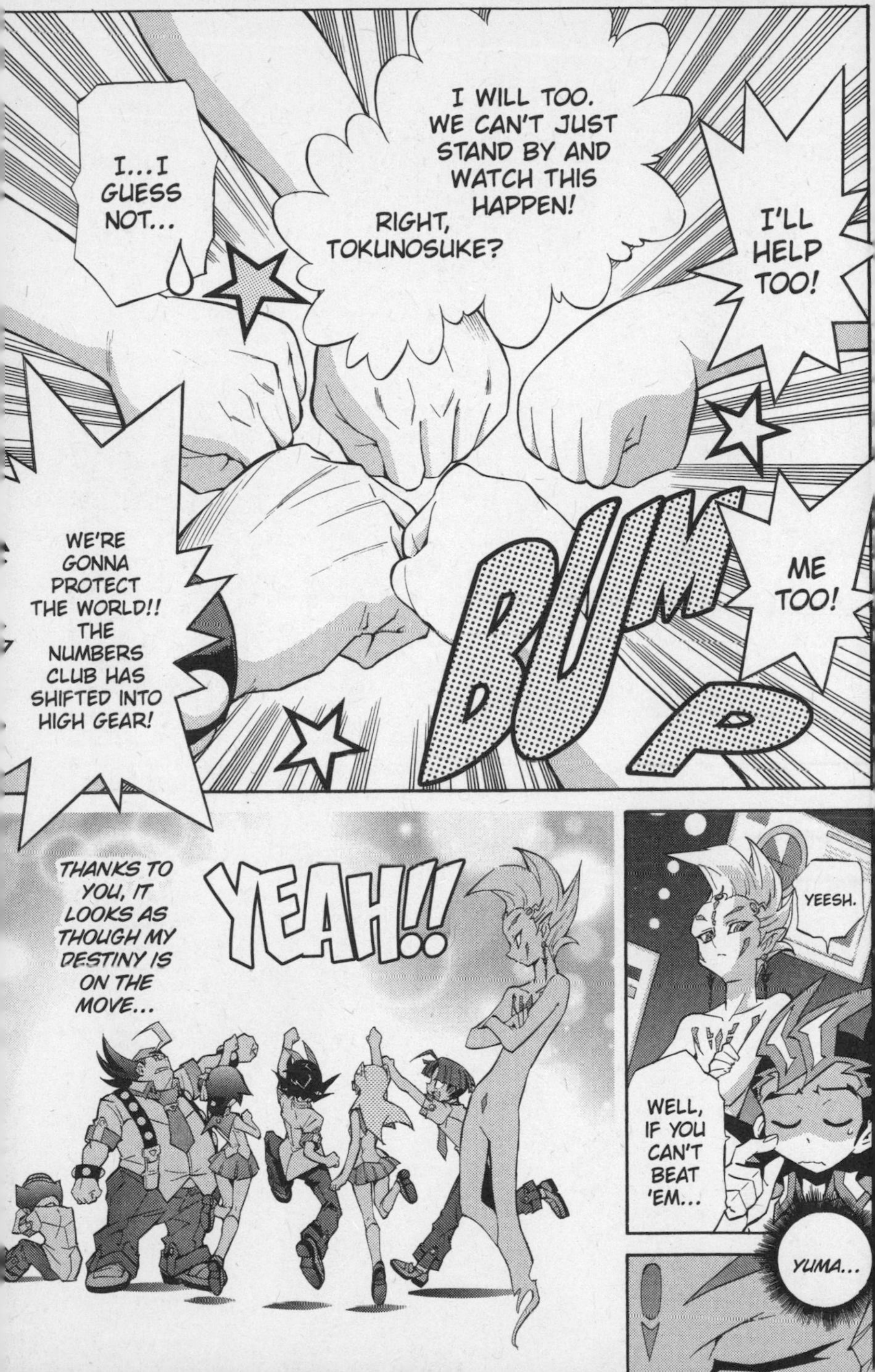
I'LL HELP TOO!
I WILL TOO. WE CAN'T JUST STAND BY AND WATCH THIS HAPPEN!
RIGHT, TOKUNOSUKE?
I...I GUESS NOT...
ME TOO!
BUMP
WE'RE GONNA PROTECT THE WORLD!! THE NUMBERS CLUB HAS SHIFTED INTO HIGH GEAR!
YEESH.
WELL, IF YOU CAN'T BEAT 'EM...
YUMA...
YEAH!!
THANKS TO YOU, IT LOOKS AS THOUGH MY DESTINY IS ON THE MOVE...

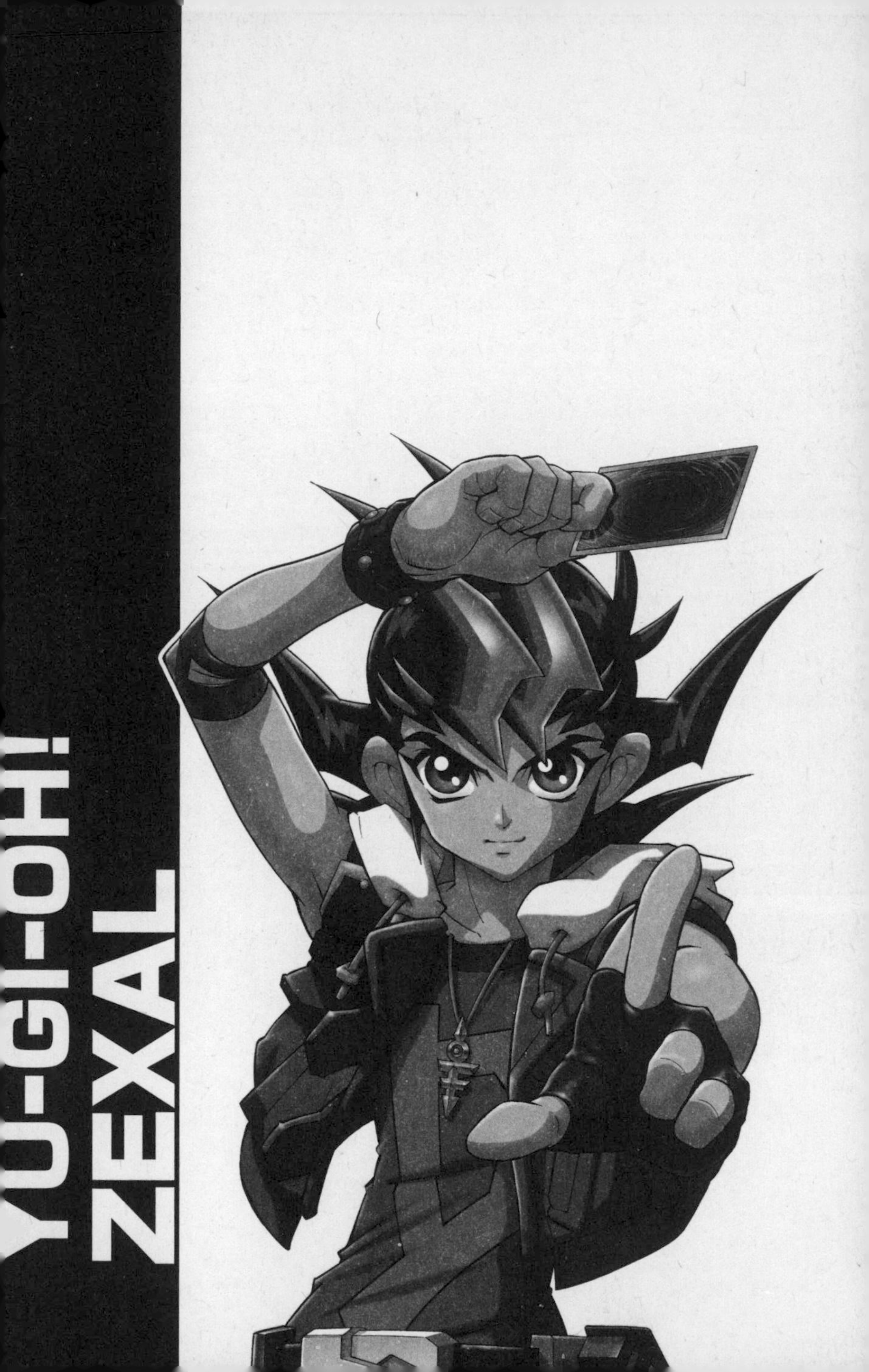
YU-GI-OH!
ZEXAL

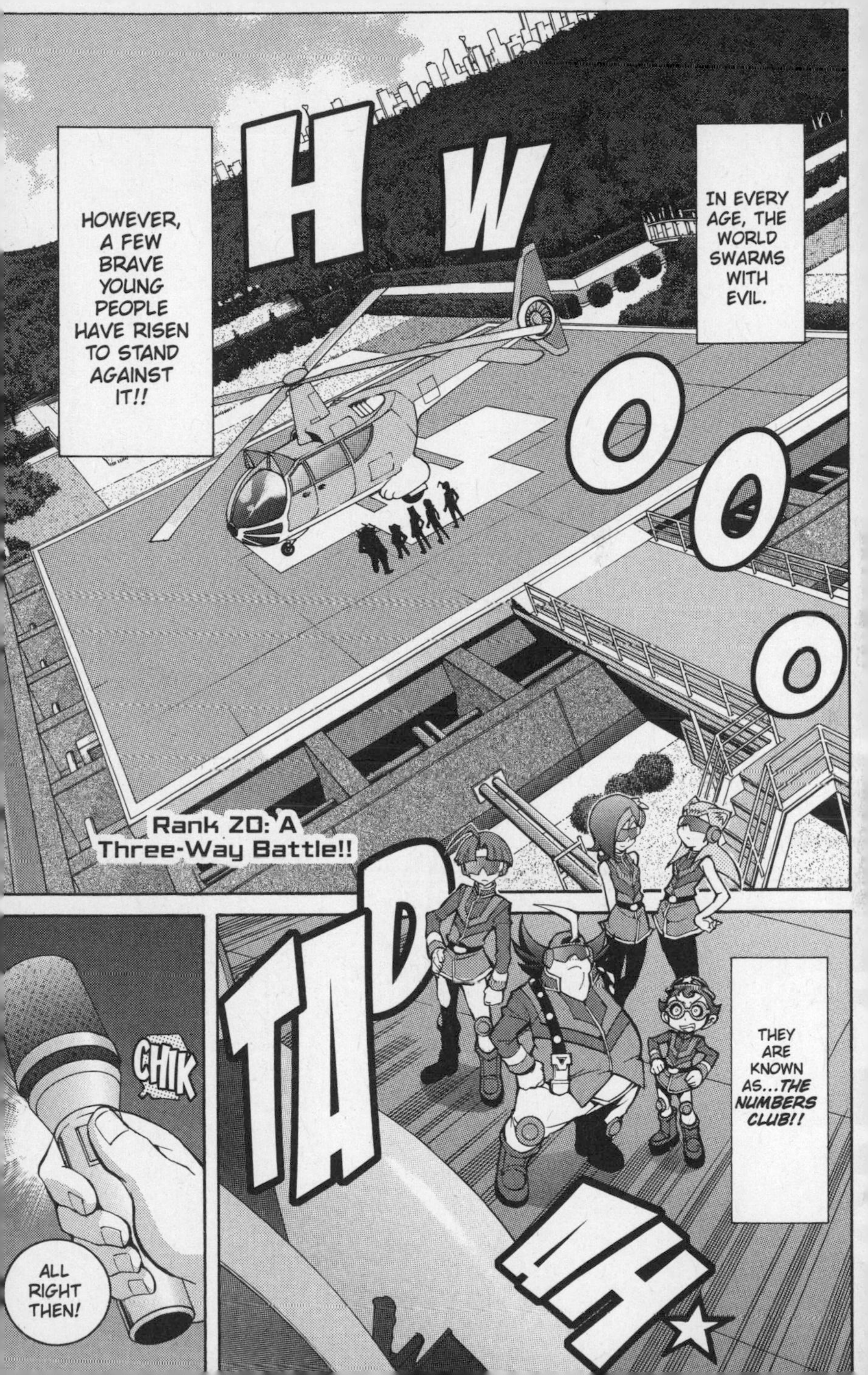
IN EVERY AGE, THE WORLD SWARMS WITH EVIL.
HWOOOO
HOWEVER, A FEW BRAVE YOUNG PEOPLE HAVE RISEN TO STAND AGAINST IT!!
Rank 20: A Three-Way Battle!!
THEY ARE KNOWN AS...*THE NUMBERS CLUB!!*
TADAH
CHIK
ALL RIGHT THEN!

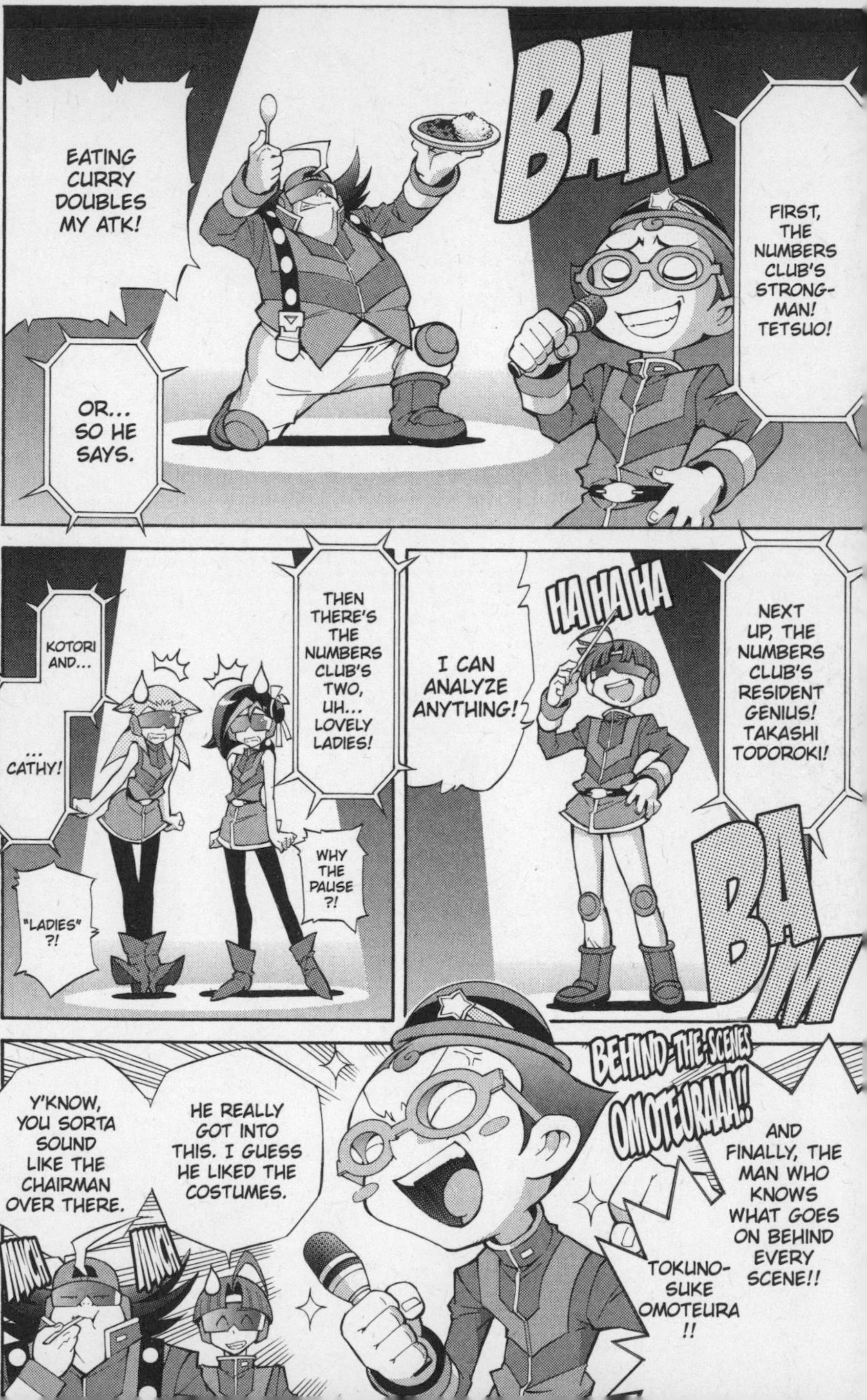
BAM
FIRST, THE NUMBERS CLUB'S STRONG-MAN! TETSUO!
EATING CURRY DOUBLES MY ATK!
OR... SO HE SAYS.
NEXT UP, THE NUMBERS CLUB'S RESIDENT GENIUS! TAKASHI TODOROKI!
HA HA HA
I CAN ANALYZE ANYTHING!
BAM
THEN THERE'S THE NUMBERS CLUB'S TWO, UH... LOVELY LADIES!
KOTORI AND...
... CATHY!
WHY THE PAUSE ?!
"LADIES" ?!
BEHIND-THE-SCENES OMOTEURAAA!!
AND FINALLY, THE MAN WHO KNOWS WHAT GOES ON BEHIND EVERY SCENE!!
TOKUNO-SUKE OMOTEURA !!
HE REALLY GOT INTO THIS. I GUESS HE LIKED THE COSTUMES.
Y'KNOW, YOU SORTA SOUND LIKE THE CHAIRMAN OVER THERE.

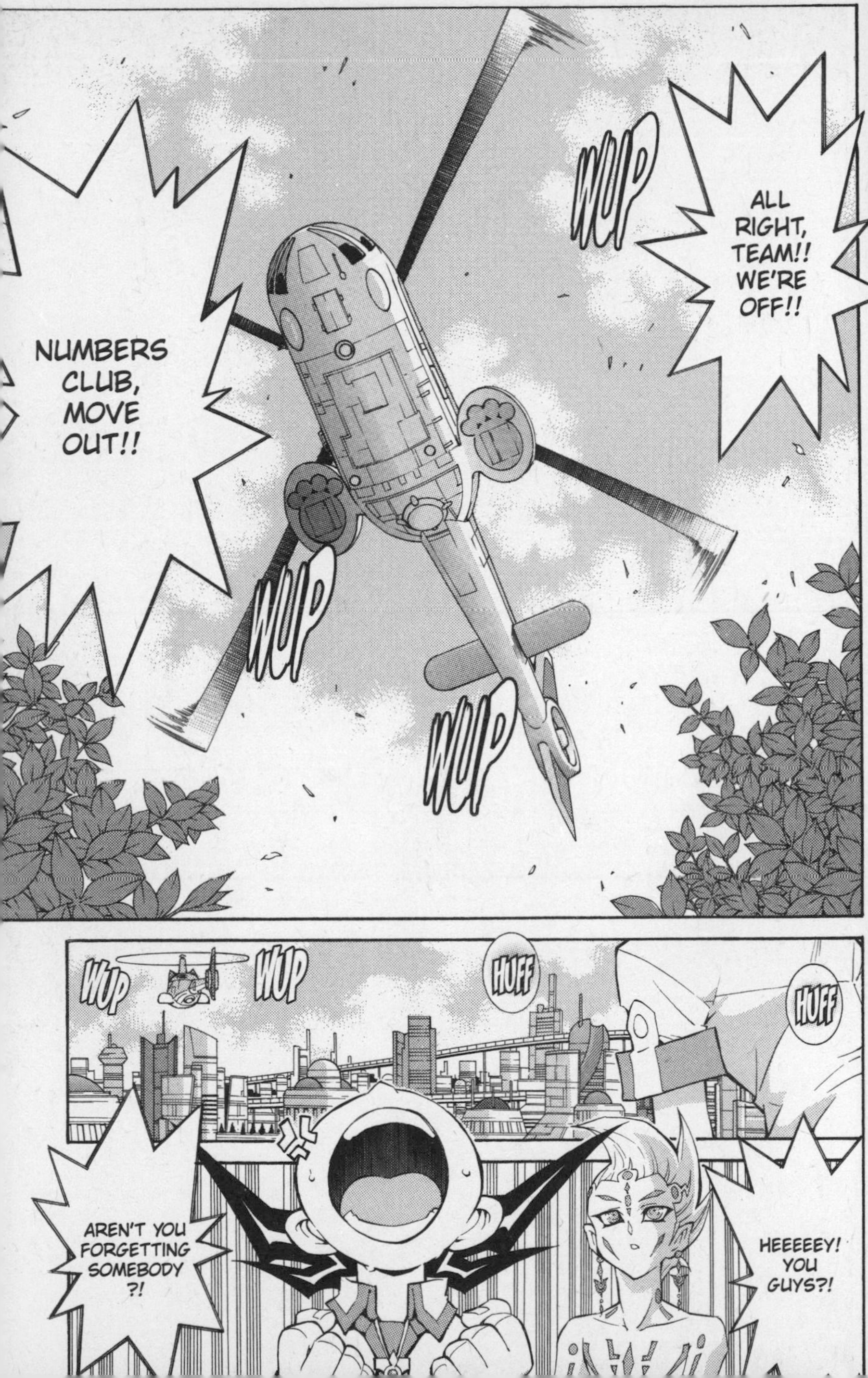
ALL RIGHT, TEAM!! WE'RE OFF!!
WUP
NUMBERS CLUB, MOVE OUT!!
WUP
WUP
HUFF
HUFF
WUP
WUP
HEEEEEY! YOU GUYS?!
AREN'T YOU FORGETTING SOMEBODY ?!

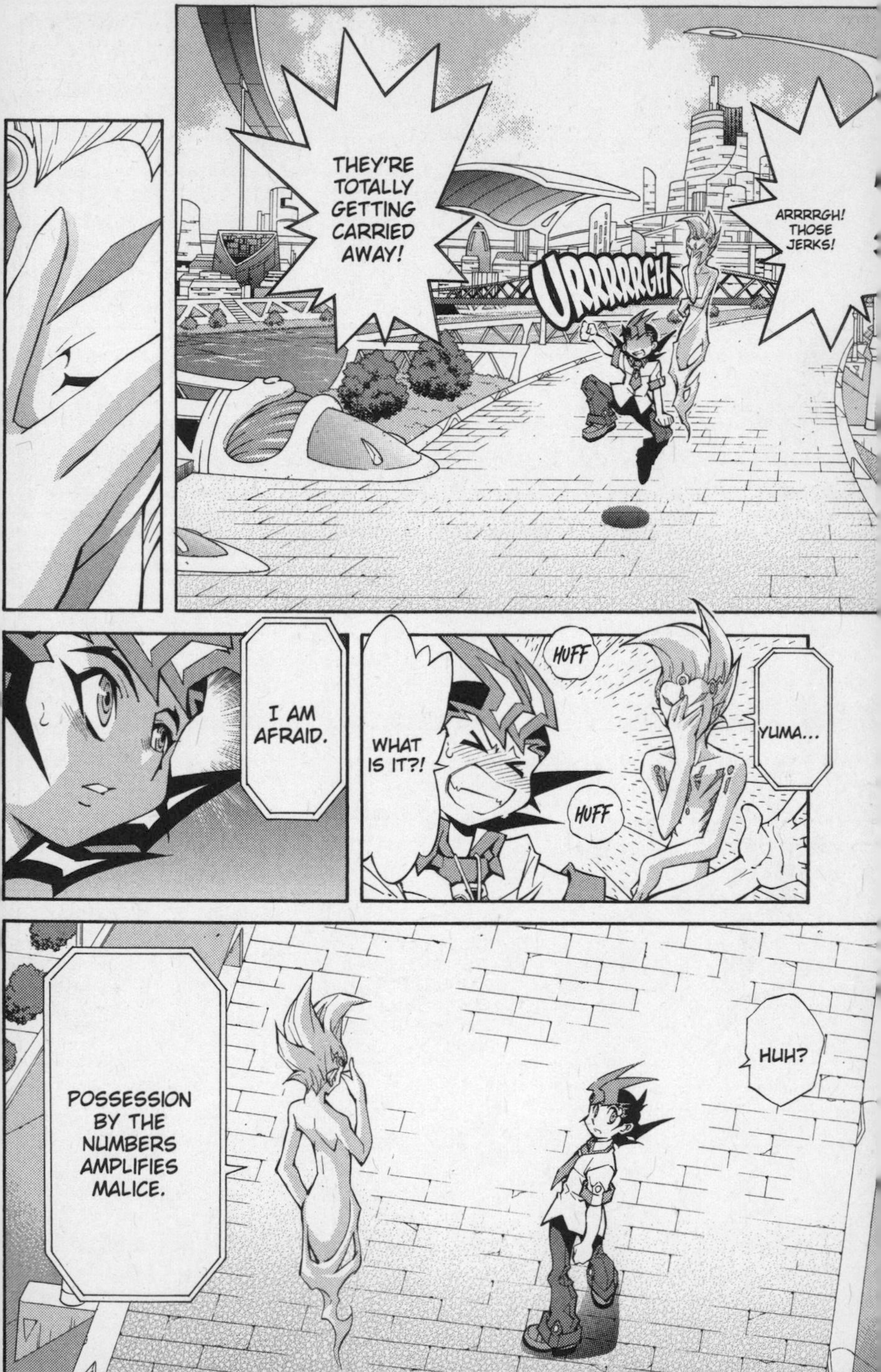
ARRRRGH! THOSE JERKS!
URRRRRGH
THEY'RE TOTALLY GETTING CARRIED AWAY!
YUMA...
HUFF
WHAT IS IT?!
HUFF
I AM AFRAID.
HUH?
POSSESSION BY THE NUMBERS AMPLIFIES MALICE.

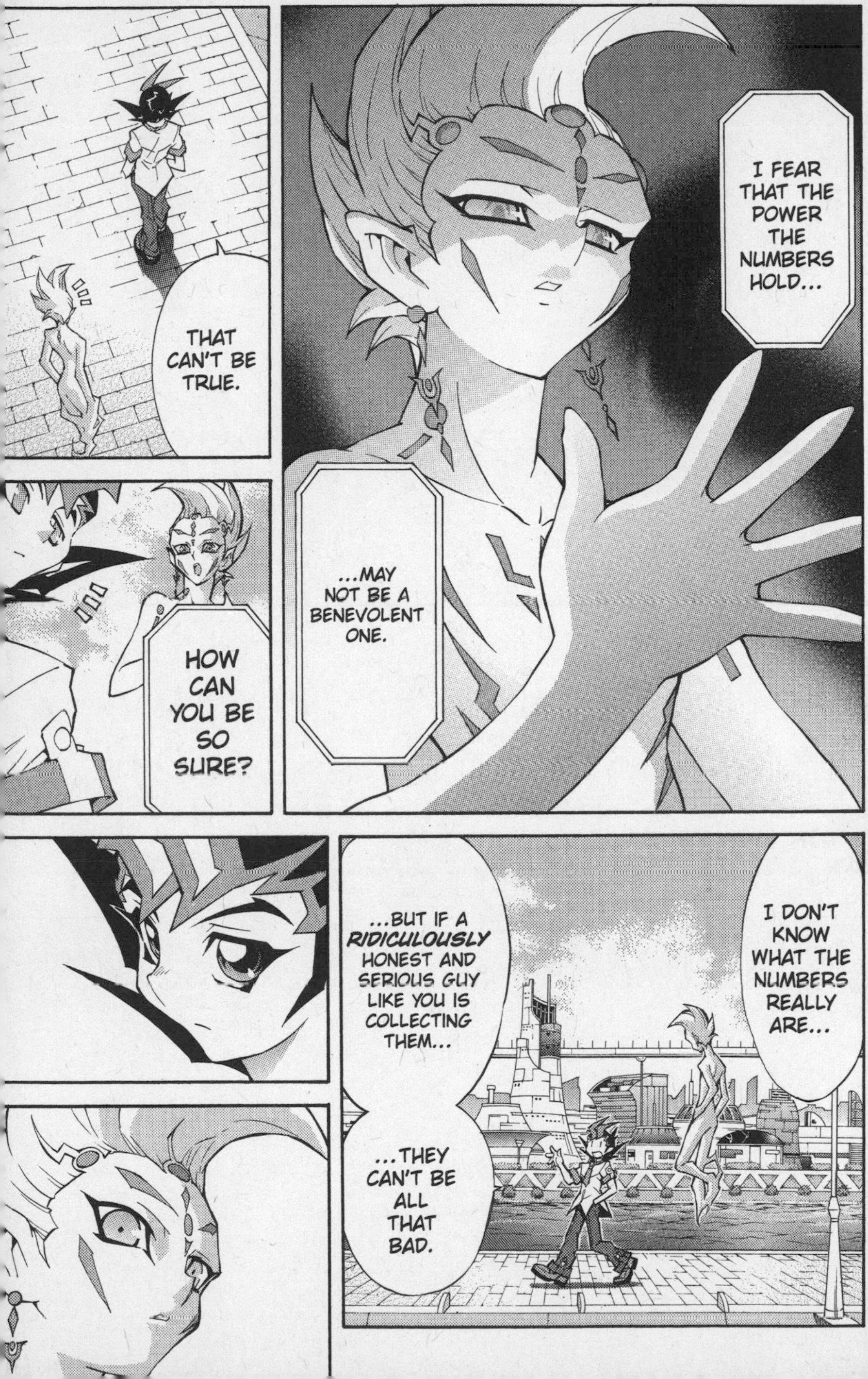
I FEAR THAT THE POWER THE NUMBERS HOLD…
…MAY NOT BE A BENEVOLENT ONE.
THAT CAN'T BE TRUE.
HOW CAN YOU BE SO SURE?
I DON'T KNOW WHAT THE NUMBERS REALLY ARE…
…BUT IF A *RIDICULOUSLY* HONEST AND SERIOUS GUY LIKE YOU IS COLLECTING THEM…
…THEY CAN'T BE ALL THAT BAD.

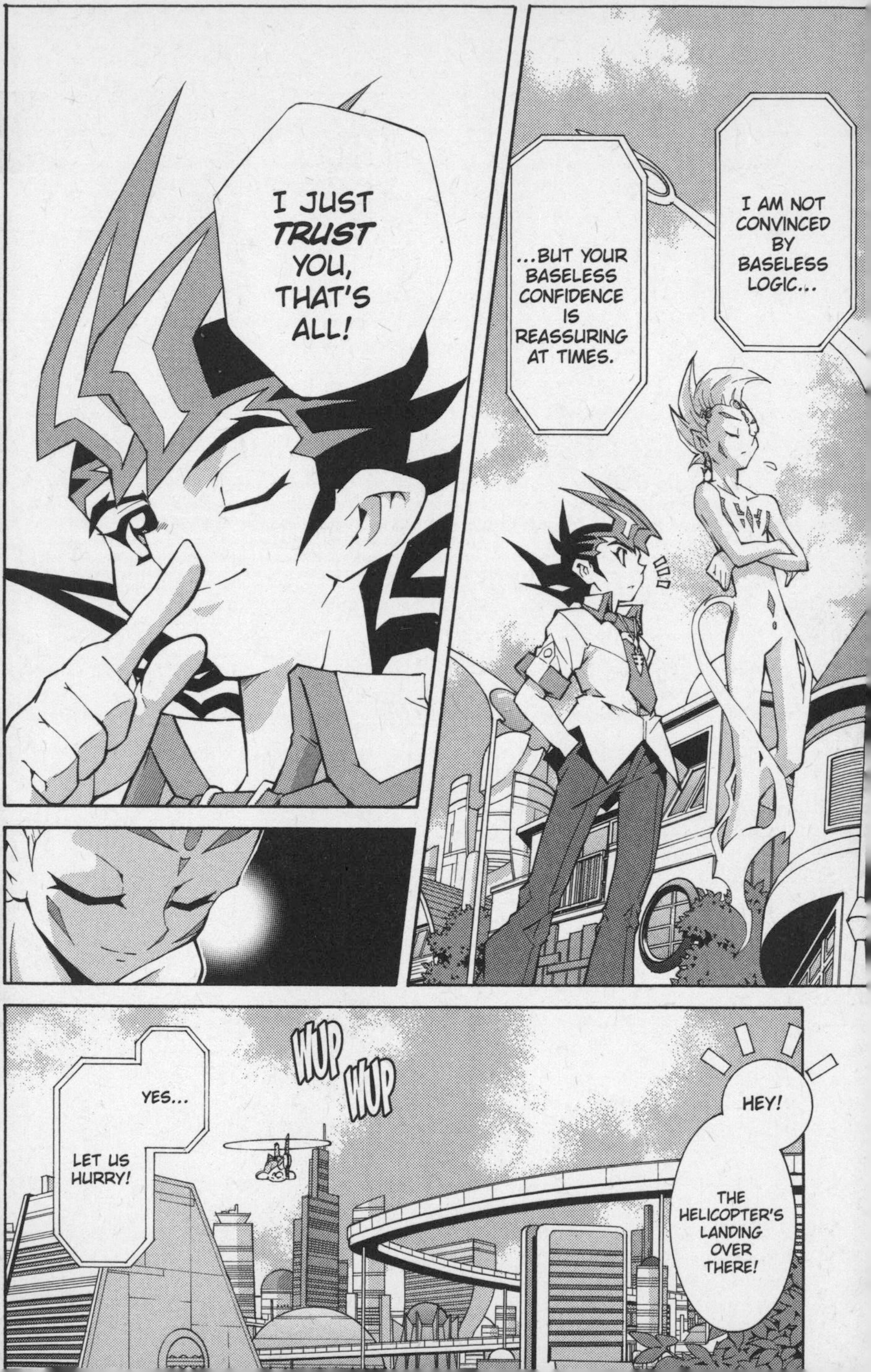
I AM NOT CONVINCED BY BASELESS LOGIC...
...BUT YOUR BASELESS CONFIDENCE IS REASSURING AT TIMES.
I JUST *TRUST* YOU, THAT'S ALL!
HEY!
THE HELICOPTER'S LANDING OVER THERE!
WUP WUP
YES...
LET US HURRY!

*SIGN: POKA POKA RESTAURANT

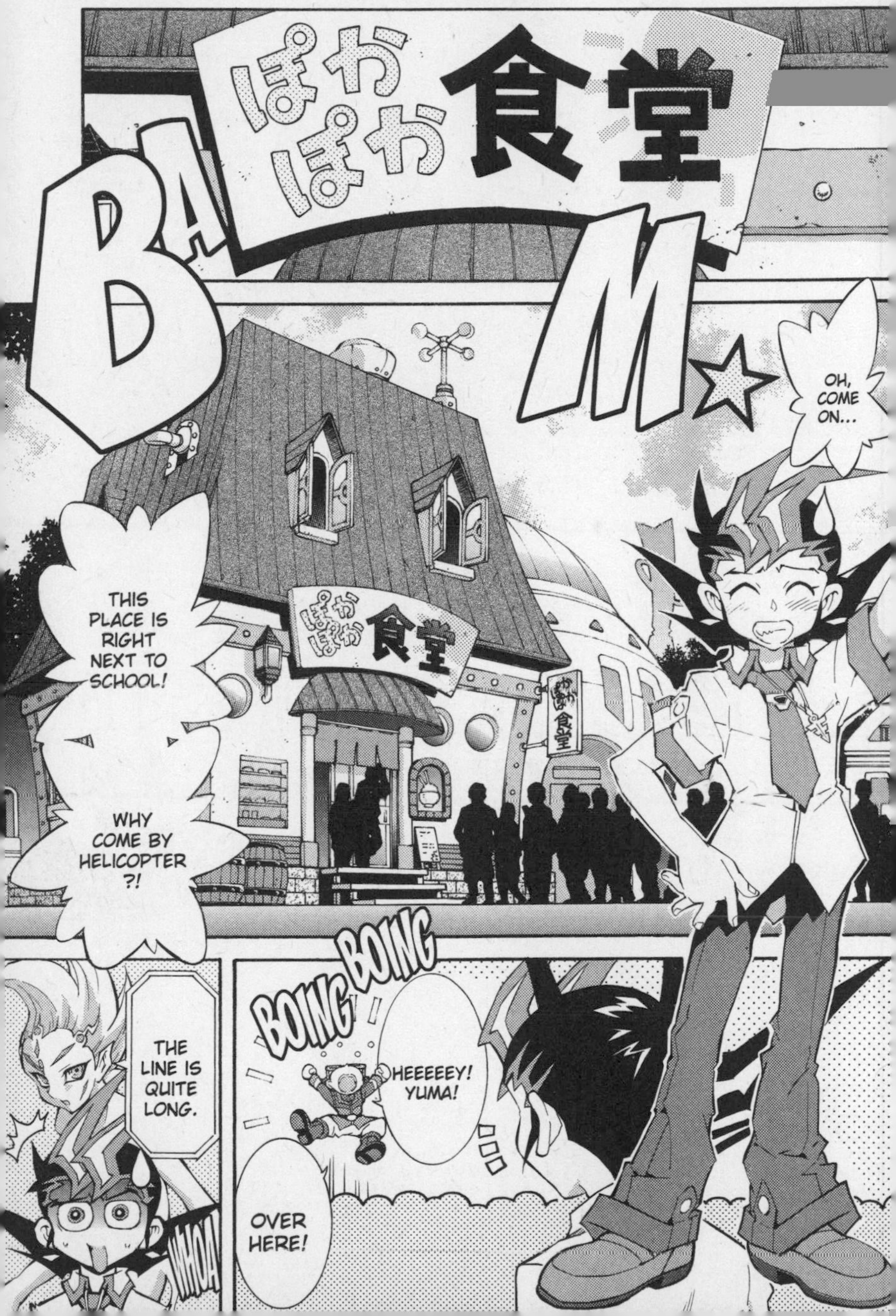
ぽかぽか食堂
BAM☆
OH, COME ON...
THIS PLACE IS RIGHT NEXT TO SCHOOL!
WHY COME BY HELICOPTER?!
BOING BOING
HEEEEEY! YUMA!
OVER HERE!
THE LINE IS QUITE LONG.
WHOA

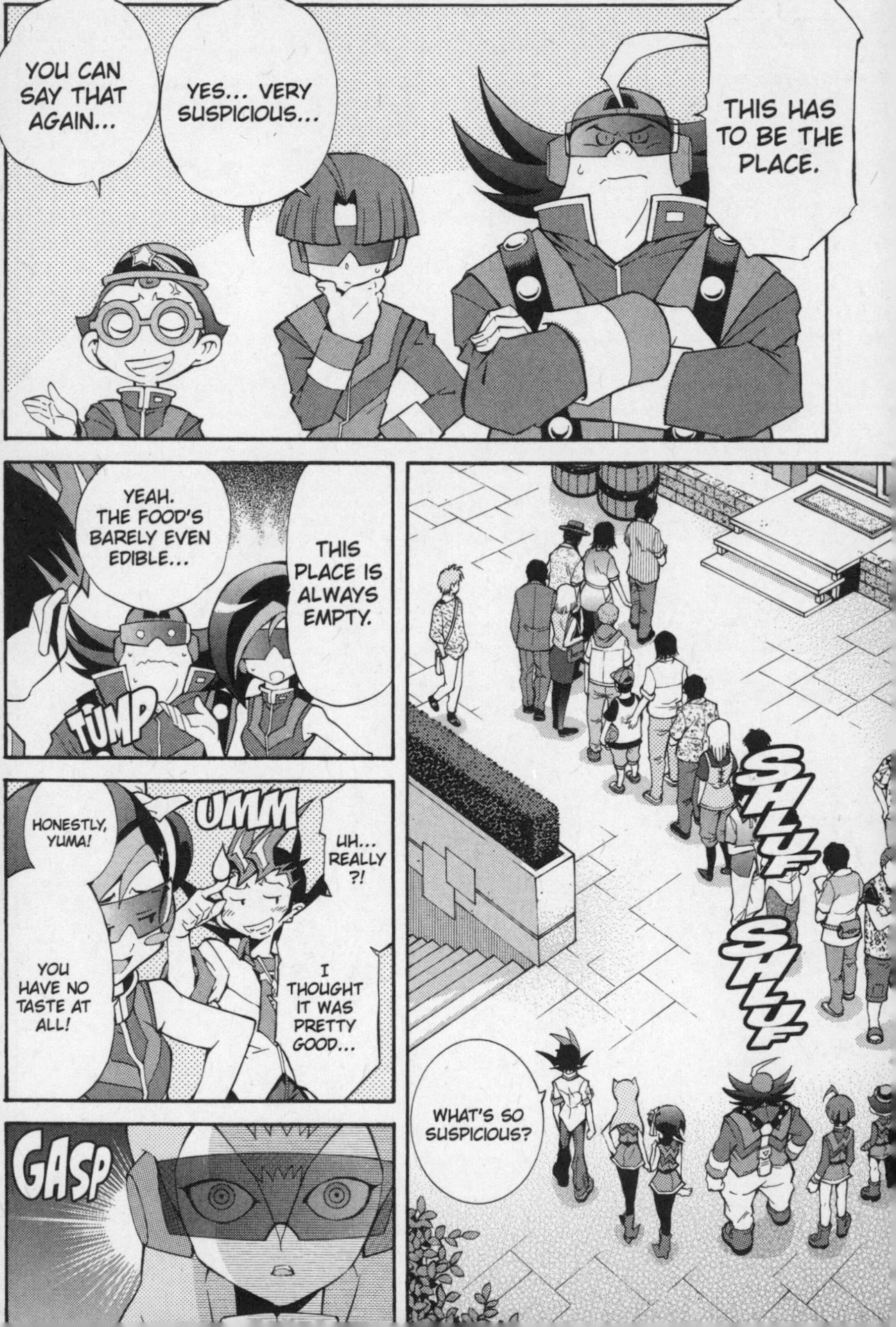
THIS HAS TO BE THE PLACE.
YES... VERY SUSPICIOUS...
YOU CAN SAY THAT AGAIN...
SHLUF
SHLUF
WHAT'S SO SUSPICIOUS?
THIS PLACE IS ALWAYS EMPTY.
YEAH. THE FOOD'S BARELY EVEN EDIBLE...
TUMP
UMM
UH... REALLY?!
HONESTLY, YUMA!
I THOUGHT IT WAS PRETTY GOOD...
YOU HAVE NO TASTE AT ALL!
GASP

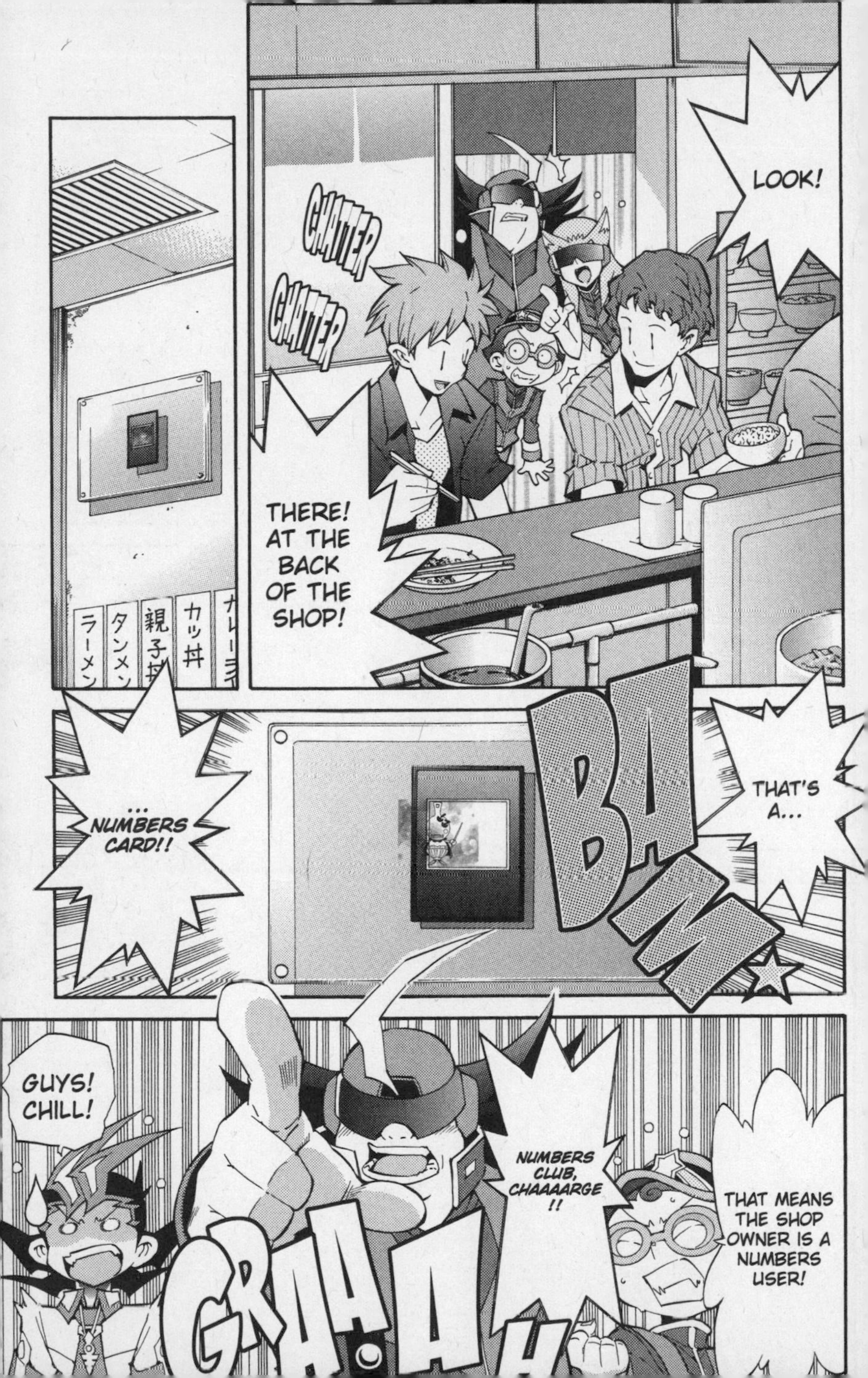
LOOK!
CHATTER
CHATTER
THERE! AT THE BACK OF THE SHOP!
カレー
カツ丼
親子丼
タンメン
ラーメン
THAT'S A...
BAM
... NUMBERS CARD!!
THAT MEANS THE SHOP OWNER IS A NUMBERS USER!
NUMBERS CLUB, CHAAAARGE!!
GUYS! CHILL!

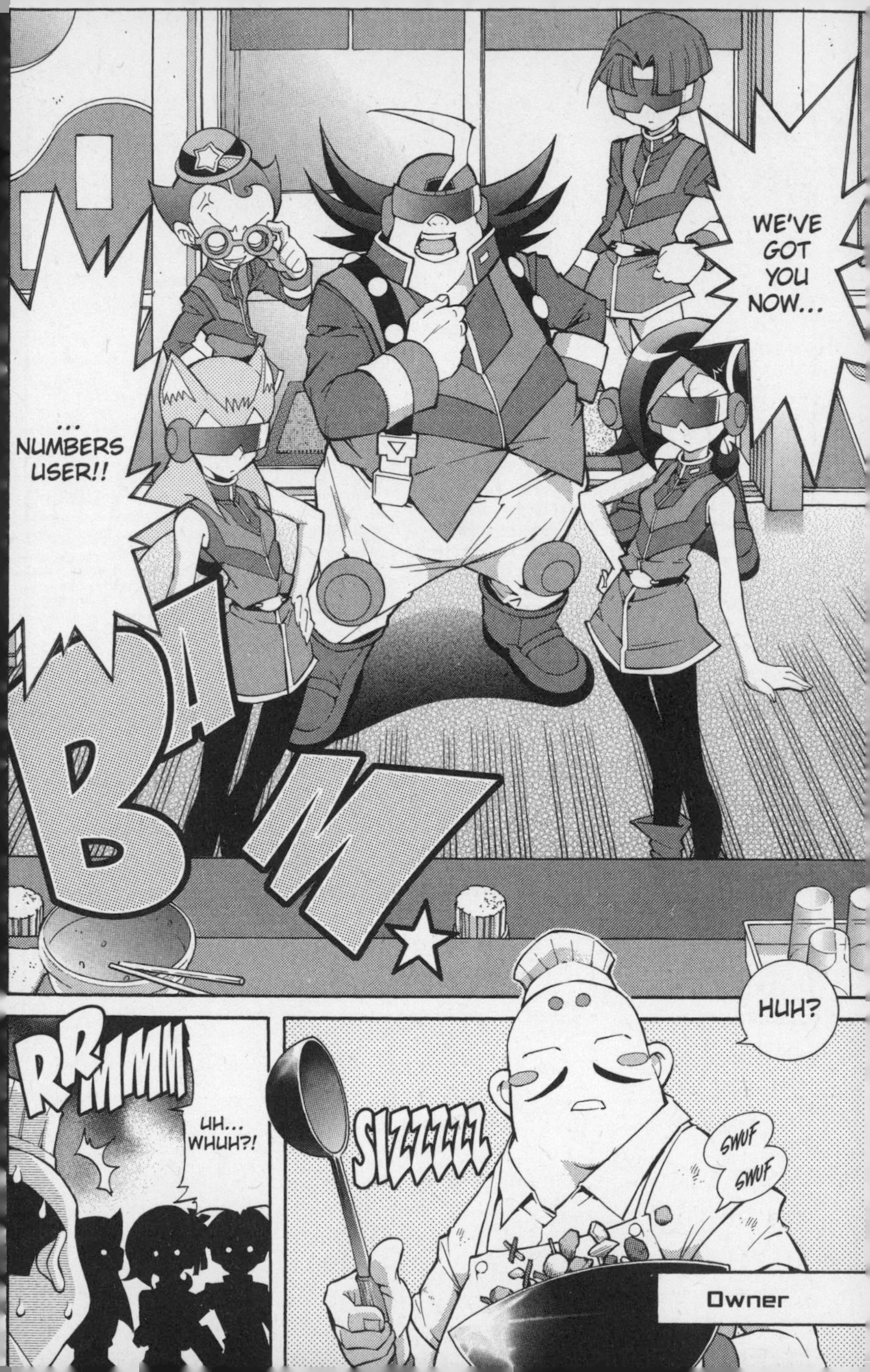
WE'VE GOT YOU NOW...
...NUMBERS USER!!
BAM
HUH?
SWUF SWUF
SIZZZZZZ
Owner
RRMMM
UH... WHUH?!

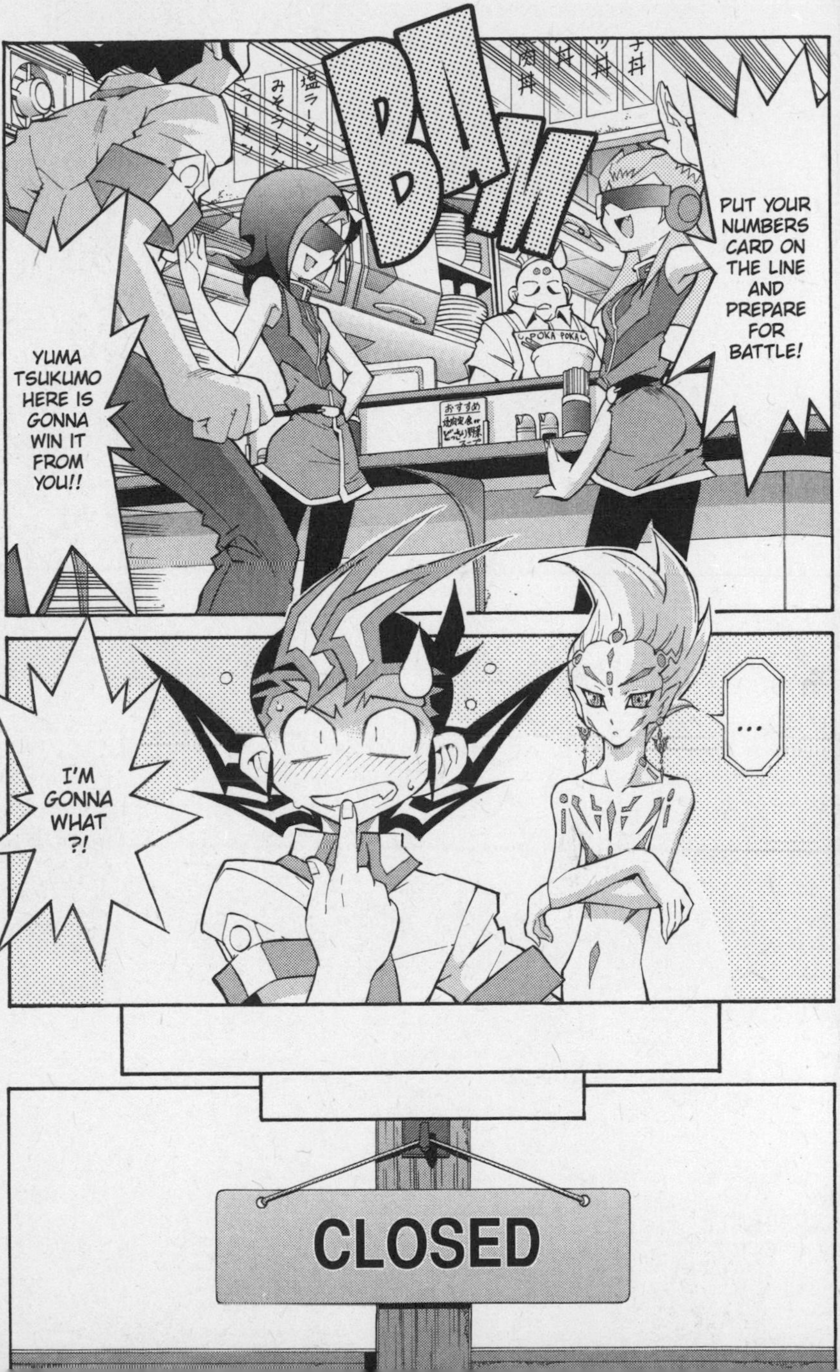
BAM
塩ラーメン
みそラーメン
POKA POKA
PUT YOUR NUMBERS CARD ON THE LINE AND PREPARE FOR BATTLE!
YUMA TSUKUMO HERE IS GONNA WIN IT FROM YOU!!
...
I'M GONNA WHAT?!
CLOSED

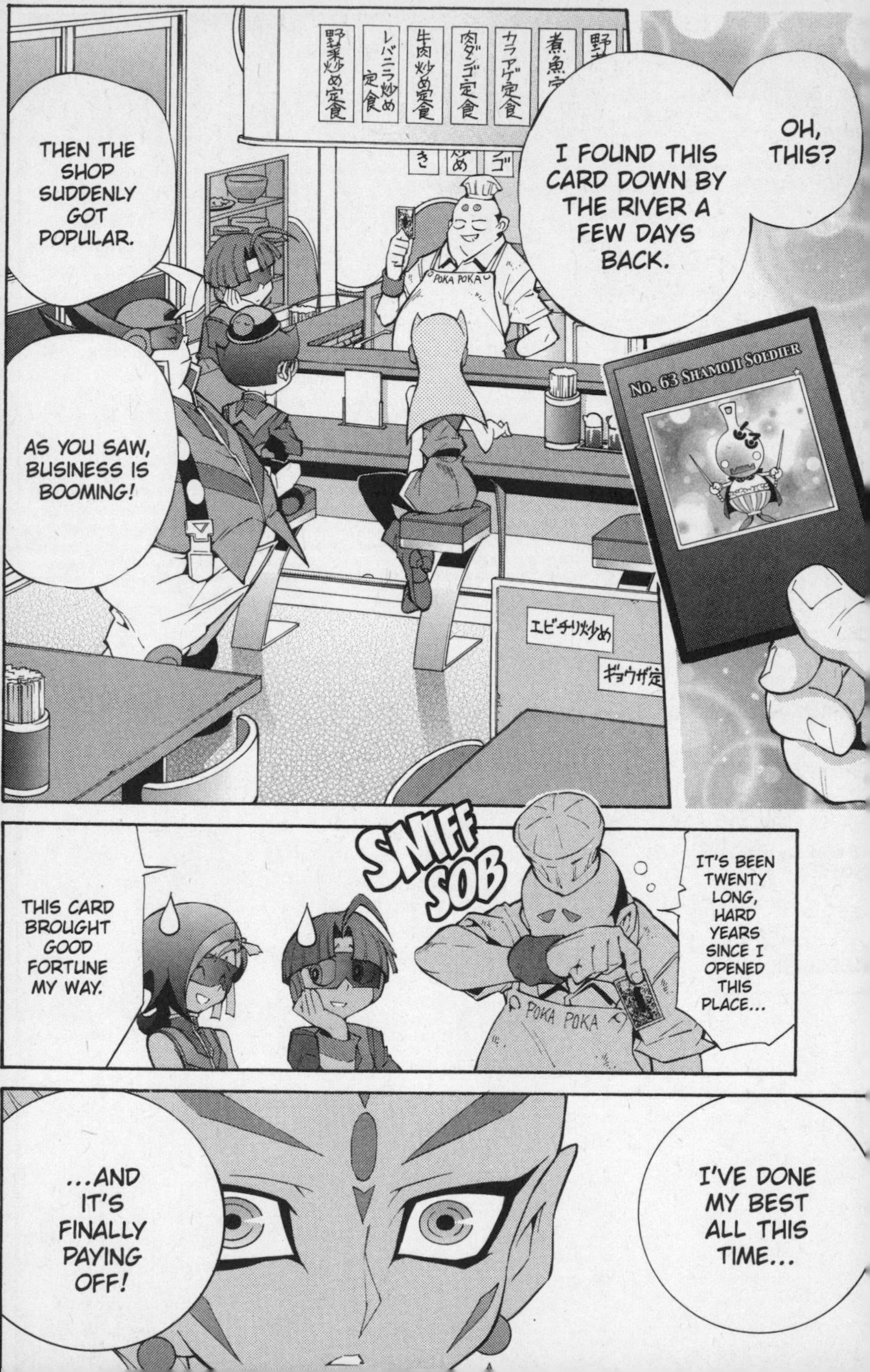

カラアゲ定食
肉ダンゴ定食
牛肉炒め定食
レバニラ炒め定食
野菜炒め定食
OH, THIS?
I FOUND THIS CARD DOWN BY THE RIVER A FEW DAYS BACK.
POKA POKA
THEN THE SHOP SUDDENLY GOT POPULAR.
No. 63 SHAMOJI SOLDIER
AS YOU SAW, BUSINESS IS BOOMING!
エビチリ炒め
ギョウザ定
IT'S BEEN TWENTY LONG, HARD YEARS SINCE I OPENED THIS PLACE...
SNIFF SOB
POKA POKA
THIS CARD BROUGHT GOOD FORTUNE MY WAY.
I'VE DONE MY BEST ALL THIS TIME...
...AND IT'S FINALLY PAYING OFF!

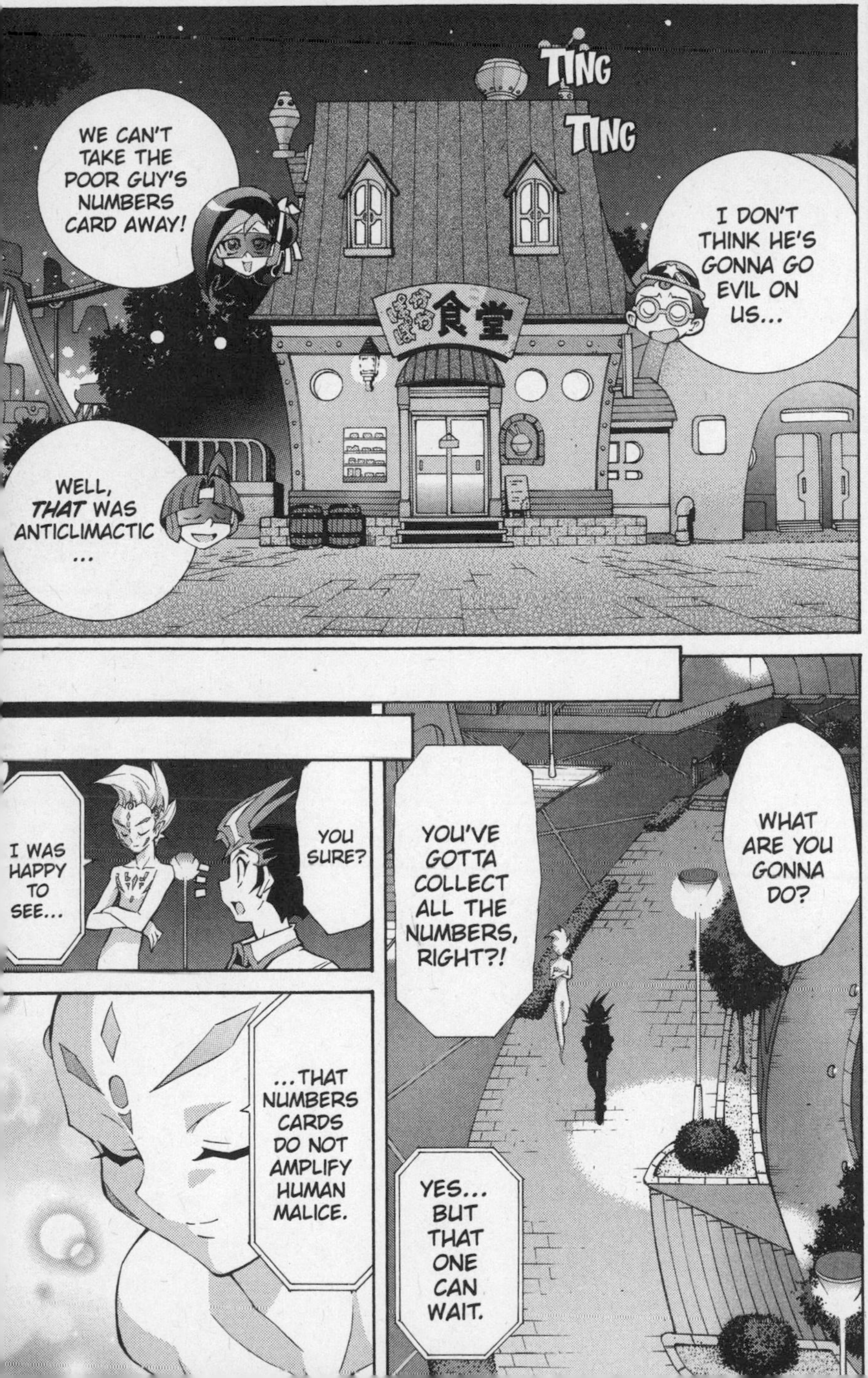
TING
TING
I DON'T THINK HE'S GONNA GO EVIL ON US...
WE CAN'T TAKE THE POOR GUY'S NUMBERS CARD AWAY!
食堂
WELL, *THAT* WAS ANTICLIMACTIC...
WHAT ARE YOU GONNA DO?
YOU'VE GOTTA COLLECT ALL THE NUMBERS, RIGHT?!
YES... BUT THAT ONE CAN WAIT.
YOU SURE?
I WAS HAPPY TO SEE...
...THAT NUMBERS CARDS DO NOT AMPLIFY HUMAN MALICE.

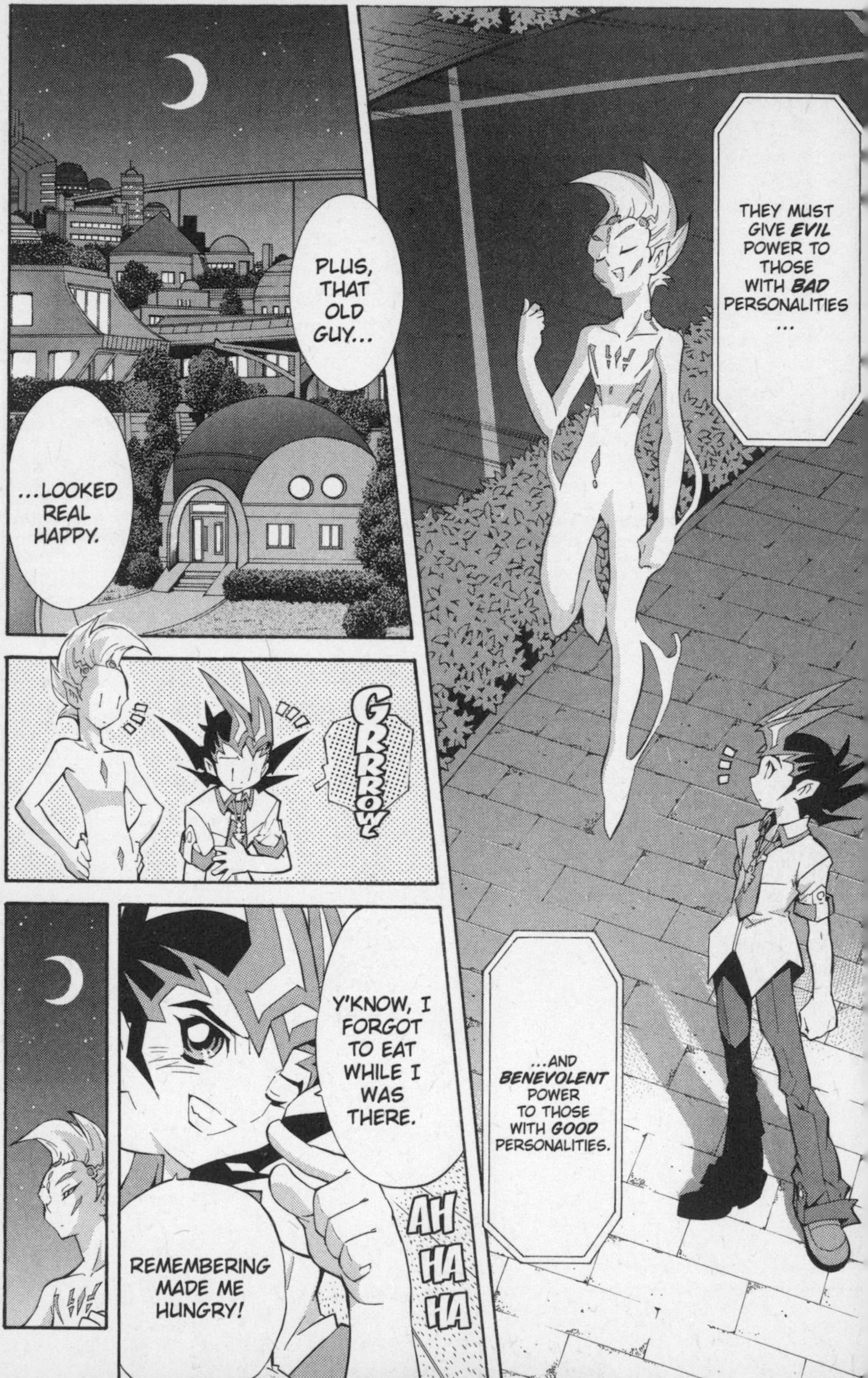
THEY MUST GIVE EVIL POWER TO THOSE WITH BAD PERSONALITIES...
...AND BENEVOLENT POWER TO THOSE WITH GOOD PERSONALITIES.
PLUS, THAT OLD GUY...
...LOOKED REAL HAPPY.
GRRROWL
Y'KNOW, I FORGOT TO EAT WHILE I WAS THERE.
AH HA HA
REMEMBERING MADE ME HUNGRY!

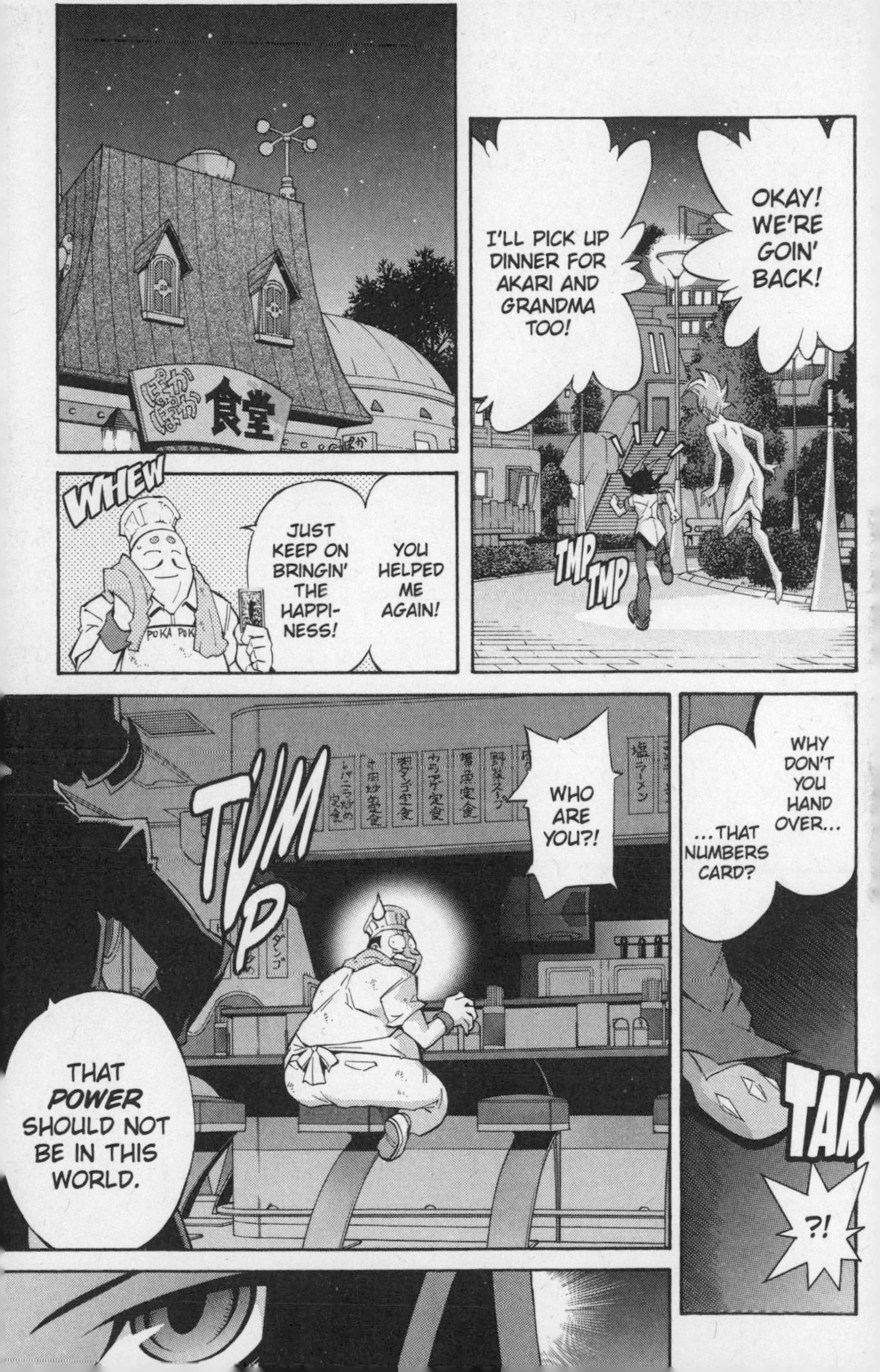
OKAY! WE'RE GOIN' BACK!
I'LL PICK UP DINNER FOR AKARI AND GRANDMA TOO!
TMP TMP
ぽかぽか食堂
YOU HELPED ME AGAIN!
JUST KEEP ON BRINGIN' THE HAPPI-NESS!
WHEW
POKA POK
WHY DON'T YOU HAND OVER...
...THAT NUMBERS CARD?
TAK
?!
WHO ARE YOU?!
TUMP
THAT POWER SHOULD NOT BE IN THIS WORLD.

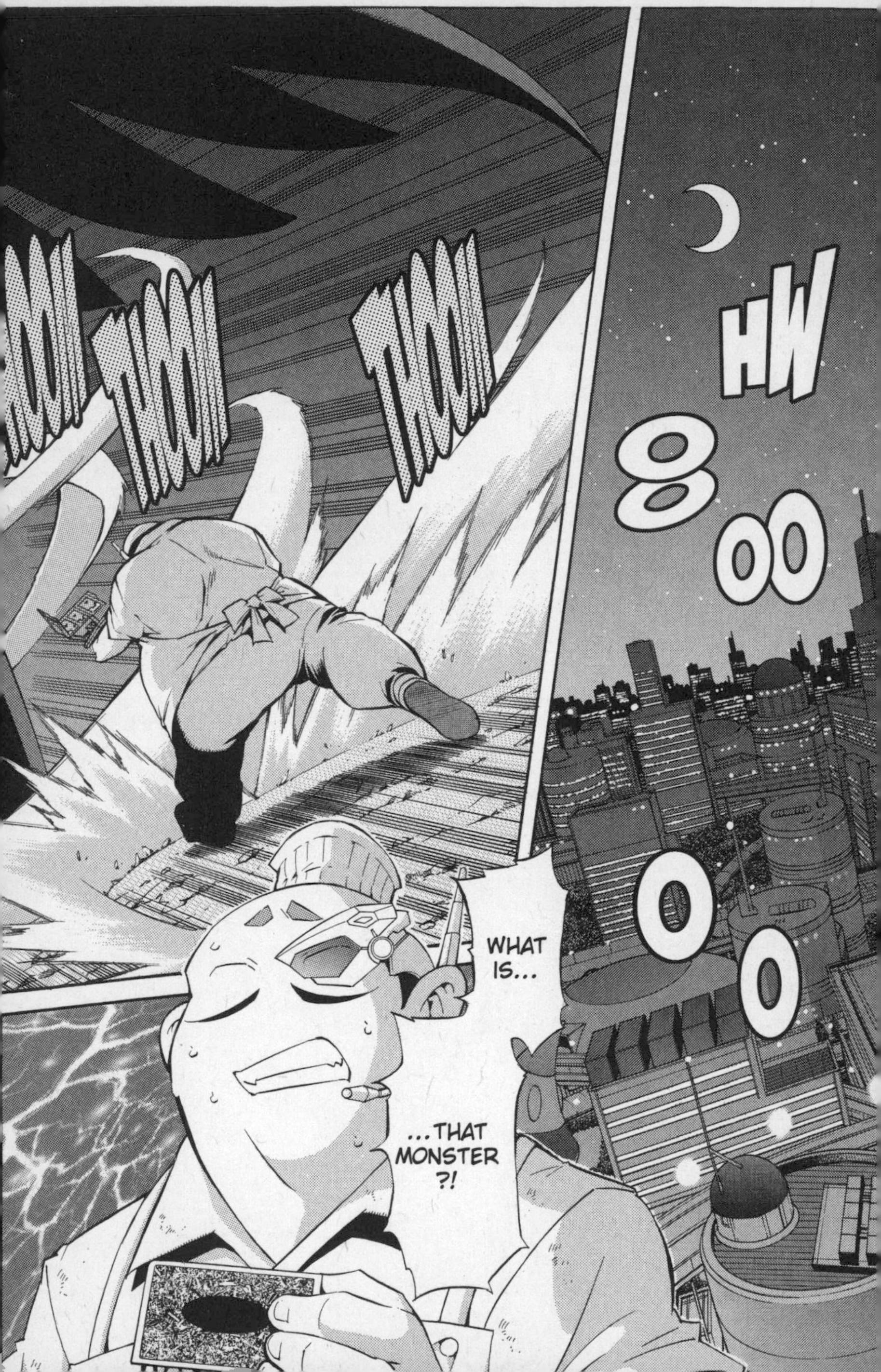
WHAT IS...
...THAT MONSTER ?!

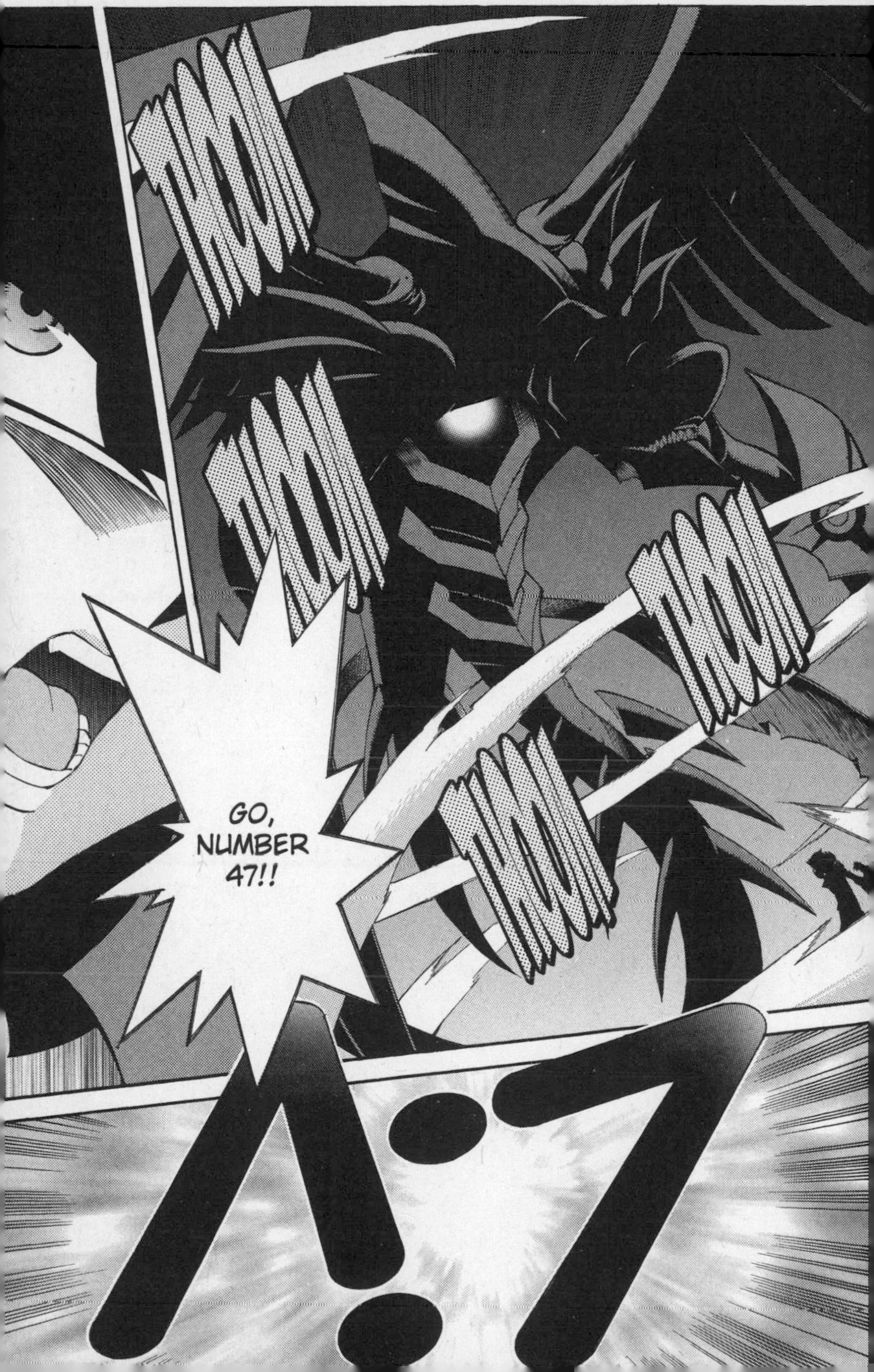
THOOM!
THOOM!
THOOM!
THOOM!
GO, NUMBER 47!!

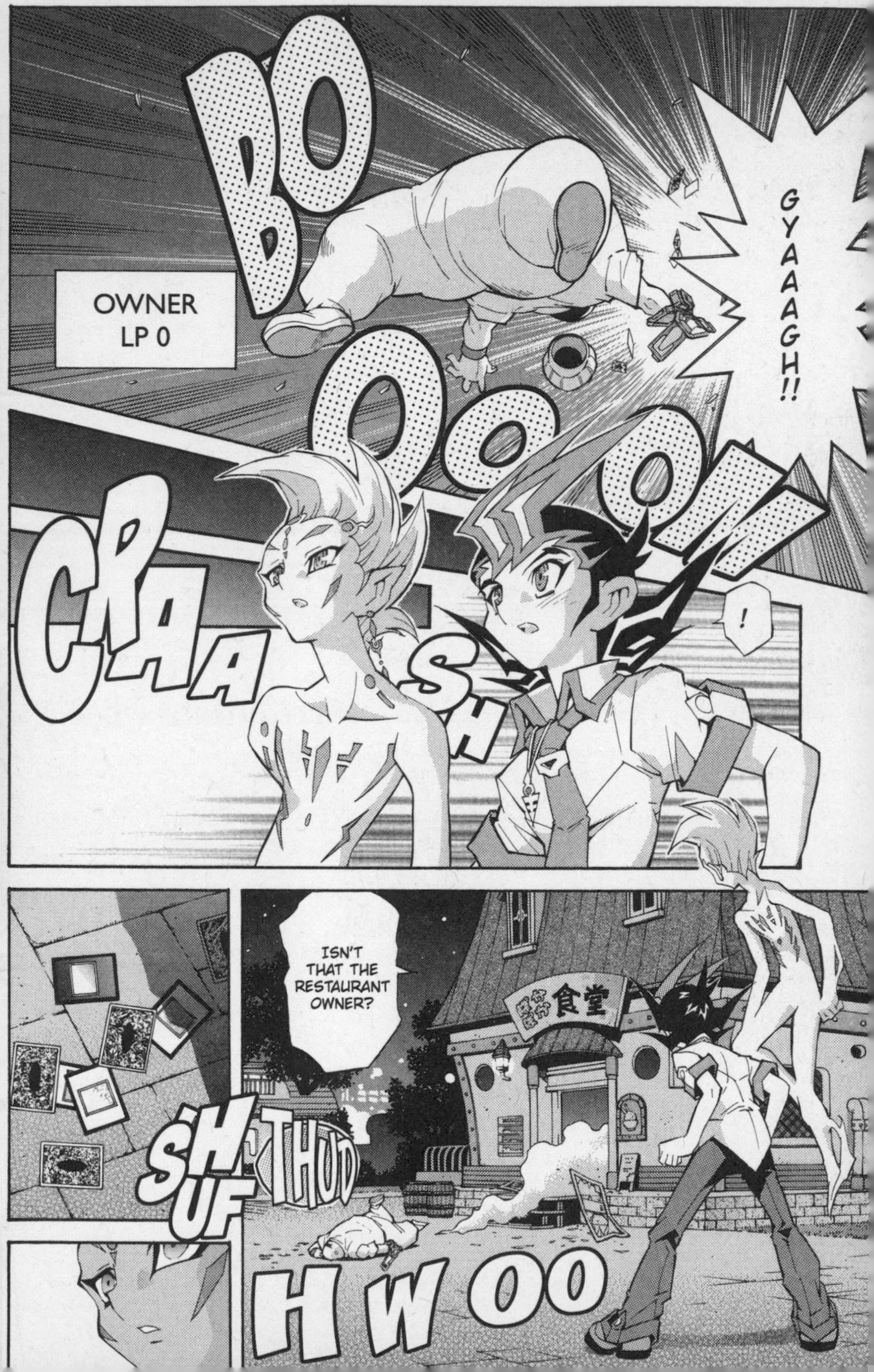
GYAAAAGH!!
BOOOOM!!
OWNER
LP 0
!
CRAASH
ISN'T THAT THE RESTAURANT OWNER?
食堂
SHUF
THUD
HWOO

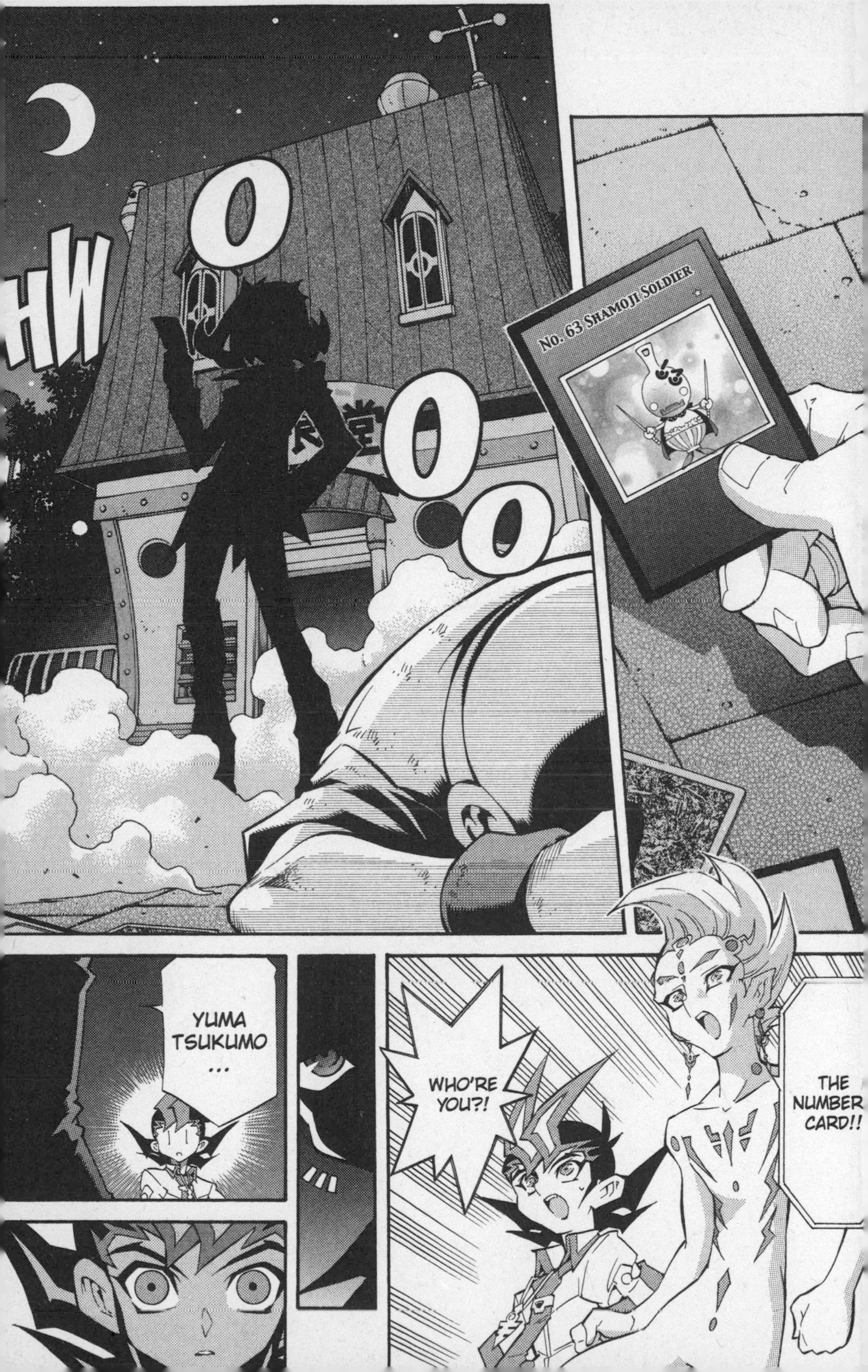
No. 63 Shamoji Soldier
HWOOOO
THE NUMBER CARD!!
WHO'RE YOU?!
YUMA TSUKUMO ...

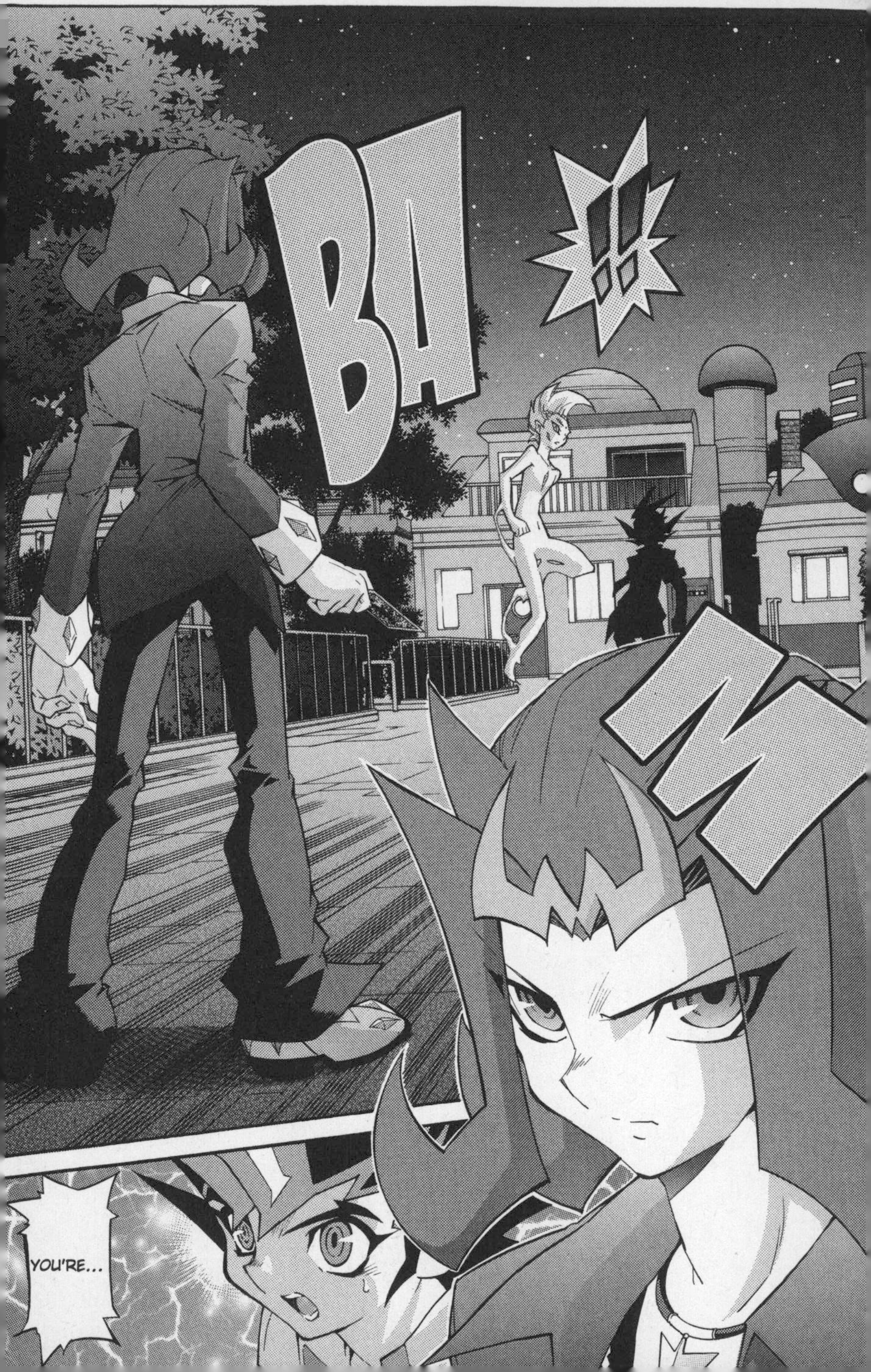
BA
!!
M
YOU'RE...

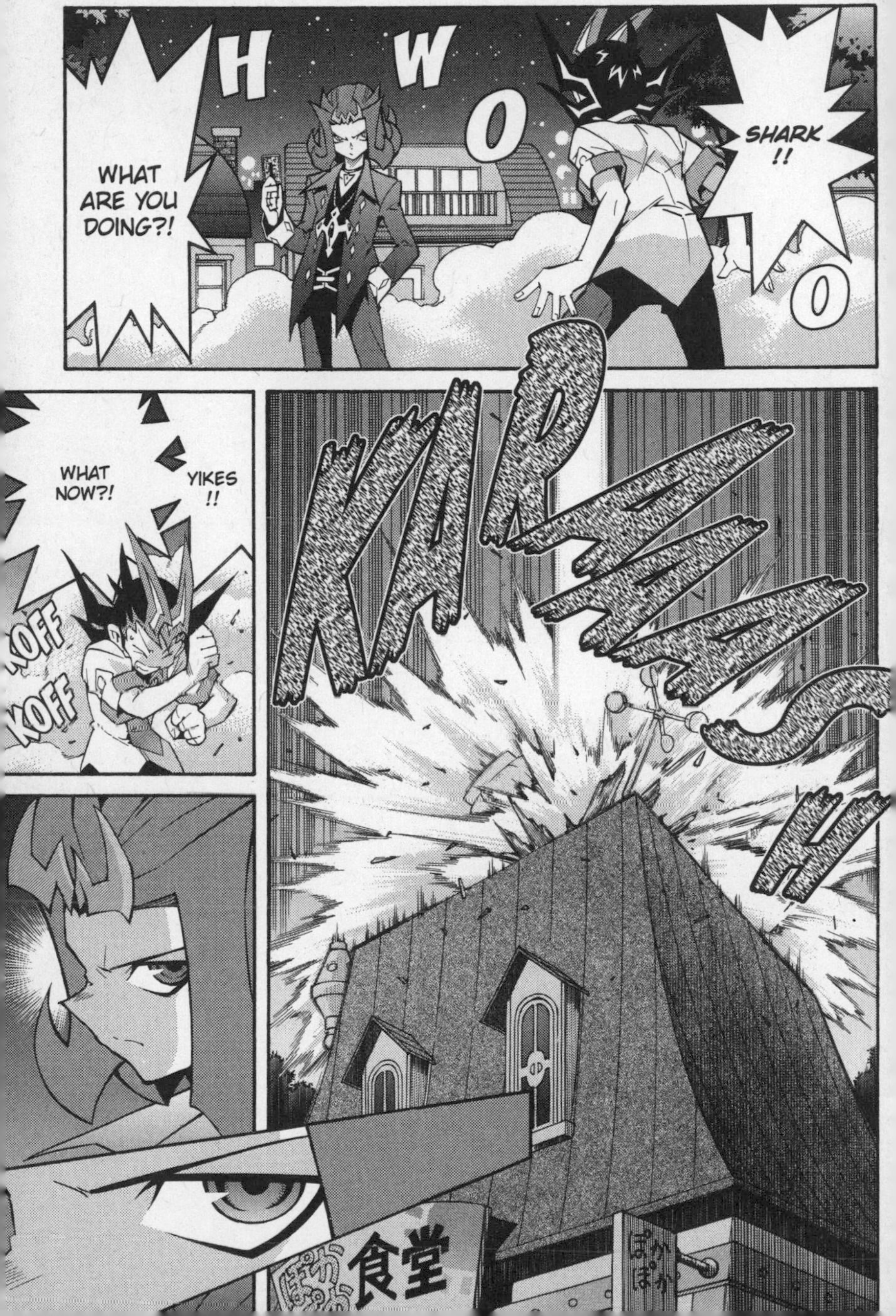
SHARK !!
WHAT ARE YOU DOING?!
KAPAAAAH
YIKES !!
WHAT NOW?!
KOFF
KOFF
ぽかぽか
食堂

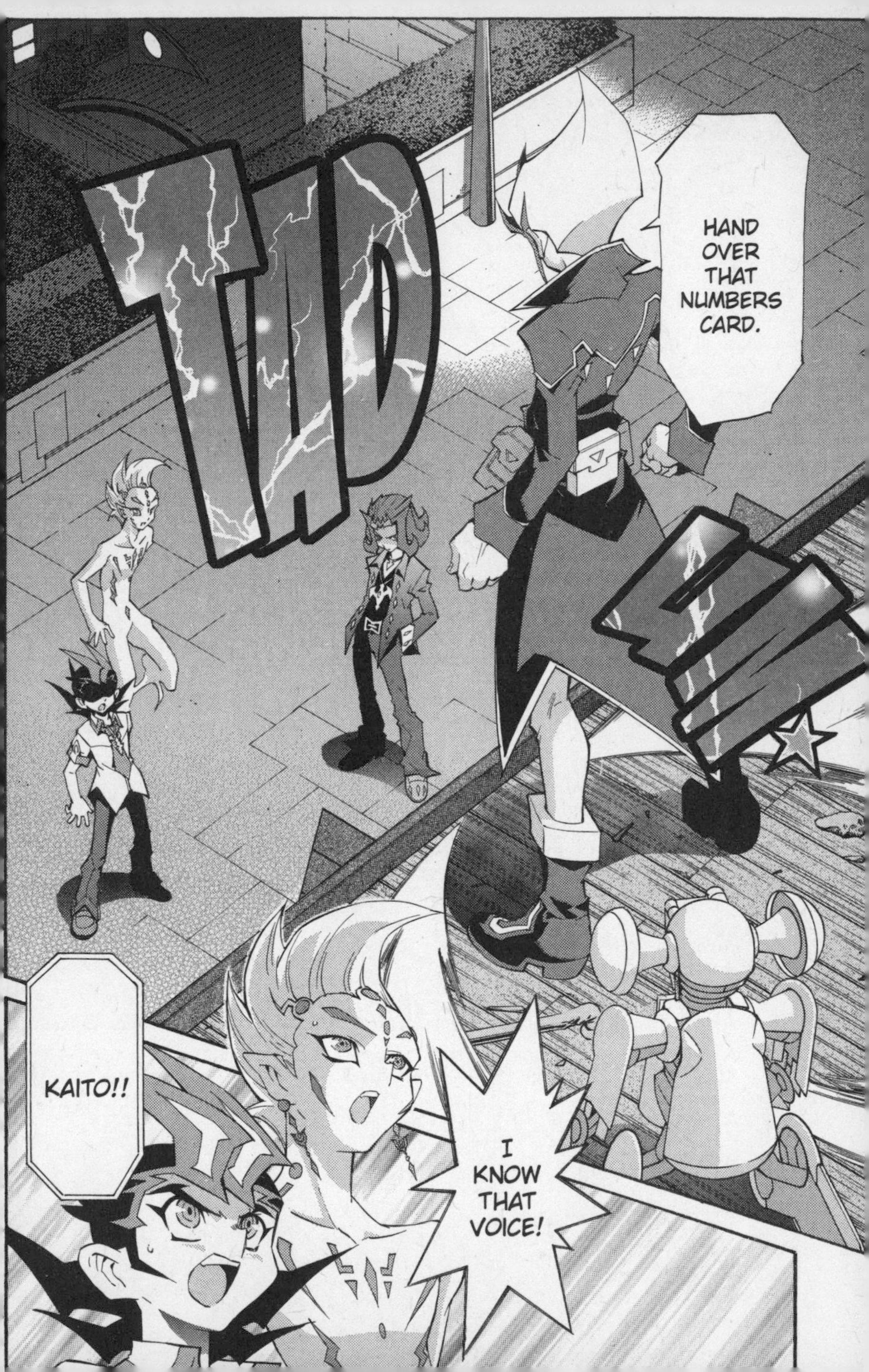
HAND OVER THAT NUMBERS CARD.
I KNOW THAT VOICE!
KAITO!!

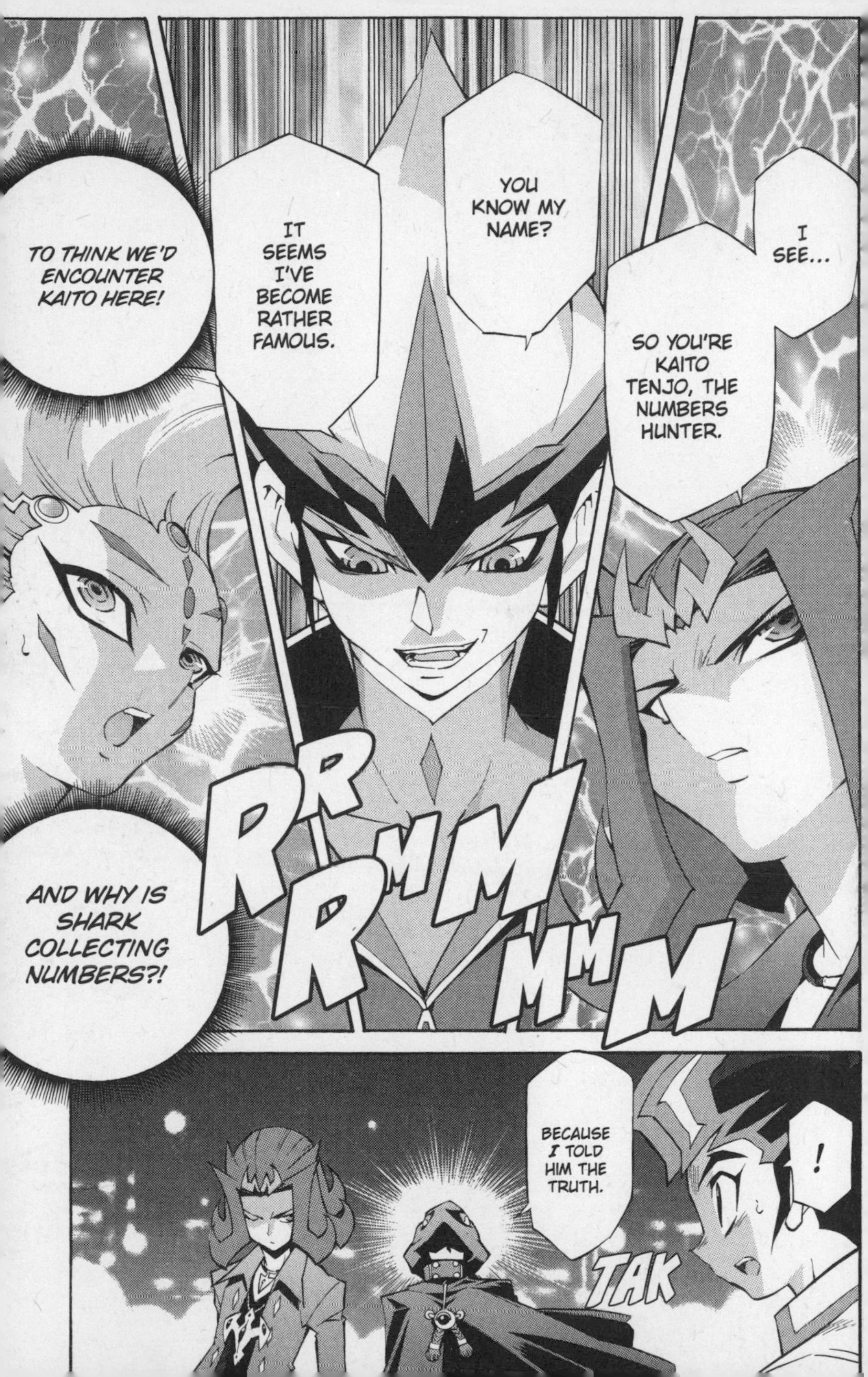
I SEE...
SO YOU'RE KAITO TENJO, THE NUMBERS HUNTER.
YOU KNOW MY NAME?
IT SEEMS I'VE BECOME RATHER FAMOUS.
TO THINK WE'D ENCOUNTER KAITO HERE!
RRRMMMMMMM
AND WHY IS SHARK COLLECTING NUMBERS?!
!
BECAUSE I TOLD HIM THE TRUTH.
TAK

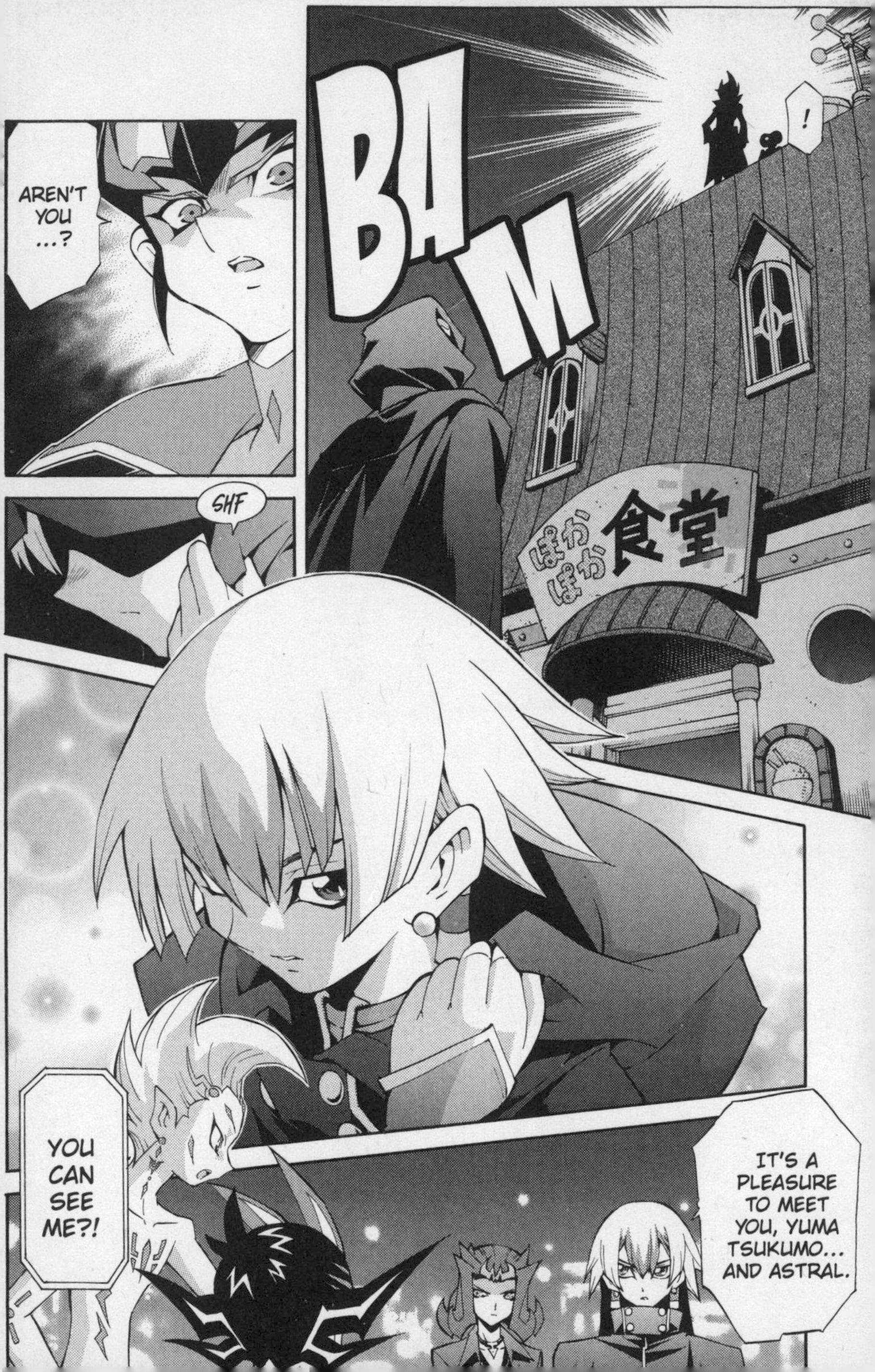
BAM
!
ぽかぽか食堂
AREN'T YOU ...?
SHF
IT'S A PLEASURE TO MEET YOU, YUMA TSUKUMO... AND ASTRAL.
YOU CAN SEE ME?!

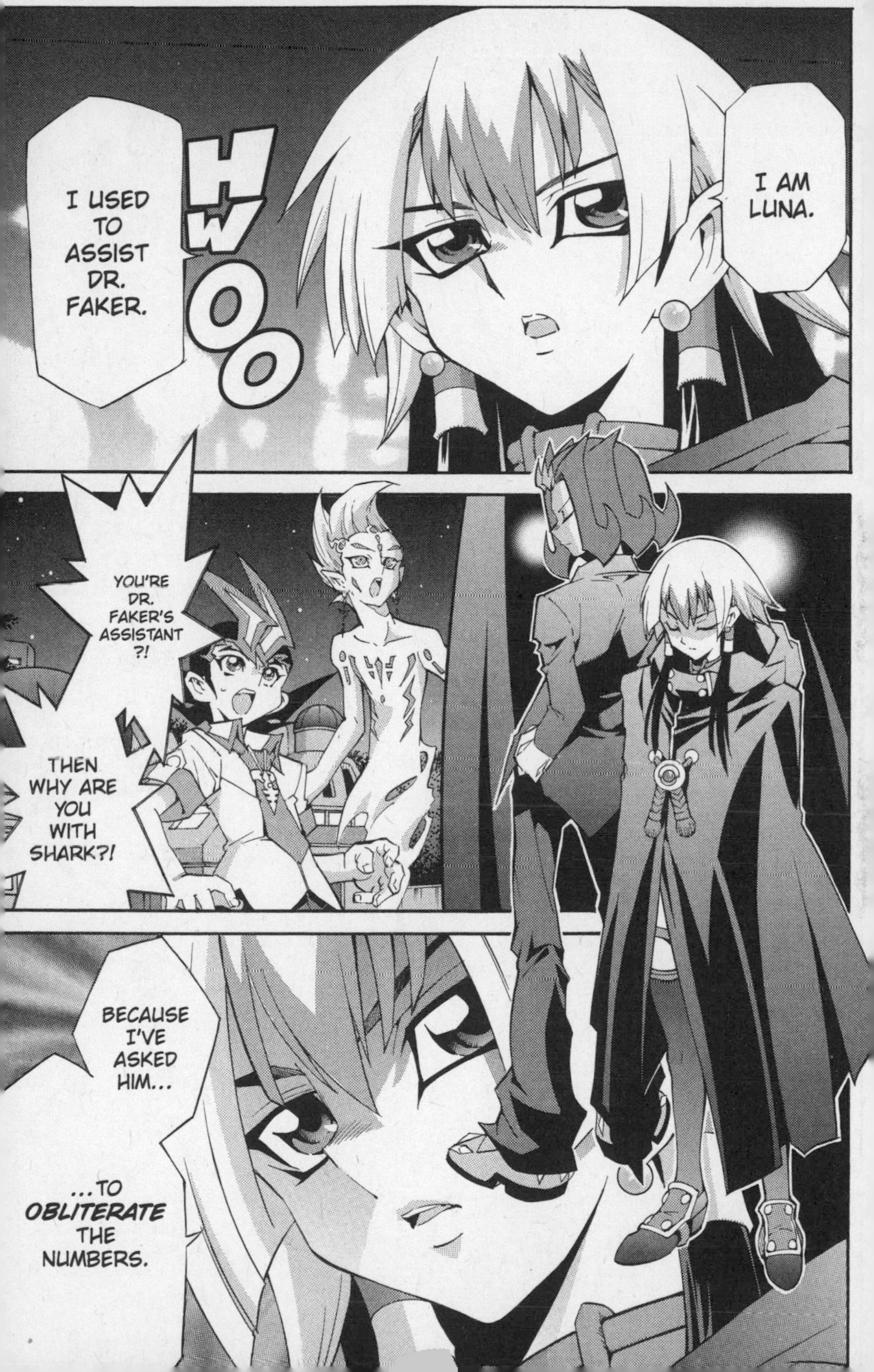
I AM LUNA.
HWOO
I USED TO ASSIST DR. FAKER.
YOU'RE DR. FAKER'S ASSISTANT?!
THEN WHY ARE YOU WITH SHARK?!
BECAUSE I'VE ASKED HIM...
...TO *OBLITERATE* THE NUMBERS.

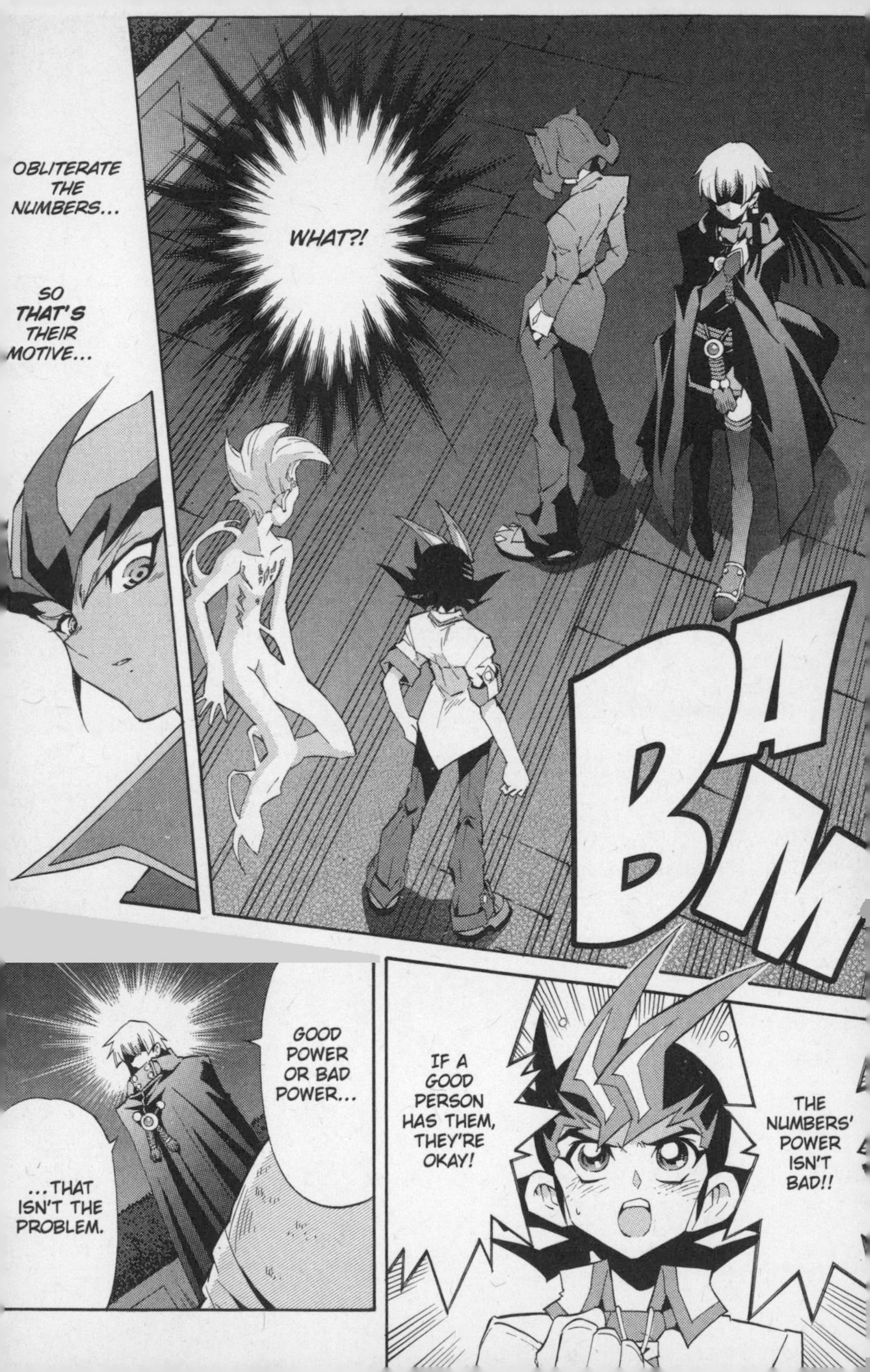
WHAT?!
BAM
OBLITERATE THE NUMBERS...
SO THAT'S THEIR MOTIVE...
THE NUMBERS' POWER ISN'T BAD!!
IF A GOOD PERSON HAS THEM, THEY'RE OKAY!
GOOD POWER OR BAD POWER...
...THAT ISN'T THE PROBLEM.

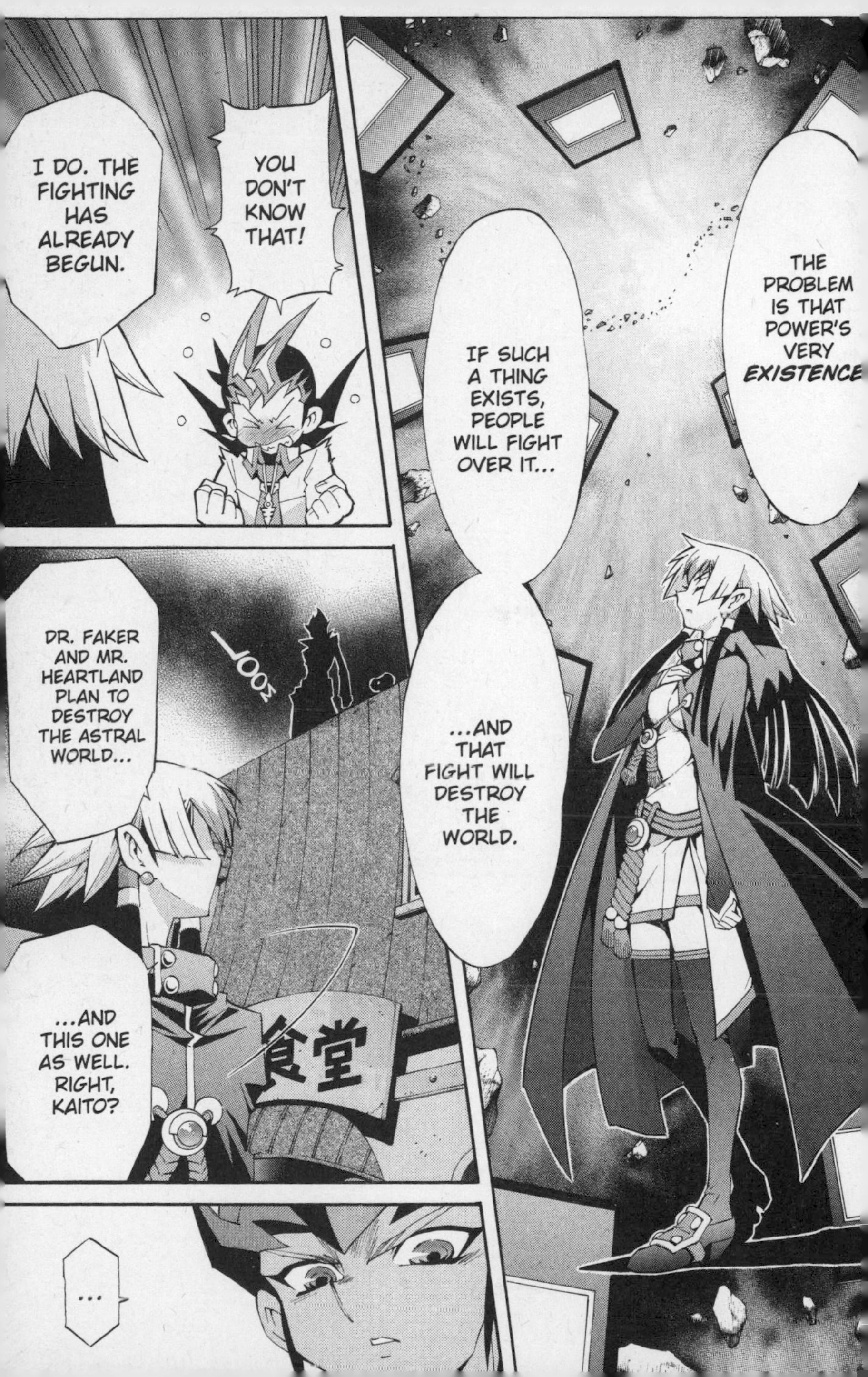
THE PROBLEM IS THAT POWER'S VERY *EXISTENCE*
IF SUCH A THING EXISTS, PEOPLE WILL FIGHT OVER IT...
...AND THAT FIGHT WILL DESTROY THE WORLD.
YOU DON'T KNOW THAT!
I DO. THE FIGHTING HAS ALREADY BEGUN.
DR. FAKER AND MR. HEARTLAND PLAN TO DESTROY THE ASTRAL WORLD...
...AND THIS ONE AS WELL. RIGHT, KAITO?
食堂
...

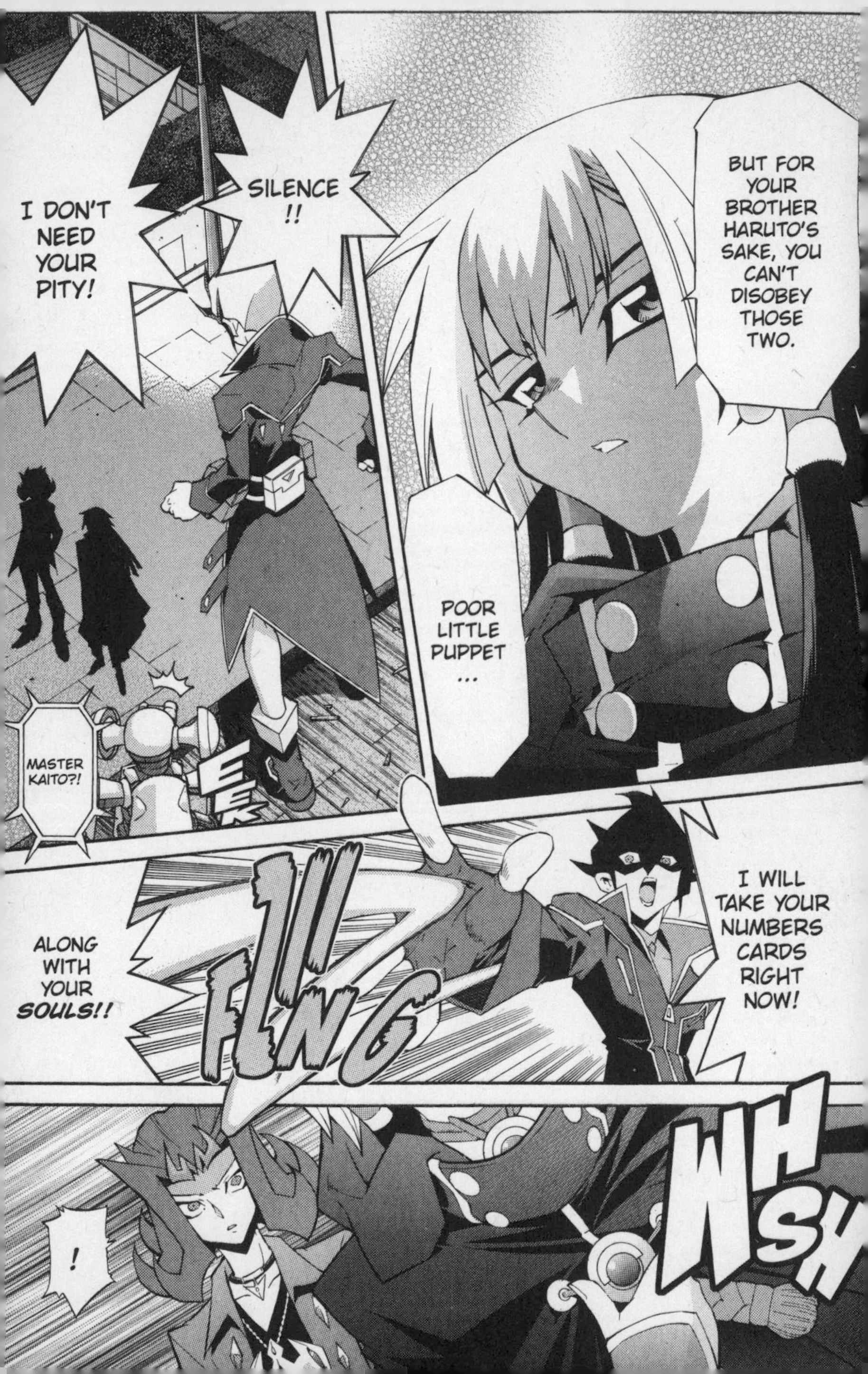
BUT FOR YOUR BROTHER HARUTO'S SAKE, YOU CAN'T DISOBEY THOSE TWO.
POOR LITTLE PUPPET ...
SILENCE !!
I DON'T NEED YOUR PITY!
EEK
MASTER KAITO?!
I WILL TAKE YOUR NUMBERS CARDS RIGHT NOW!
ALONG WITH YOUR *SOULS!!*
FLING
WHSH
!

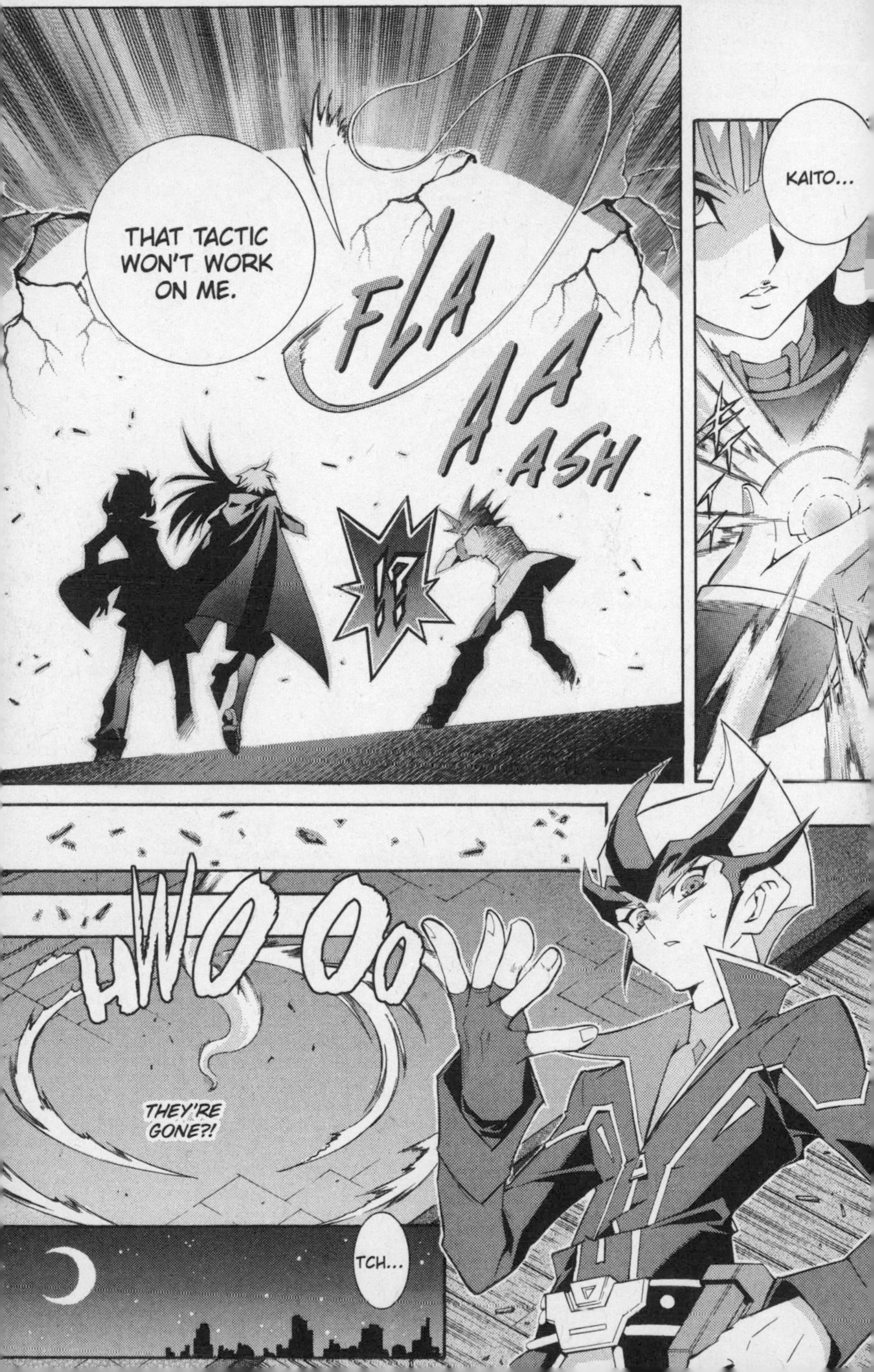

KAITO...
THAT TACTIC WON'T WORK ON ME.
FLAAAASH
!?
HWOOO
THEY'RE GONE?!
TCH...

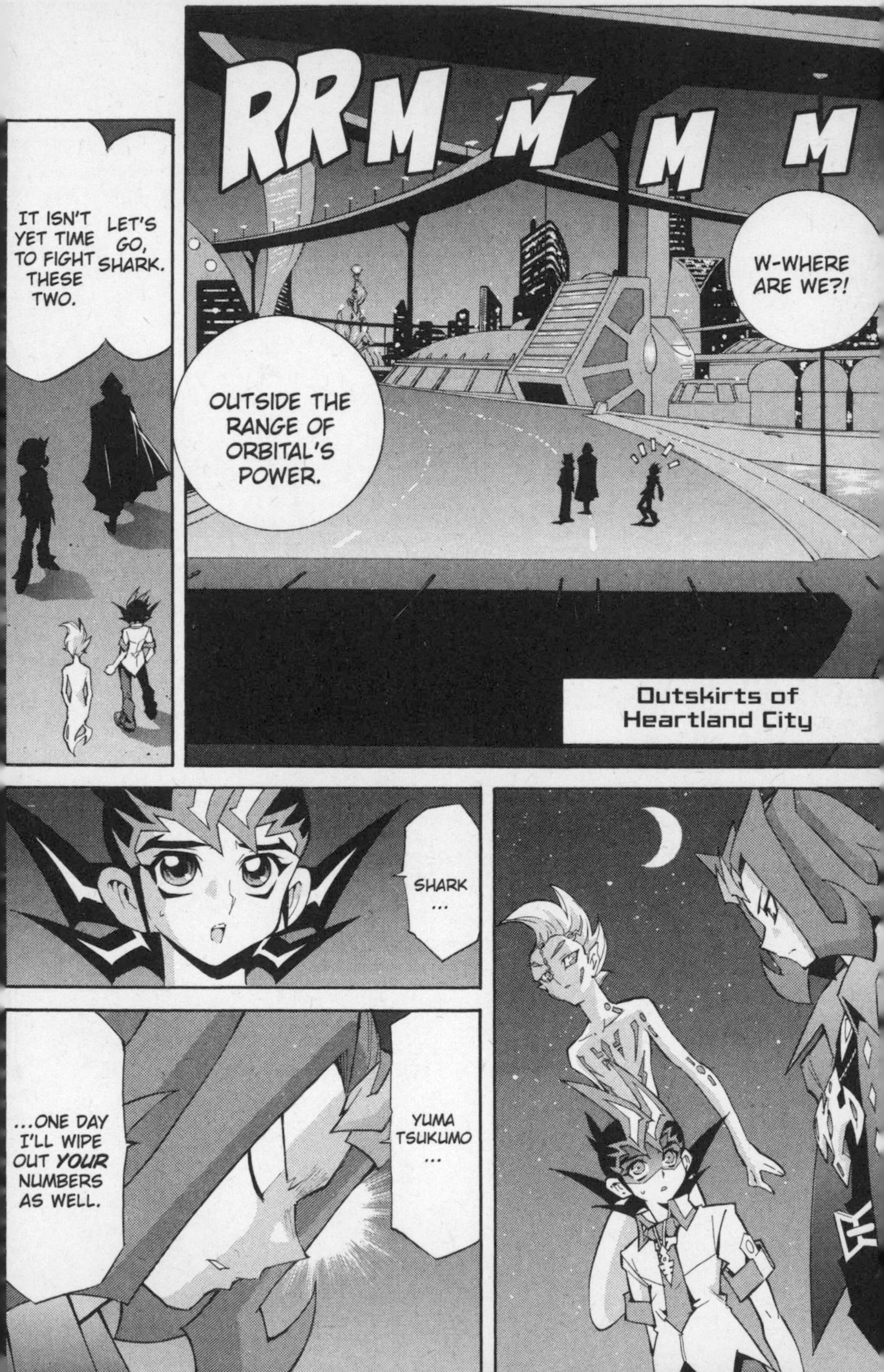
RRMMMM
W-WHERE ARE WE?!
OUTSIDE THE RANGE OF ORBITAL'S POWER.
Outskirts of Heartland City
IT ISN'T YET TIME TO FIGHT THESE TWO. LET'S GO, SHARK.
SHARK ...
YUMA TSUKUMO ...
...ONE DAY I'LL WIPE OUT *YOUR* NUMBERS AS WELL.

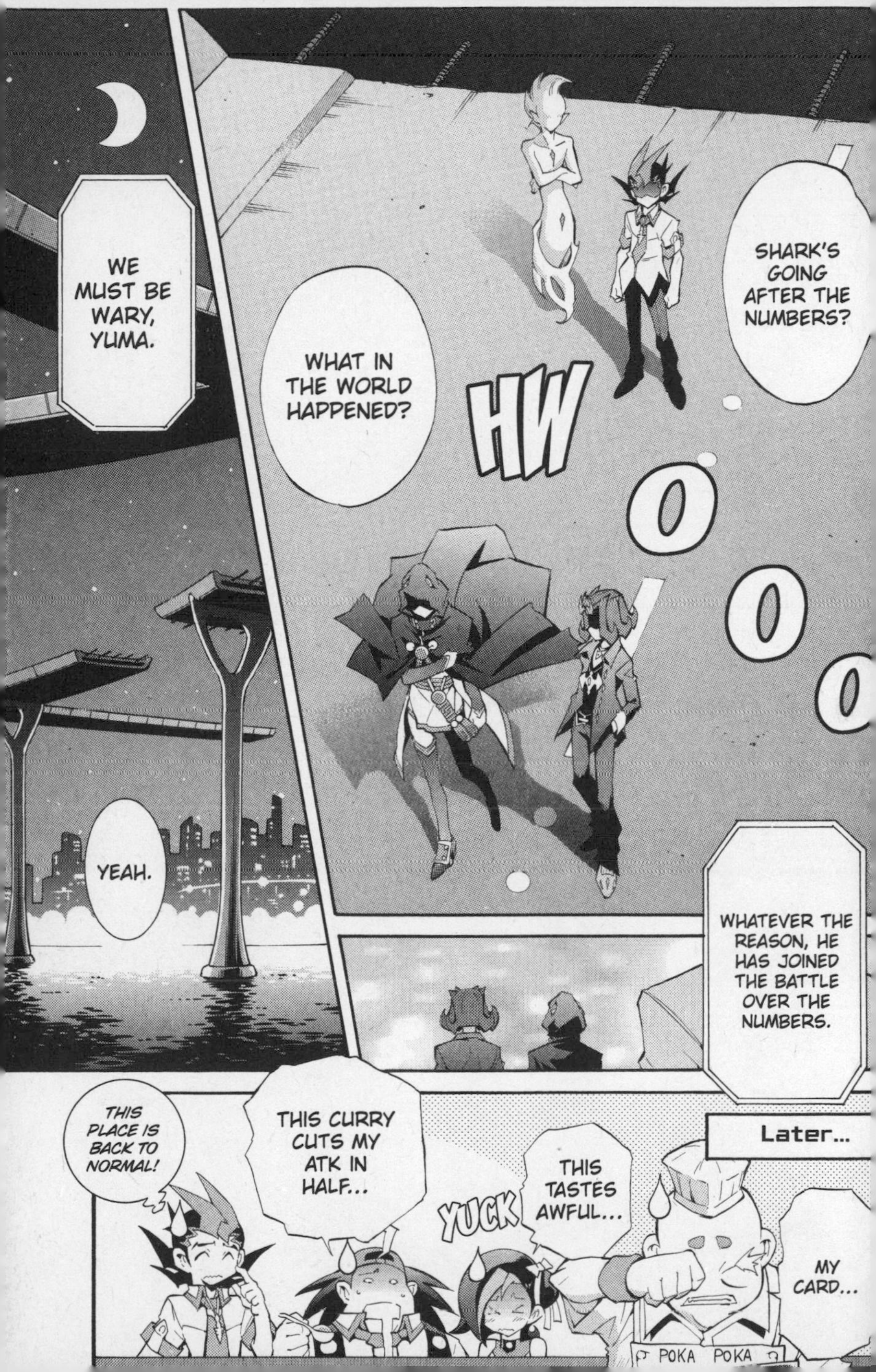
SHARK'S GOING AFTER THE NUMBERS?
WHAT IN THE WORLD HAPPENED?
HWOOOO
WHATEVER THE REASON, HE HAS JOINED THE BATTLE OVER THE NUMBERS.
WE MUST BE WARY, YUMA.
YEAH.
Later...
MY CARD...
POKA POKA
THIS TASTES AWFUL...
YUCK
THIS CURRY CUTS MY ATK IN HALF...
THIS PLACE IS BACK TO NORMAL!

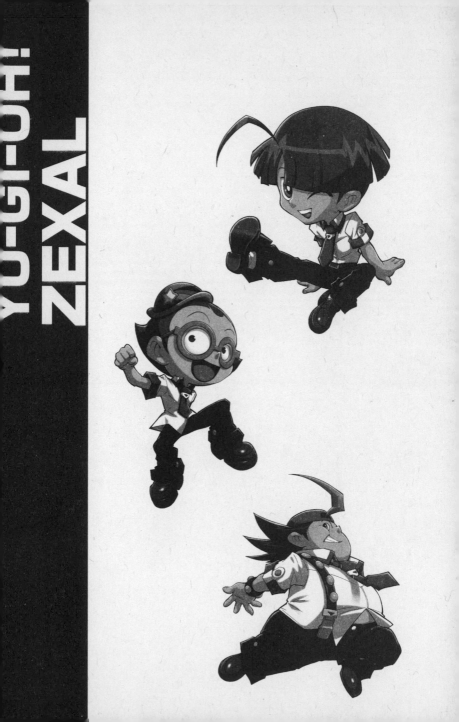

YU-GI-OH! ZEXAL

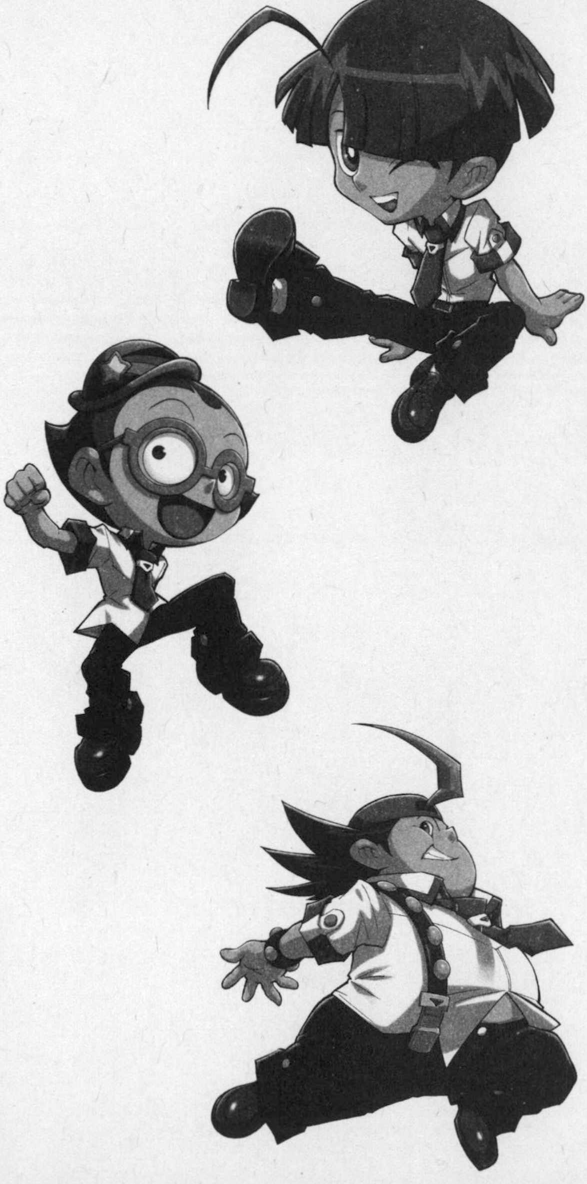

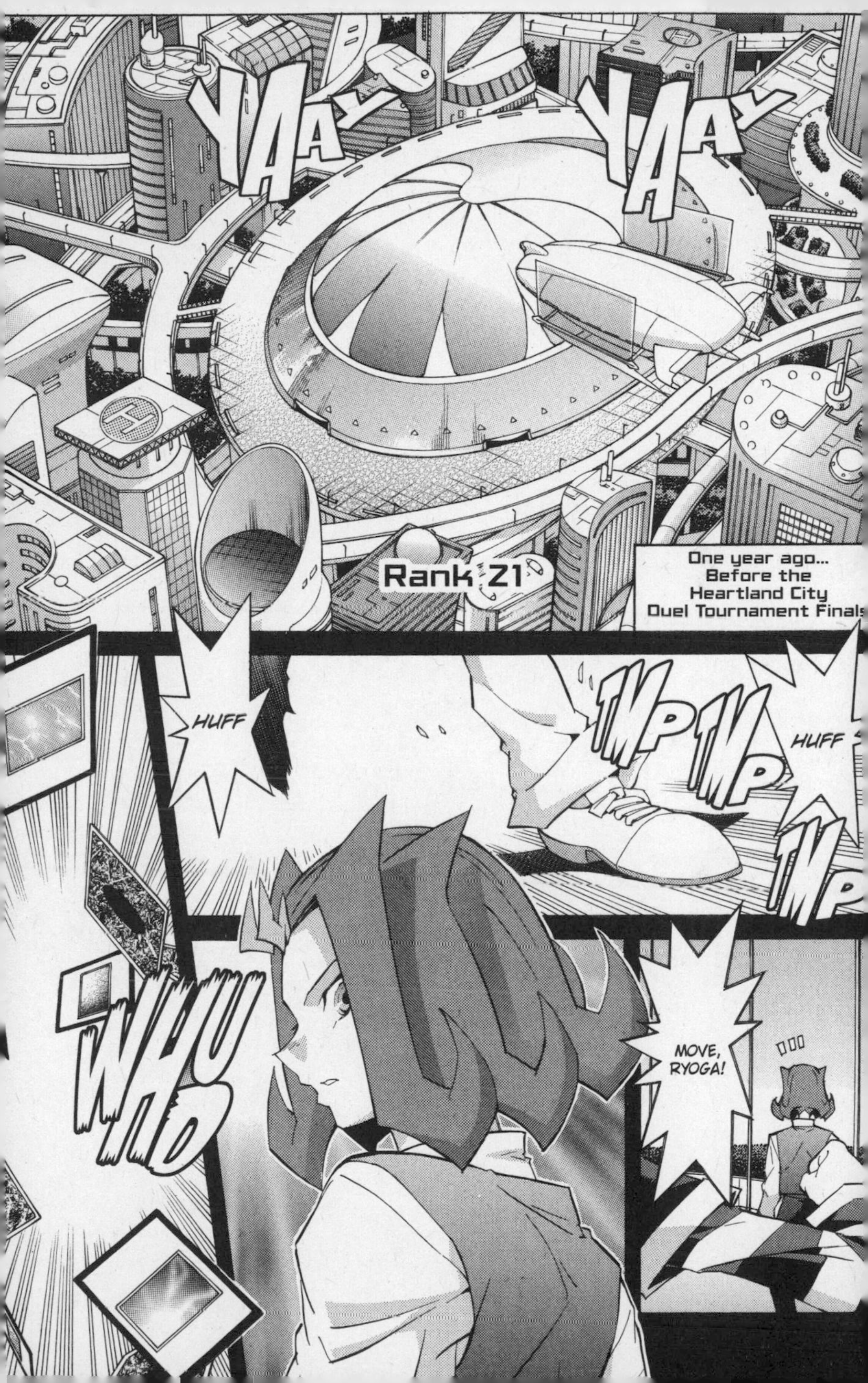
YAAY
YAAY
One year ago...
Before the
Heartland City
Duel Tournament Finals
Rank 21
HUFF
TMP TMP TMP
HUFF
MOVE, RYOGA!

Rank 21: Kyoji Yagumo!!

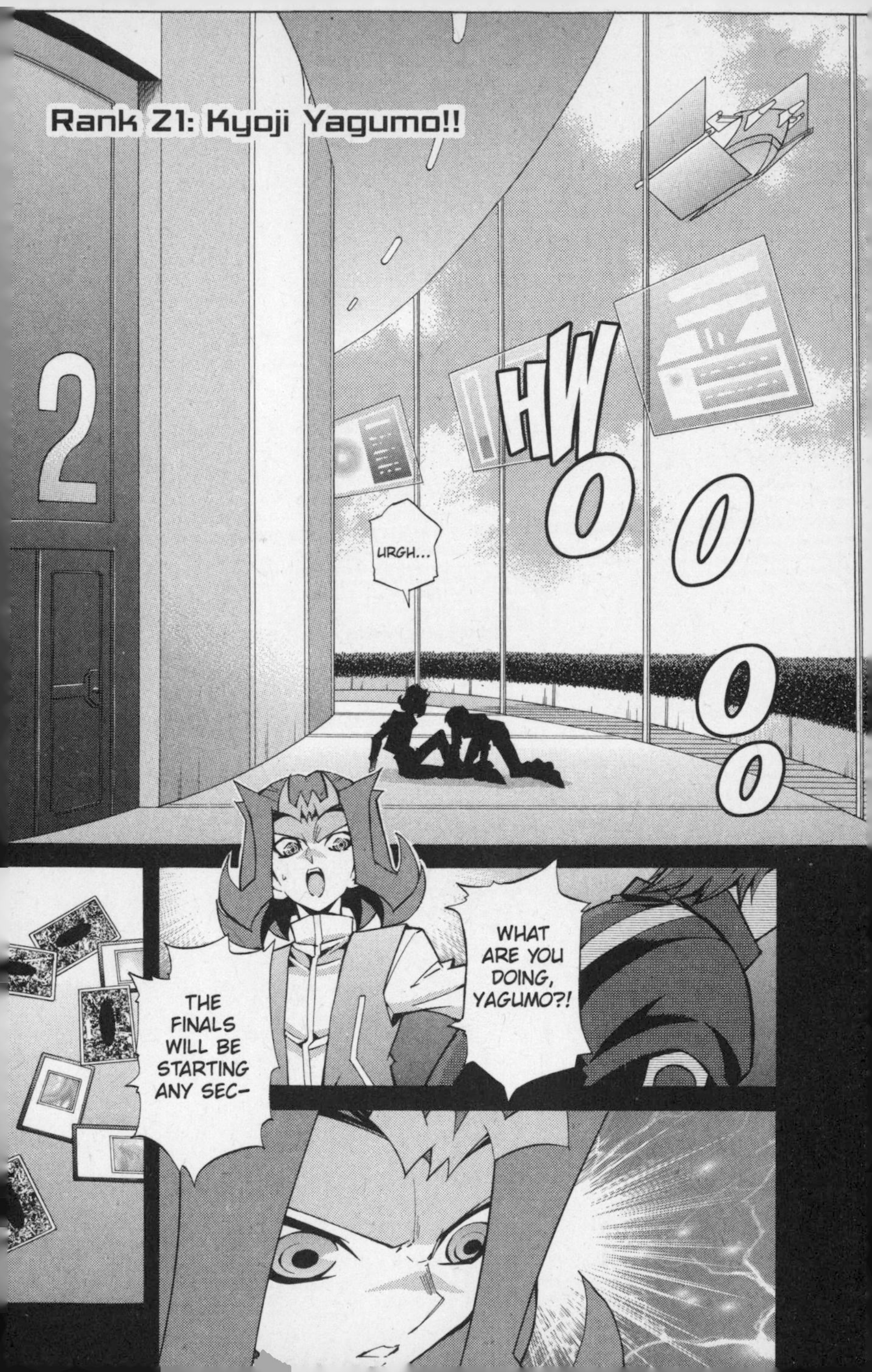
HWOOOO
URGH...
WHAT ARE YOU DOING, YAGUMO?!
THE FINALS WILL BE STARTING ANY SEC-

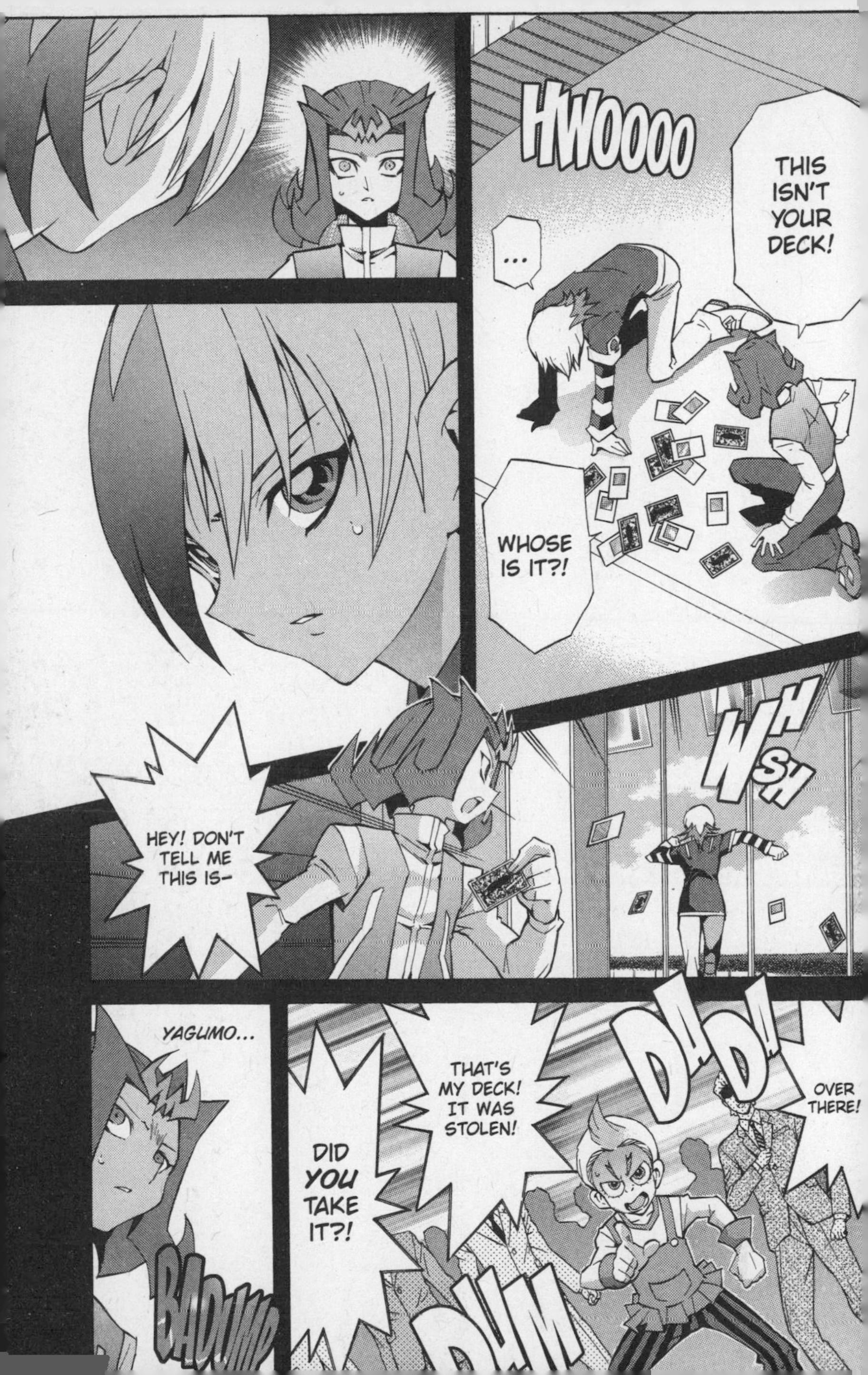
HWOOOO
THIS ISN'T YOUR DECK!
...
WHOSE IS IT?!
WHSH
HEY! DON'T TELL ME THIS IS-
OVER THERE!
THAT'S MY DECK! IT WAS STOLEN!
DID YOU TAKE IT?!
YAGUMO...

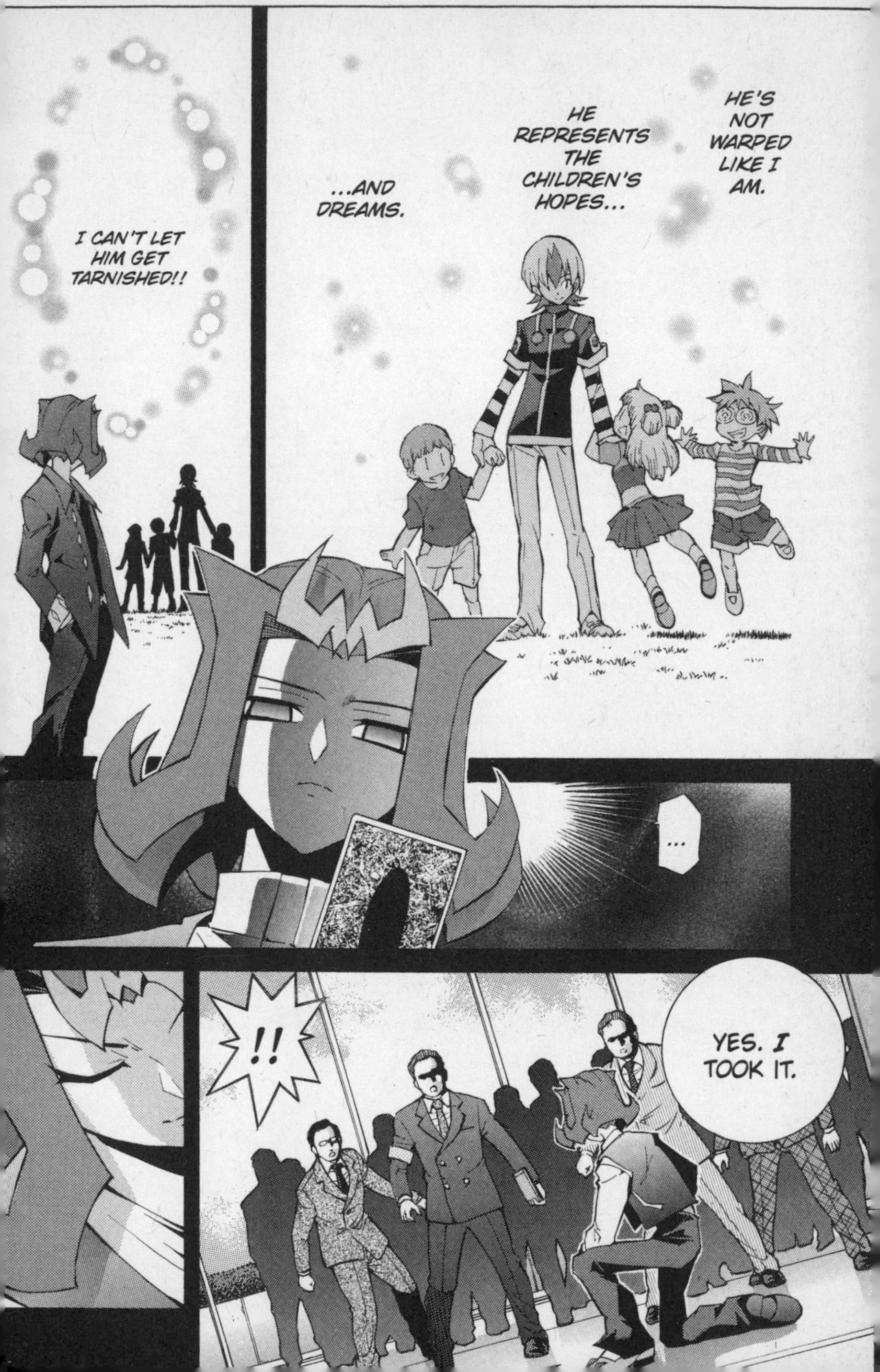
HE'S NOT WARPED LIKE I AM.
HE REPRESENTS THE CHILDREN'S HOPES...
...AND DREAMS.
I CAN'T LET HIM GET TARNISHED!!
...
YES. I TOOK IT.
!!

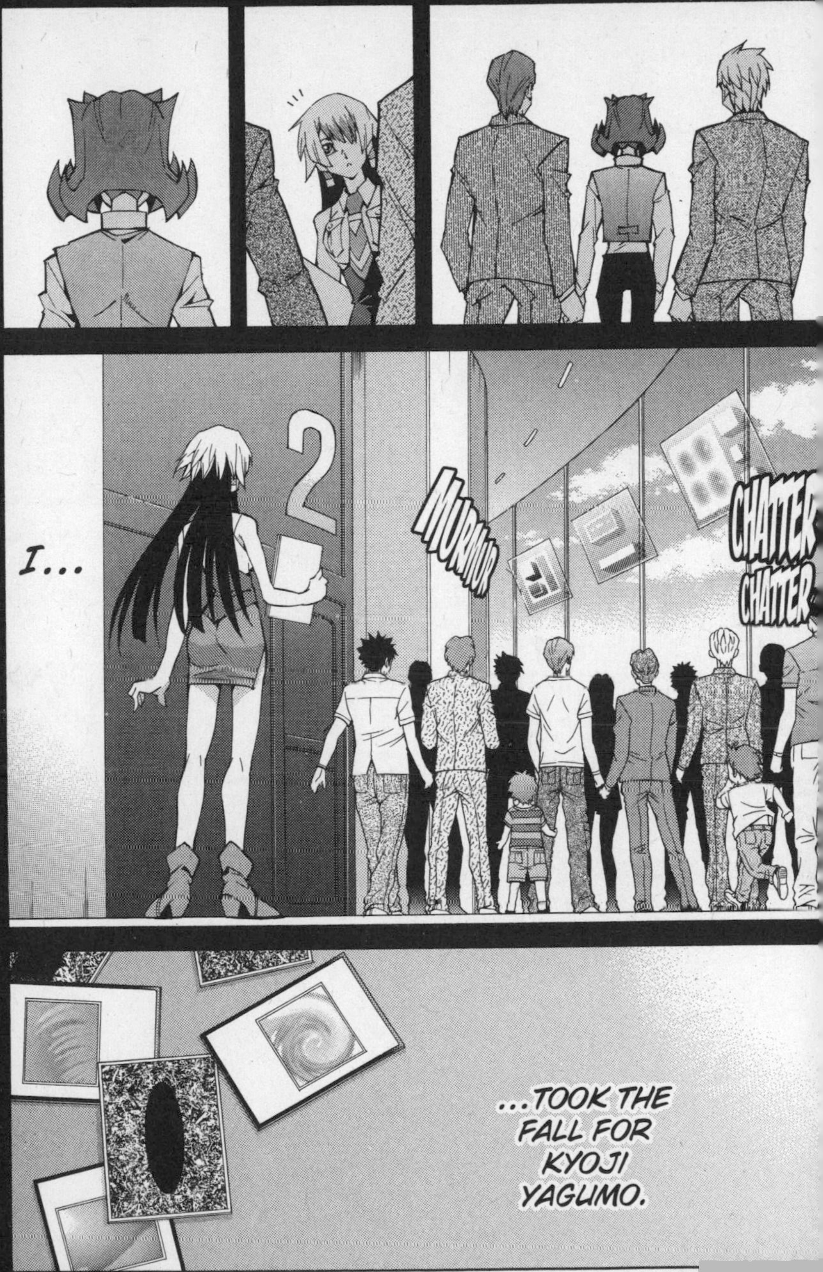
CHATTER
CHATTER
CHATTER
MURMUR
I...
...TOOK THE FALL FOR KYOJI YAGUMO.

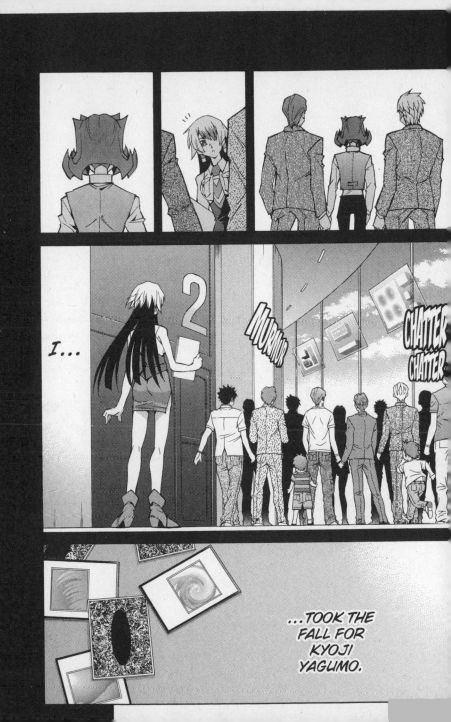

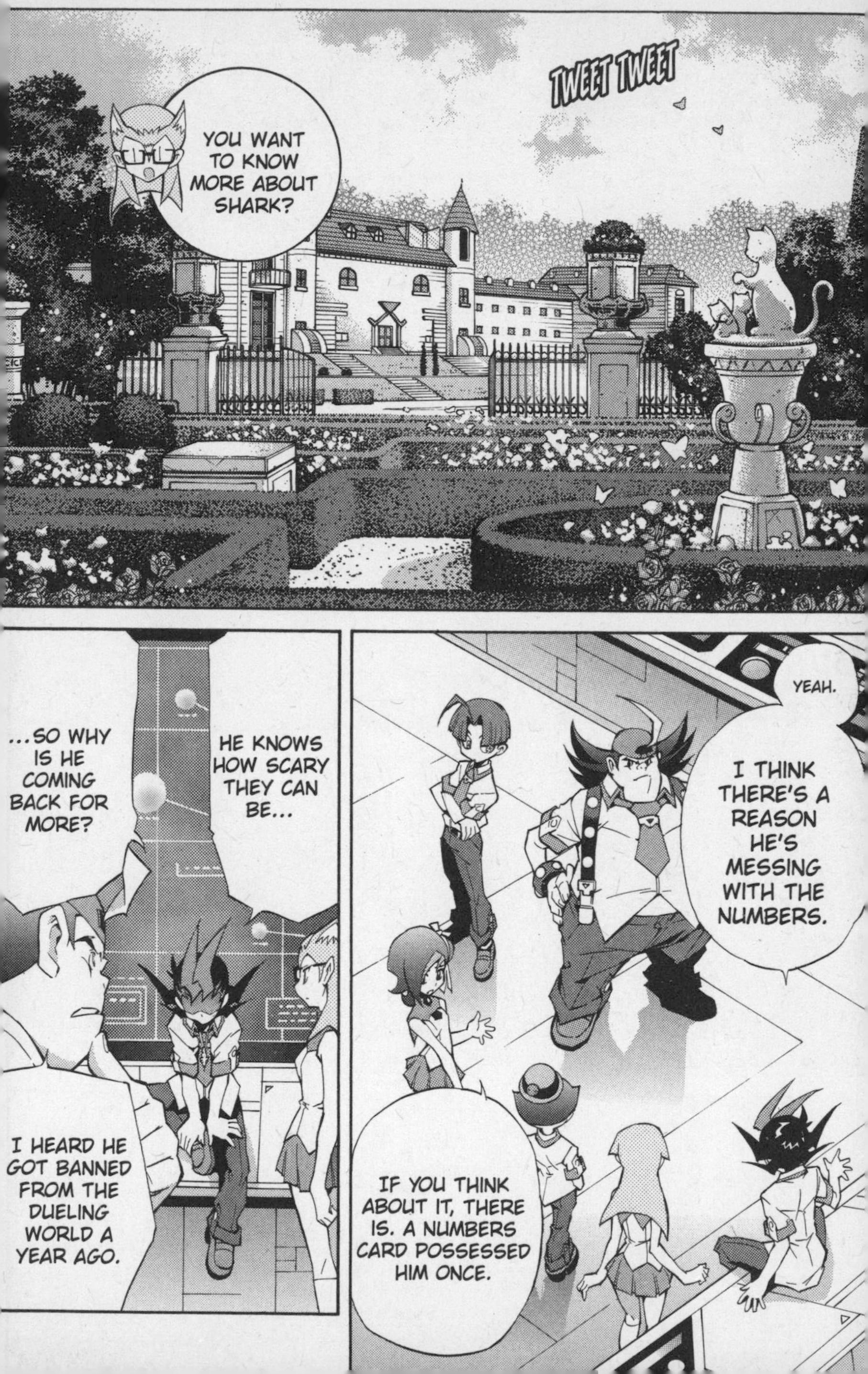
TWEET TWEET
YOU WANT TO KNOW MORE ABOUT SHARK?
YEAH.
I THINK THERE'S A REASON HE'S MESSING WITH THE NUMBERS.
IF YOU THINK ABOUT IT, THERE IS. A NUMBERS CARD POSSESSED HIM ONCE.
HE KNOWS HOW SCARY THEY CAN BE...
...SO WHY IS HE COMING BACK FOR MORE?
I HEARD HE GOT BANNED FROM THE DUELING WORLD A YEAR AGO.

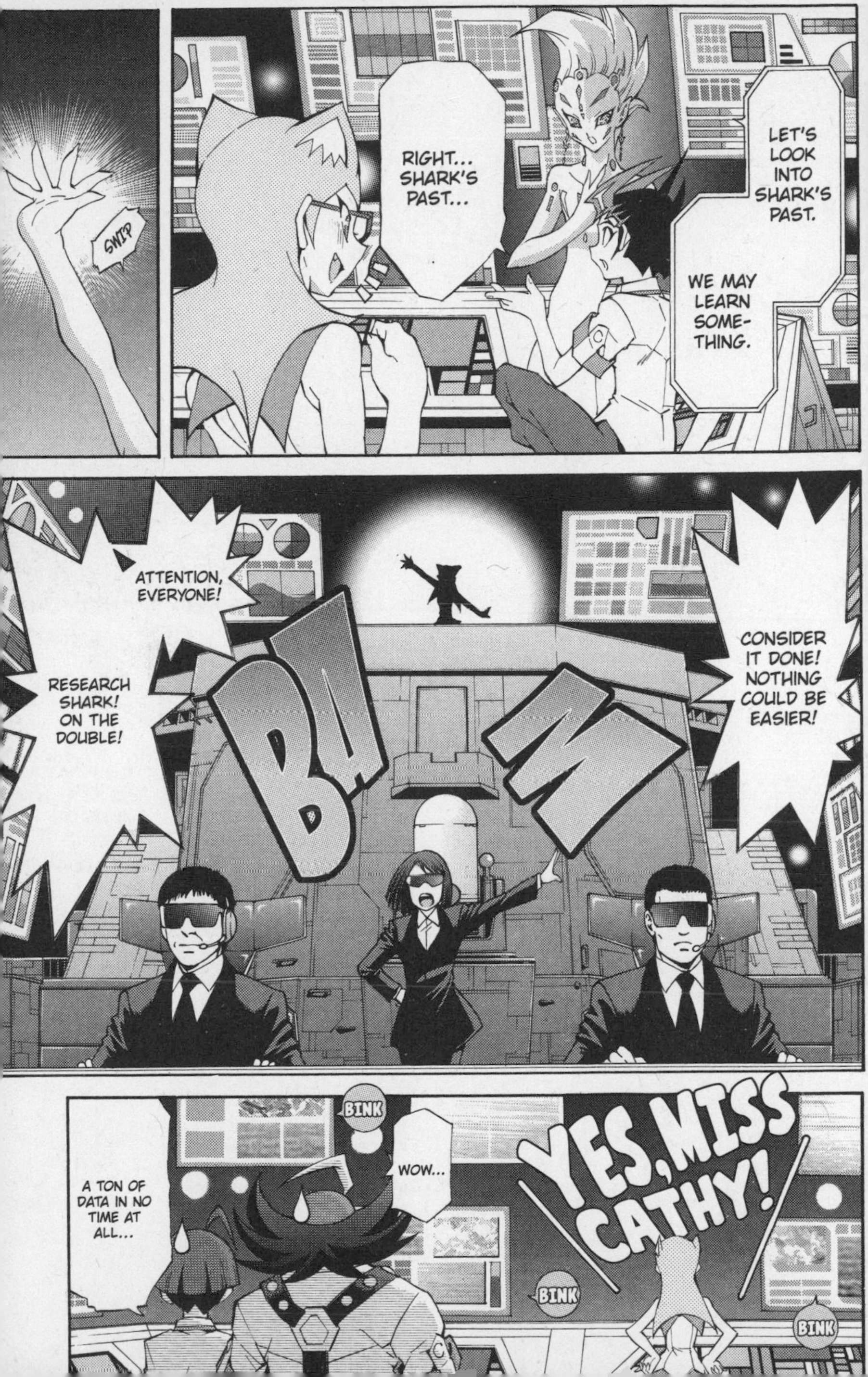
LET'S LOOK INTO SHARK'S PAST.
WE MAY LEARN SOME-THING.
RIGHT... SHARK'S PAST...
SWIP
ATTENTION, EVERYONE!
RESEARCH SHARK! ON THE DOUBLE!
BAM
CONSIDER IT DONE! NOTHING COULD BE EASIER!
YES, MISS CATHY!
BINK
WOW...
A TON OF DATA IN NO TIME AT ALL...
BINK
BINK

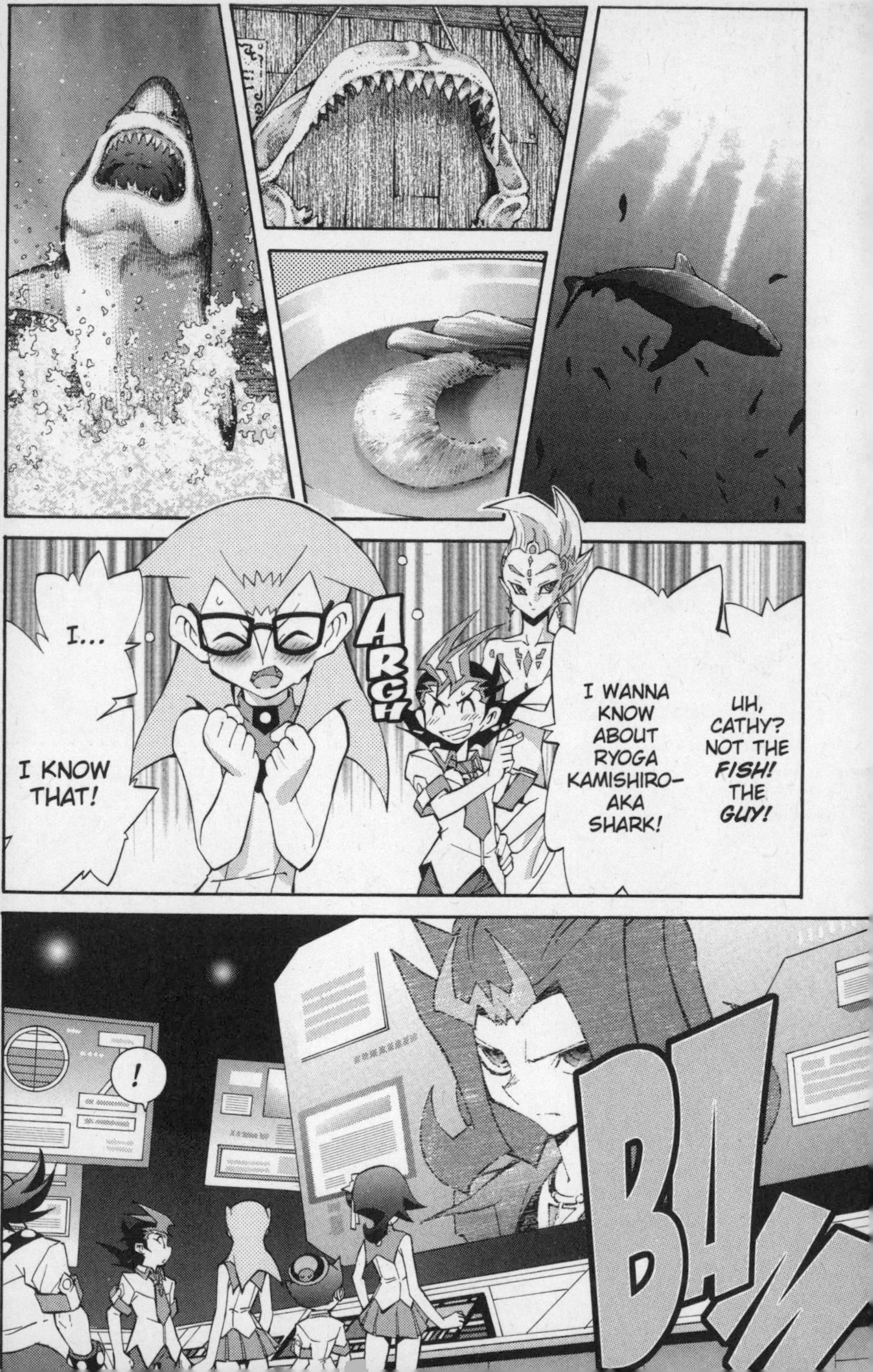
UH, CATHY? NOT THE *FISH!* THE *GUY!*
I WANNA KNOW ABOUT RYOGA KAMISHIRO-AKA SHARK!
ARGH
I...
I KNOW THAT!
BAM
!

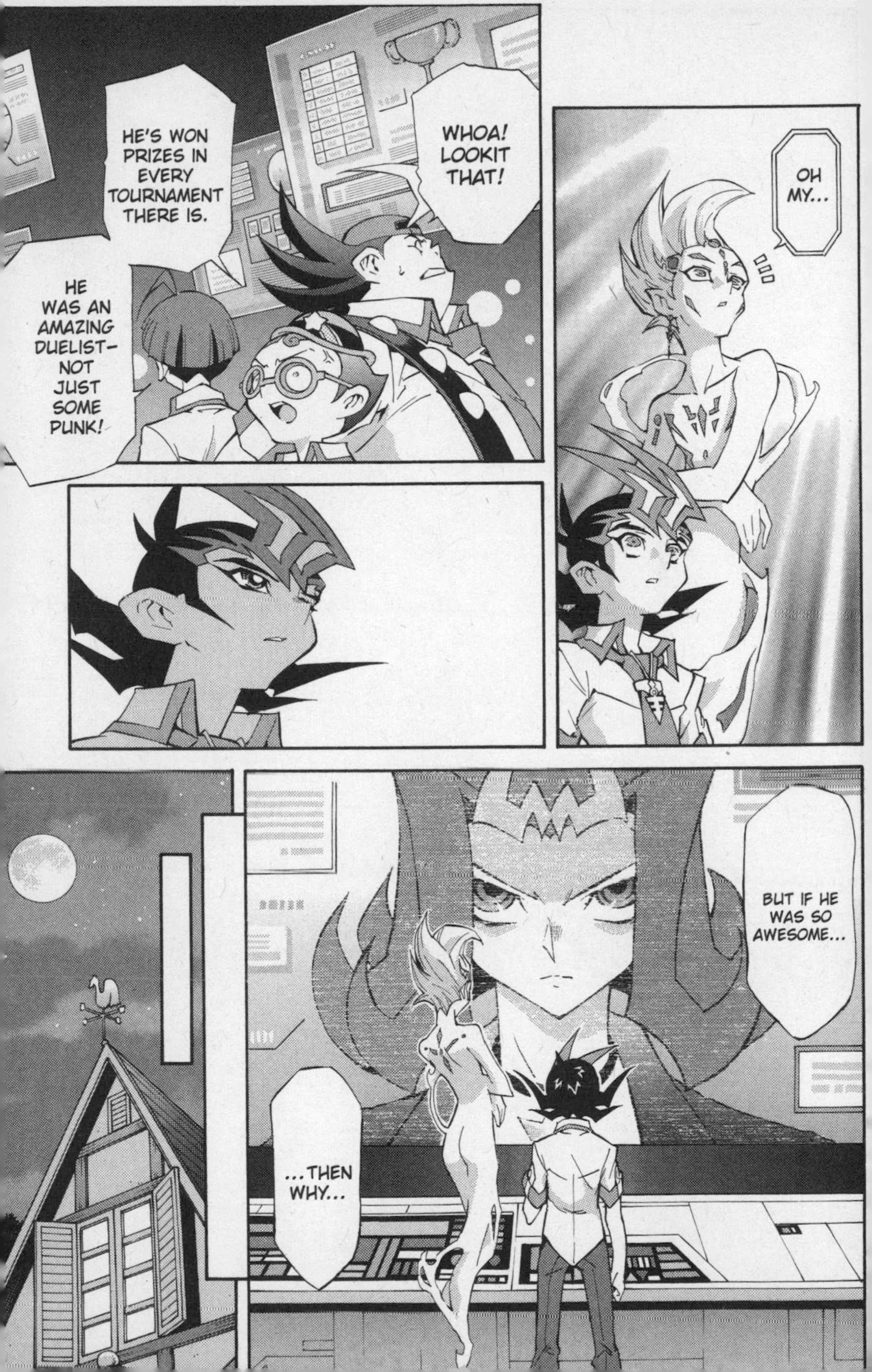
WHOA! LOOKIT THAT!
HE'S WON PRIZES IN EVERY TOURNAMENT THERE IS.
HE WAS AN AMAZING DUELIST—NOT JUST SOME PUNK!
OH MY...
BUT IF HE WAS SO AWESOME...
...THEN WHY...

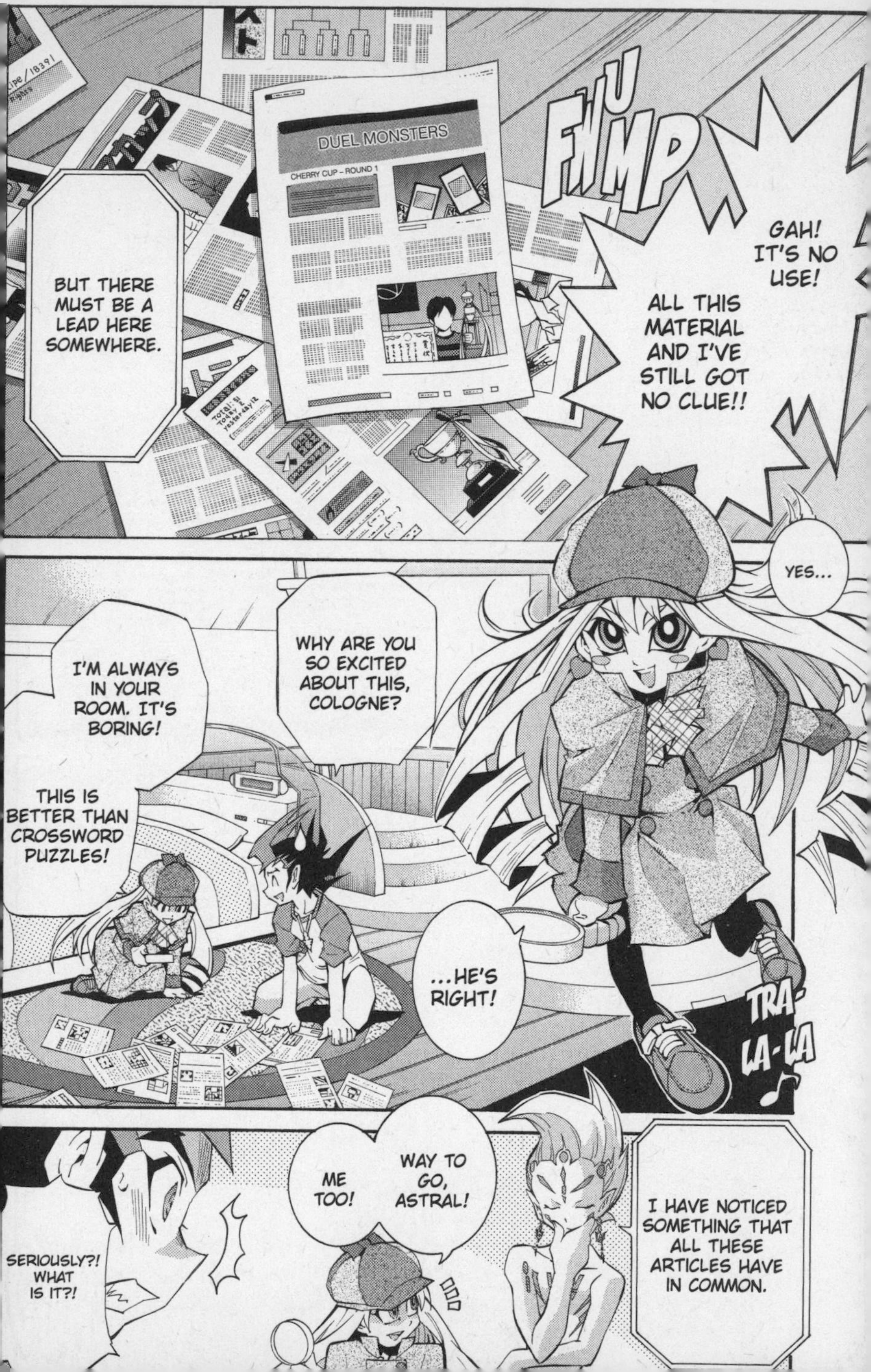
DUEL MONSTERS
CHERRY CUP – ROUND 1
FWUMP
GAH! IT'S NO USE!
ALL THIS MATERIAL AND I'VE STILL GOT NO CLUE!!
BUT THERE MUST BE A LEAD HERE SOMEWHERE.
YES...
TRA-LA-LA
...HE'S RIGHT!
WHY ARE YOU SO EXCITED ABOUT THIS, COLOGNE?
I'M ALWAYS IN YOUR ROOM. IT'S BORING!
THIS IS BETTER THAN CROSSWORD PUZZLES!
I HAVE NOTICED SOMETHING THAT ALL THESE ARTICLES HAVE IN COMMON.
WAY TO GO, ASTRAL!
ME TOO!
SERIOUSLY?! WHAT IS IT?!

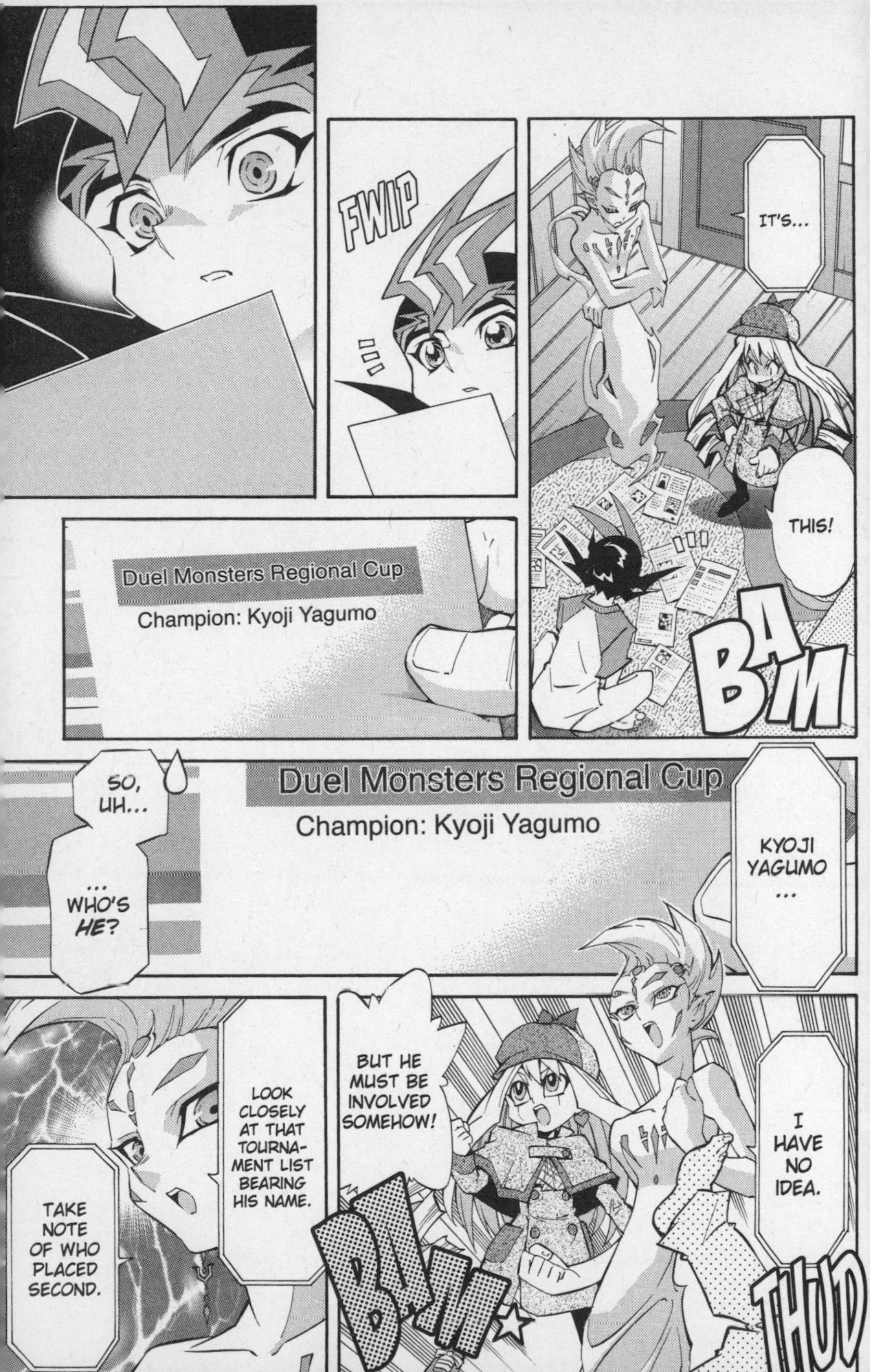
IT'S...
THIS!
BAM
FWIP
Duel Monsters Regional Cup
Champion: Kyoji Yagumo
KYOJI YAGUMO...
Duel Monsters Regional Cup
Champion: Kyoji Yagumo
SO, UH...
...WHO'S *HE*?
I HAVE NO IDEA.
THUD
BUT HE MUST BE INVOLVED SOMEHOW!
BAM
LOOK CLOSELY AT THAT TOURNAMENT LIST BEARING HIS NAME.
TAKE NOTE OF WHO PLACED SECOND.

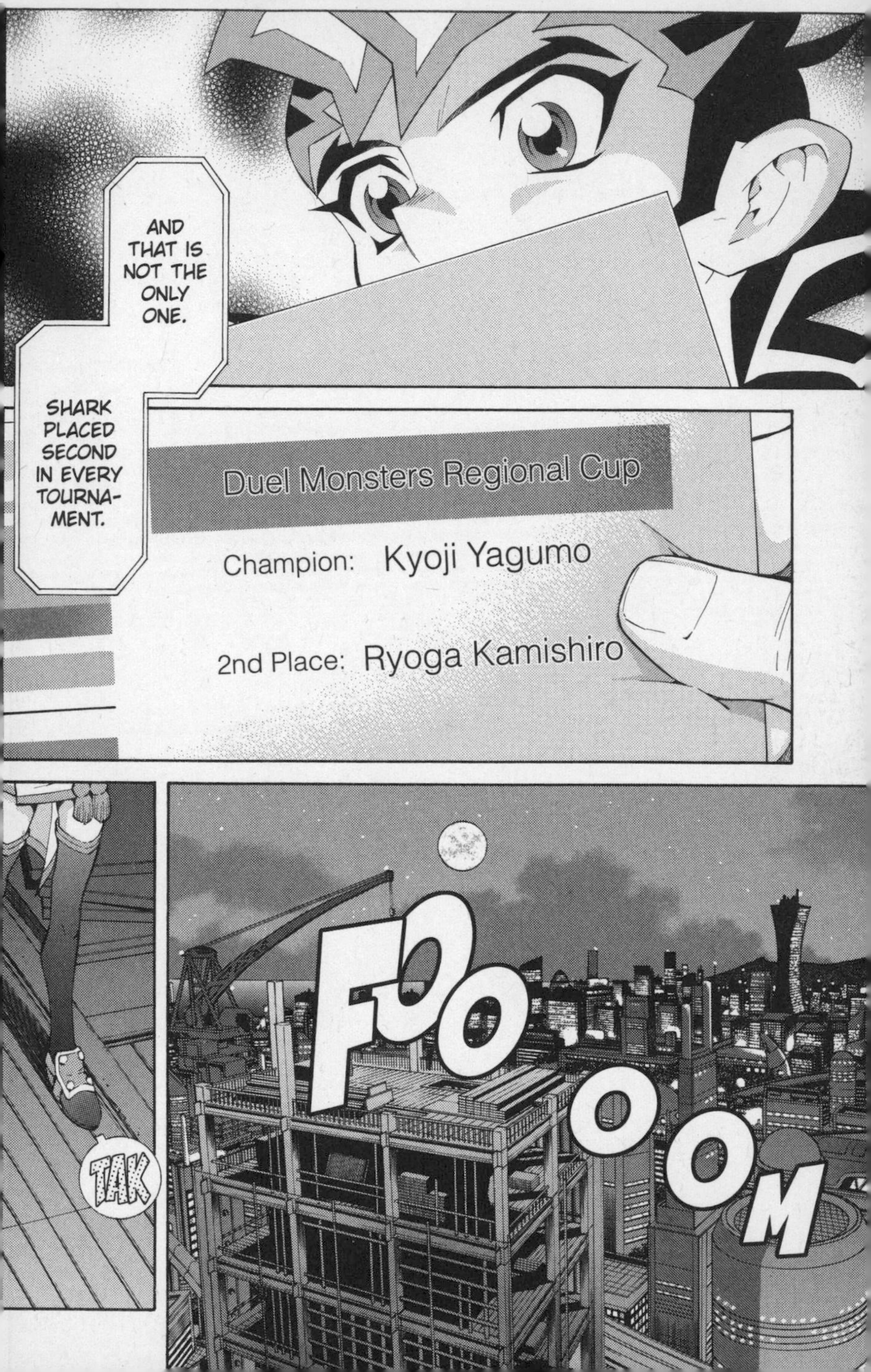
AND THAT IS NOT THE ONLY ONE.
SHARK PLACED SECOND IN EVERY TOURNA- MENT.
Duel Monsters Regional Cup
Champion: Kyoji Yagumo
2nd Place: Ryoga Kamishiro
FOOOOOM
TAK

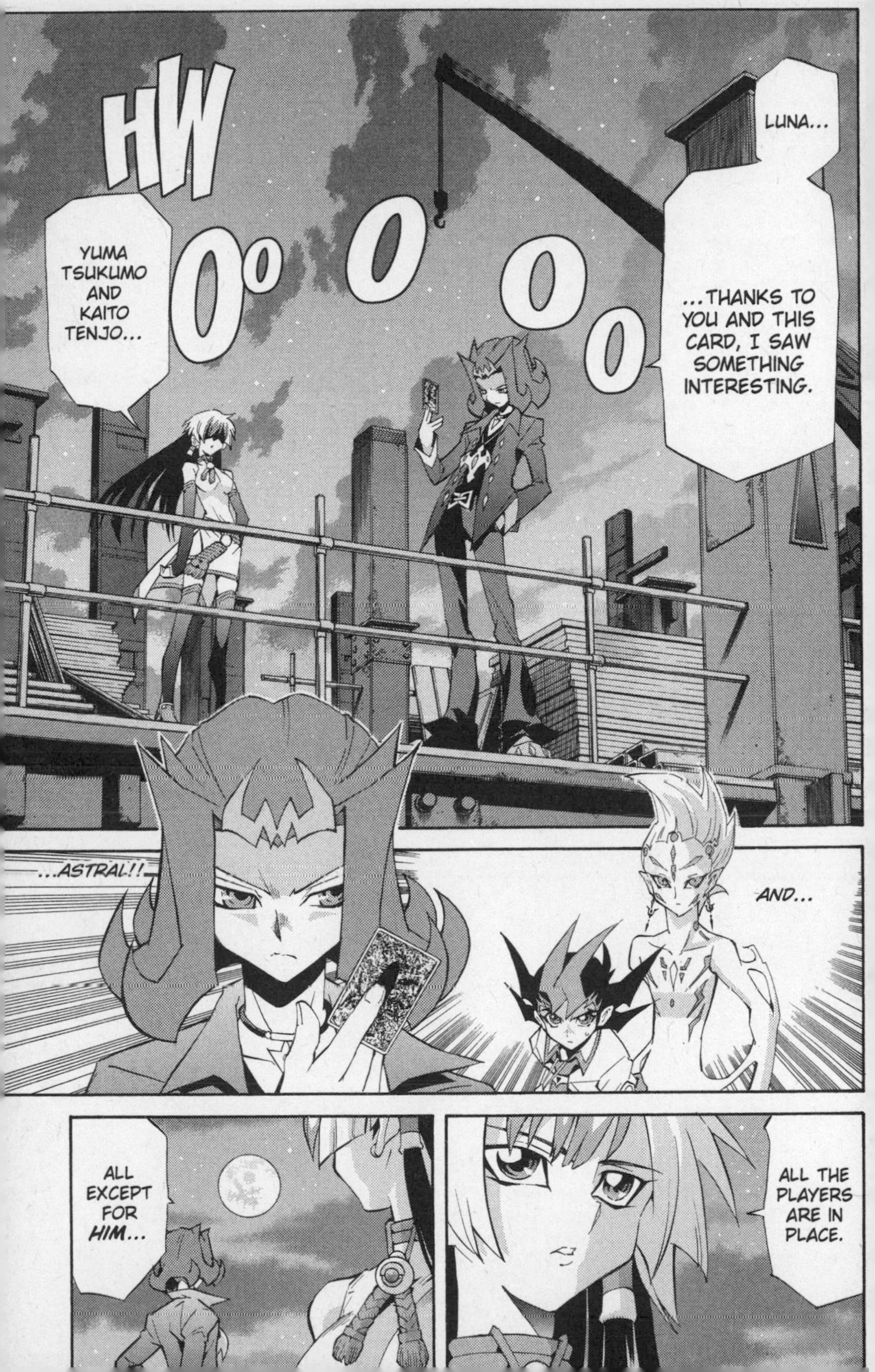
LUNA...
...THANKS TO YOU AND THIS CARD, I SAW SOMETHING INTERESTING.
HWOOOOO
YUMA TSUKUMO AND KAITO TENJO...
AND...
...ASTRAL!!
ALL THE PLAYERS ARE IN PLACE.
ALL EXCEPT FOR *HIM*...

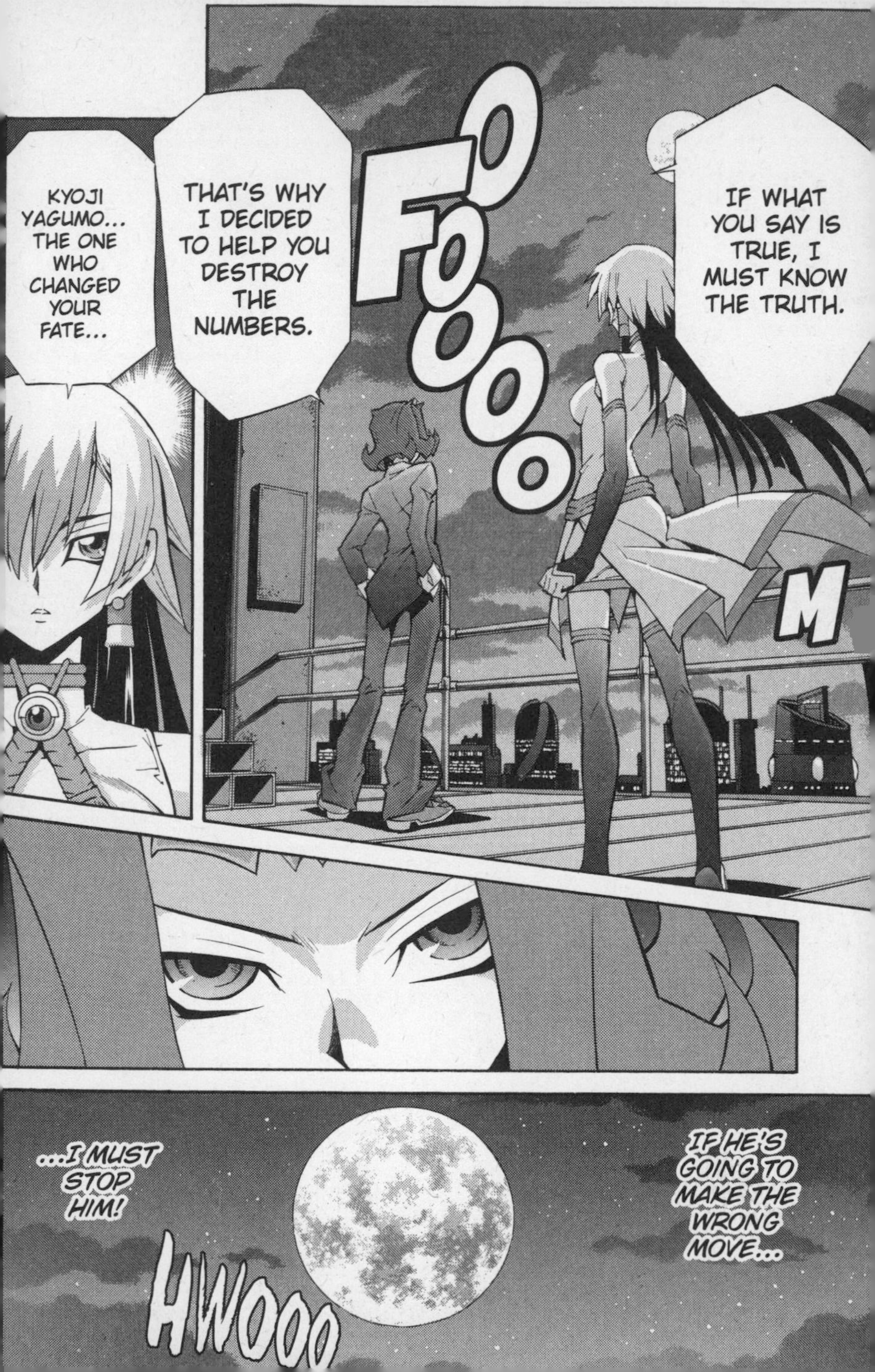
IF WHAT YOU SAY IS TRUE, I MUST KNOW THE TRUTH.
FOOOOOO
M
THAT'S WHY I DECIDED TO HELP YOU DESTROY THE NUMBERS.
KYOJI YAGUMO... THE ONE WHO CHANGED YOUR FATE...
IF HE'S GOING TO MAKE THE WRONG MOVE...
...I MUST STOP HIM!
HWOOO

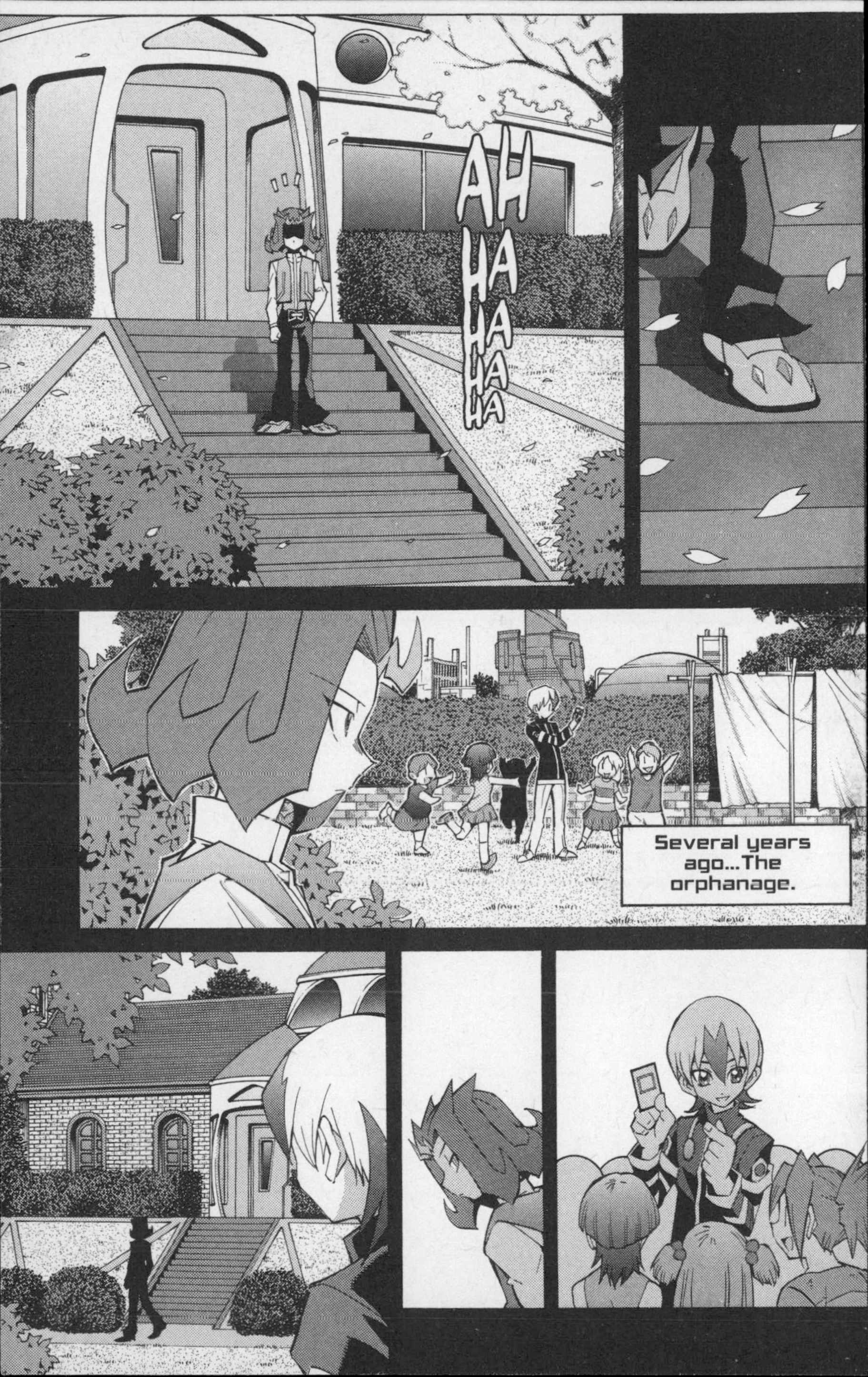
AH HA HA HA HA HA HA
Several years ago...The orphanage.

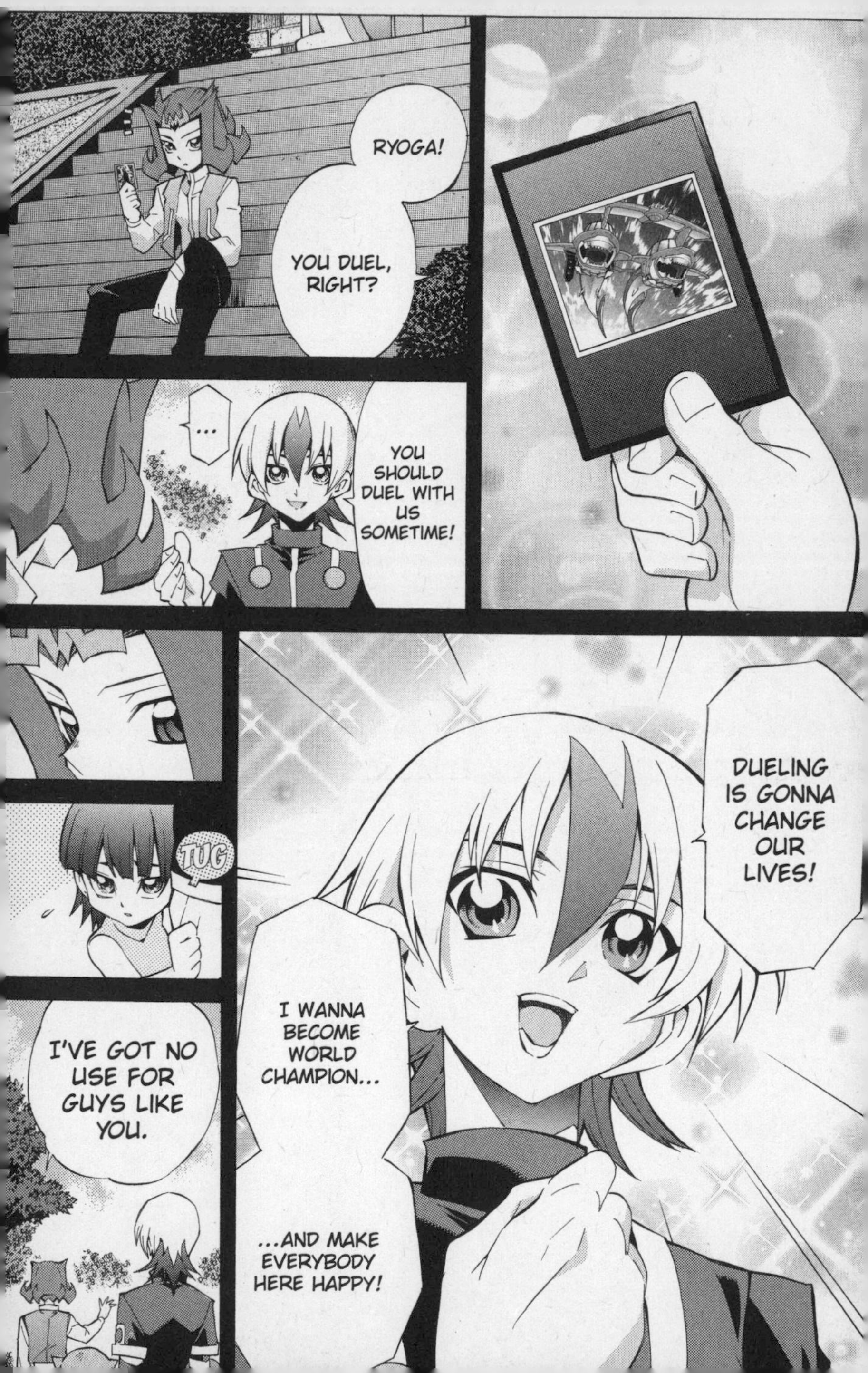
RYOGA!
YOU DUEL, RIGHT?
YOU SHOULD DUEL WITH US SOMETIME!
...
DUELING IS GONNA CHANGE OUR LIVES!
I WANNA BECOME WORLD CHAMPION...
...AND MAKE EVERYBODY HERE HAPPY!
TUG
I'VE GOT NO USE FOR GUYS LIKE YOU.

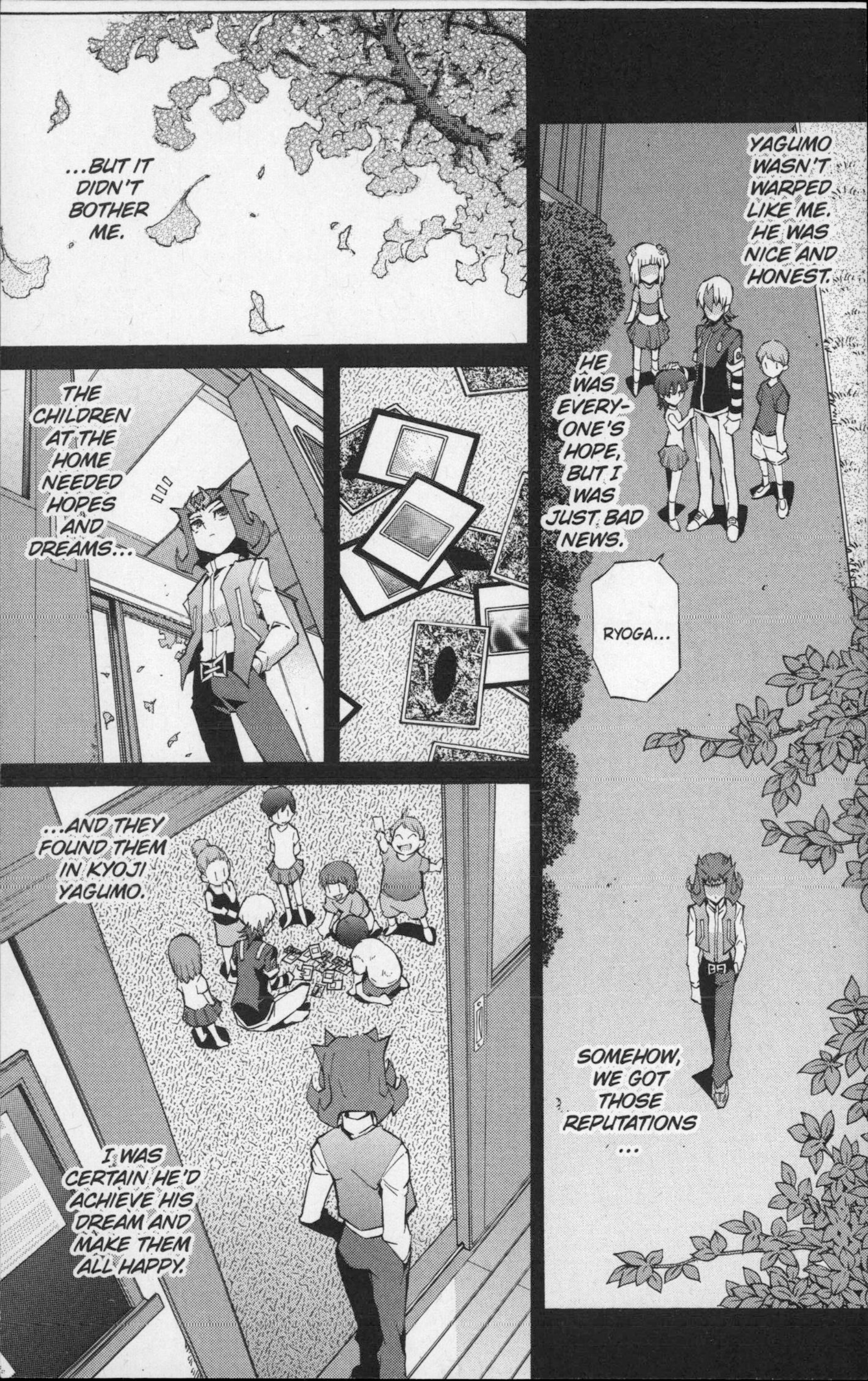
YAGUMO WASN'T WARPED LIKE ME. HE WAS NICE AND HONEST.
HE WAS EVERYONE'S HOPE, BUT I WAS JUST BAD NEWS.
RYOGA...
SOMEHOW, WE GOT THOSE REPUTATIONS...
...BUT IT DIDN'T BOTHER ME.
THE CHILDREN AT THE HOME NEEDED HOPES AND DREAMS...
...AND THEY FOUND THEM IN KYOJI YAGUMO.
I WAS CERTAIN HE'D ACHIEVE HIS DREAM AND MAKE THEM ALL HAPPY.

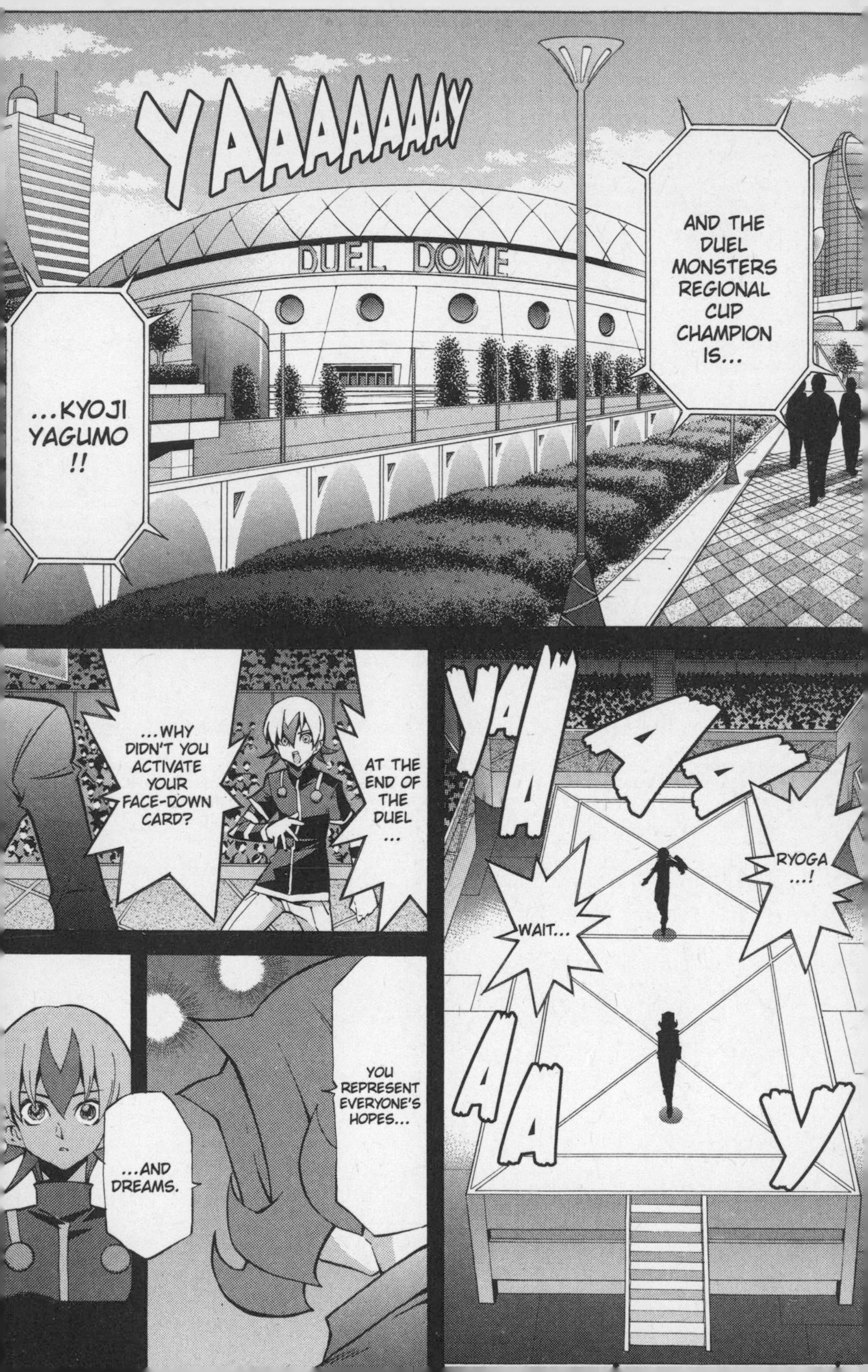
AND THE DUEL MONSTERS REGIONAL CUP CHAMPION IS...
YAAAAAAAY
DUEL DOME
...KYOJI YAGUMO !!
YAAAAAAAY
RYOGA ...!
WAIT...
AT THE END OF THE DUEL ...
...WHY DIDN'T YOU ACTIVATE YOUR FACE-DOWN CARD?
YOU REPRESENT EVERYONE'S HOPES...
...AND DREAMS.

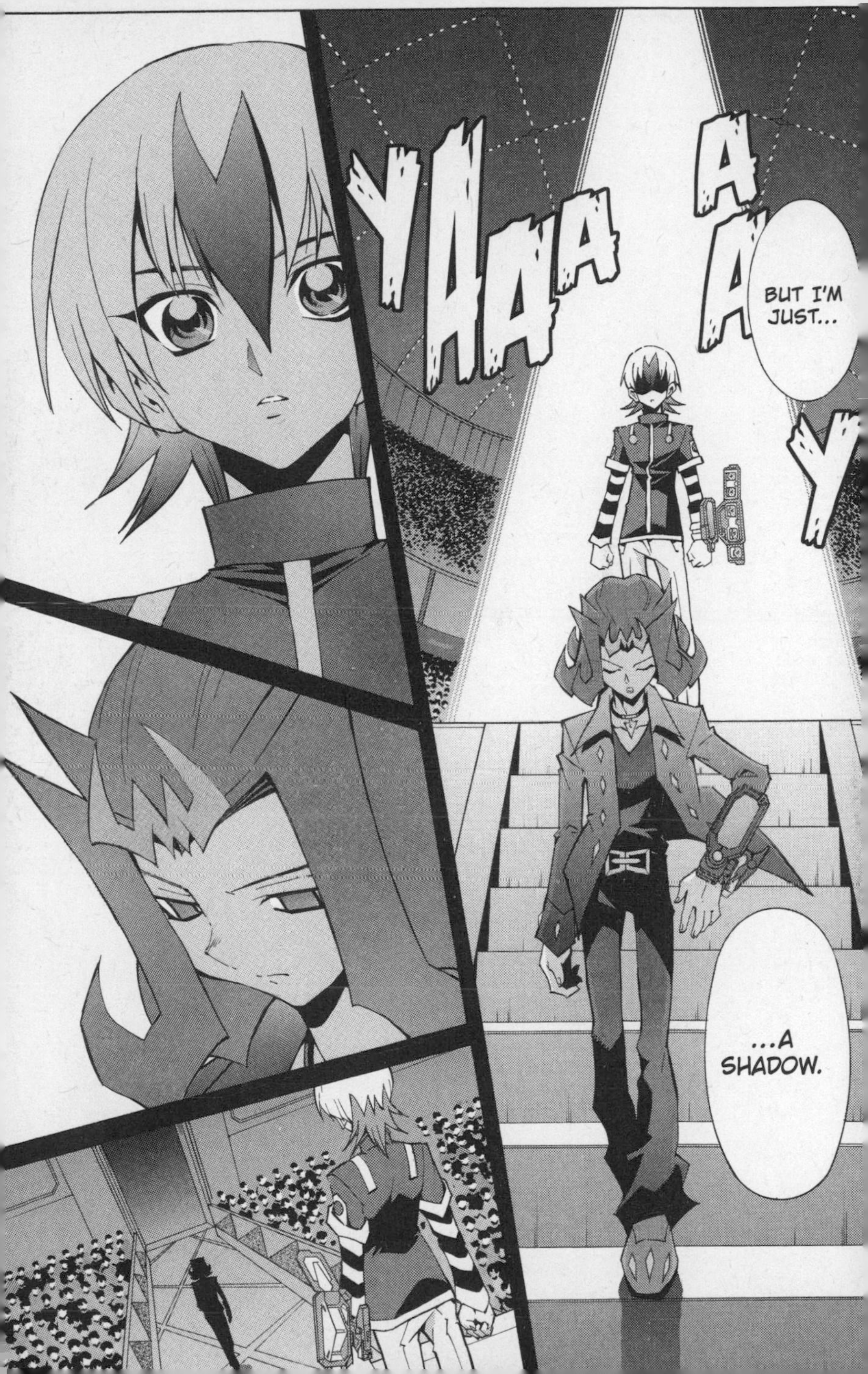
YAAAAAY
BUT I'M JUST...
...A SHADOW.

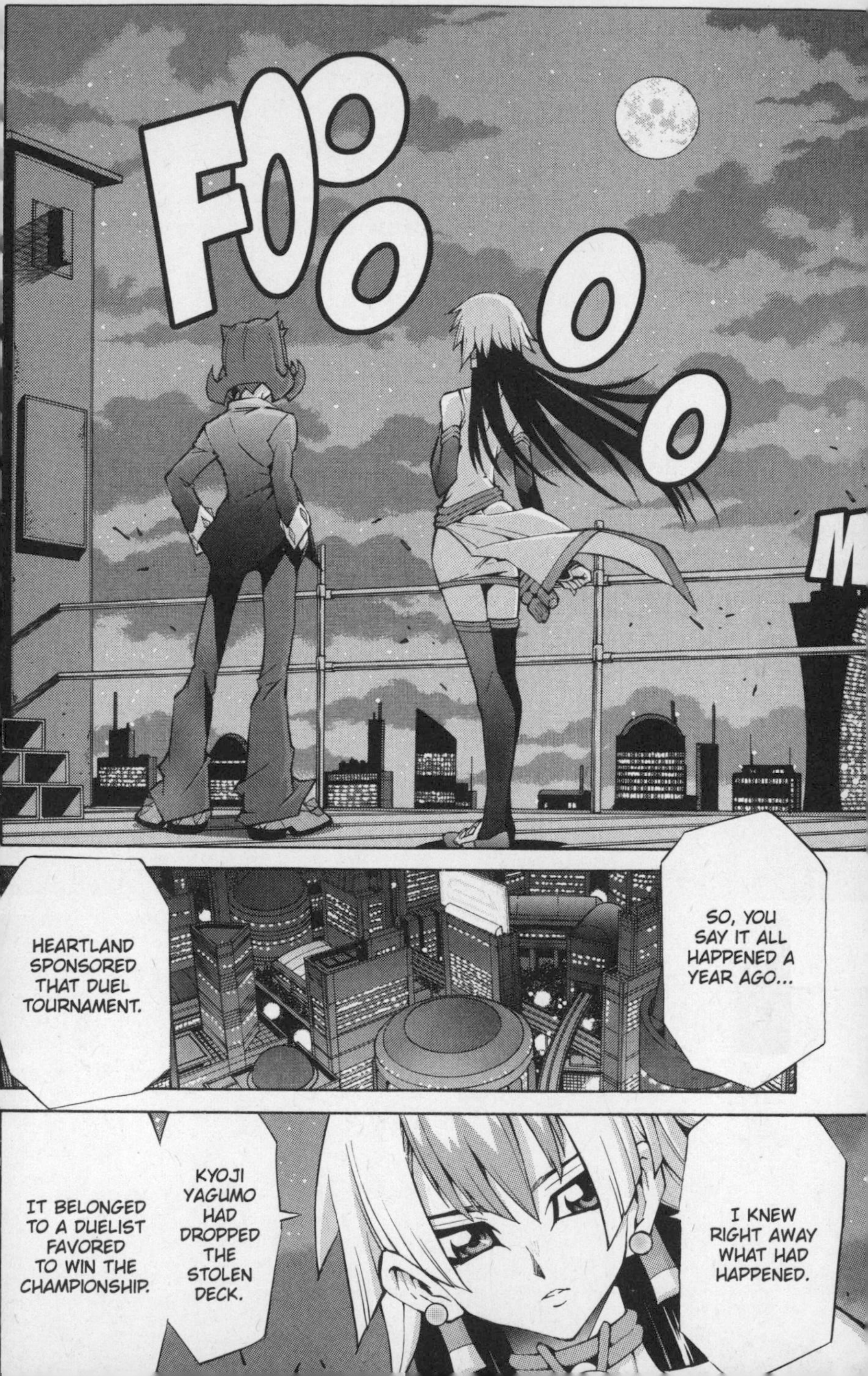
FOOOOOOO
SO, YOU SAY IT ALL HAPPENED A YEAR AGO...
HEARTLAND SPONSORED THAT DUEL TOURNAMENT.
I KNEW RIGHT AWAY WHAT HAD HAPPENED.
KYOJI YAGUMO HAD DROPPED THE STOLEN DECK.
IT BELONGED TO A DUELIST FAVORED TO WIN THE CHAMPIONSHIP.

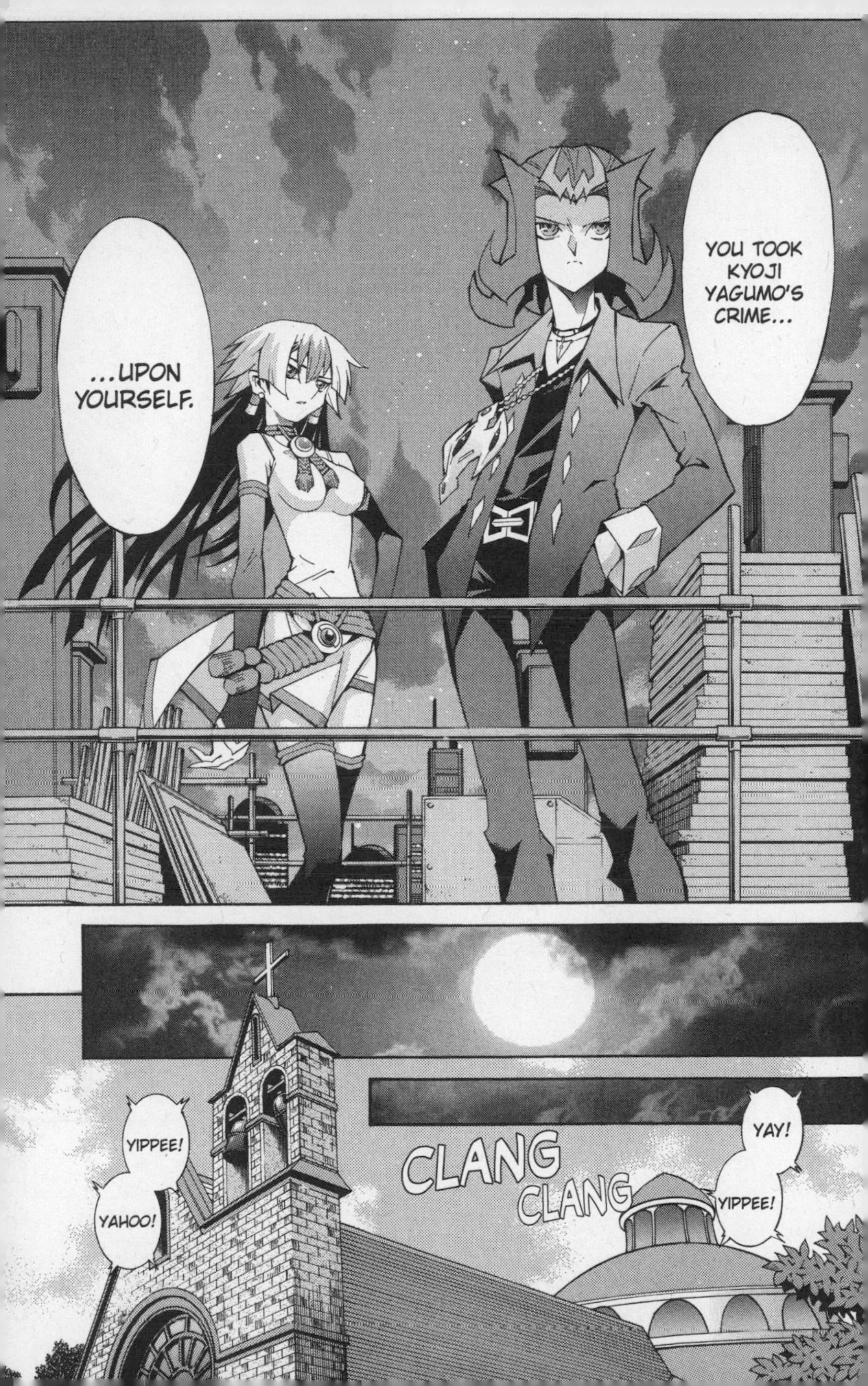
YOU TOOK KYOJI YAGUMO'S CRIME...
...UPON YOURSELF.
CLANG
CLANG
YAY!
YIPPEE!
YIPPEE!
YAHOO!

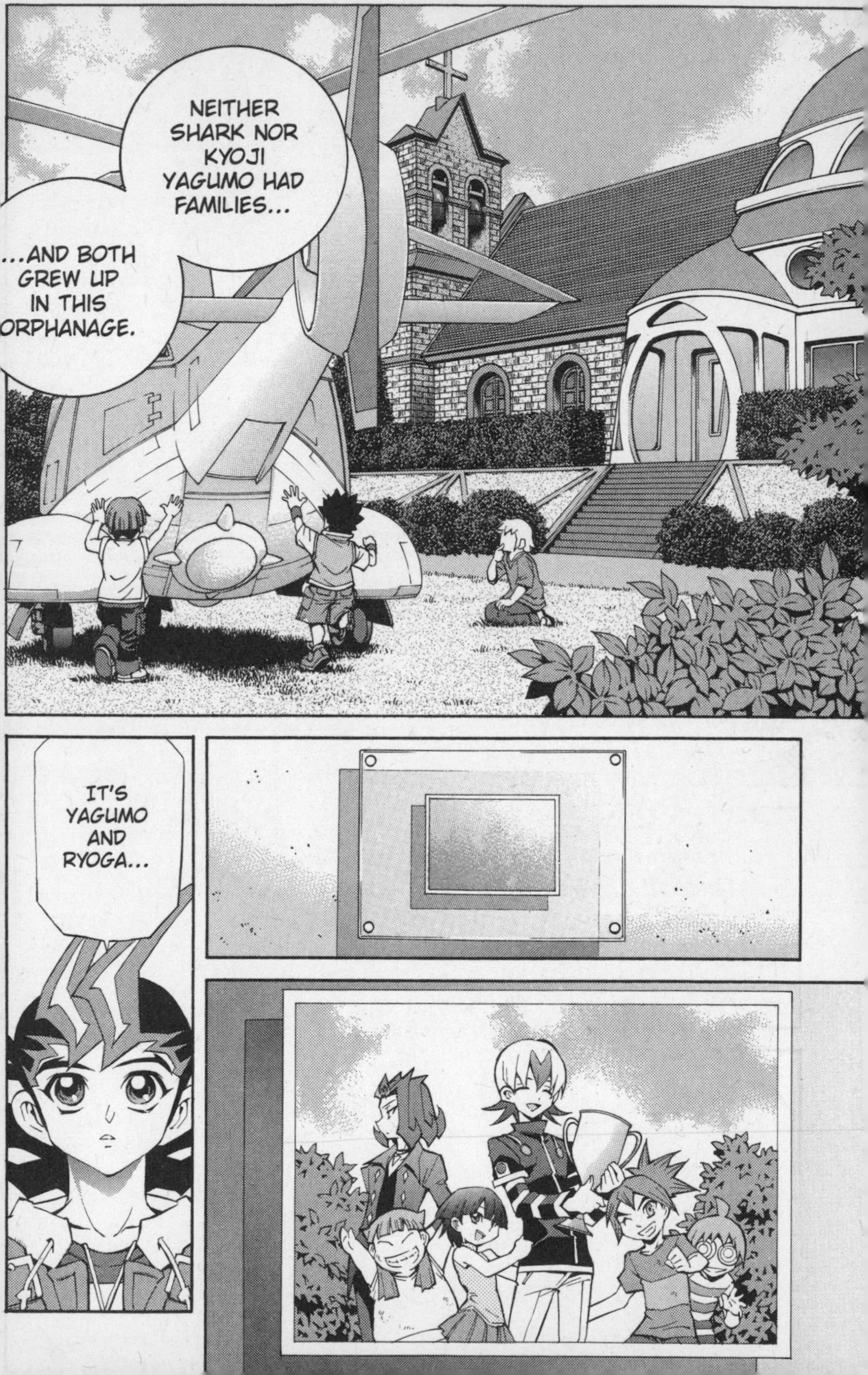
NEITHER SHARK NOR KYOJI YAGUMO HAD FAMILIES...
...AND BOTH GREW UP IN THIS ORPHANAGE.
IT'S YAGUMO AND RYOGA...

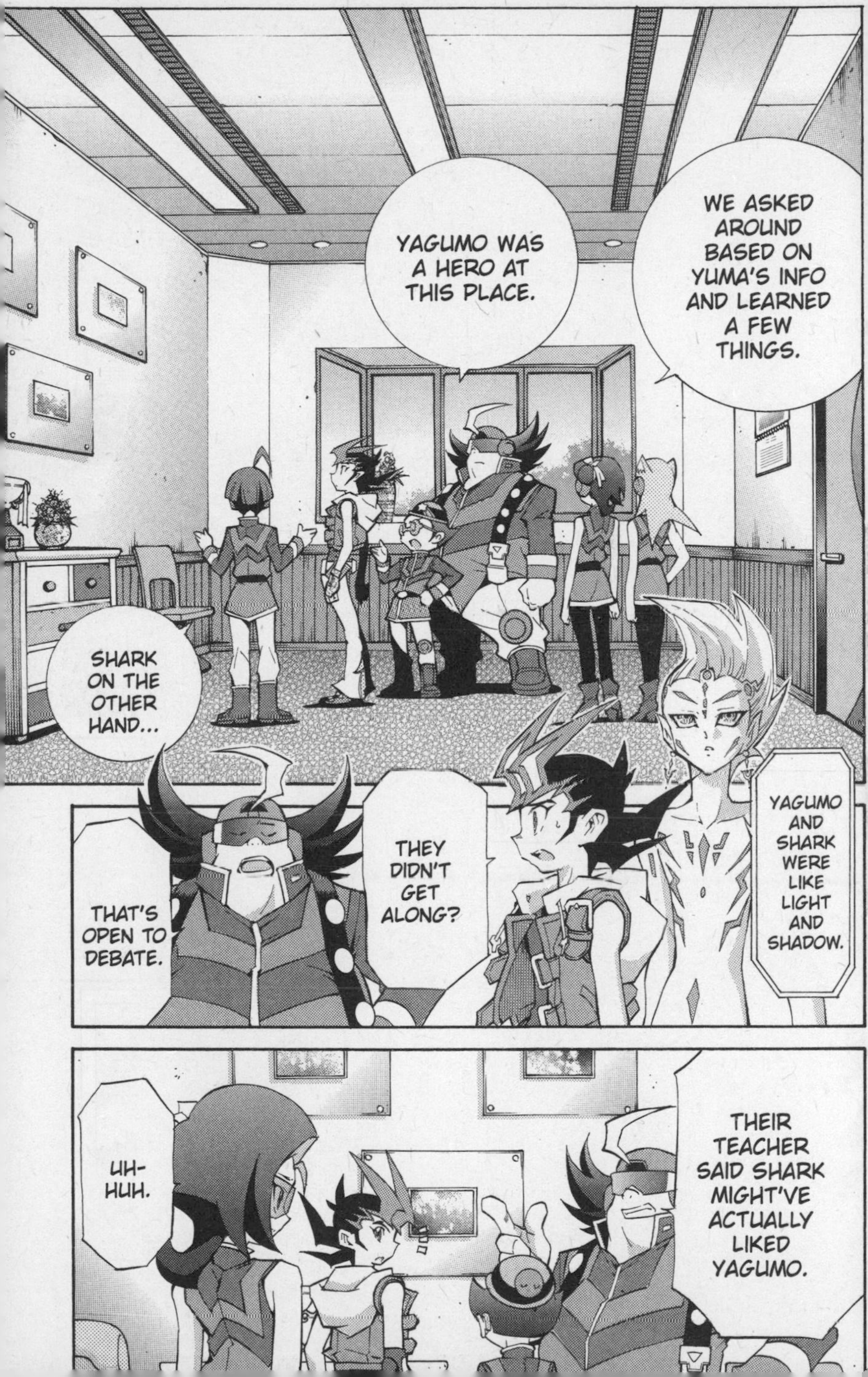
WE ASKED AROUND BASED ON YUMA'S INFO AND LEARNED A FEW THINGS.
YAGUMO WAS A HERO AT THIS PLACE.
SHARK ON THE OTHER HAND...
YAGUMO AND SHARK WERE LIKE LIGHT AND SHADOW.
THEY DIDN'T GET ALONG?
THAT'S OPEN TO DEBATE.
THEIR TEACHER SAID SHARK MIGHT'VE ACTUALLY LIKED YAGUMO.
UH-HUH.

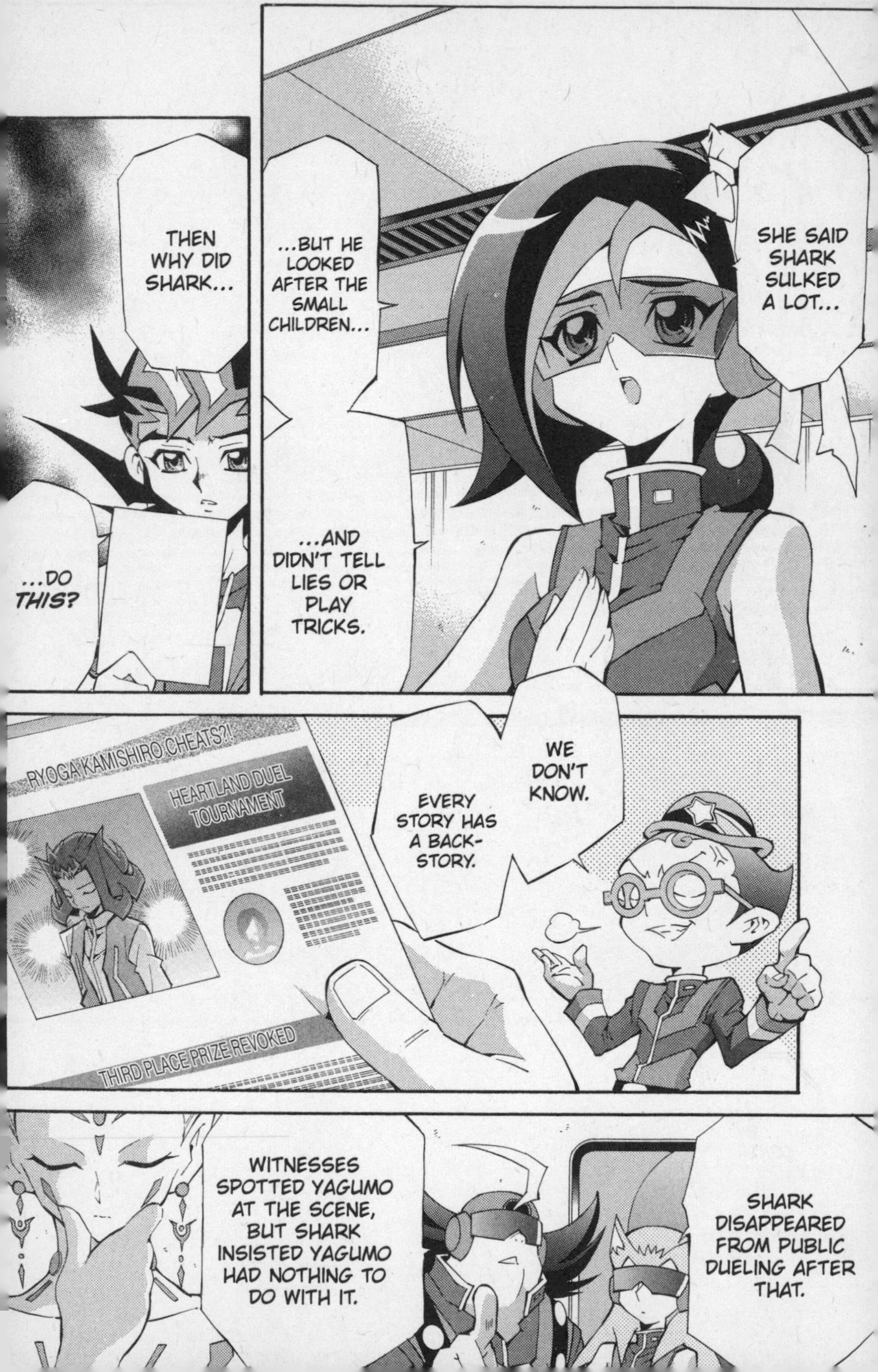
SHE SAID SHARK SULKED A LOT...
...BUT HE LOOKED AFTER THE SMALL CHILDREN...
...AND DIDN'T TELL LIES OR PLAY TRICKS.
THEN WHY DID SHARK...
...DO *THIS?*
WE DON'T KNOW.
EVERY STORY HAS A BACK-STORY.
RYOGA KAMISHIRO CHEATS?!
HEARTLAND DUEL TOURNAMENT
THIRD PLACE PRIZE REVOKED
SHARK DISAPPEARED FROM PUBLIC DUELING AFTER THAT.
WITNESSES SPOTTED YAGUMO AT THE SCENE, BUT SHARK INSISTED YAGUMO HAD NOTHING TO DO WITH IT.

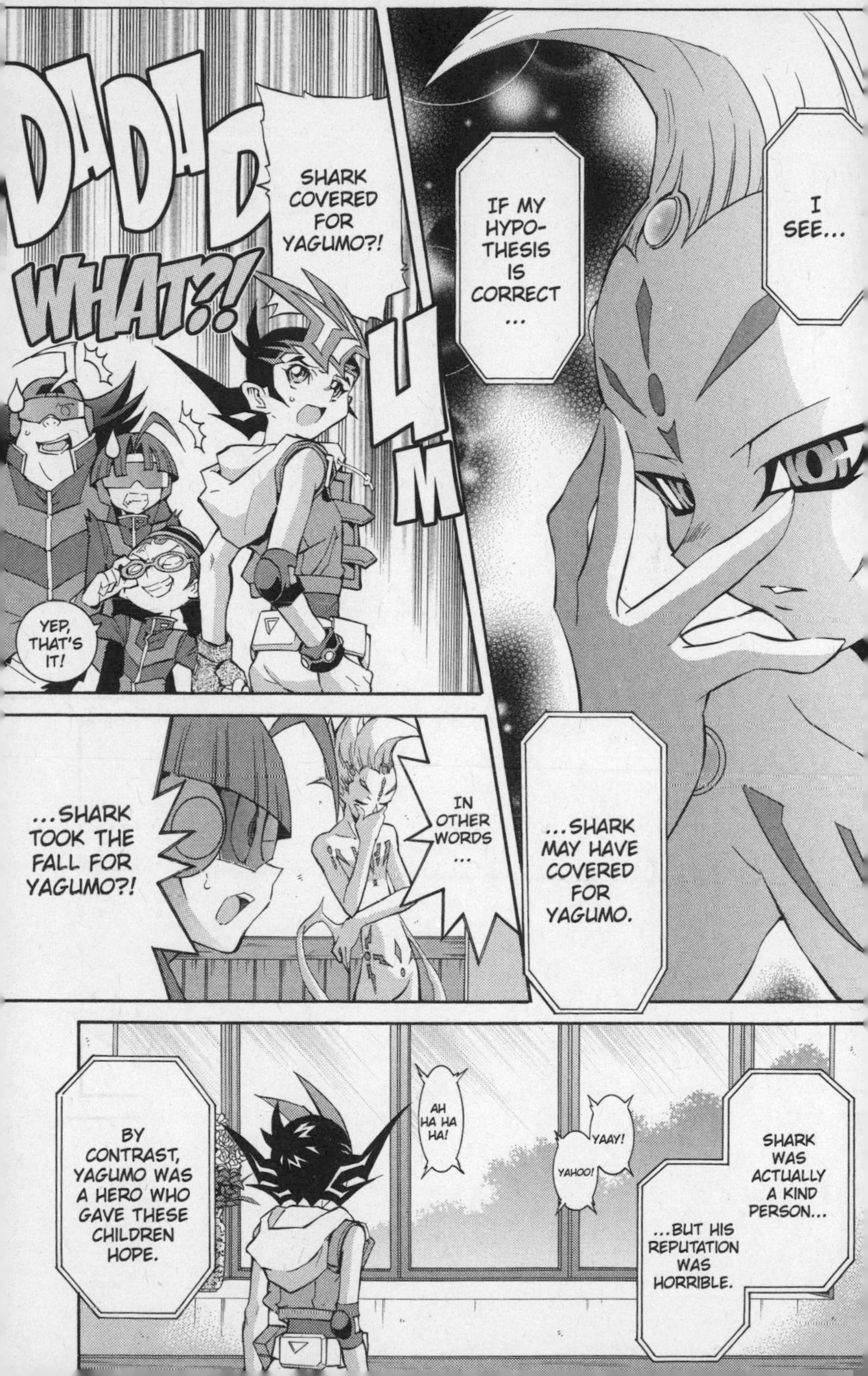

I SEE...
IF MY HYPOTHESIS IS CORRECT...
...SHARK MAY HAVE COVERED FOR YAGUMO.
DADADUM
SHARK COVERED FOR YAGUMO?!
WHAT?!
YEP, THAT'S IT!
IN OTHER WORDS...
...SHARK TOOK THE FALL FOR YAGUMO?!
SHARK WAS ACTUALLY A KIND PERSON...
...BUT HIS REPUTATION WAS HORRIBLE.
YAAY!
YAHOO!
AH HA HA HA!
BY CONTRAST, YAGUMO WAS A HERO WHO GAVE THESE CHILDREN HOPE.

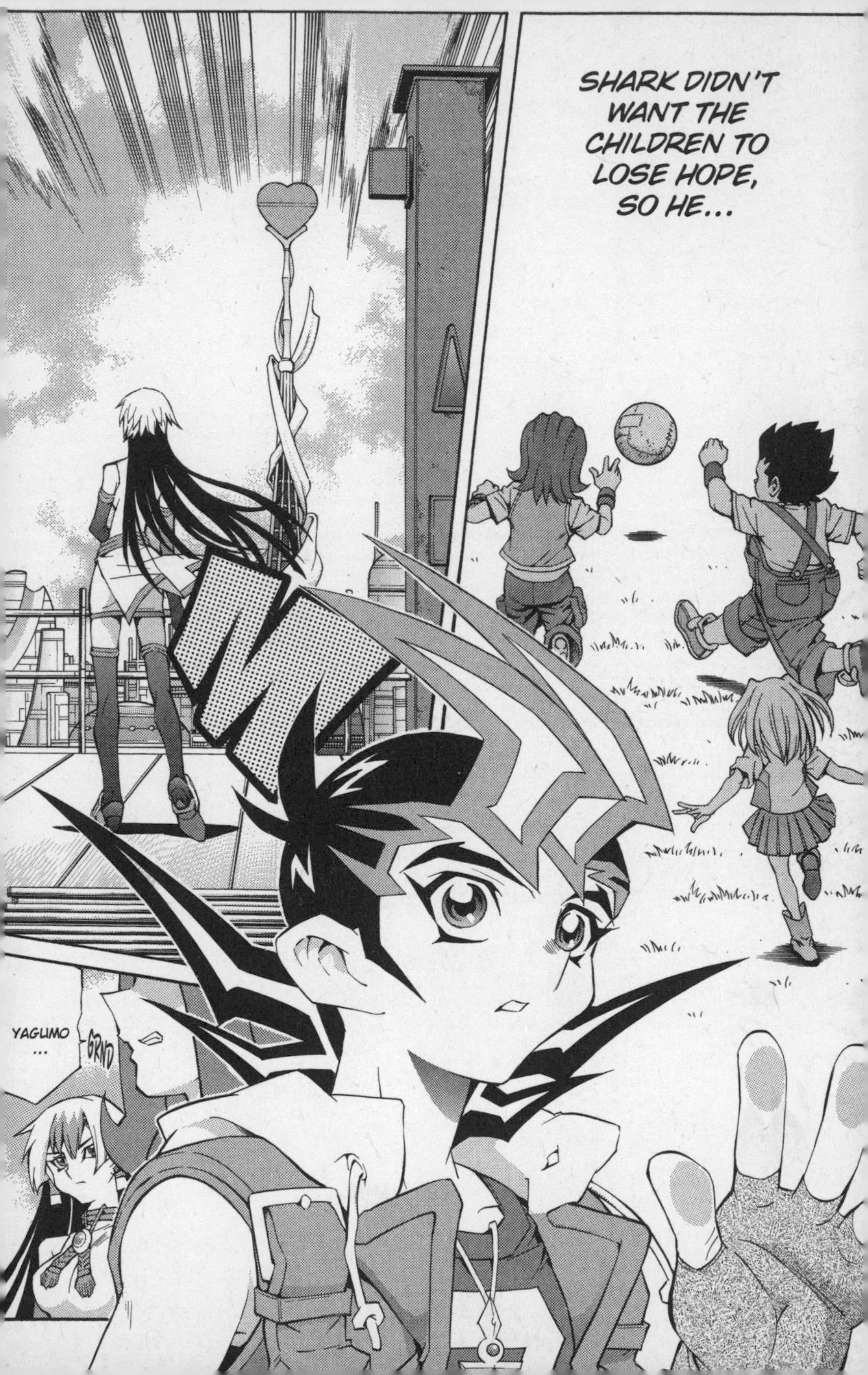
SHARK DIDN'T WANT THE CHILDREN TO LOSE HOPE, SO HE...
YAGUMO ...
GRND

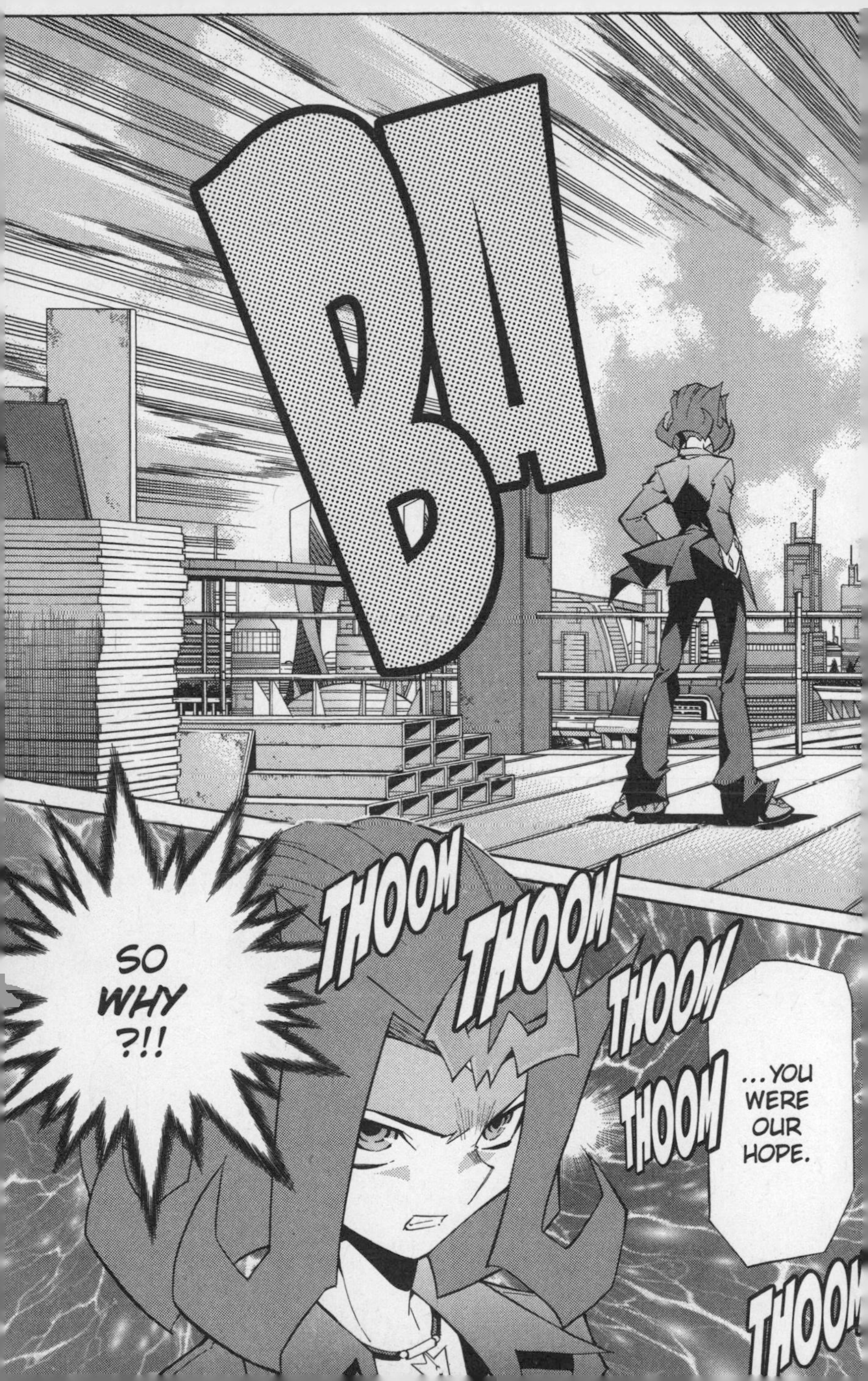
BA!
...YOU WERE OUR HOPE.
THOOM
THOOM
THOOM
THOOM
THOOM
SO WHY?!!

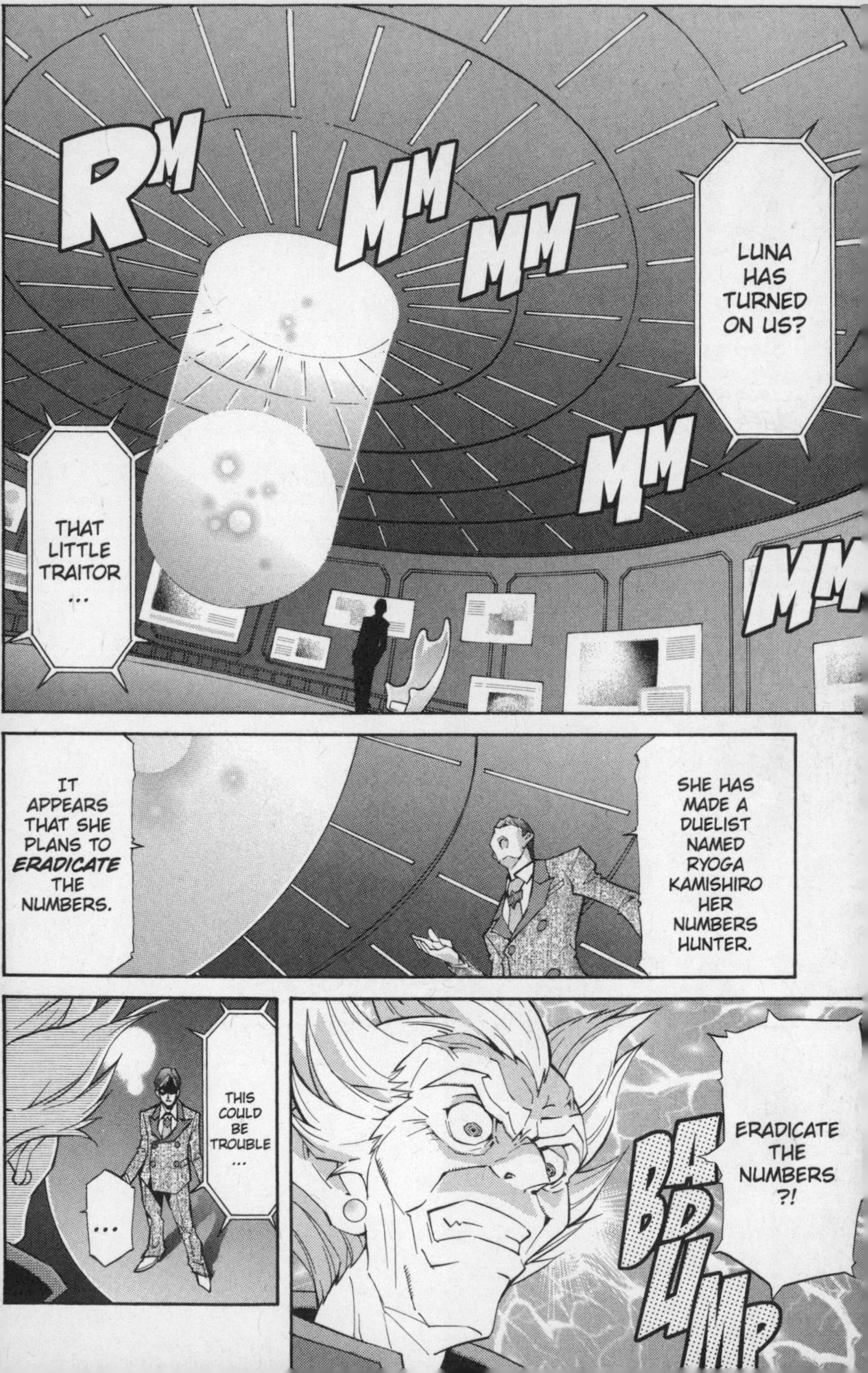
LUNA HAS TURNED ON US?
RMMMMMMMMMMM
THAT LITTLE TRAITOR...
SHE HAS MADE A DUELIST NAMED RYOGA KAMISHIRO HER NUMBERS HUNTER.
IT APPEARS THAT SHE PLANS TO *ERADICATE* THE NUMBERS.
ERADICATE THE NUMBERS?!
THIS COULD BE TROUBLE...
...

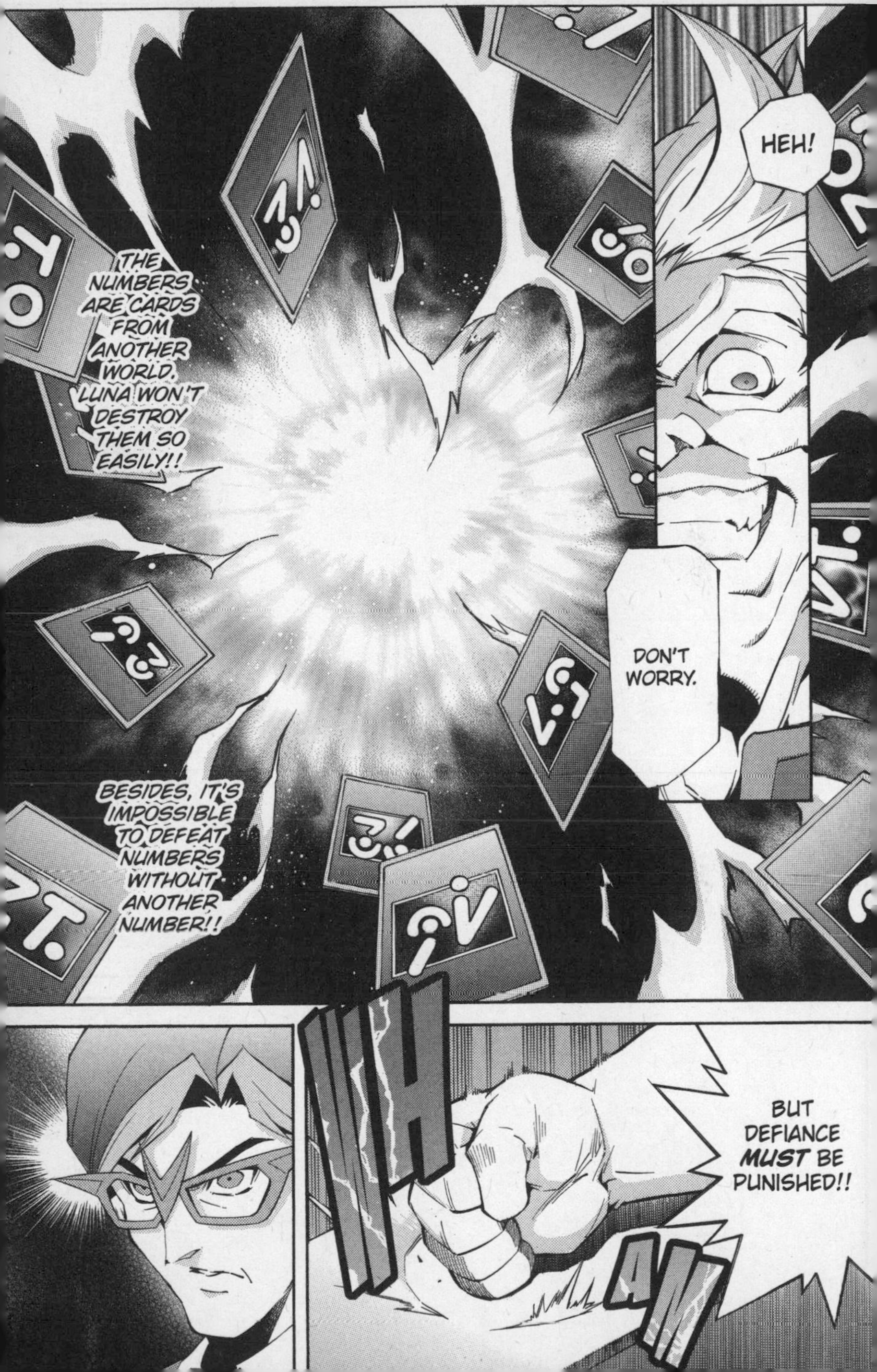
HEH!
DON'T WORRY.
THE NUMBERS ARE CARDS FROM ANOTHER WORLD. LUNA WON'T DESTROY THEM SO EASILY!!
BESIDES, IT'S IMPOSSIBLE TO DEFEAT NUMBERS WITHOUT ANOTHER NUMBER!!
BUT DEFIANCE **MUST** BE PUNISHED!!

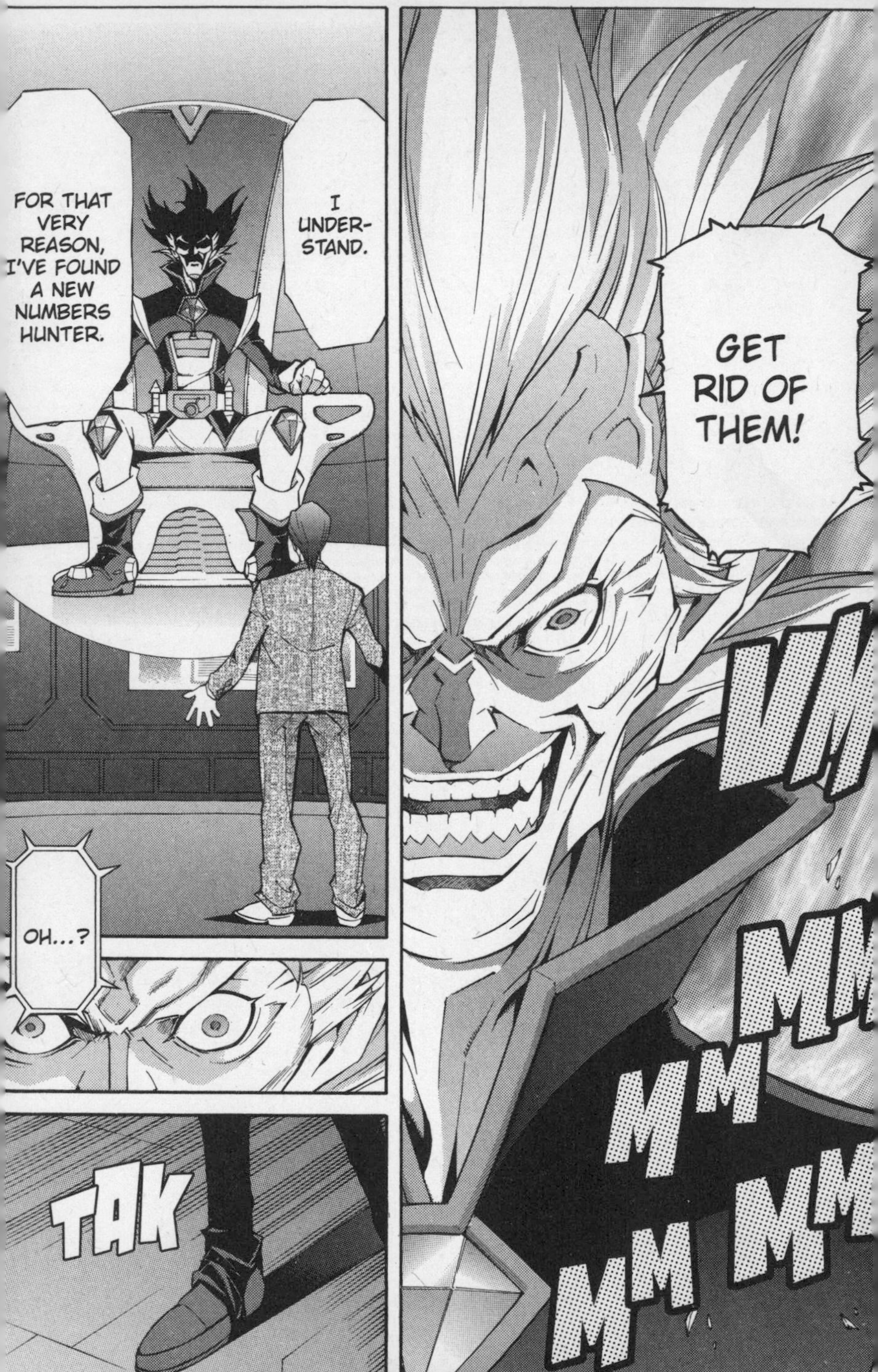
GET RID OF THEM!
UM MM MM MM MM
I UNDERSTAND.
FOR THAT VERY REASON, I'VE FOUND A NEW NUMBERS HUNTER.
OH...?
TAK

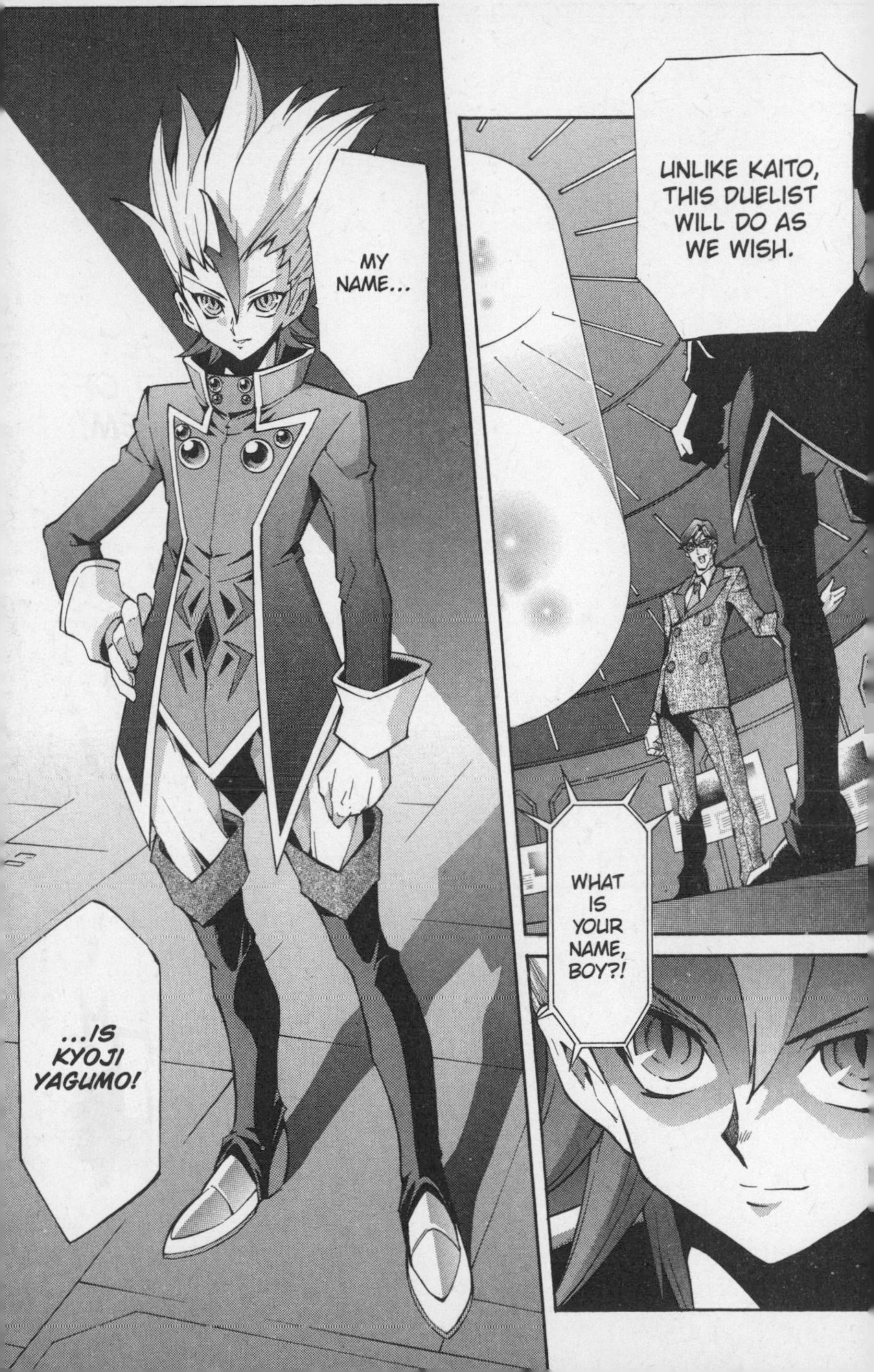
UNLIKE KAITO, THIS DUELIST WILL DO AS WE WISH.
WHAT IS YOUR NAME, BOY?!
MY NAME...
...IS KYOJI YAGUMO!

YU-GI-OH!
ZEXAL

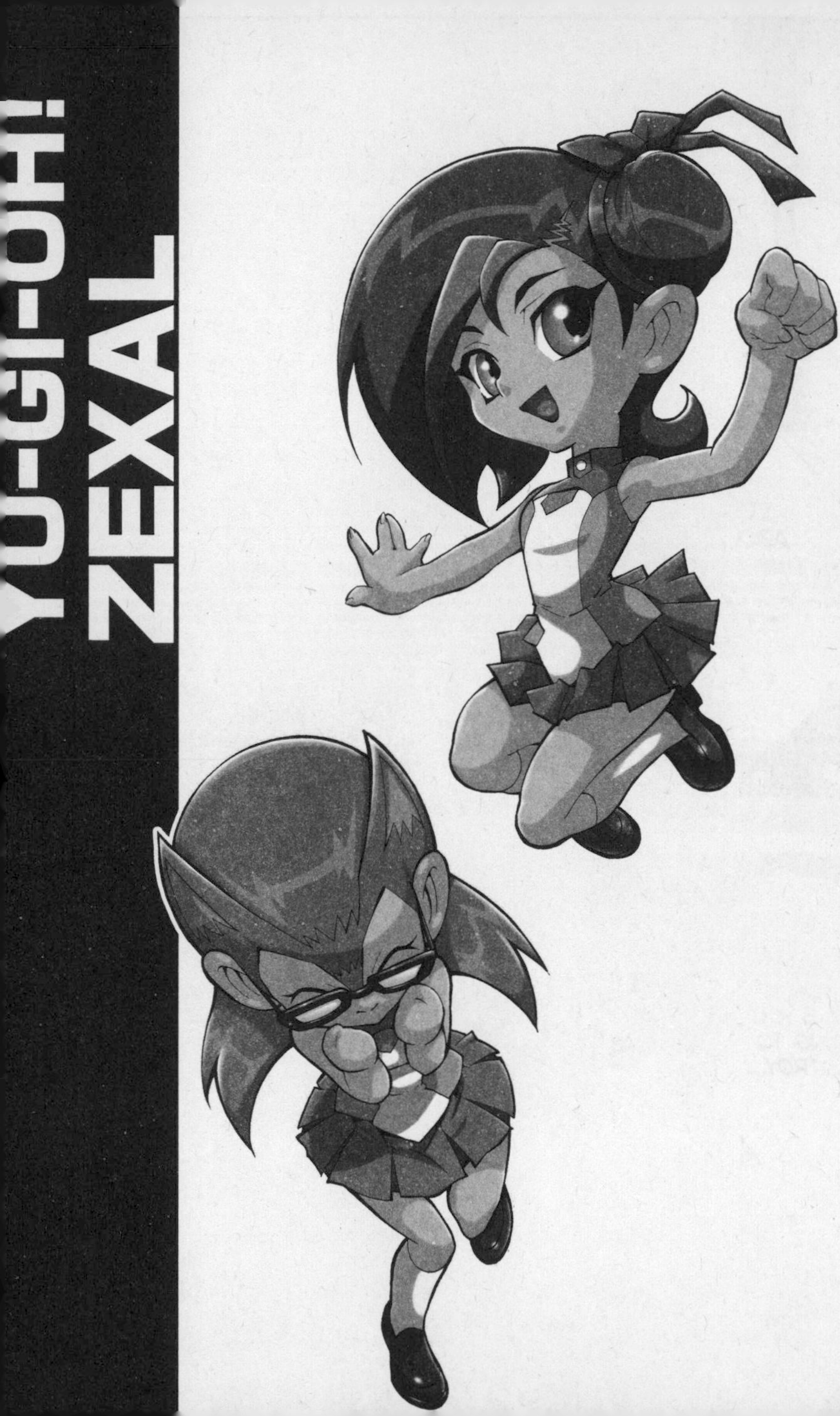

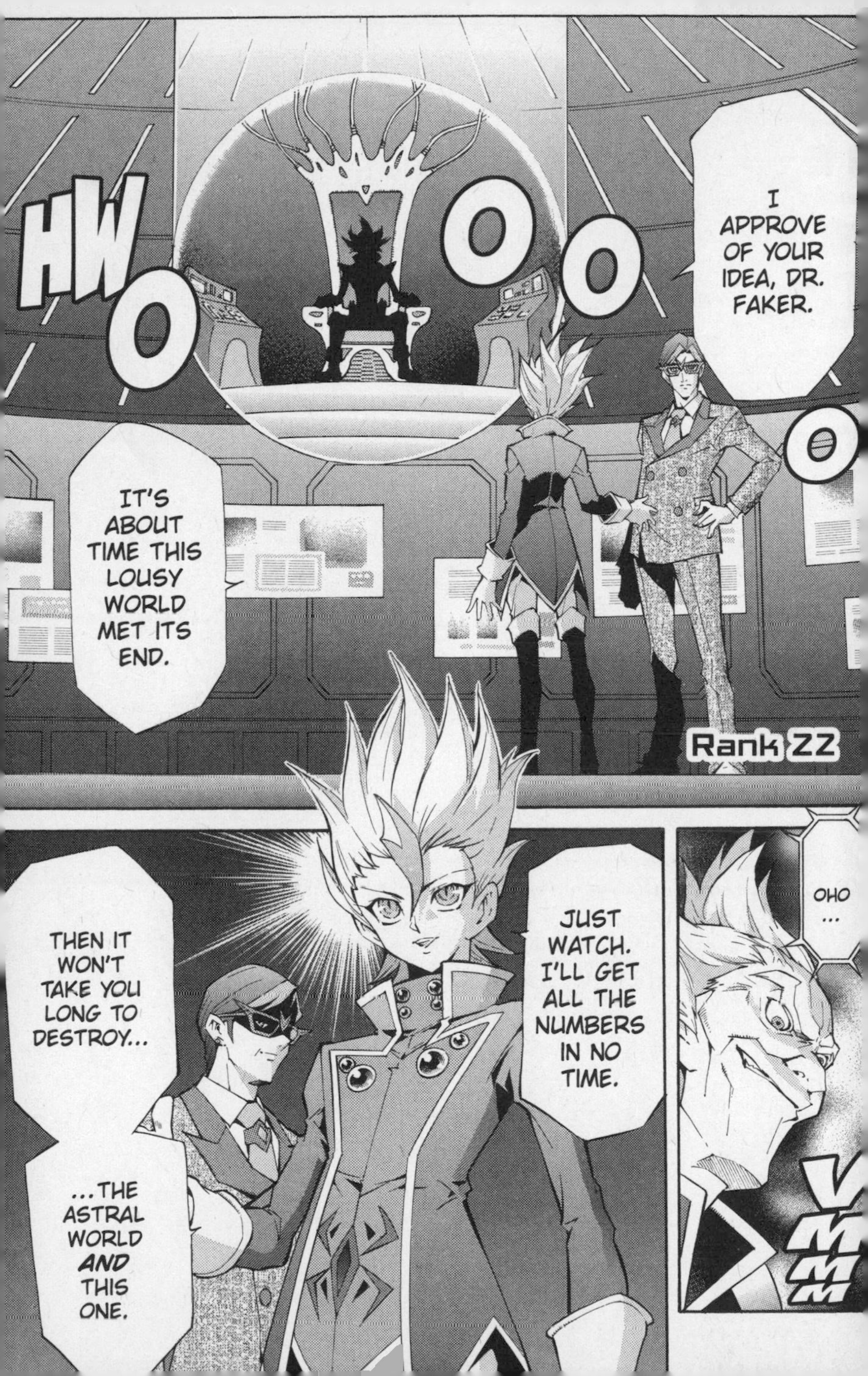
I APPROVE OF YOUR IDEA, DR. FAKER.
HWOOOOO
IT'S ABOUT TIME THIS LOUSY WORLD MET ITS END.
Rank 22
OHO...
VMMM
JUST WATCH. I'LL GET ALL THE NUMBERS IN NO TIME.
THEN IT WON'T TAKE YOU LONG TO DESTROY...
...THE ASTRAL WORLD *AND* THIS ONE.

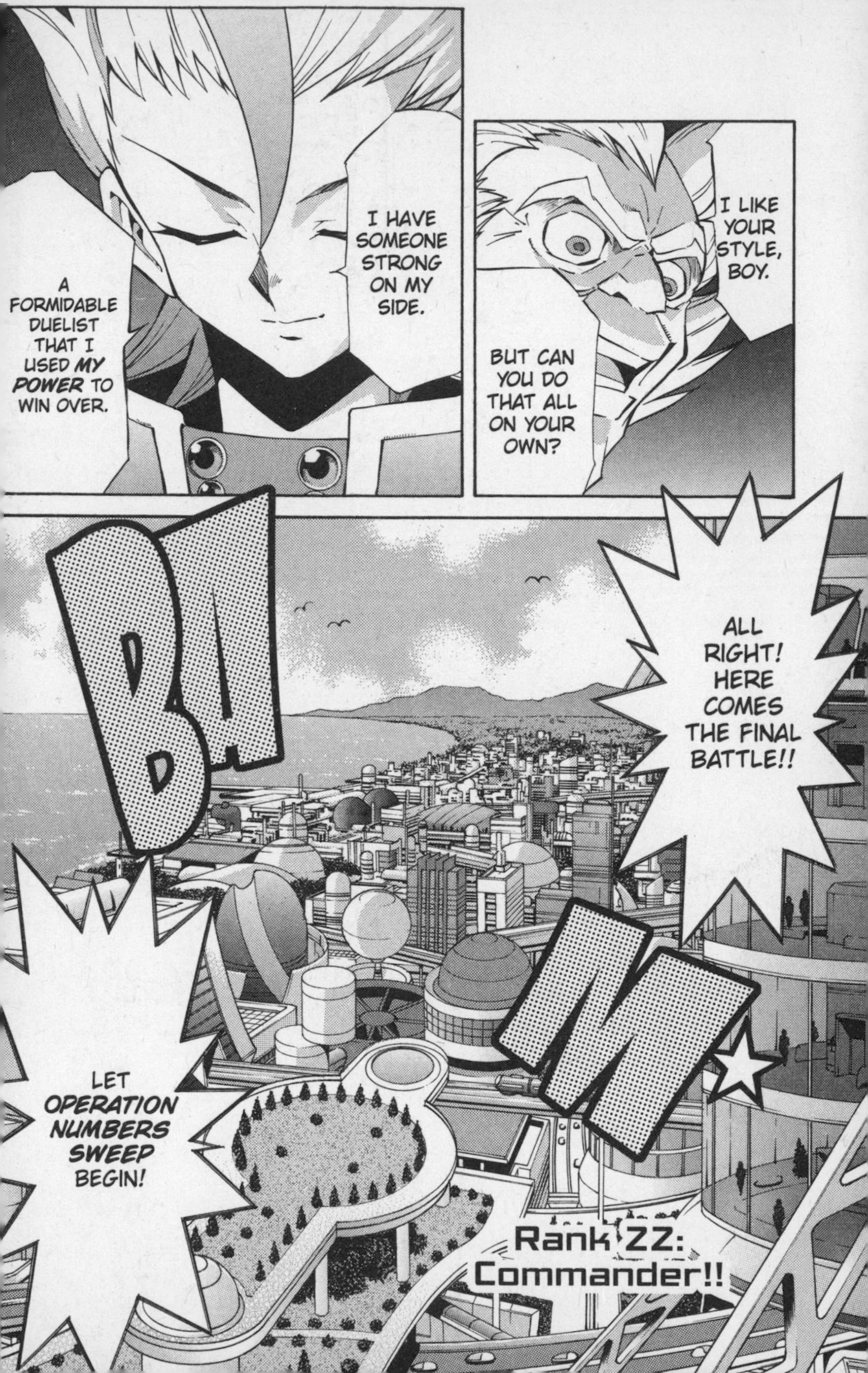

I LIKE YOUR STYLE, BOY.
BUT CAN YOU DO THAT ALL ON YOUR OWN?
I HAVE SOMEONE STRONG ON MY SIDE.
A FORMIDABLE DUELIST THAT I USED *MY POWER* TO WIN OVER.
ALL RIGHT! HERE COMES THE FINAL BATTLE!!
BAM★
LET *OPERATION NUMBERS SWEEP* BEGIN!
Rank 22: Commander!!

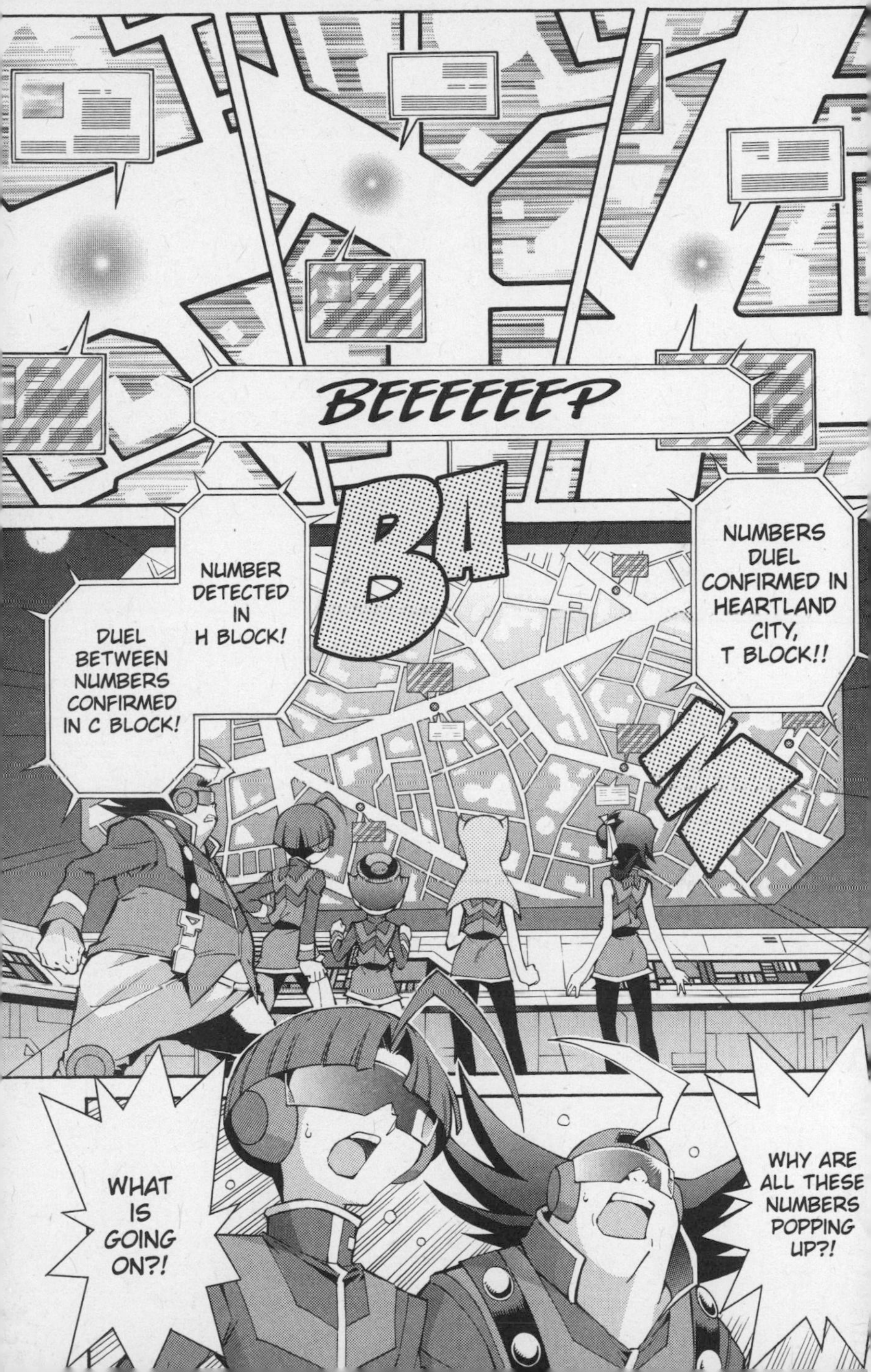
BEEEEEEP
NUMBERS DUEL CONFIRMED IN HEARTLAND CITY, T BLOCK!!
BA
NUMBER DETECTED IN H BLOCK!
DUEL BETWEEN NUMBERS CONFIRMED IN C BLOCK!
WHY ARE ALL THESE NUMBERS POPPING UP?!
WHAT IS GOING ON?!

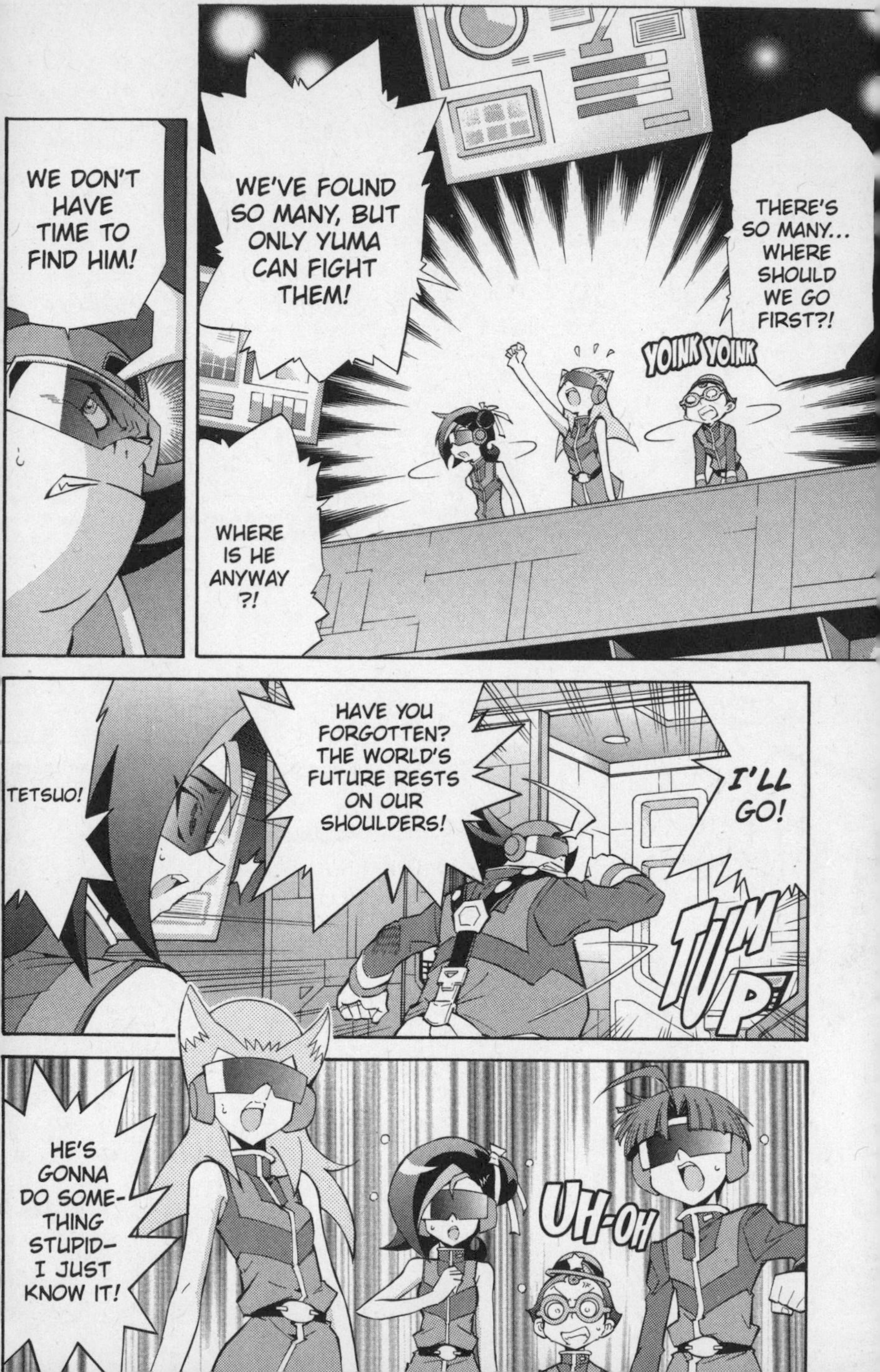
THERE'S SO MANY... WHERE SHOULD WE GO FIRST?!
YOINK YOINK
WE'VE FOUND SO MANY, BUT ONLY YUMA CAN FIGHT THEM!
WHERE IS HE ANYWAY?!
WE DON'T HAVE TIME TO FIND HIM!
I'LL GO!
TUMP
HAVE YOU FORGOTTEN? THE WORLD'S FUTURE RESTS ON OUR SHOULDERS!
TETSUO!
UH-OH
HE'S GONNA DO SOME-THING STUPID— I JUST KNOW IT!

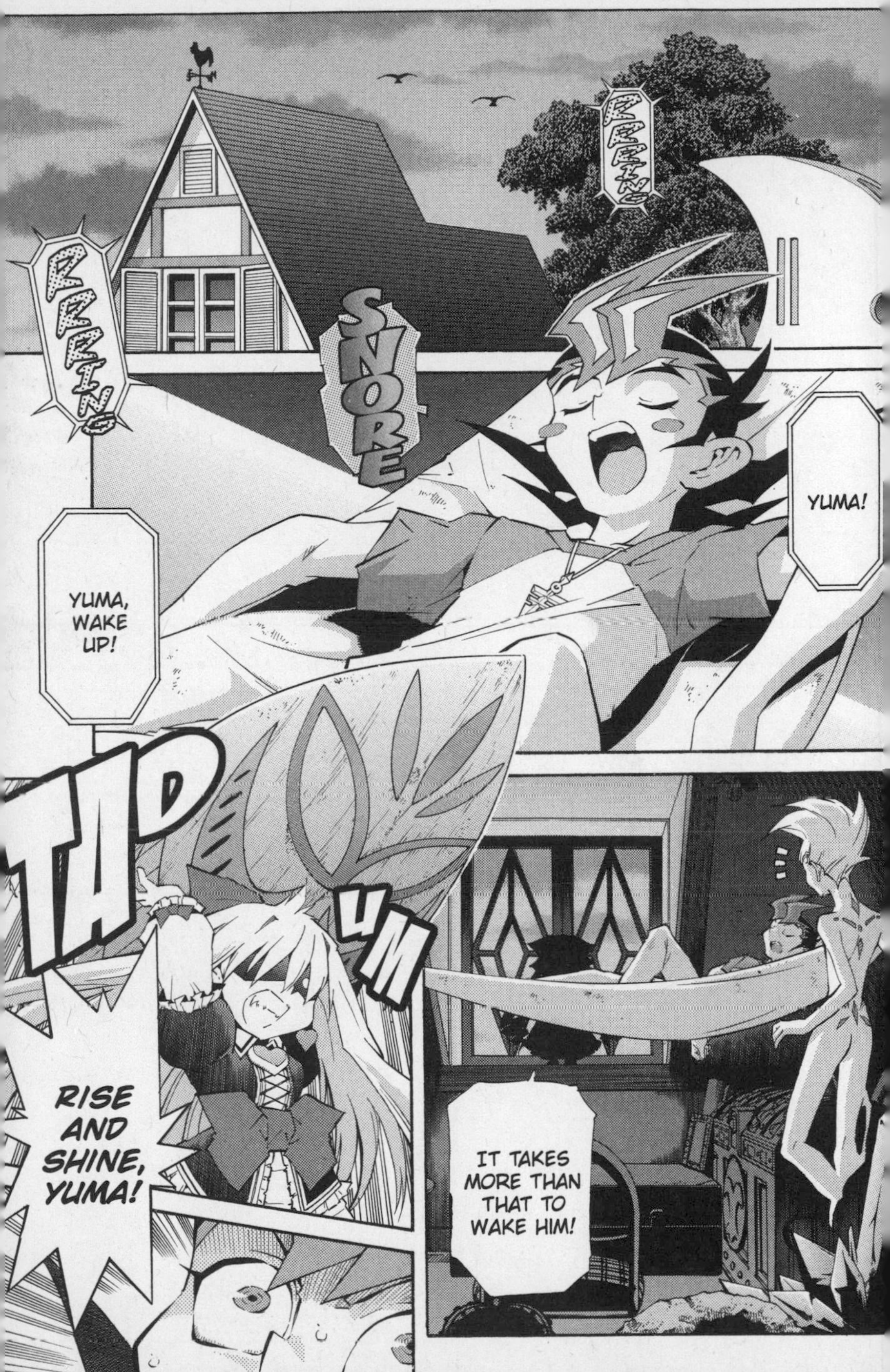

RRRING
YUMA!
SNORE
RRRING
YUMA, WAKE UP!
IT TAKES MORE THAN THAT TO WAKE HIM!
TAD
UM
RISE AND SHINE, YUMA!

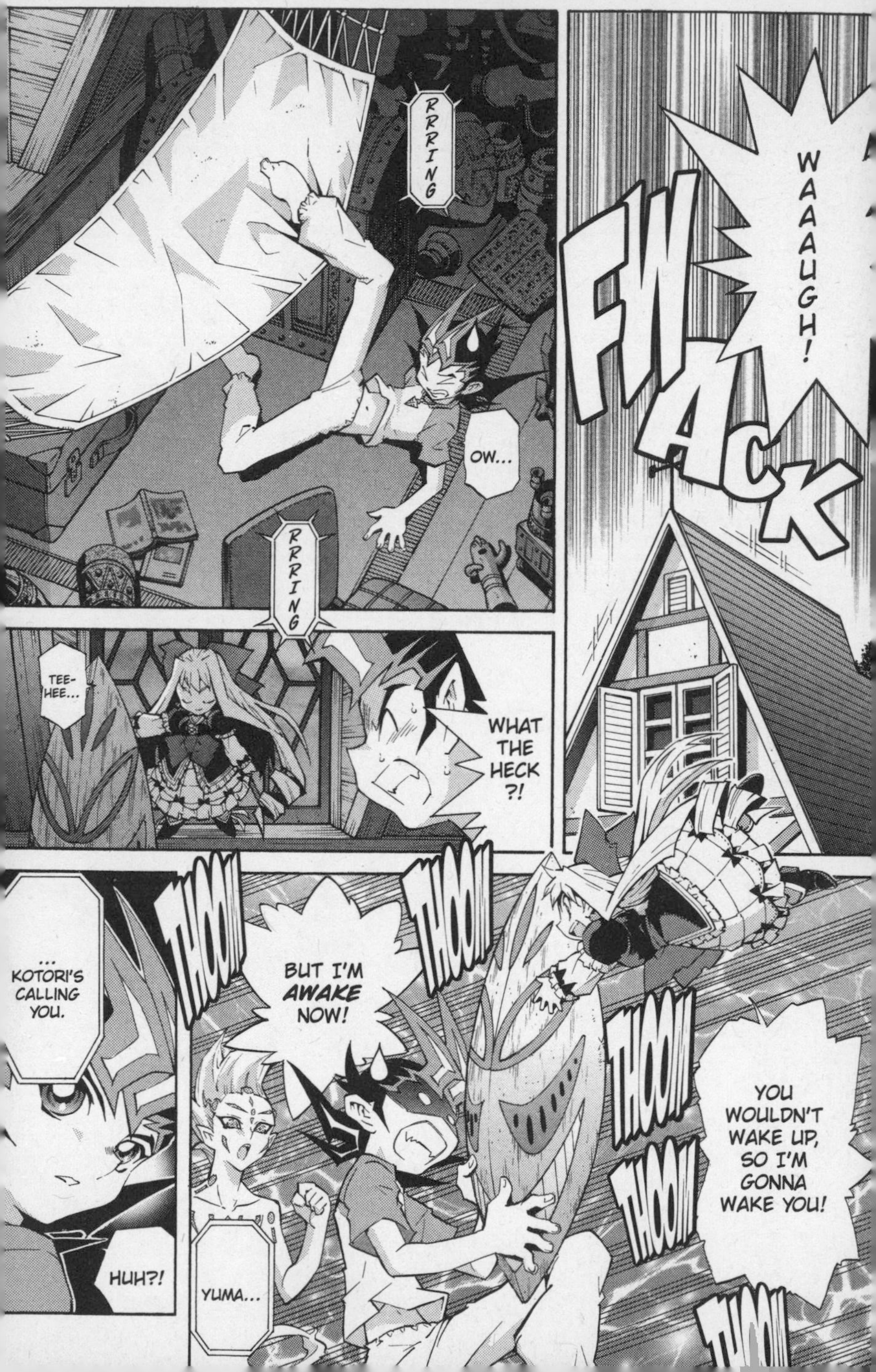
WAAAAUGH!
FWACK
RRRING
OW...
RRRING
WHAT THE HECK?!
TEE-HEE...
THOOM
THOOM
YOU WOULDN'T WAKE UP, SO I'M GONNA WAKE YOU!
THOOM
THOOM
BUT I'M AWAKE NOW!
THOOM
YUMA...
... KOTORI'S CALLING YOU.
HUH?!

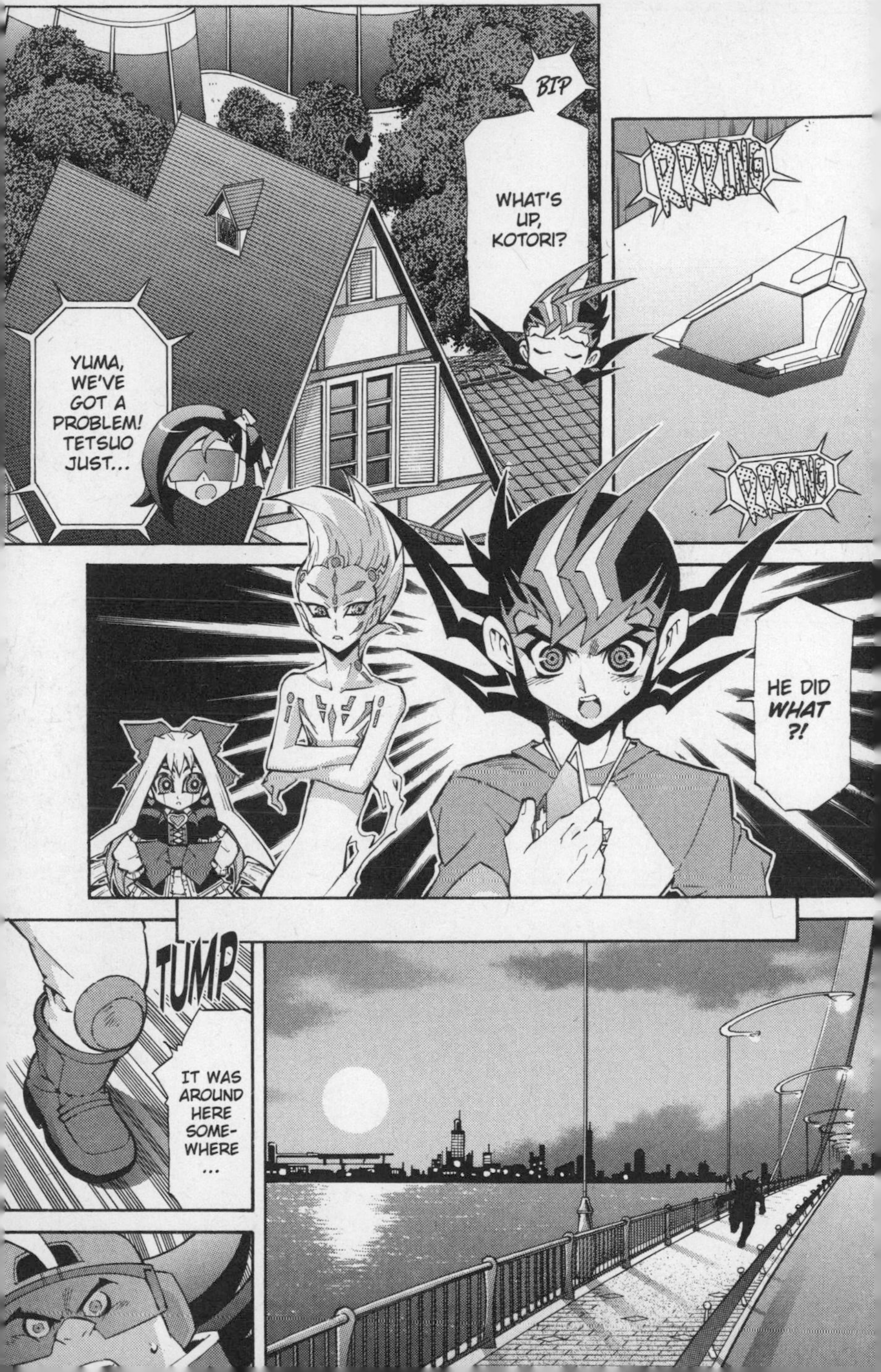
RRRING
RRRING
BIP
WHAT'S UP, KOTORI?
YUMA, WE'VE GOT A PROBLEM! TETSUO JUST...
HE DID WHAT?!
TUMP
IT WAS AROUND HERE SOME-WHERE...

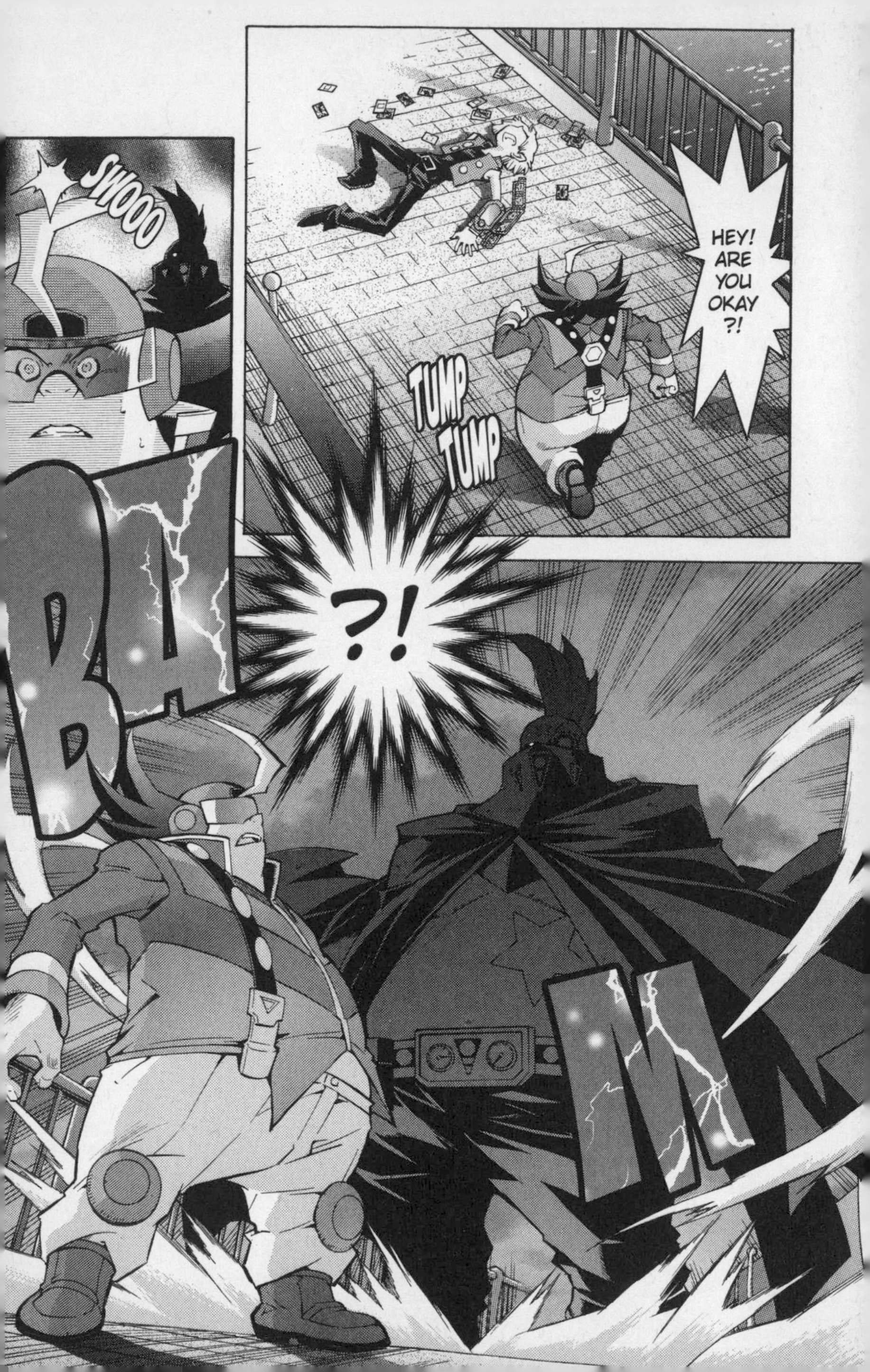
HEY! ARE YOU OKAY ?!
TUMP TUMP
SWOOO
?!
BA
M

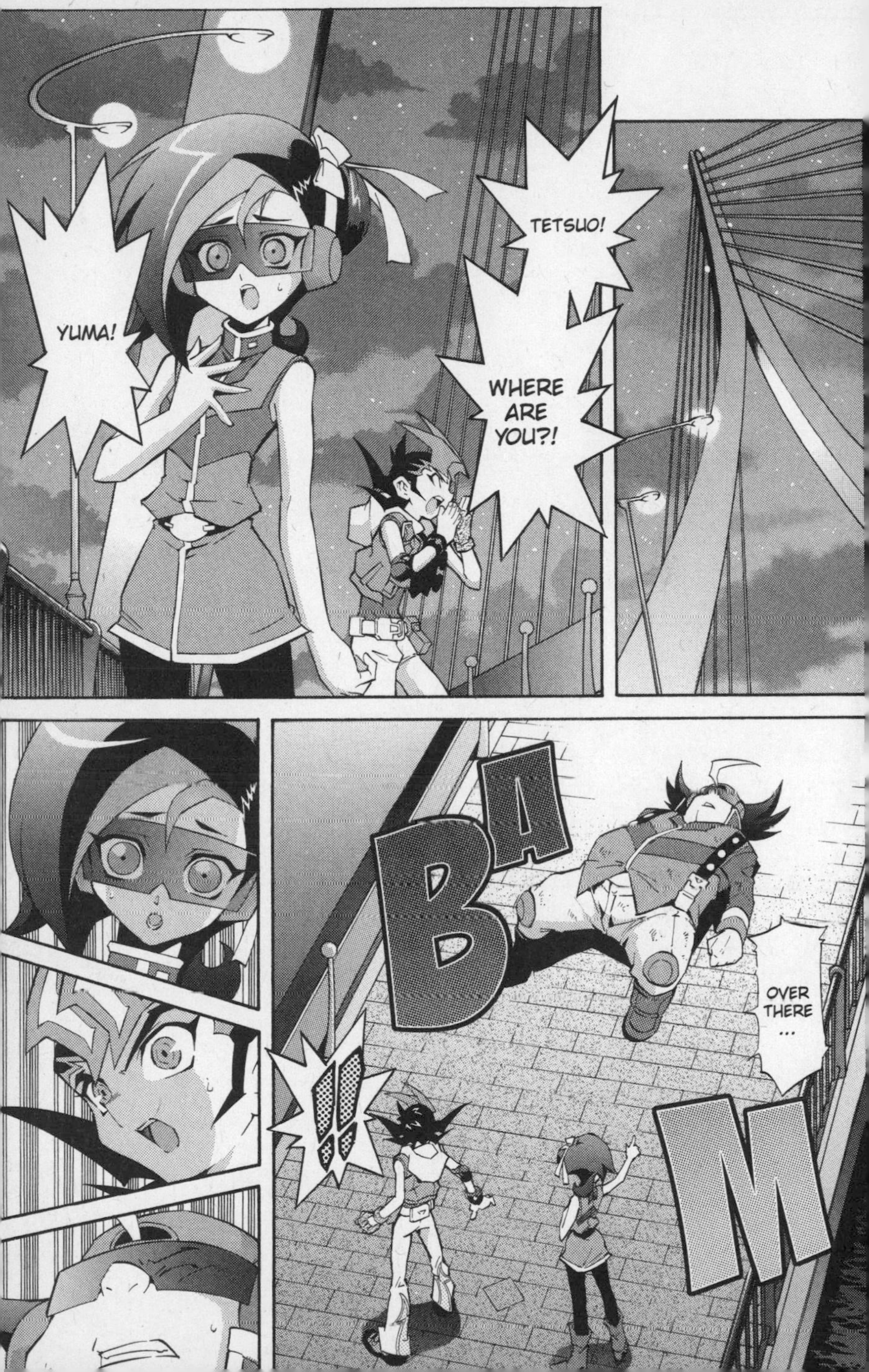
TETSUO!
WHERE ARE YOU?!
YUMA!
BA
OVER THERE ...
M
!!

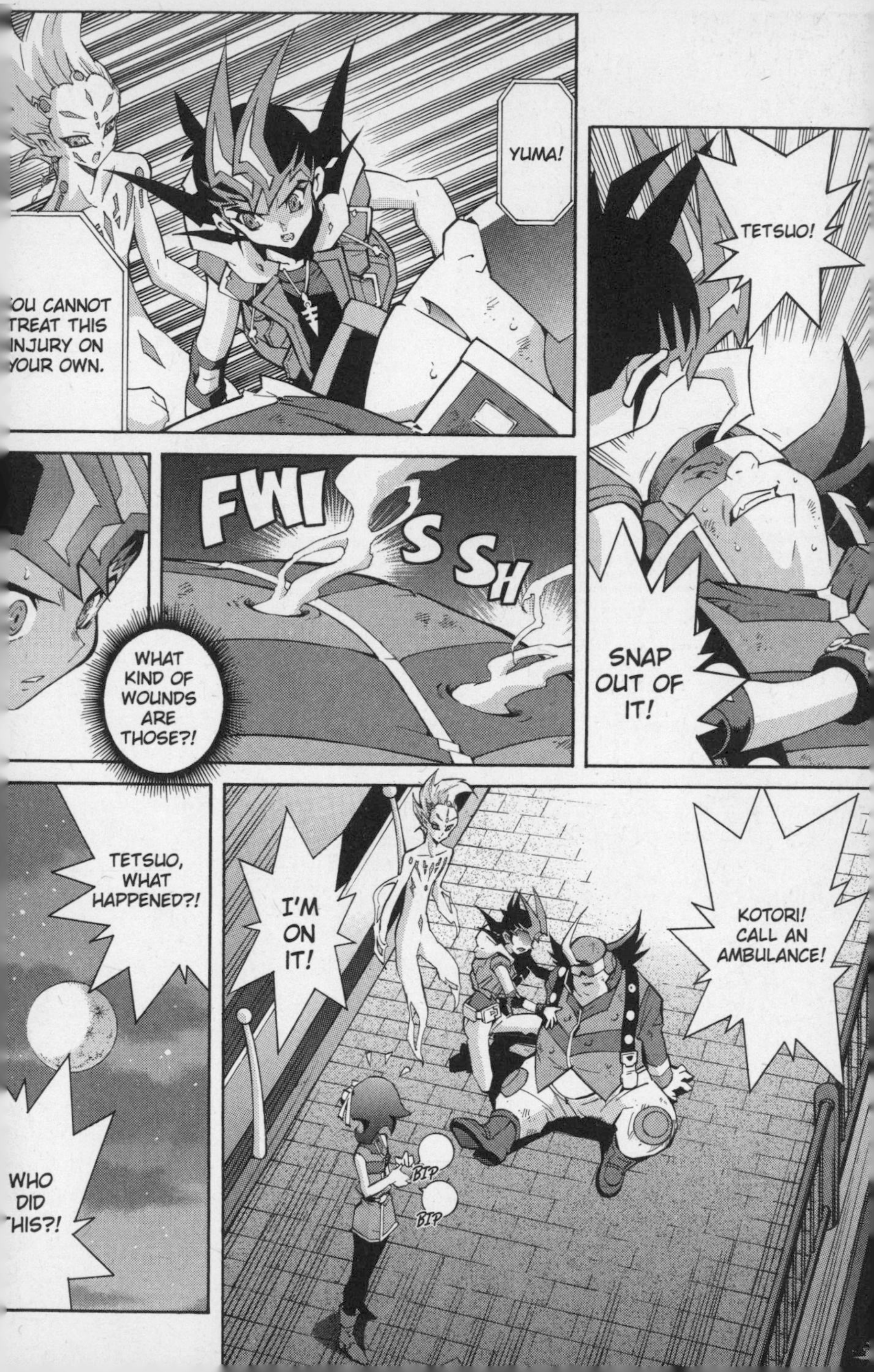
TETSUO!
SNAP OUT OF IT!
YUMA!
YOU CANNOT TREAT THIS INJURY ON YOUR OWN.
FWISSSH
WHAT KIND OF WOUNDS ARE THOSE?!
KOTORI! CALL AN AMBULANCE!
I'M ON IT!
BIP
BIP
TETSUO, WHAT HAPPENED?!
WHO DID THIS?!

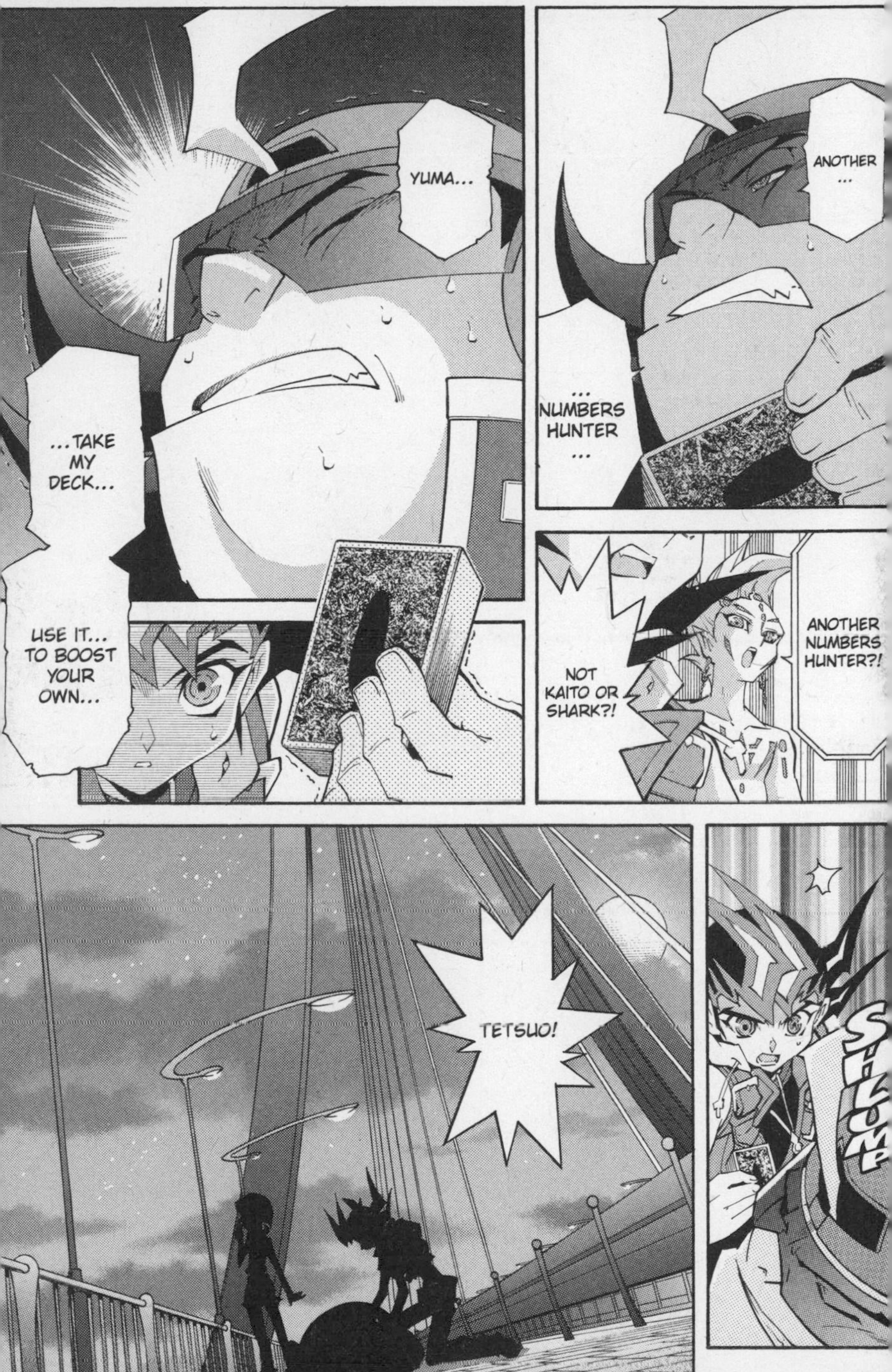
ANOTHER ...
... NUMBERS HUNTER ...
ANOTHER NUMBERS HUNTER?!
NOT KAITO OR SHARK?!
YUMA...
...TAKE MY DECK...
USE IT... TO BOOST YOUR OWN...
SHLUMP
TETSUO!

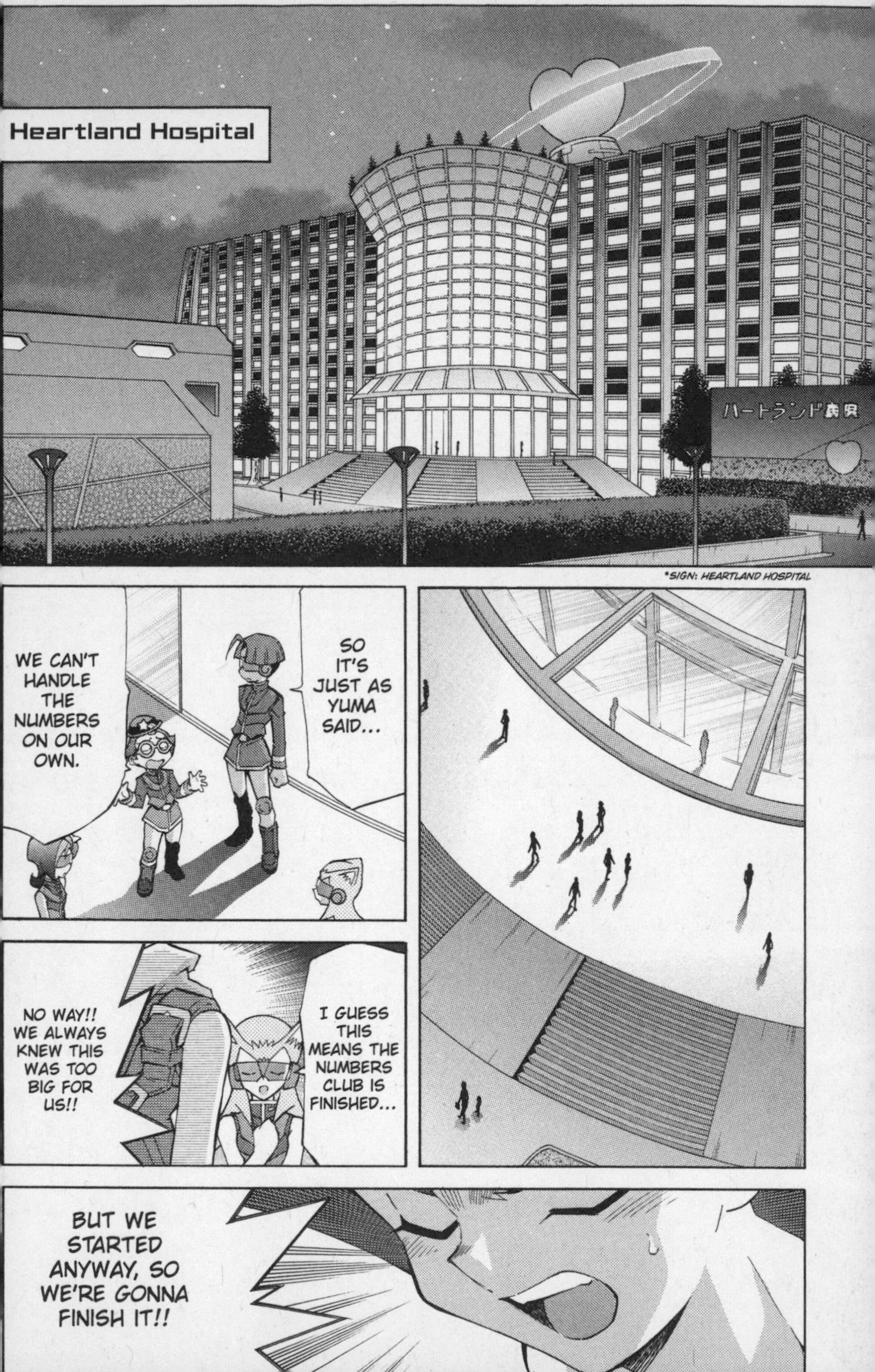
Heartland Hospital
ハートランド病院
*SIGN: HEARTLAND HOSPITAL
SO IT'S JUST AS YUMA SAID...
WE CAN'T HANDLE THE NUMBERS ON OUR OWN.
I GUESS THIS MEANS THE NUMBERS CLUB IS FINISHED...
NO WAY!! WE ALWAYS KNEW THIS WAS TOO BIG FOR US!!
BUT WE STARTED ANYWAY, SO WE'RE GONNA FINISH IT!!

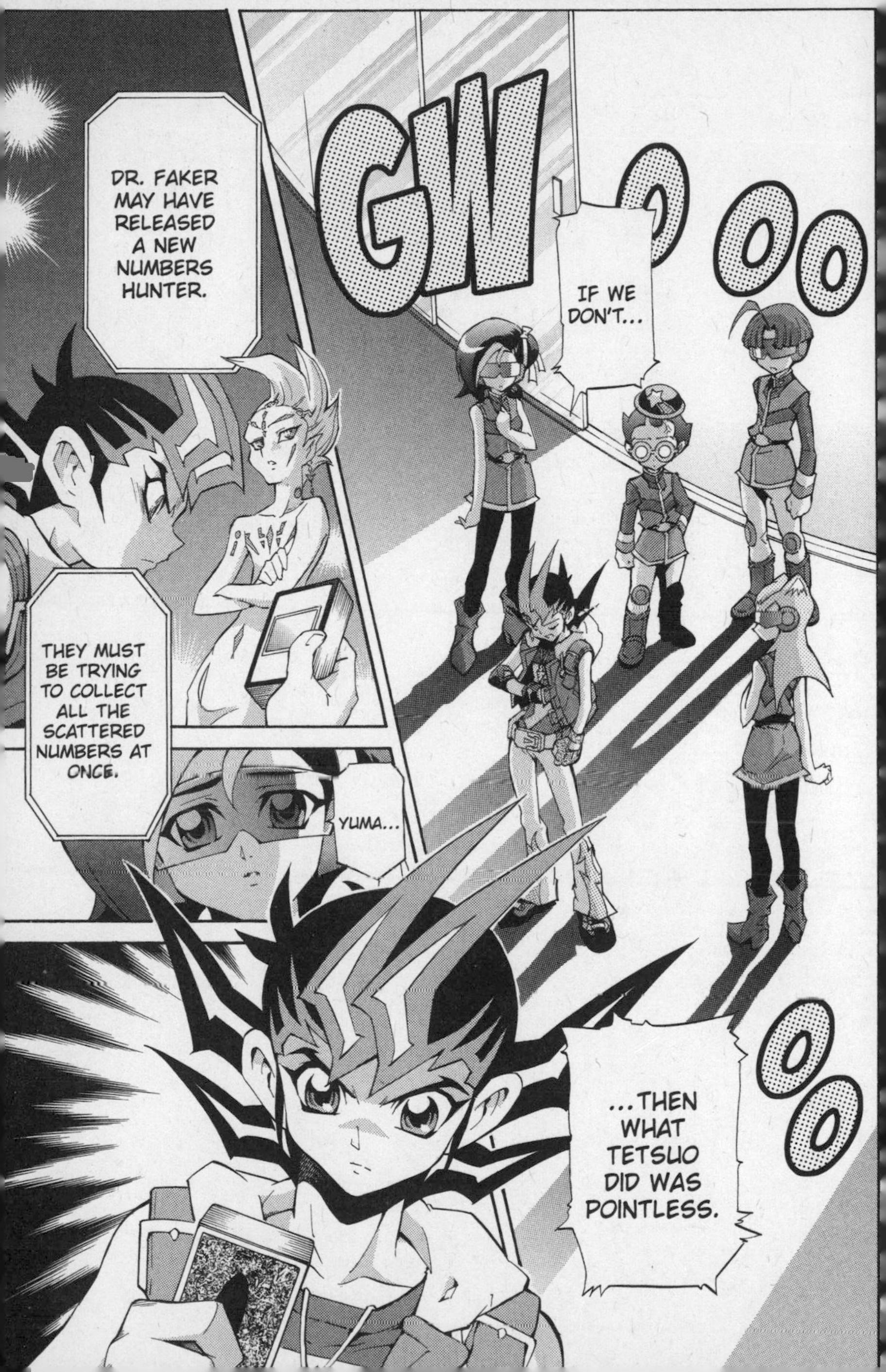
GWOOOOO
IF WE DON'T...
DR. FAKER MAY HAVE RELEASED A NEW NUMBERS HUNTER.
THEY MUST BE TRYING TO COLLECT ALL THE SCATTERED NUMBERS AT ONCE.
YUMA...
...THEN WHAT TETSUO DID WAS POINTLESS.

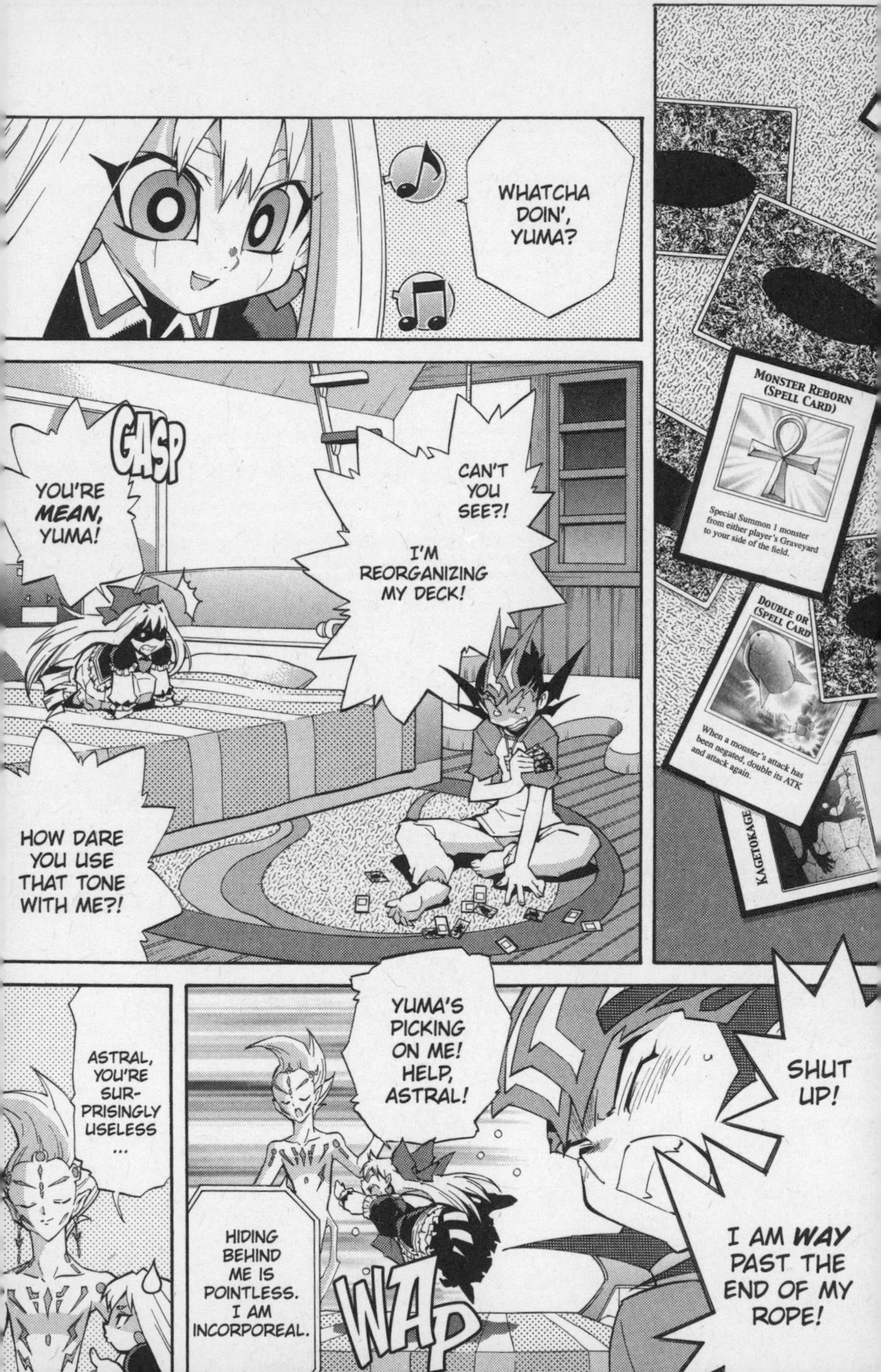
MONSTER REBORN (SPELL CARD)
Special Summon 1 monster from either player's Graveyard to your side of the field.
DOUBLE OR (SPELL CARD
When a monster's attack has been negated, double its ATK and attack again.
KAGETOKAGE
WHATCHA DOIN', YUMA?
CAN'T YOU SEE?!
I'M REORGANIZING MY DECK!
GASP
YOU'RE *MEAN,* YUMA!
HOW DARE YOU USE THAT TONE WITH ME?!
SHUT UP!
I AM *WAY* PAST THE END OF MY ROPE!
YUMA'S PICKING ON ME! HELP, ASTRAL!
HIDING BEHIND ME IS POINTLESS. I AM INCORPOREAL.
WAP
ASTRAL, YOU'RE SUR-PRISINGLY USELESS ...

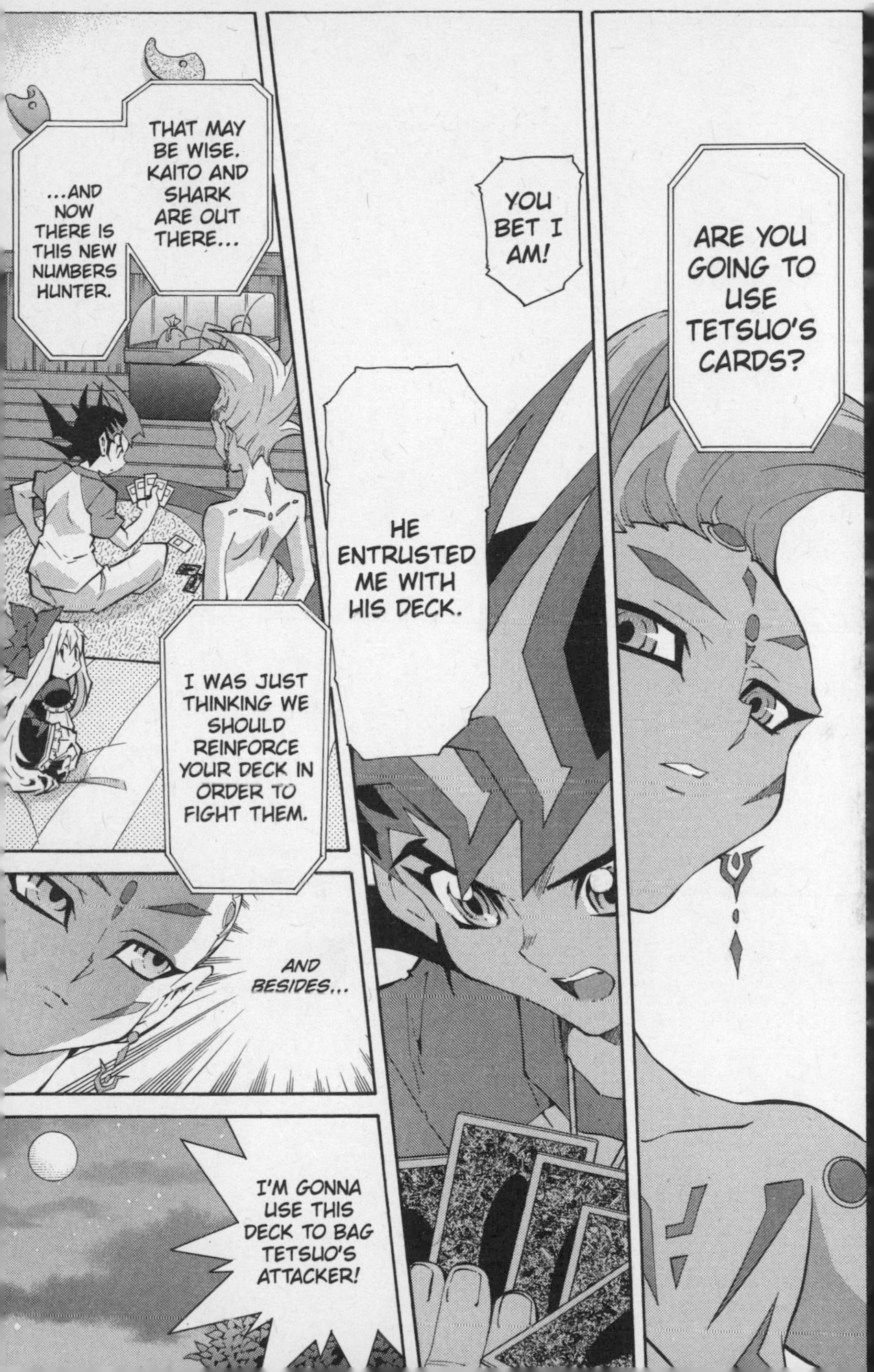
ARE YOU GOING TO USE TETSUO'S CARDS?
YOU BET I AM!
HE ENTRUSTED ME WITH HIS DECK.
THAT MAY BE WISE. KAITO AND SHARK ARE OUT THERE...
...AND NOW THERE IS THIS NEW NUMBERS HUNTER.
I WAS JUST THINKING WE SHOULD REINFORCE YOUR DECK IN ORDER TO FIGHT THEM.
AND BESIDES...
I'M GONNA USE THIS DECK TO BAG TETSUO'S ATTACKER!

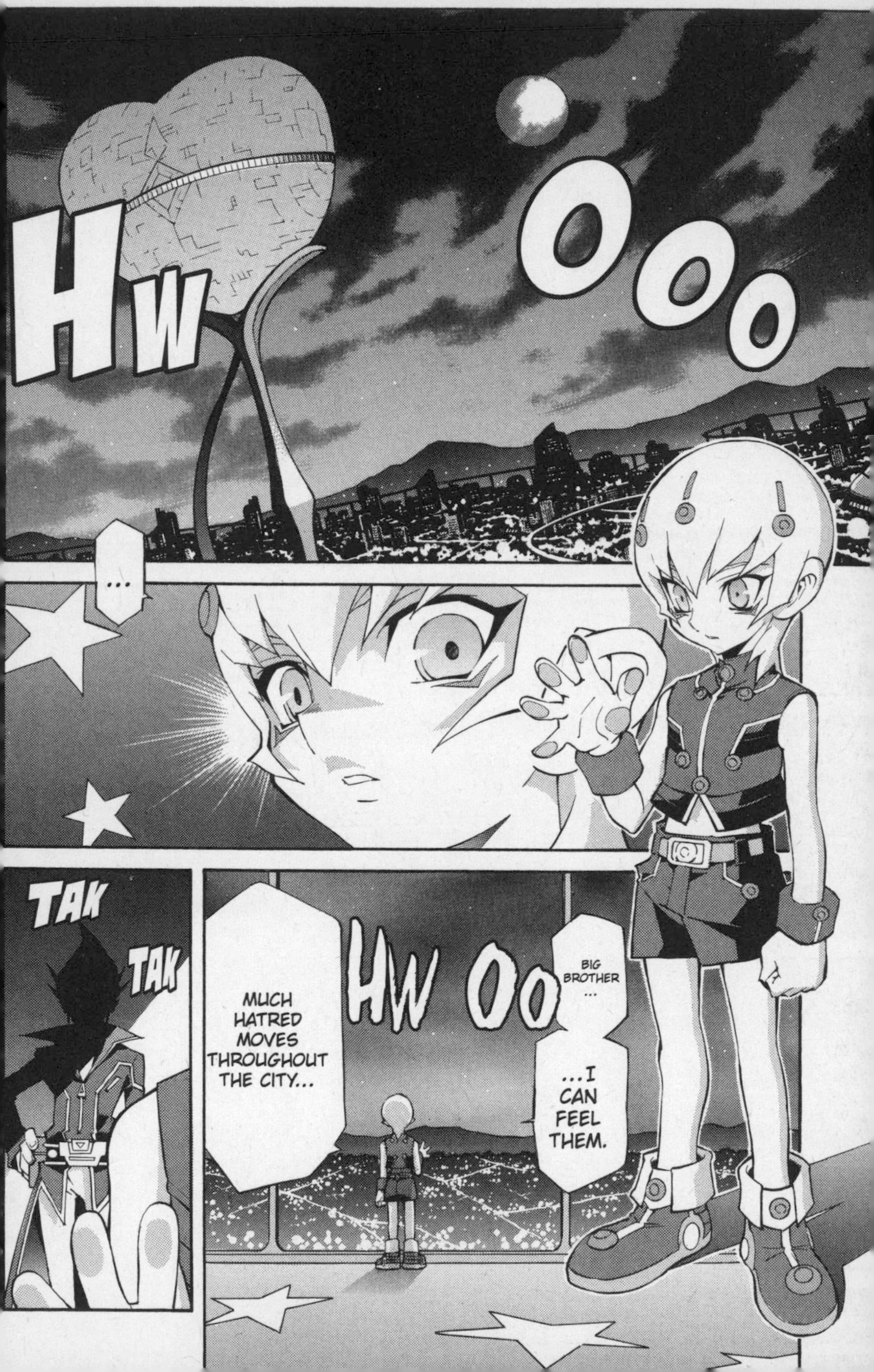
HWOOO
...
BIG BROTHER ...
HW OO
MUCH HATRED MOVES THROUGHOUT THE CITY...
...I CAN FEEL THEM.
TAK
TAK

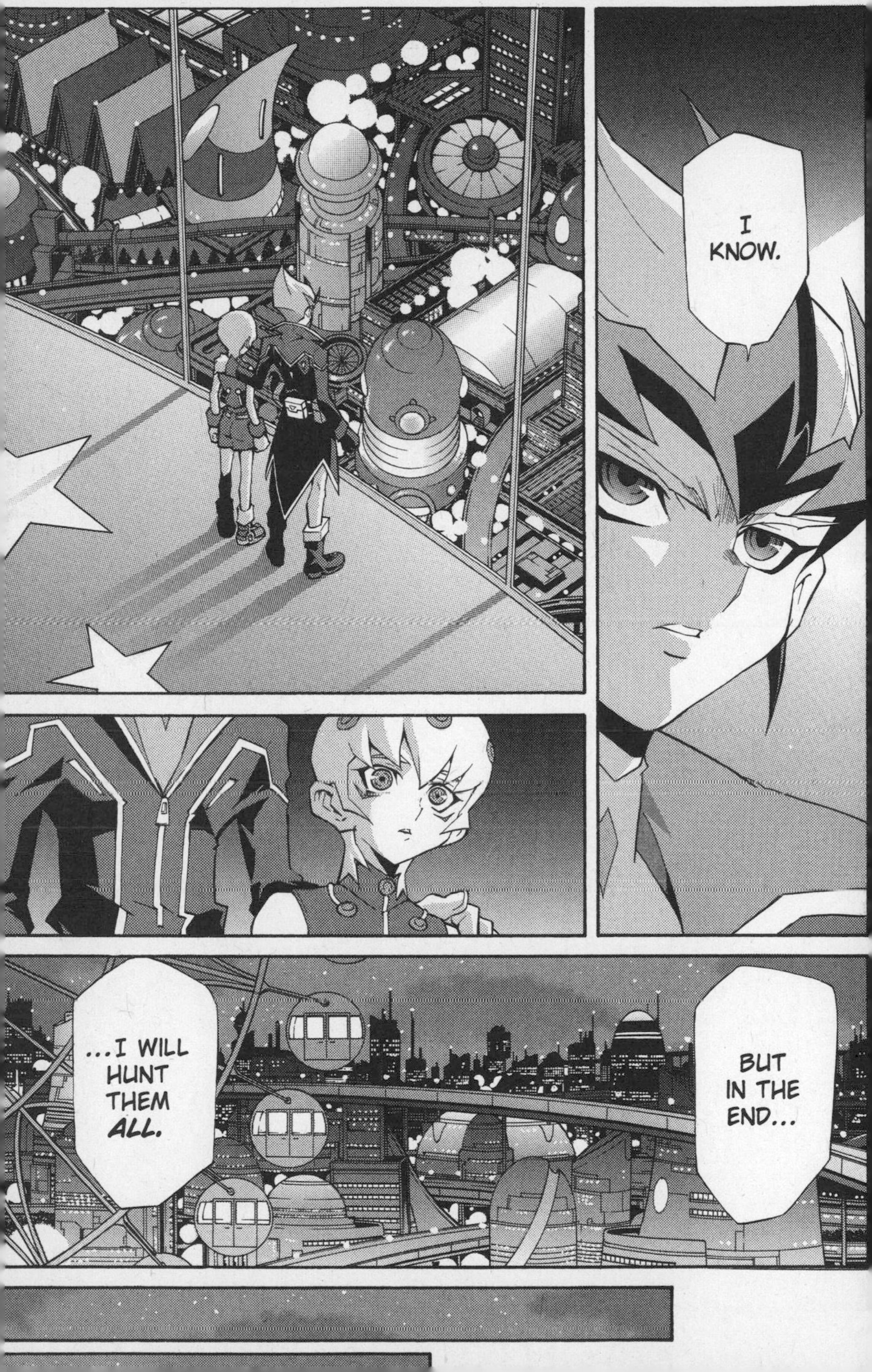
I KNOW.
BUT IN THE END...
...I WILL HUNT THEM ALL.

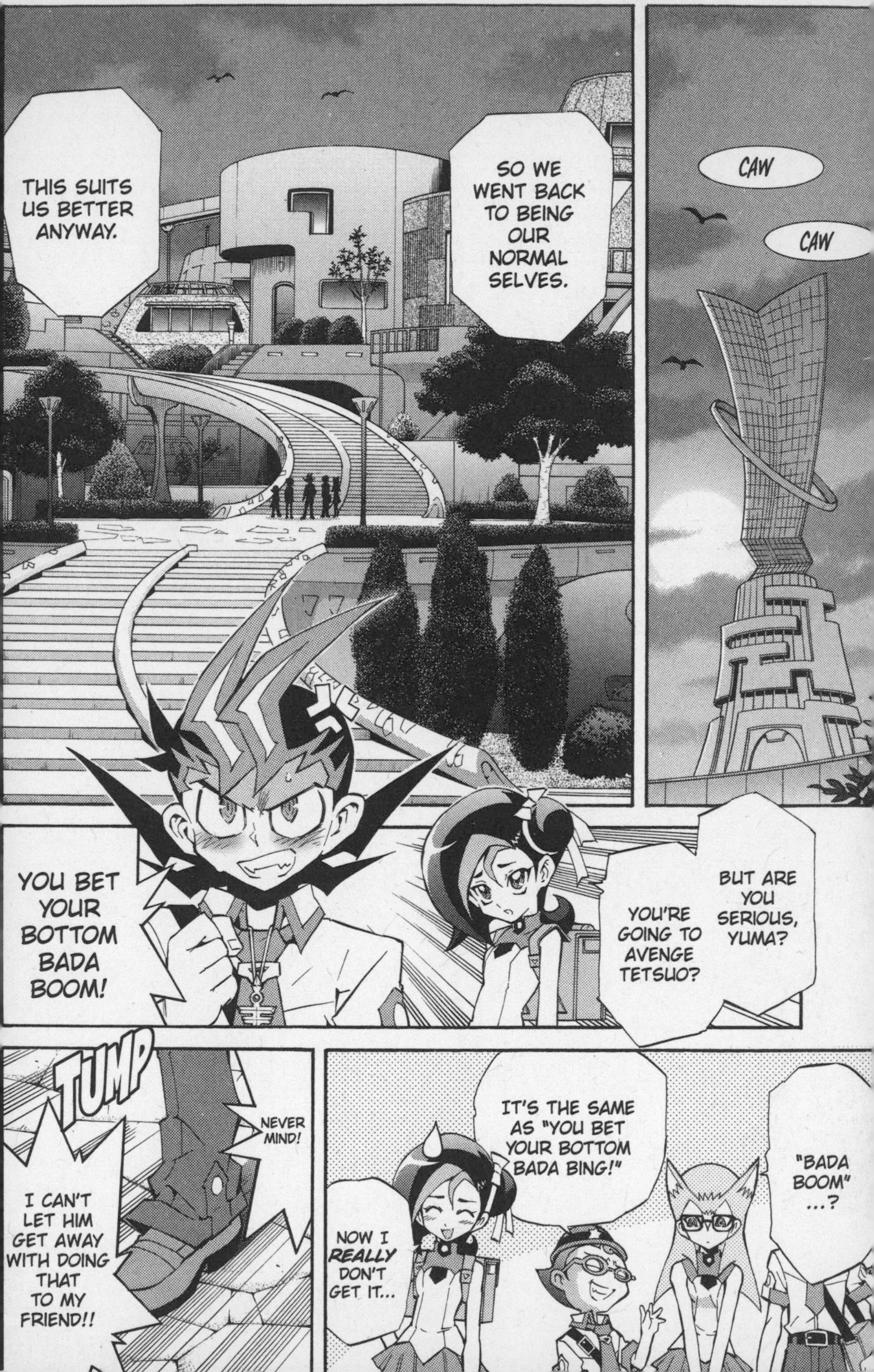
CAW
CAW
SO WE WENT BACK TO BEING OUR NORMAL SELVES.
THIS SUITS US BETTER ANYWAY.
BUT ARE YOU SERIOUS, YUMA?
YOU'RE GOING TO AVENGE TETSUO?
YOU BET YOUR BOTTOM BADA BOOM!
"BADA BOOM" ...?
IT'S THE SAME AS "YOU BET YOUR BOTTOM BADA BING!"
NOW I *REALLY* DON'T GET IT...
TUMP
NEVER MIND!
I CAN'T LET HIM GET AWAY WITH DOING THAT TO MY FRIEND!!

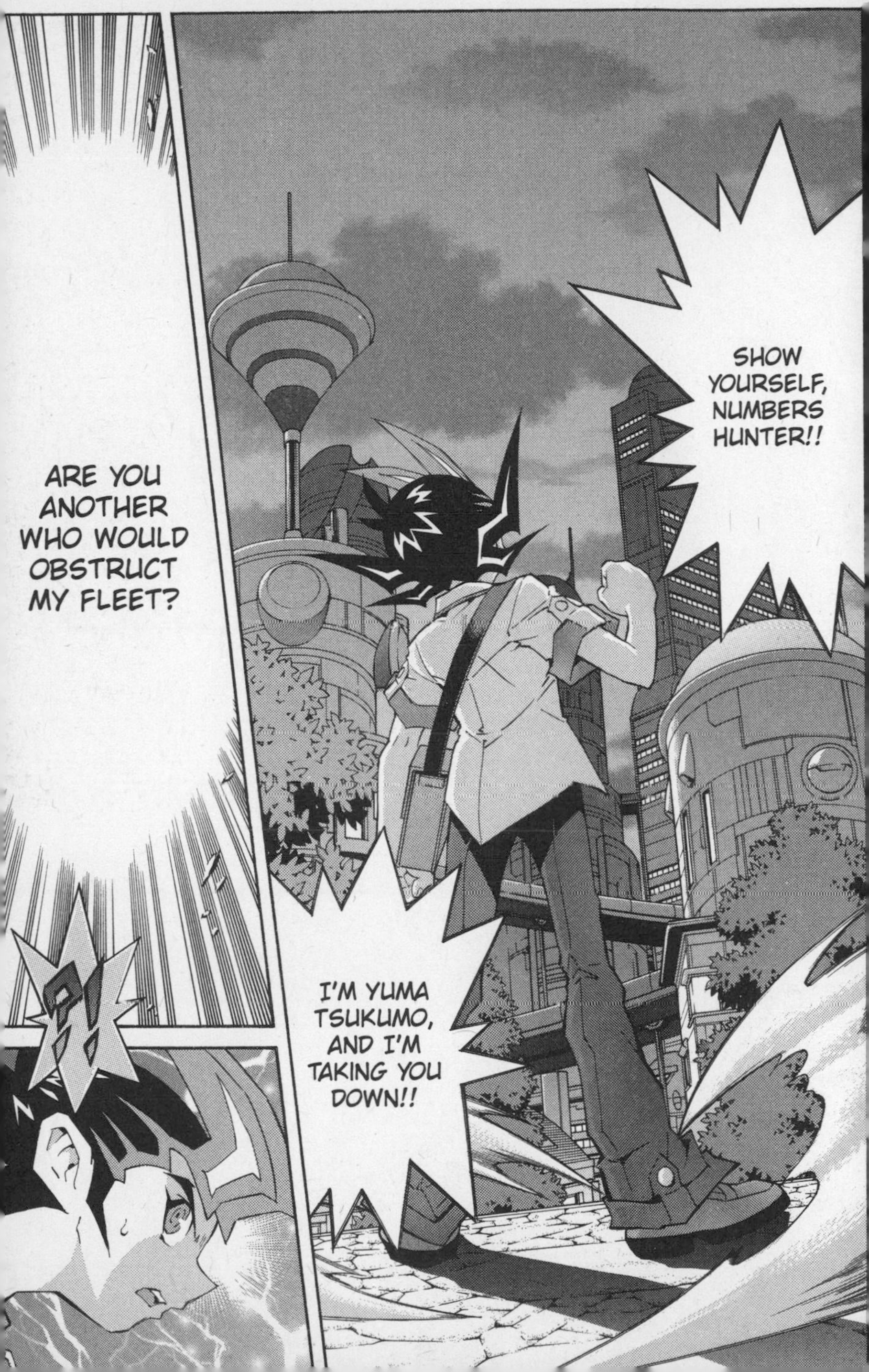
SHOW YOURSELF, NUMBERS HUNTER!!
I'M YUMA TSUKUMO, AND I'M TAKING YOU DOWN!!
ARE YOU ANOTHER WHO WOULD OBSTRUCT MY FLEET?
?!

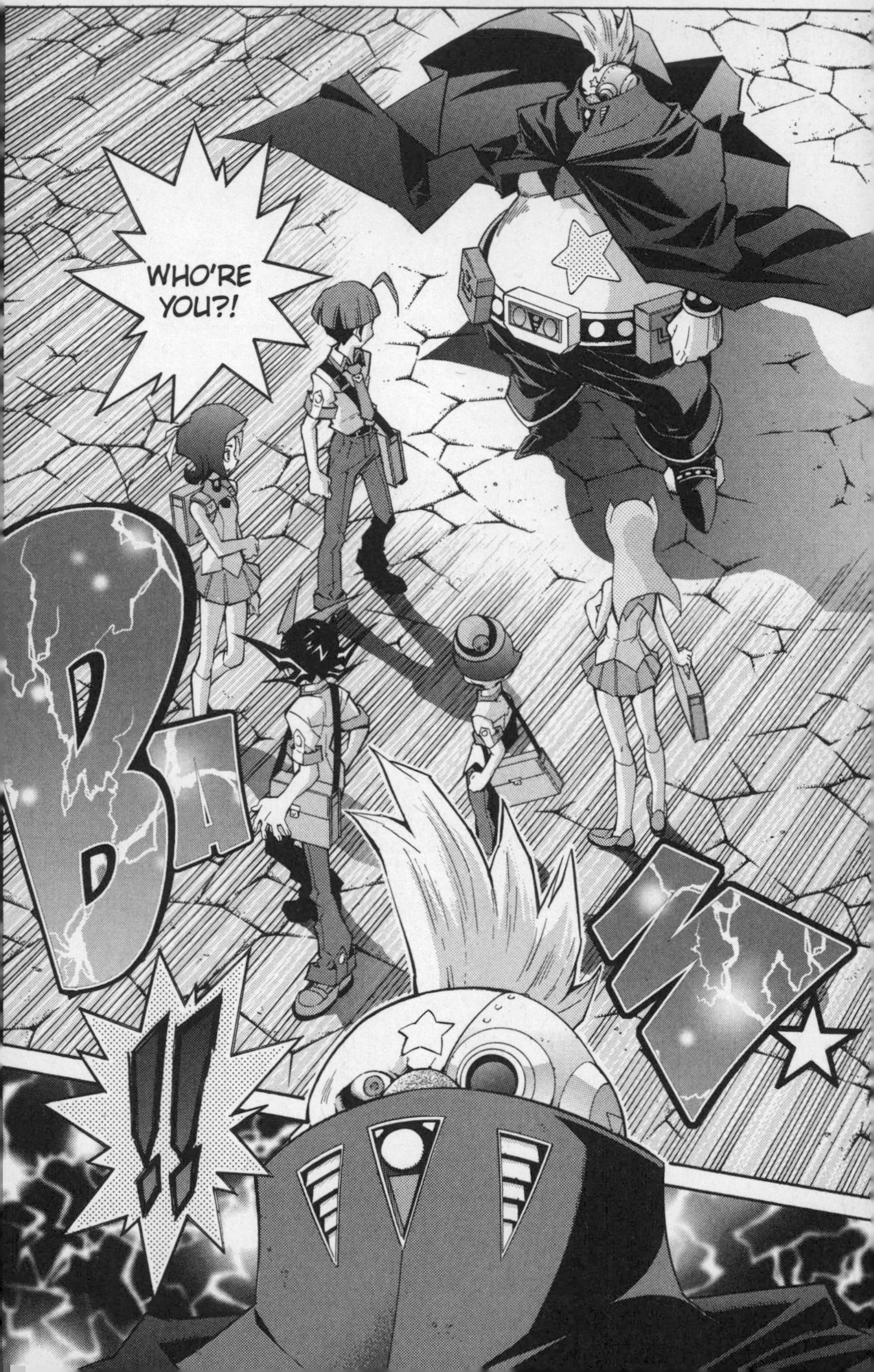
WHO'RE YOU?!
!!
BAM

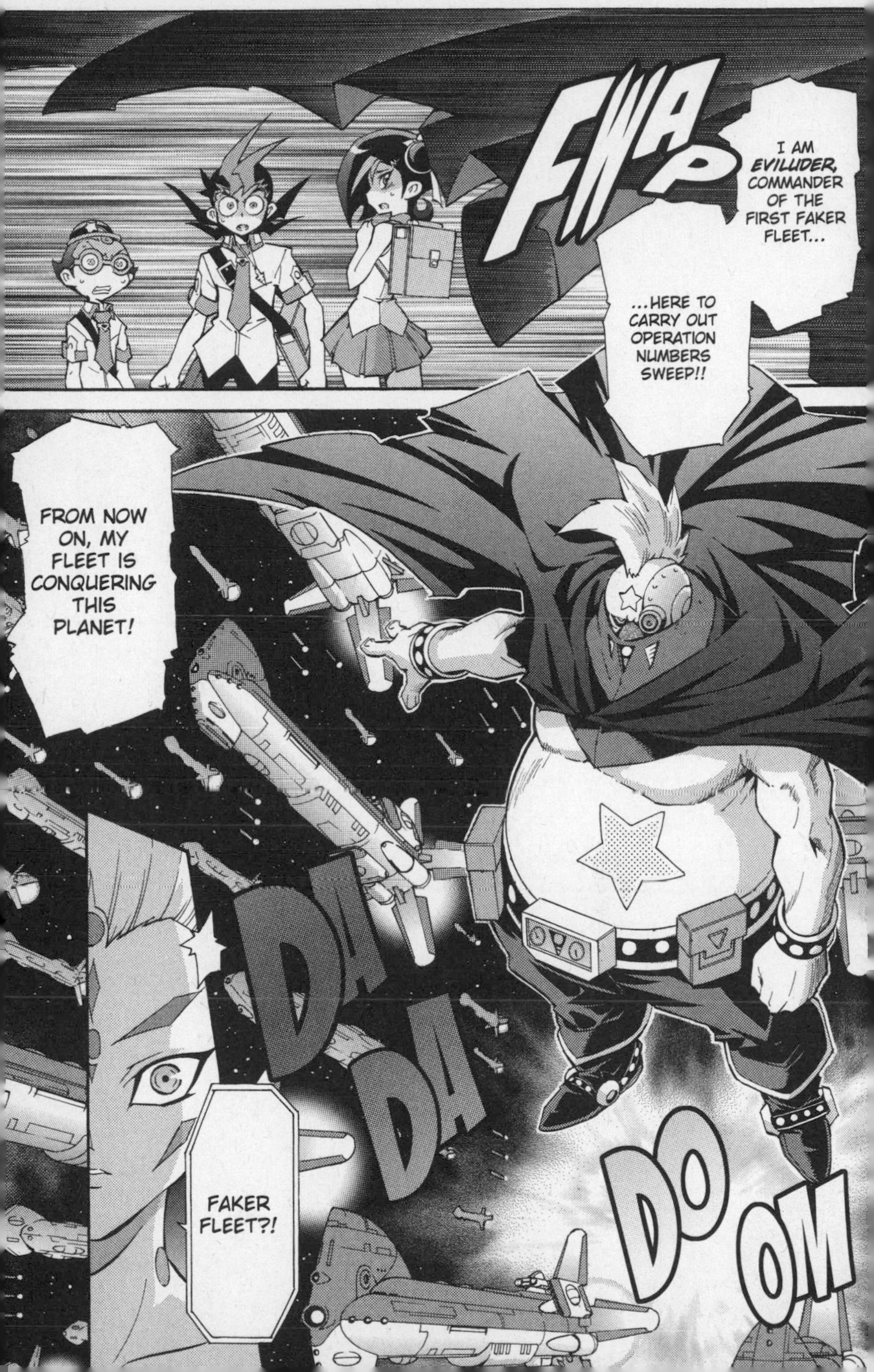
FWAP
I AM *EVILUDER,* COMMANDER OF THE FIRST FAKER FLEET...
...HERE TO CARRY OUT OPERATION NUMBERS SWEEP!!
FROM NOW ON, MY FLEET IS CONQUERING THIS PLANET!
DOOM
DA DA
FAKER FLEET?!

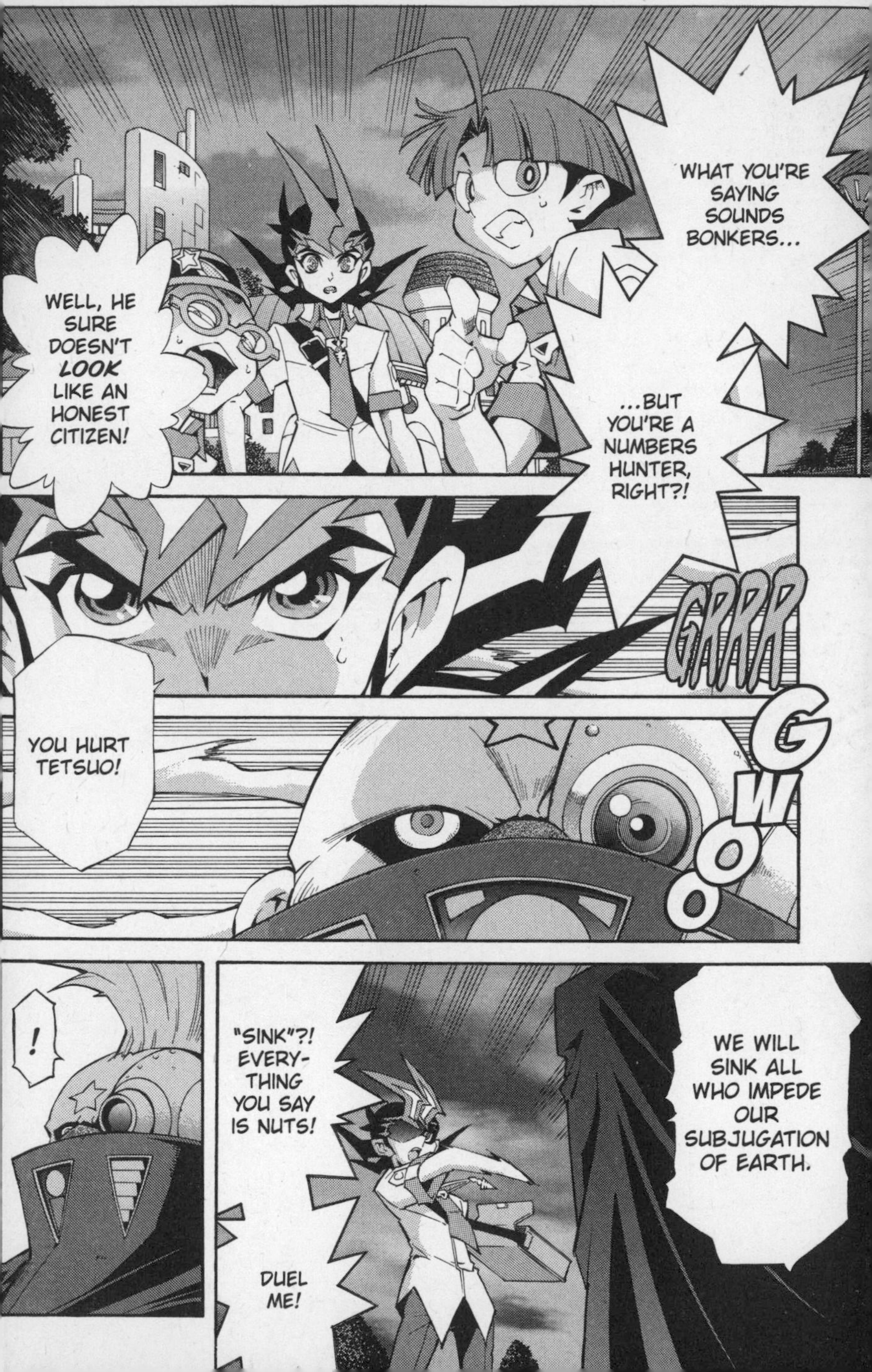
WHAT YOU'RE SAYING SOUNDS BONKERS...
...BUT YOU'RE A NUMBERS HUNTER, RIGHT?!
WELL, HE SURE DOESN'T *LOOK* LIKE AN HONEST CITIZEN!
GRRR
GWOOO
YOU HURT TETSUO!
WE WILL SINK ALL WHO IMPEDE OUR SUBJUGATION OF EARTH.
"SINK"?! EVERY-THING YOU SAY IS NUTS!
DUEL ME!
!

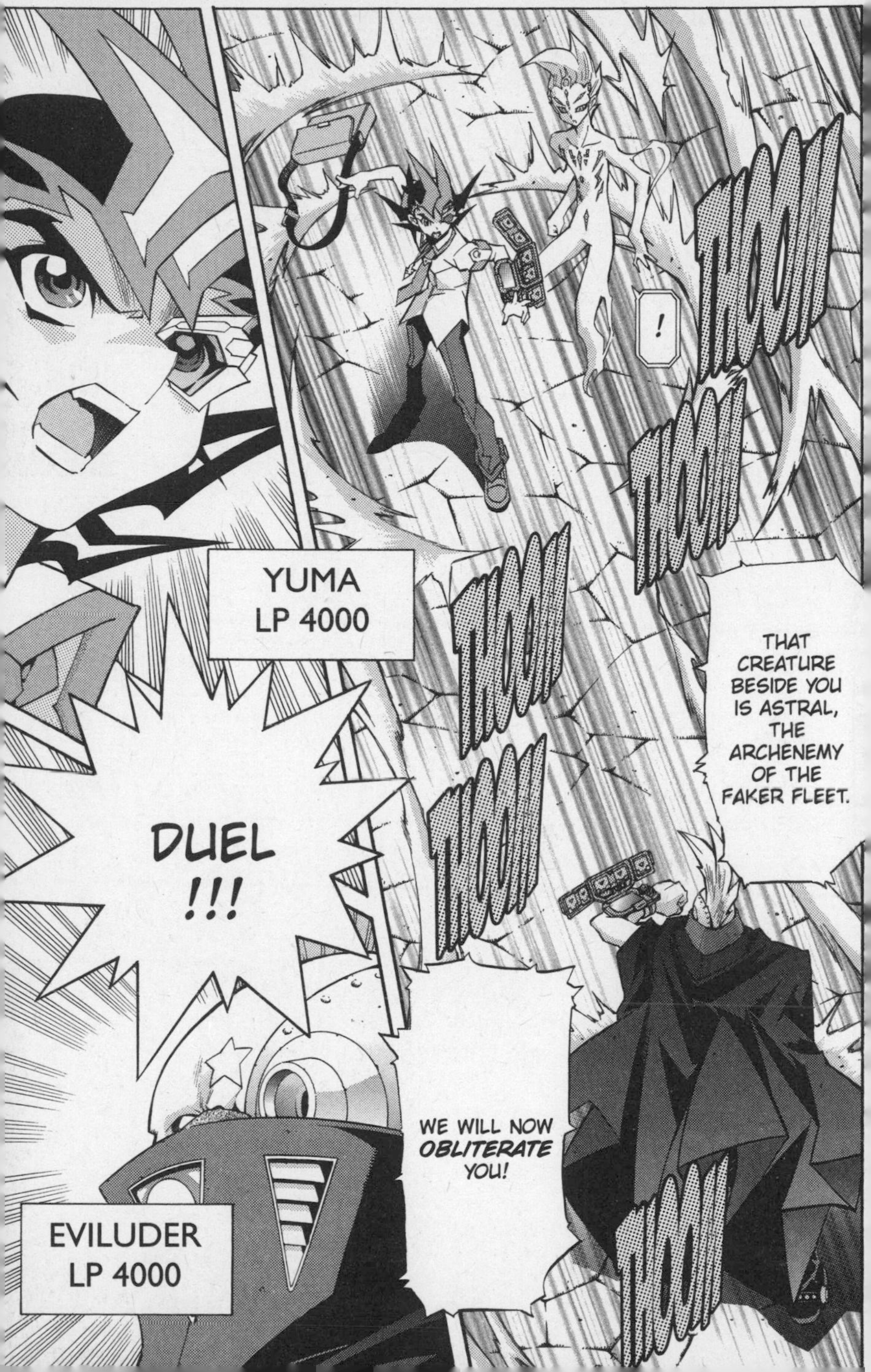
!
THOOM
THOOM
THOOM
THOOM
THAT CREATURE BESIDE YOU IS ASTRAL, THE ARCHENEMY OF THE FAKER FLEET.
WE WILL NOW *OBLITERATE* YOU!
THOOM
YUMA LP 4000
DUEL !!!
EVILUDER LP 4000

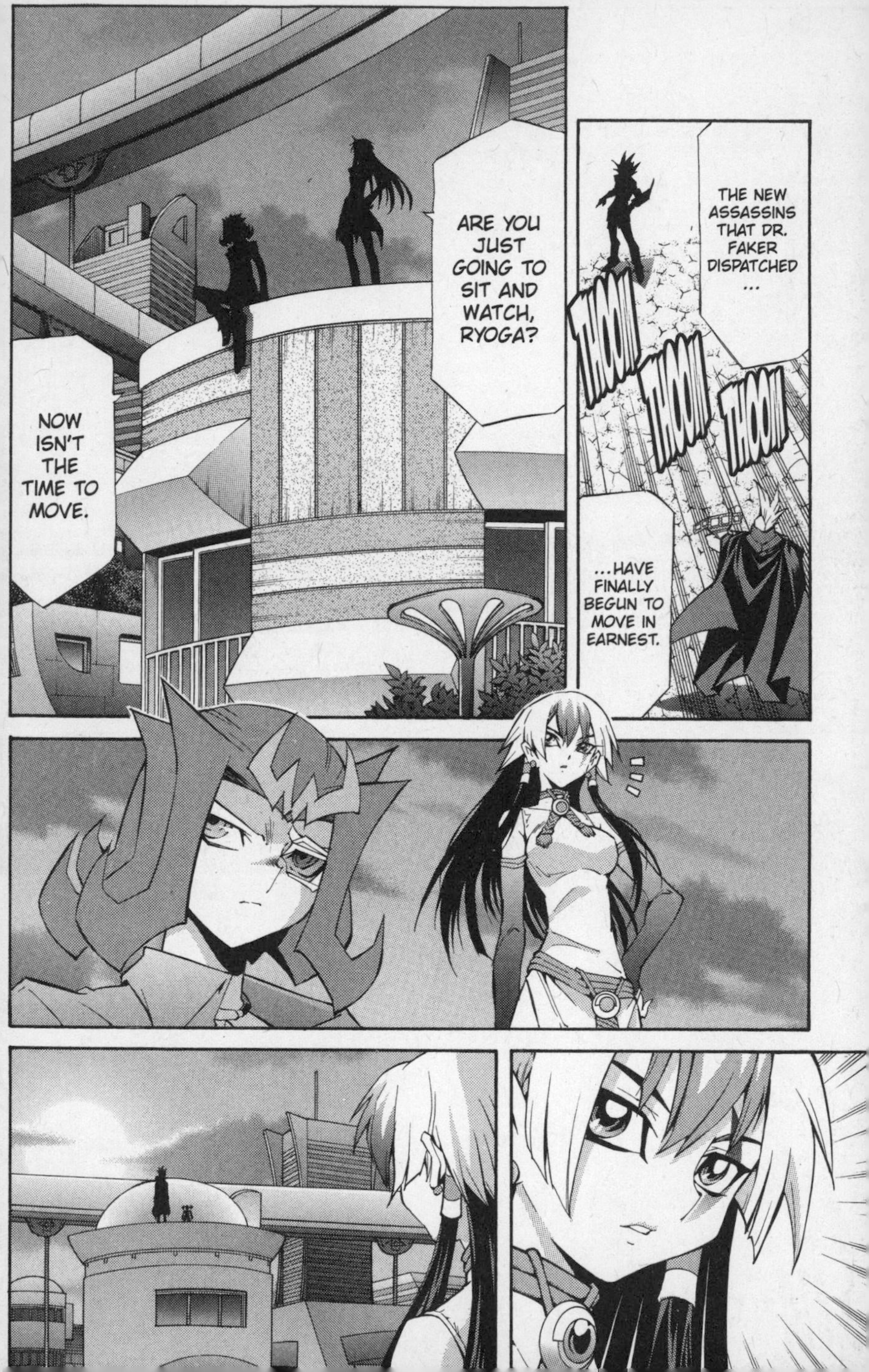
THE NEW ASSASSINS THAT DR. FAKER DISPATCHED ...
THOOM THOOM THOOM
...HAVE FINALLY BEGUN TO MOVE IN EARNEST.
ARE YOU JUST GOING TO SIT AND WATCH, RYOGA?
NOW ISN'T THE TIME TO MOVE.

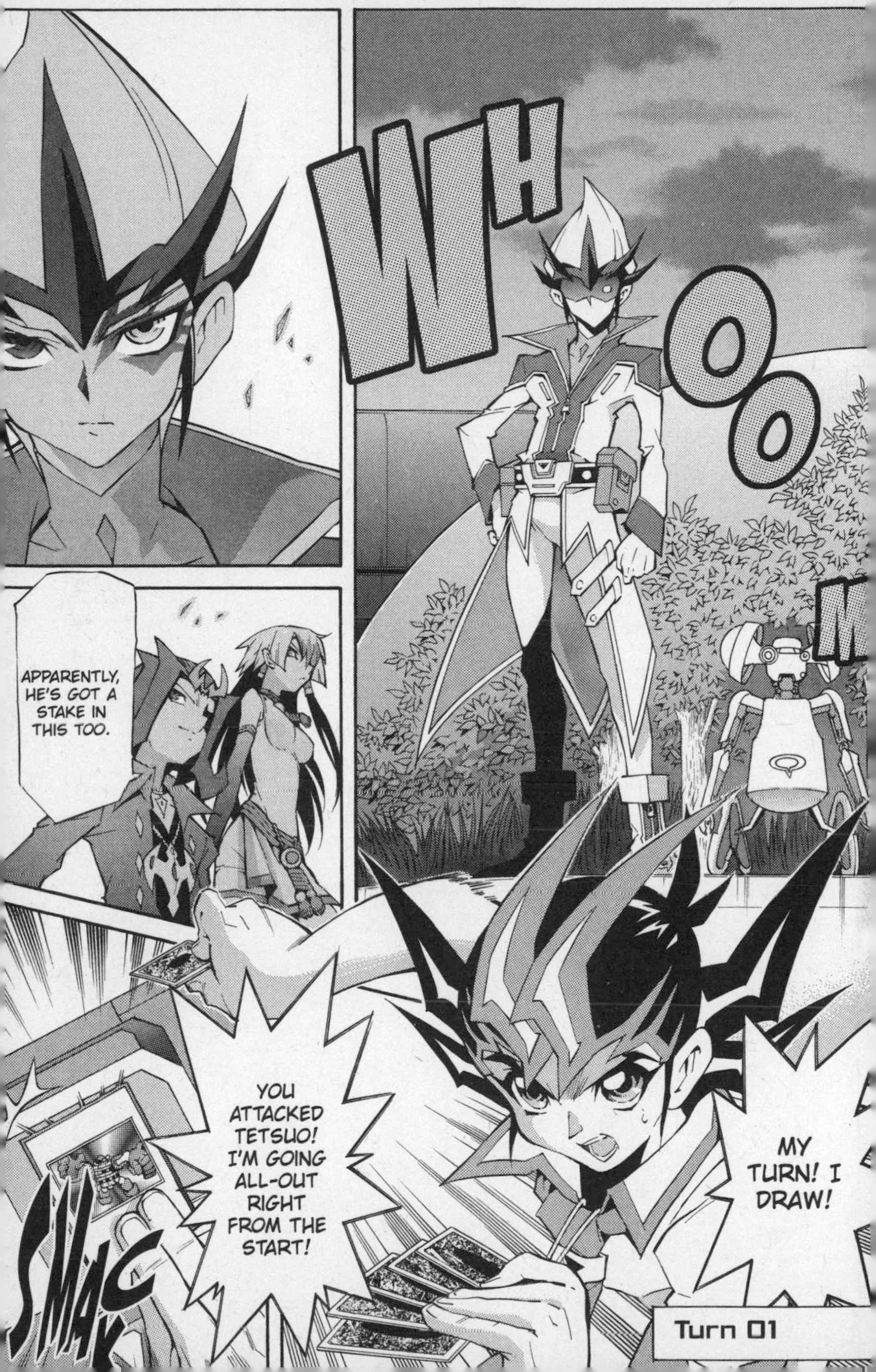
WHOOOM
APPARENTLY, HE'S GOT A STAKE IN THIS TOO.
MY TURN! I DRAW!
YOU ATTACKED TETSUO! I'M GOING ALL-OUT RIGHT FROM THE START!
SMAC

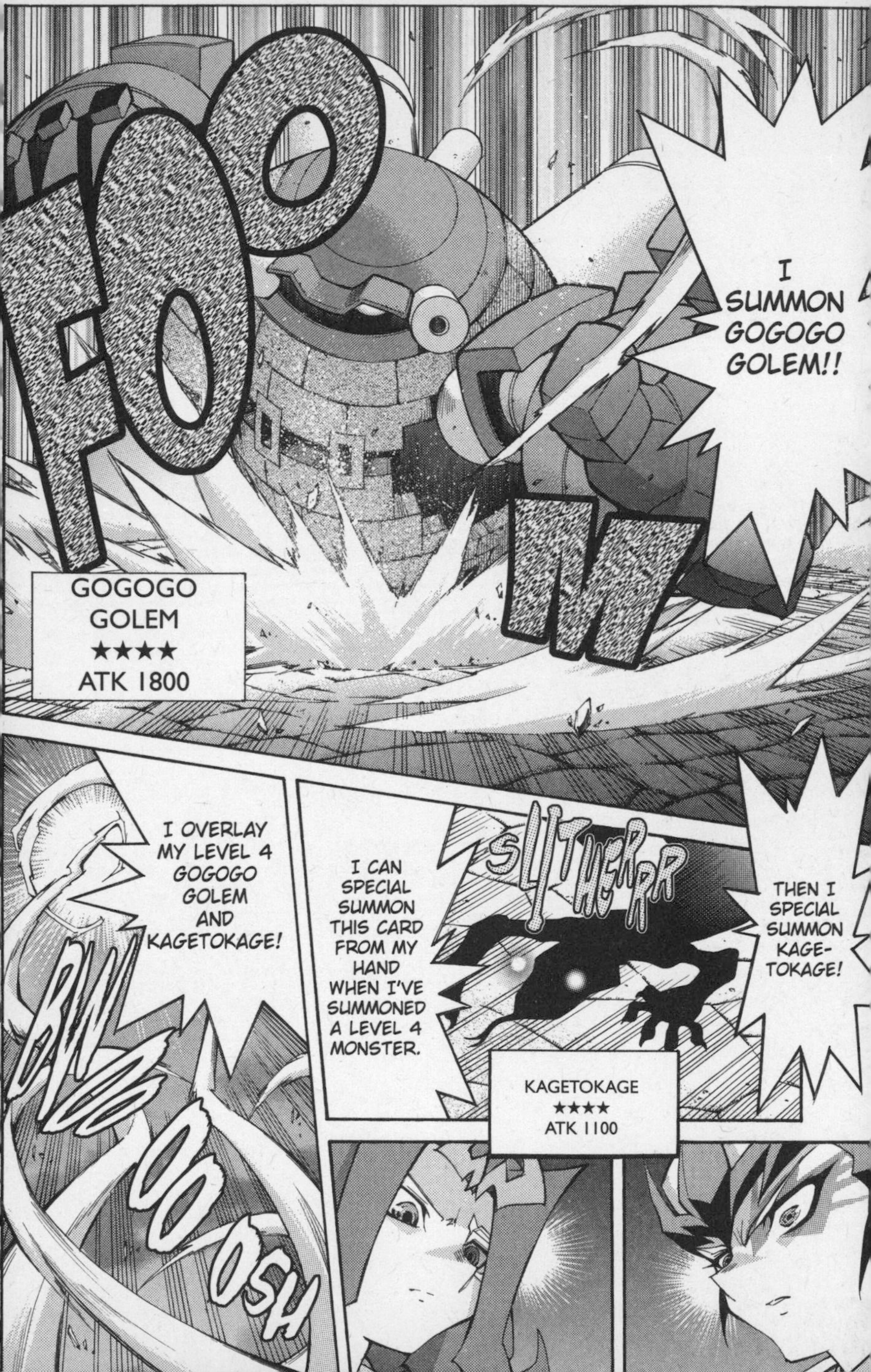
I SUMMON GOGOGO GOLEM!!
FOOM
GOGOGO GOLEM ★★★★ ATK 1800
THEN I SPECIAL SUMMON KAGE-TOKAGE!
SLITHERRR
I CAN SPECIAL SUMMON THIS CARD FROM MY HAND WHEN I'VE SUMMONED A LEVEL 4 MONSTER.
KAGETOKAGE ★★★★ ATK 1100
I OVERLAY MY LEVEL 4 GOGOGO GOLEM AND KAGETOKAGE!
BWOOOOOSH

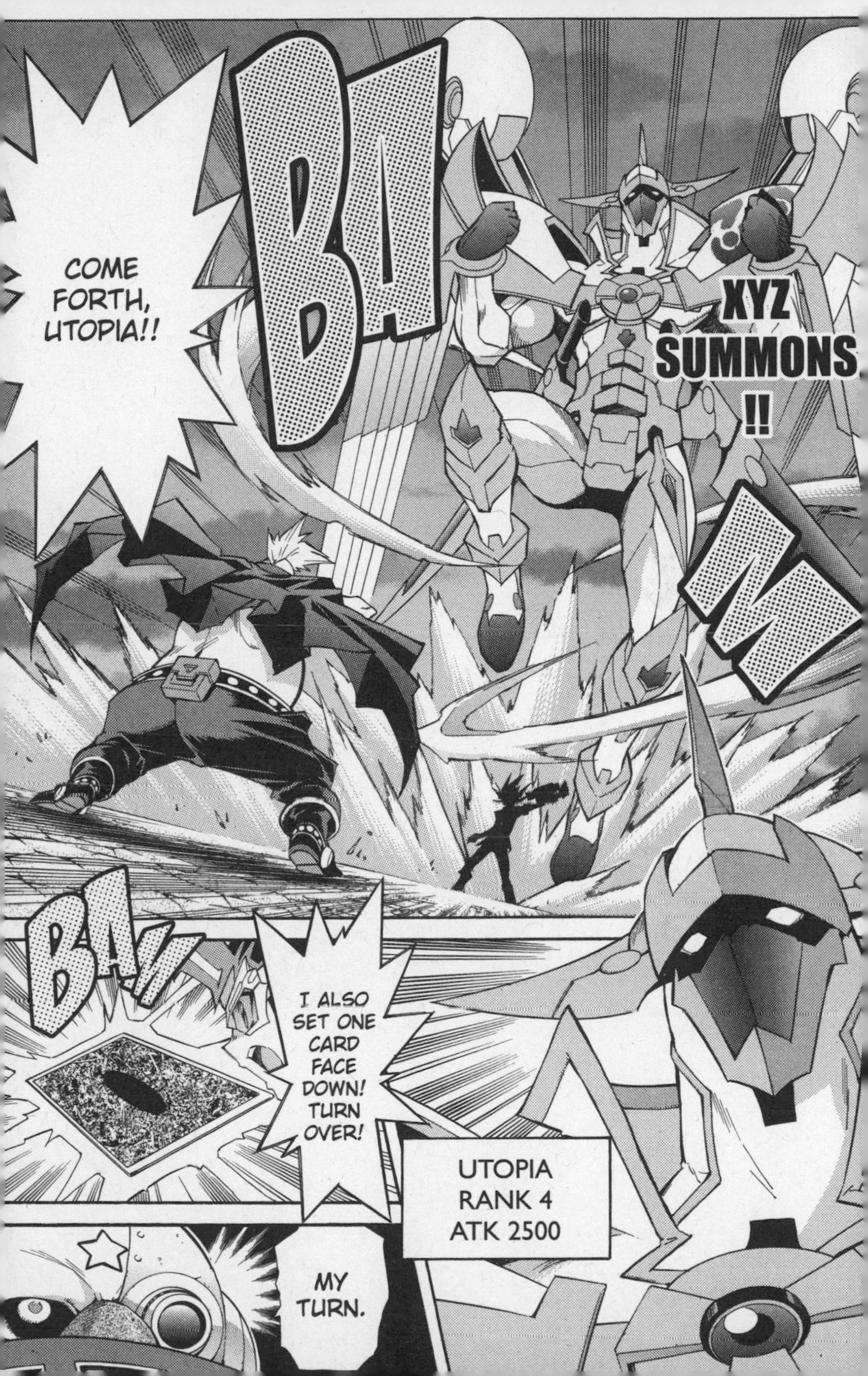
XYZ SUMMONS!!
BA
COME FORTH, UTOPIA!!
M
UTOPIA RANK 4 ATK 2500
I ALSO SET ONE CARD FACE DOWN! TURN OVER!
BA!!
MY TURN.

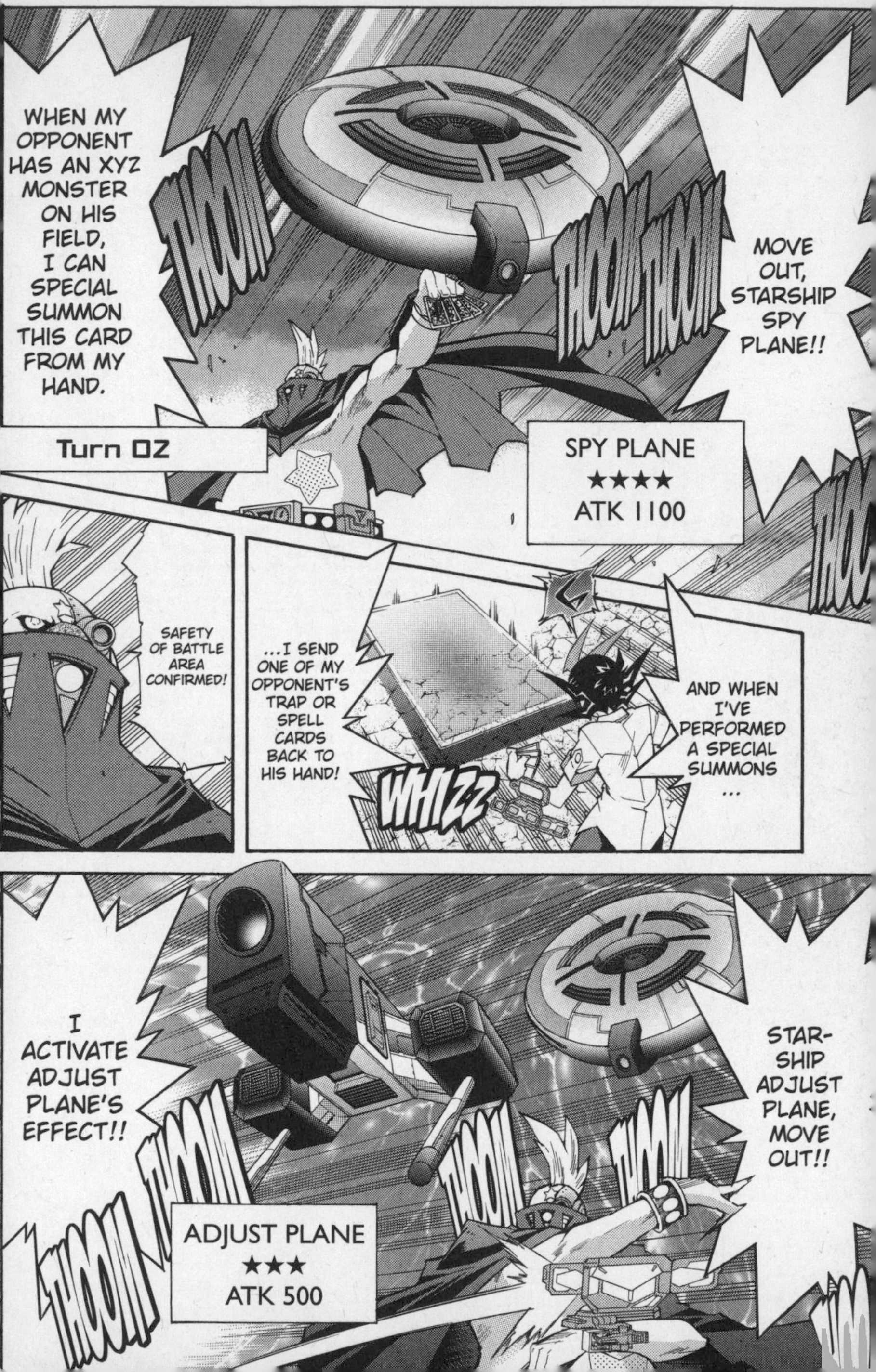
WHEN MY OPPONENT HAS AN XYZ MONSTER ON HIS FIELD, I CAN SPECIAL SUMMON THIS CARD FROM MY HAND.
THOOM THOOM
THOOM
MOVE OUT, STARSHIP SPY PLANE!!
SPY PLANE ★★★★ ATK 1100
Turn 02
AND WHEN I'VE PERFORMED A SPECIAL SUMMONS ...
...I SEND ONE OF MY OPPONENT'S TRAP OR SPELL CARDS BACK TO HIS HAND!
WHIZZ
SAFETY OF BATTLE AREA CONFIRMED!
STAR-SHIP ADJUST PLANE, MOVE OUT!!
I ACTIVATE ADJUST PLANE'S EFFECT!!
THOOM THOOM
THOOM THOOM
ADJUST PLANE ★★★ ATK 500

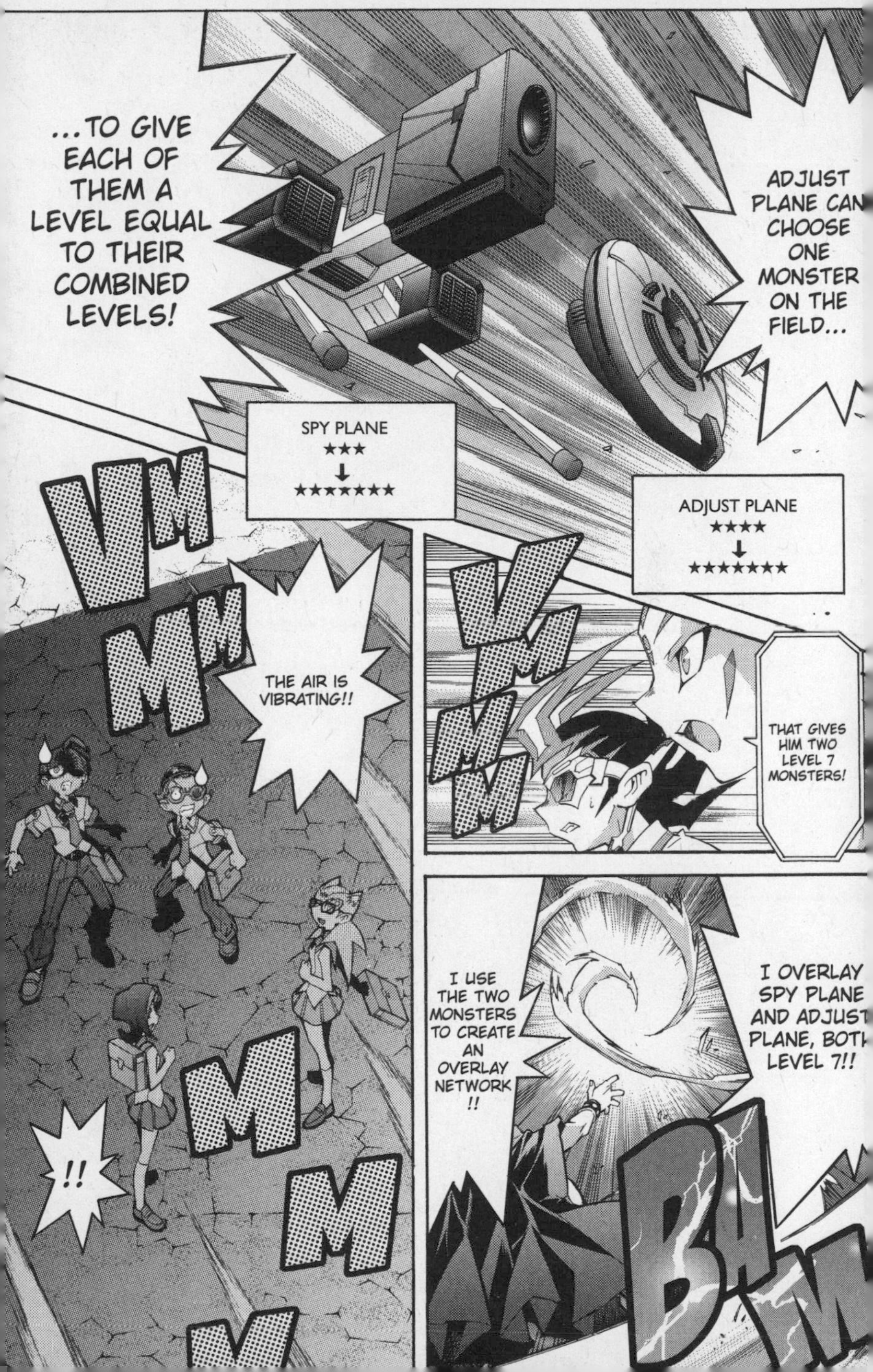
ADJUST PLANE CA CHOOSE ONE MONSTER ON THE FIELD...
...TO GIVE EACH OF THEM A LEVEL EQUAL TO THEIR COMBINED LEVELS!
SPY PLANE ★★★ ↓ ★★★★★★★
ADJUST PLANE ★★★★ ↓ ★★★★★★★
VMMM
THAT GIVES HIM TWO LEVEL 7 MONSTERS!
I OVERLAY SPY PLANE AND ADJUS PLANE, BOT LEVEL 7!!
I USE THE TWO MONSTERS TO CREATE AN OVERLAY NETWORK !!
BA
VMMM
THE AIR IS VIBRATING!!
MMM
!!

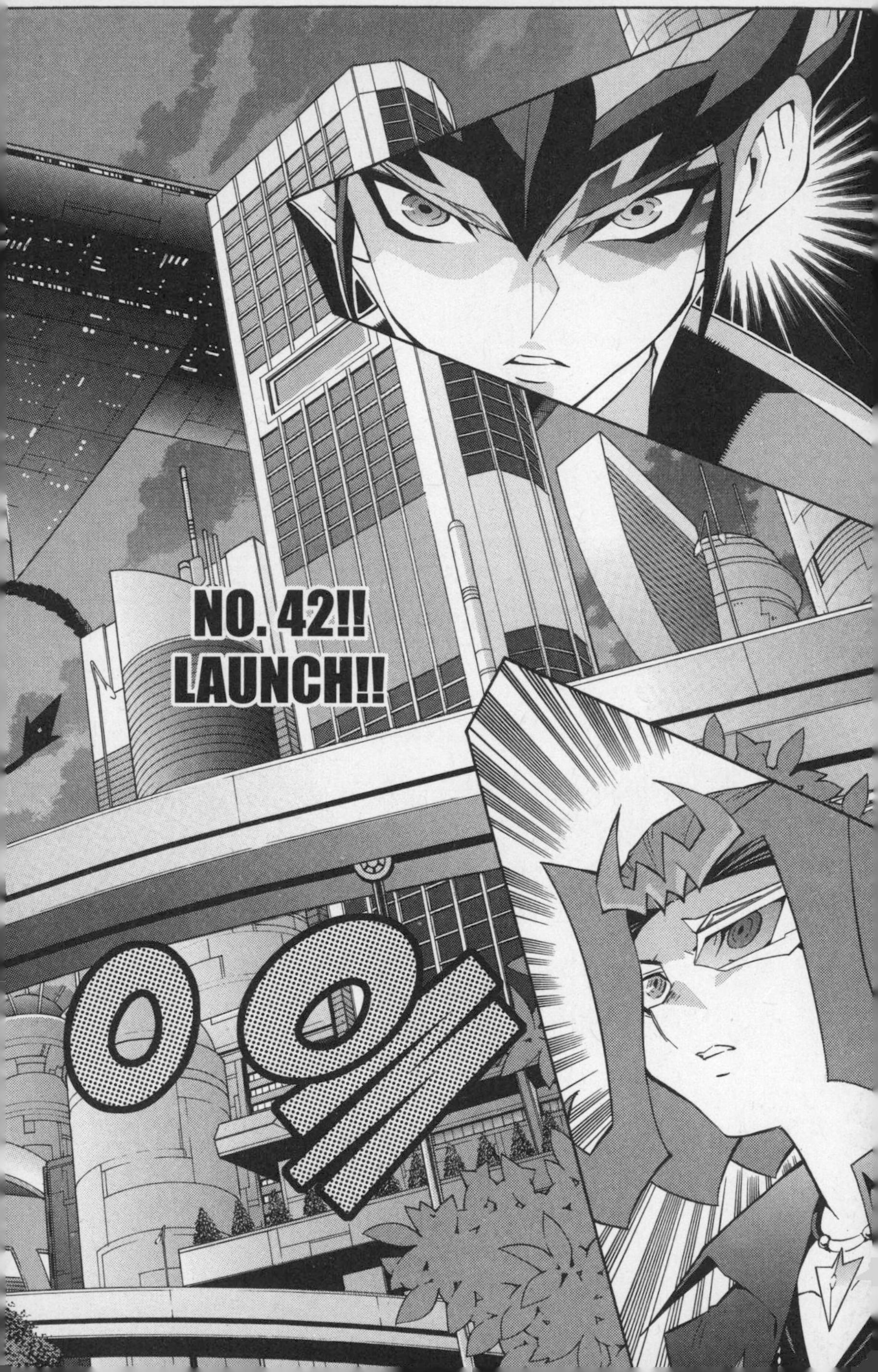
NO. 42!!
LAUNCH!!

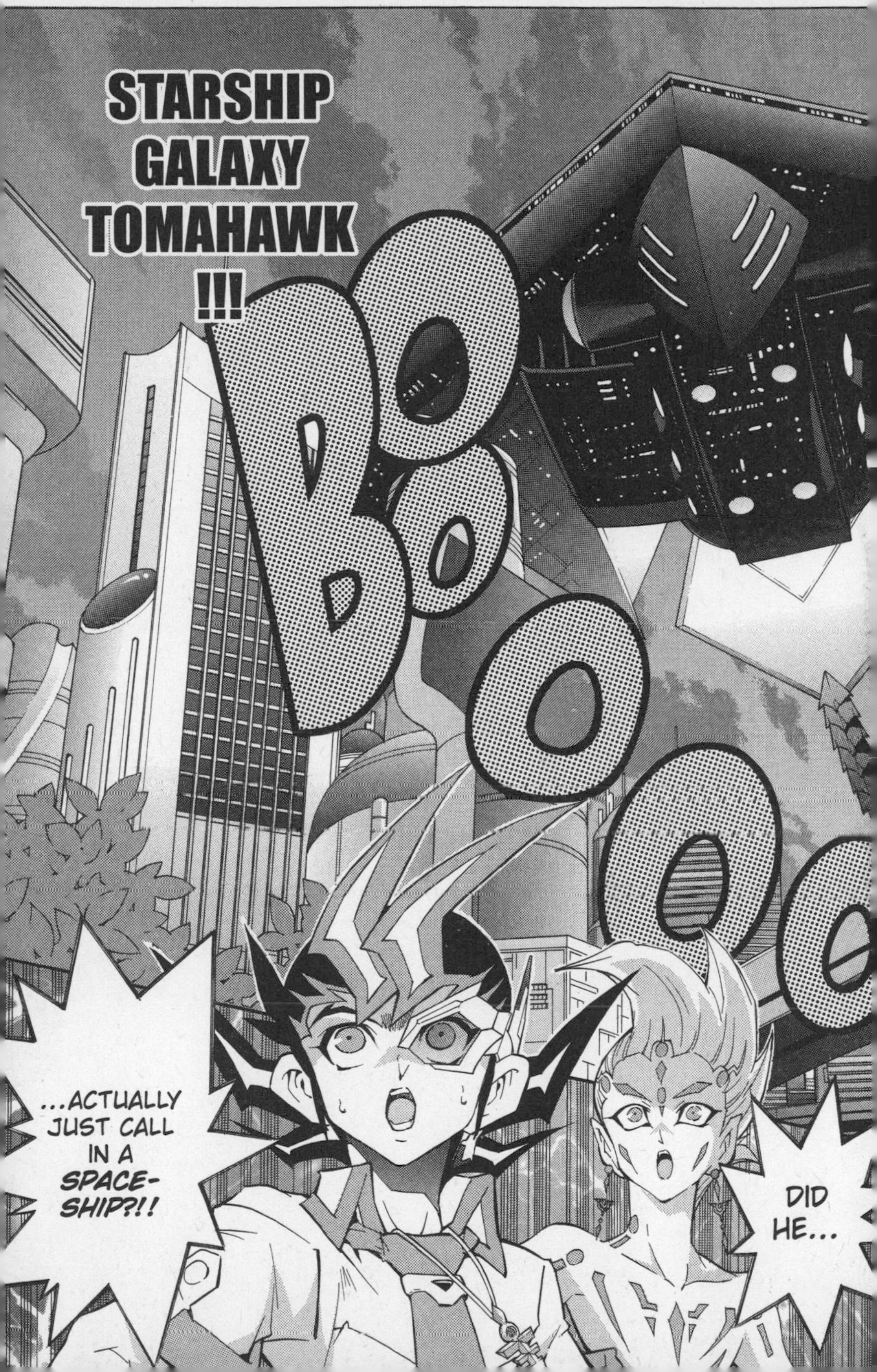
STARSHIP GALAXY TOMAHAWK!!!
DID HE...
...ACTUALLY JUST CALL IN A SPACE-SHIP?!!

YU-GI-OH!
ZEXAL

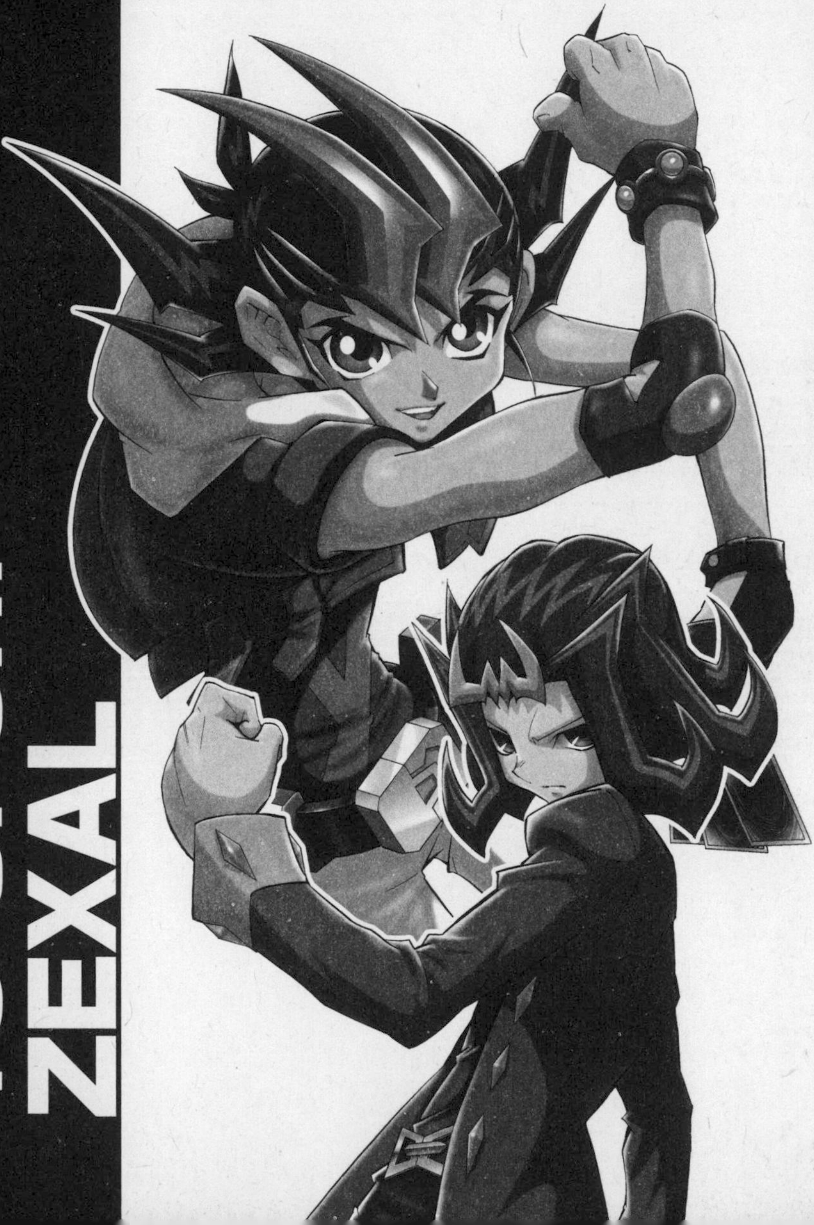

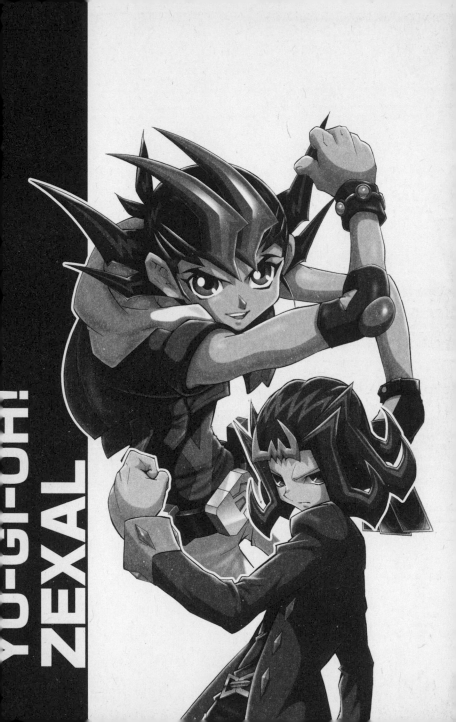

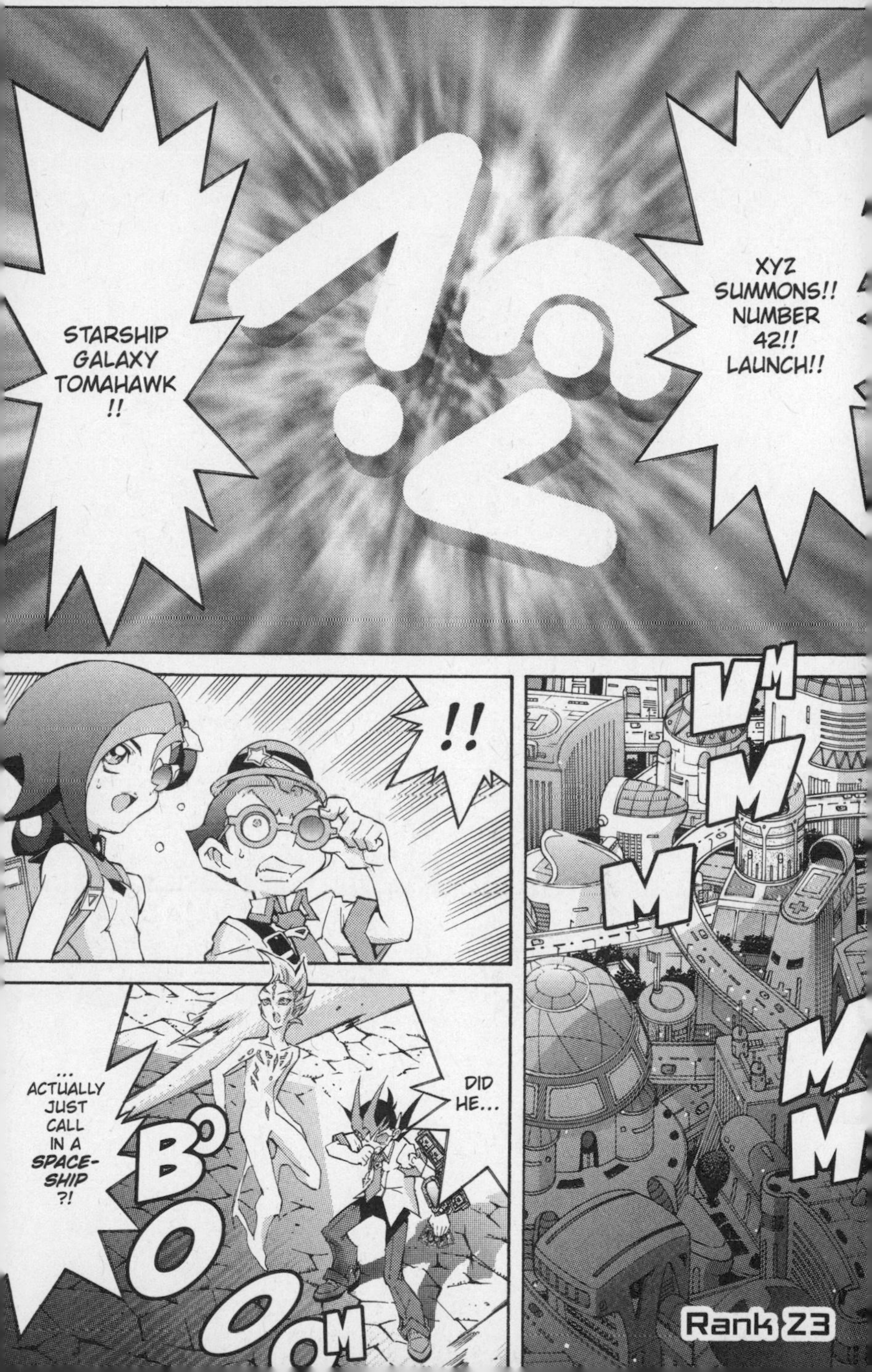
XYZ SUMMONS!! NUMBER 42!! LAUNCH!!
STARSHIP GALAXY TOMAHAWK!!
VMMMMMM
!!
DID HE...
...ACTUALLY JUST CALL IN A SPACESHIP?!
BOOOOM

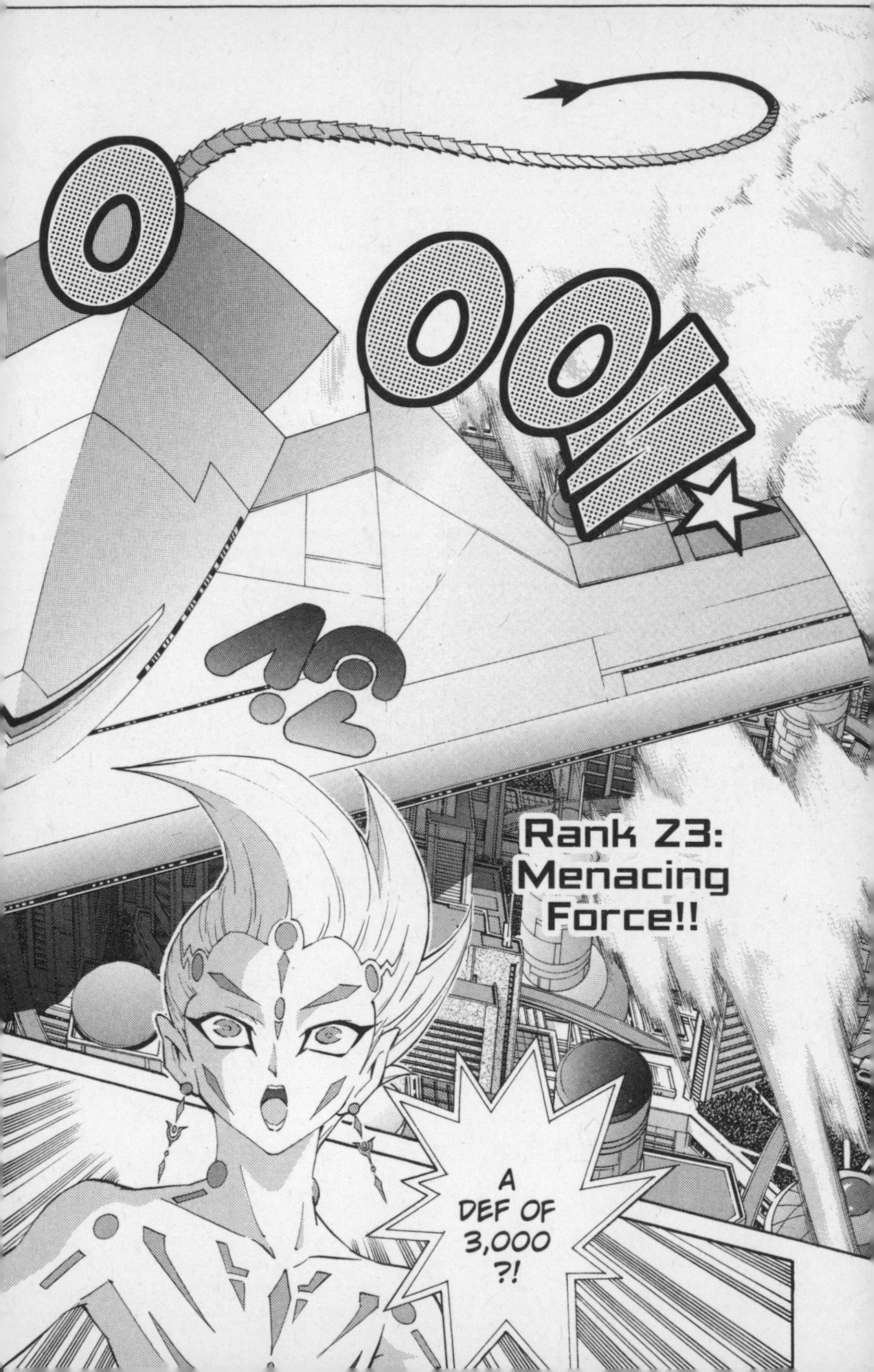
Rank 23: Menacing Force!!
A DEF OF 3,000 ?!

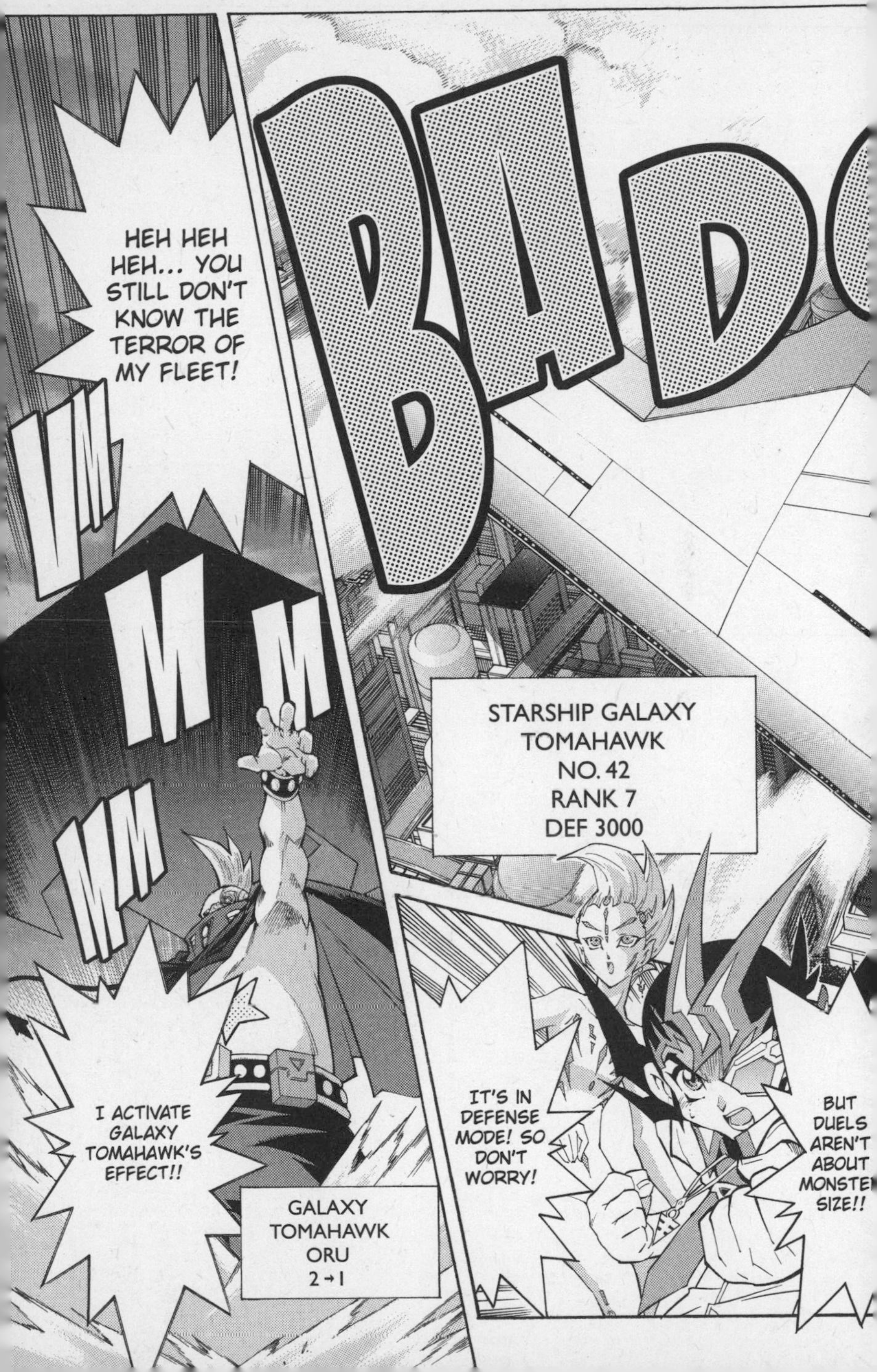
BAD
STARSHIP GALAXY TOMAHAWK NO. 42 RANK 7 DEF 3000
BUT DUELS AREN'T ABOUT MONSTE SIZE!!
IT'S IN DEFENSE MODE! SO DON'T WORRY!
HEH HEH HEH... YOU STILL DON'T KNOW THE TERROR OF MY FLEET!
VMMMMMM
I ACTIVATE GALAXY TOMAHAWK'S EFFECT!!
GALAXY TOMAHAWK ORU 2→1

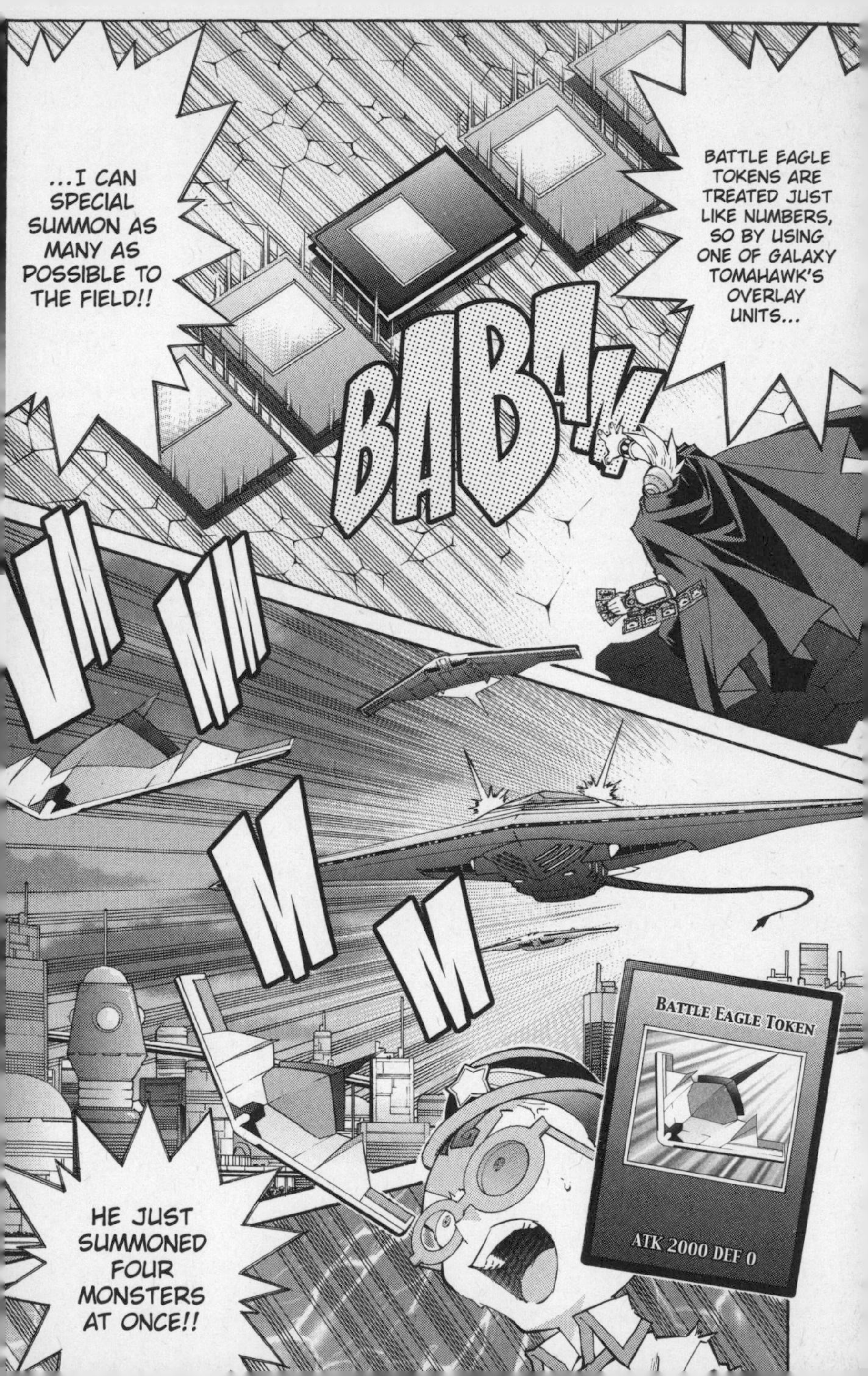
BATTLE EAGLE TOKENS ARE TREATED JUST LIKE NUMBERS, SO BY USING ONE OF GALAXY TOMAHAWK'S OVERLAY UNITS...
...I CAN SPECIAL SUMMON AS MANY AS POSSIBLE TO THE FIELD!!
BABA!!
VM VMM M M
BATTLE EAGLE TOKEN
ATK 2000 DEF 0
HE JUST SUMMONED FOUR MONSTERS AT ONCE!!

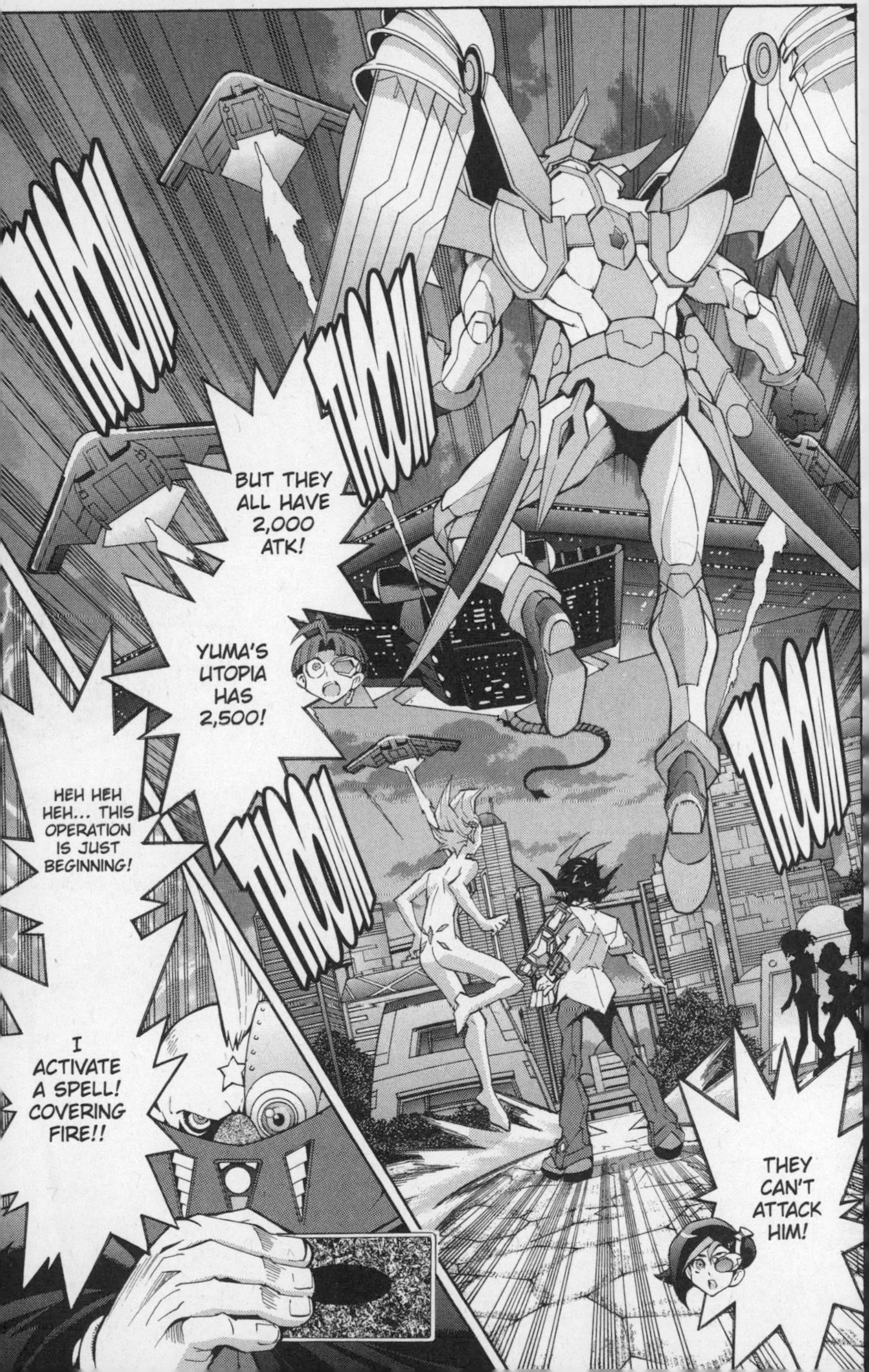
THOOM
THOOM
BUT THEY ALL HAVE 2,000 ATK!
YUMA'S UTOPIA HAS 2,500!
THOOM
THOOM
HEH HEH HEH... THIS OPERATION IS JUST BEGINNING!
THEY CAN'T ATTACK HIM!
I ACTIVATE A SPELL! COVERING FIRE!!

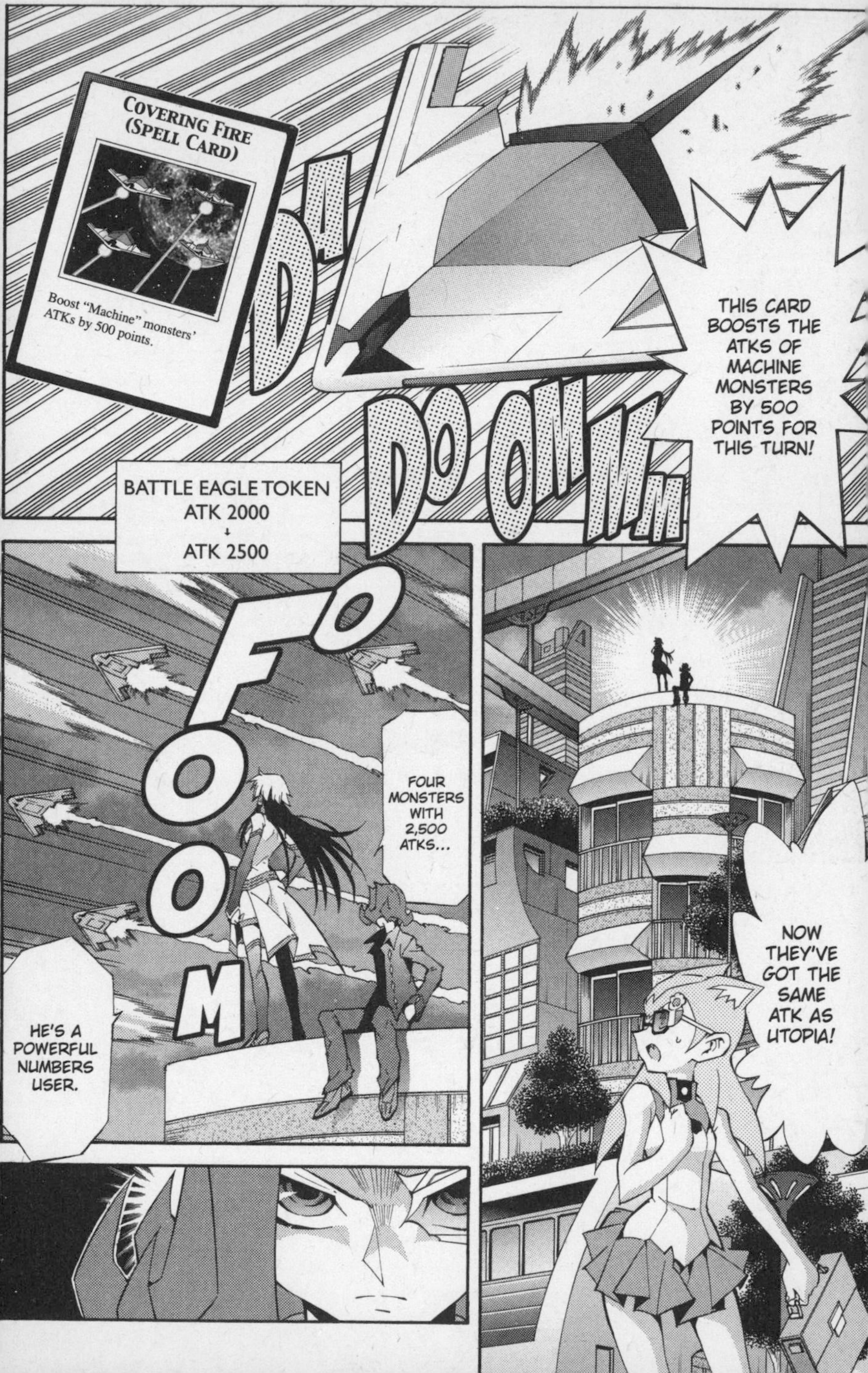
THIS CARD BOOSTS THE ATKS OF MACHINE MONSTERS BY 500 POINTS FOR THIS TURN!
COVERING FIRE (SPELL CARD)
Boost "Machine" monsters' ATKs by 500 points.
DA
DOOMMM
BATTLE EAGLE TOKEN ATK 2000 ↓ ATK 2500
NOW THEY'VE GOT THE SAME ATK AS UTOPIA!
FOUR MONSTERS WITH 2,500 ATKS...
FOOOOM
HE'S A POWERFUL NUMBERS USER.

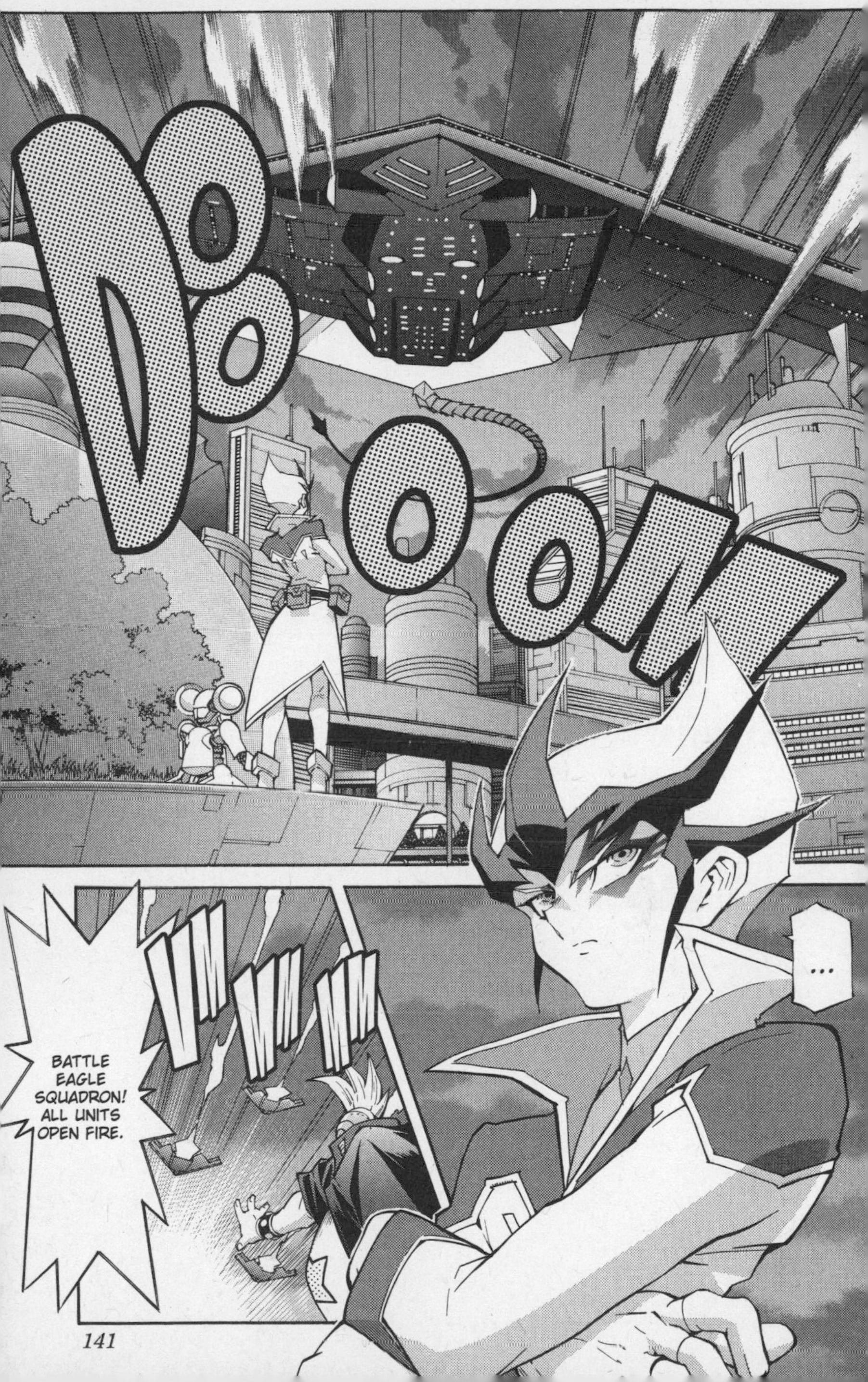
DOOOOM
...
VMMMMMM
BATTLE EAGLE SQUADRON! ALL UNITS OPEN FIRE.

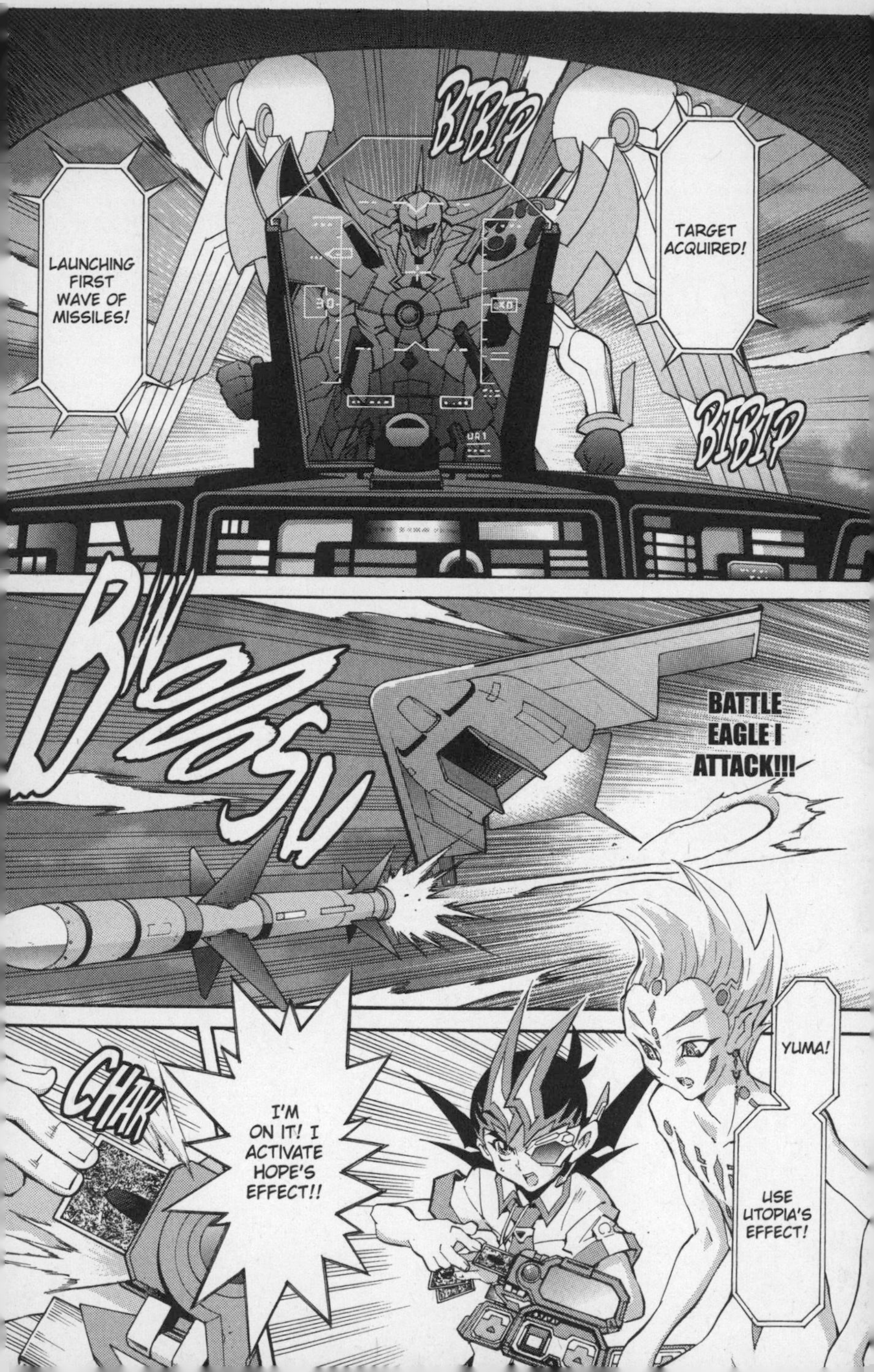
BIBIP
TARGET ACQUIRED!
LAUNCHING FIRST WAVE OF MISSILES!
BIBIP
BATTLE EAGLE I ATTACK!!!
BWOOSH
YUMA!
USE UTOPIA'S EFFECT!
I'M ON IT! I ACTIVATE HOPE'S EFFECT!!
CHAK

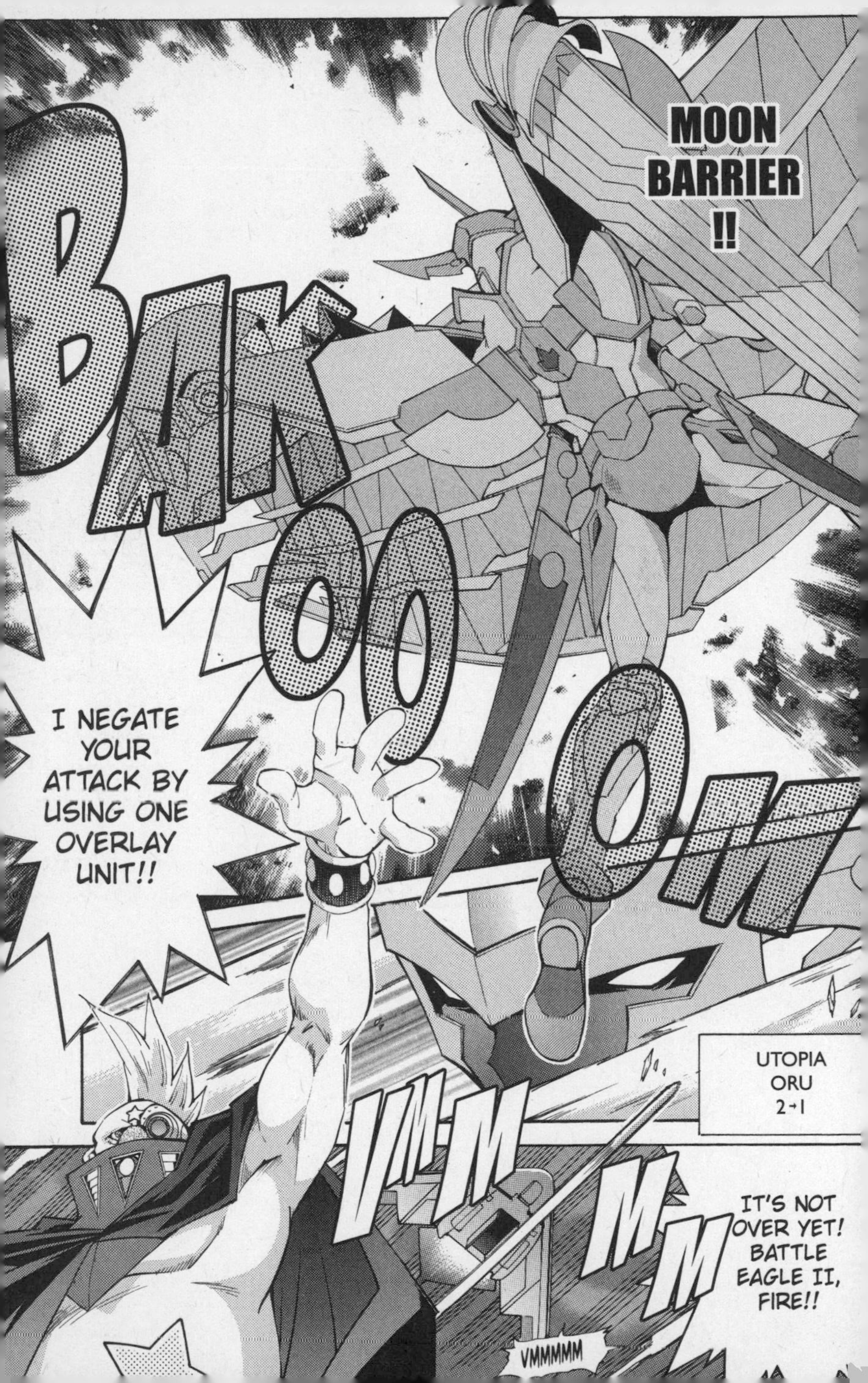
MOON BARRIER!!
BAKOOOM
I NEGATE YOUR ATTACK BY USING ONE OVERLAY UNIT!!
UTOPIA ORU 2→1
IT'S NOT OVER YET! BATTLE EAGLE II, FIRE!!
VMMMMM

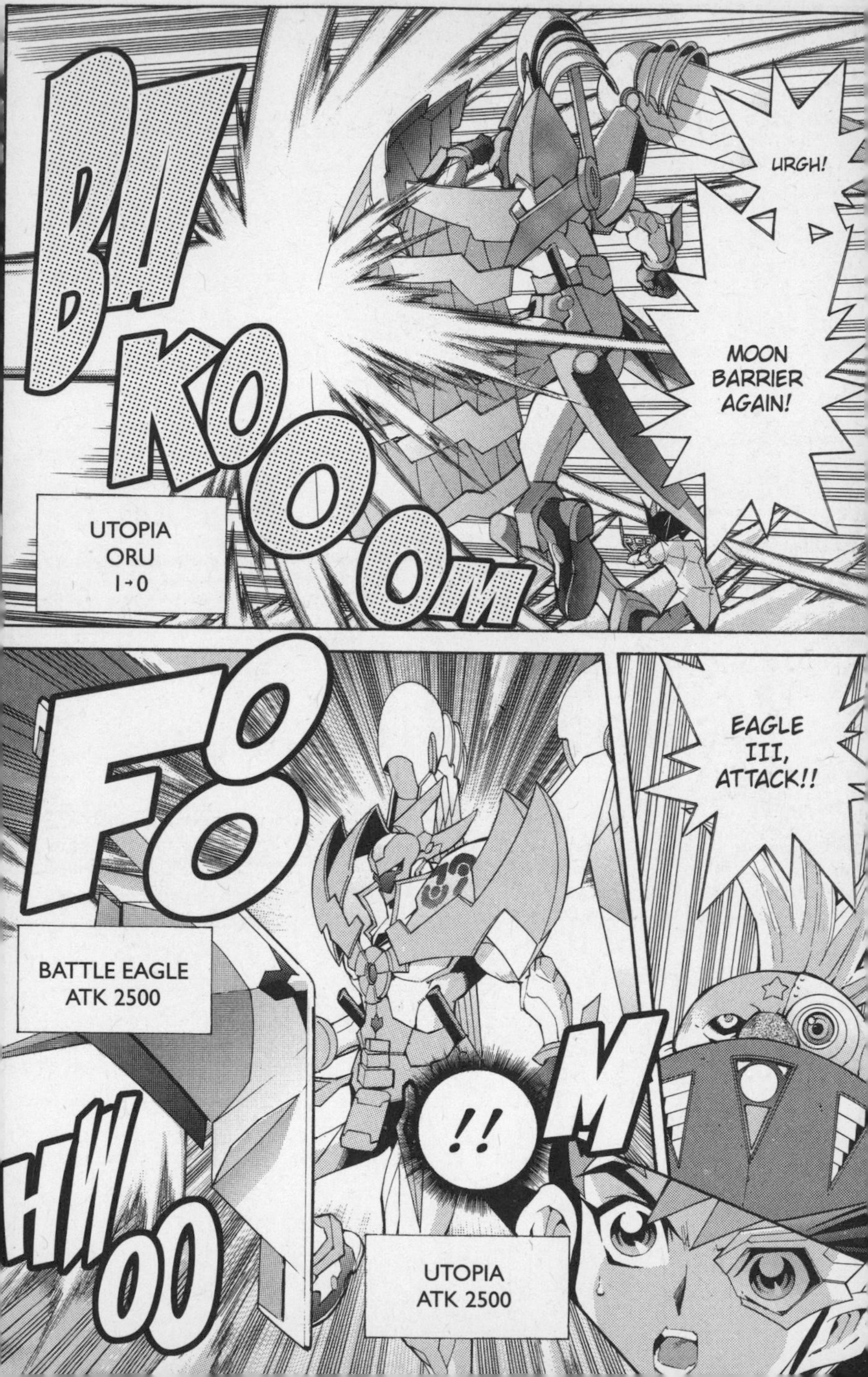
URGH!
MOON BARRIER AGAIN!
BA KOOOOM
UTOPIA ORU 1→0
EAGLE III, ATTACK!!
FOO
BATTLE EAGLE ATK 2500
M
!!
UTOPIA ATK 2500

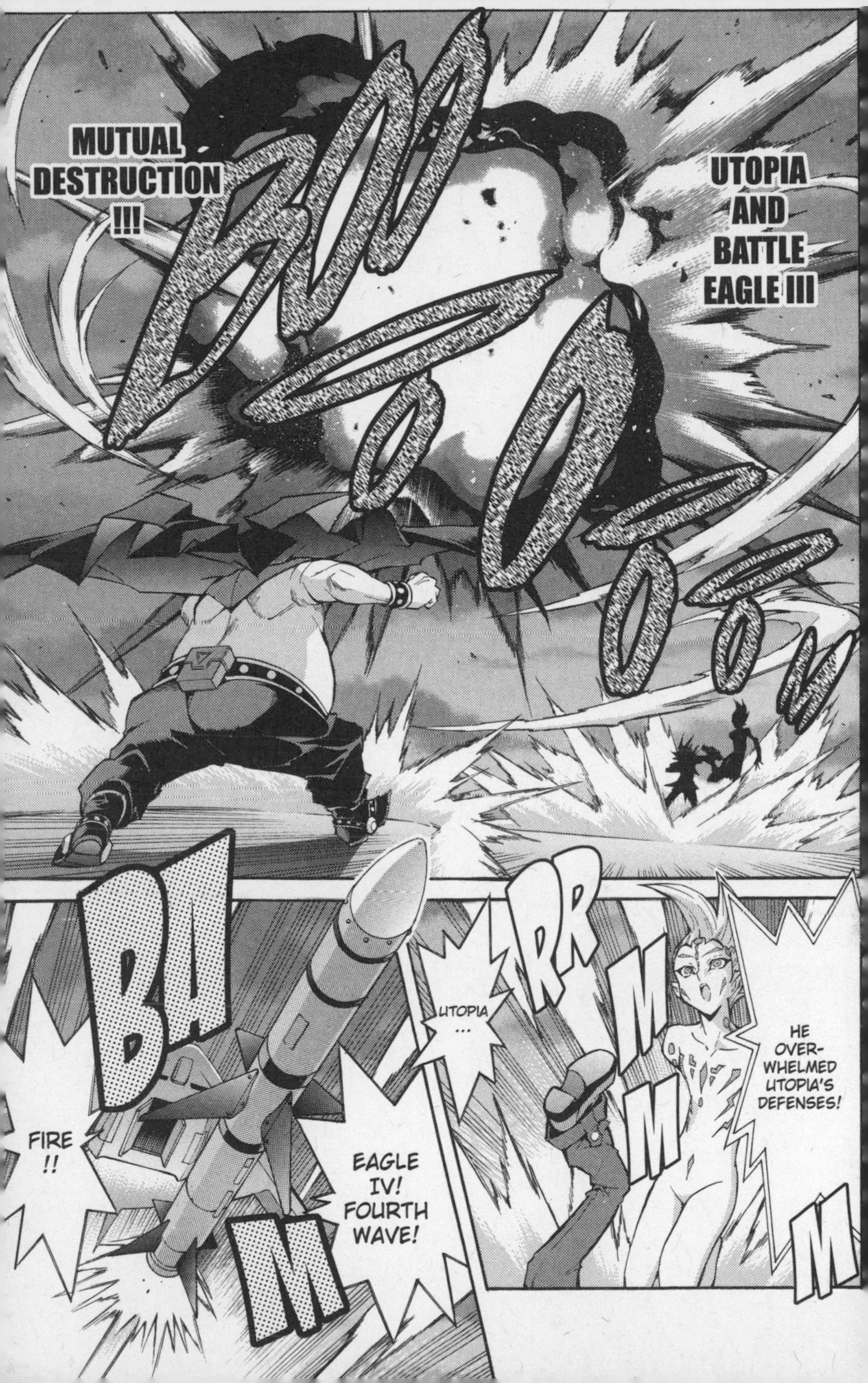
UTOPIA AND BATTLE EAGLE III
MUTUAL DESTRUCTION!!!
HE OVER-WHELMED UTOPIA'S DEFENSES!
RRMMM
UTOPIA...
EAGLE IV! FOURTH WAVE!
FIRE!!
BAM

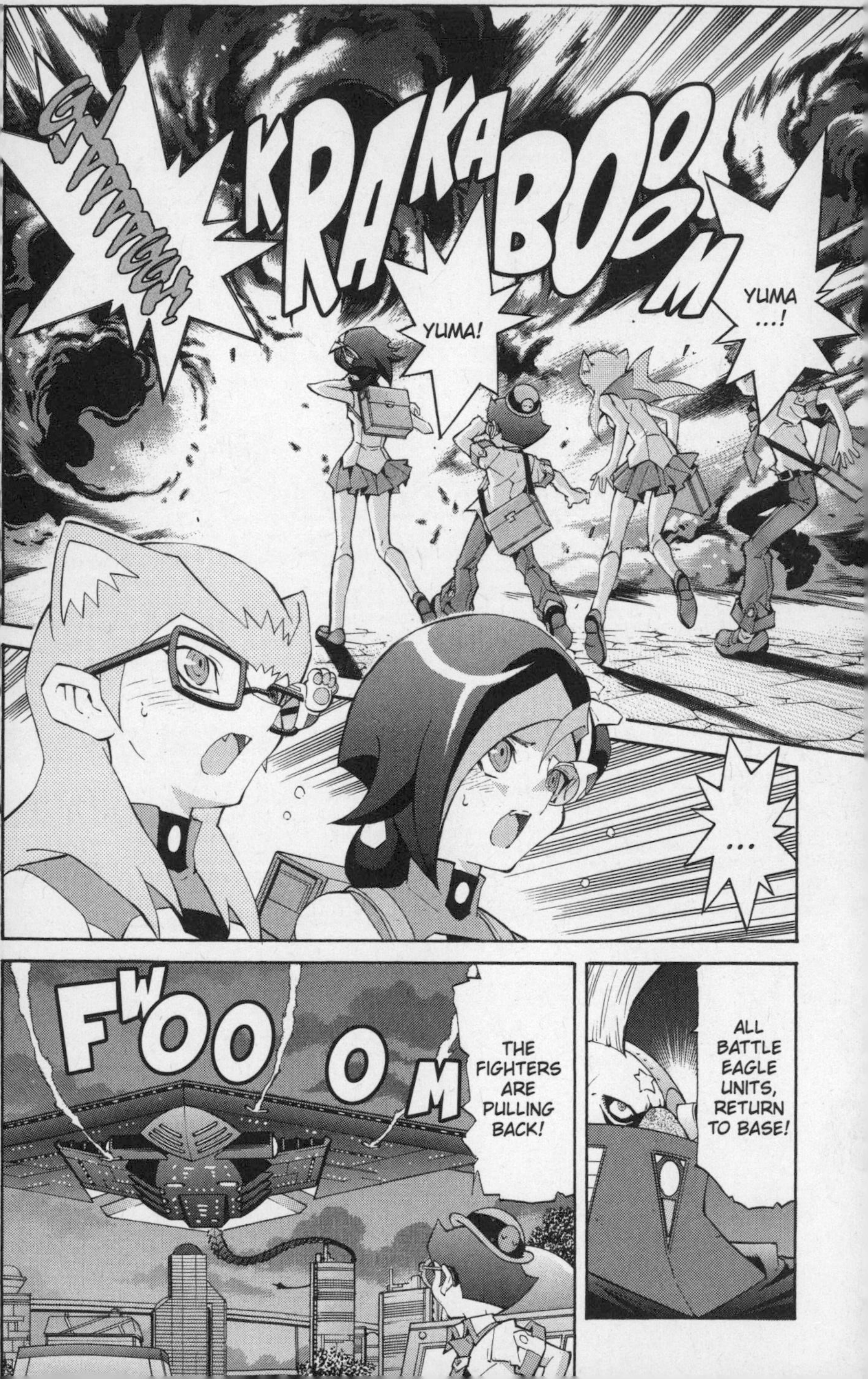
YUMA ...!
KRAKABOOOOM
GWAAAAGH!
YUMA!
...
ALL BATTLE EAGLE UNITS, RETURN TO BASE!
FWOOOOM
THE FIGHTERS ARE PULLING BACK!

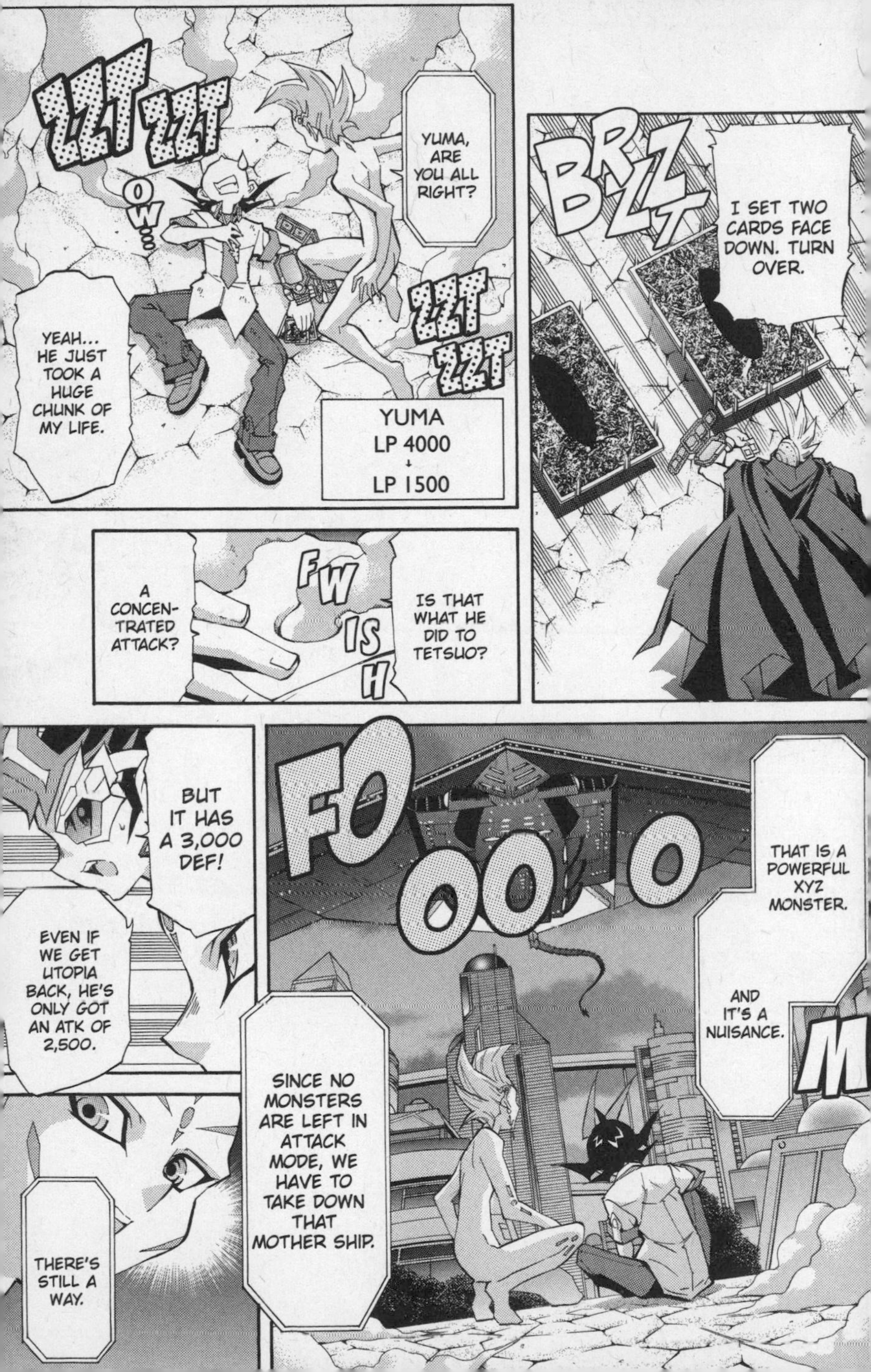
BRZZT
I SET TWO CARDS FACE DOWN. TURN OVER.
ZZT ZZT
YUMA, ARE YOU ALL RIGHT?
OW...
YEAH... HE JUST TOOK A HUGE CHUNK OF MY LIFE.
ZZT ZZT
YUMA
LP 4000
↓
LP 1500
IS THAT WHAT HE DID TO TETSUO?
FWISH
A CONCEN-TRATED ATTACK?
FOOOO
THAT IS A POWERFUL XYZ MONSTER.
AND IT'S A NUISANCE.
M
SINCE NO MONSTERS ARE LEFT IN ATTACK MODE, WE HAVE TO TAKE DOWN THAT MOTHER SHIP.
BUT IT HAS A 3,000 DEF!
EVEN IF WE GET UTOPIA BACK, HE'S ONLY GOT AN ATK OF 2,500.
THERE'S STILL A WAY.

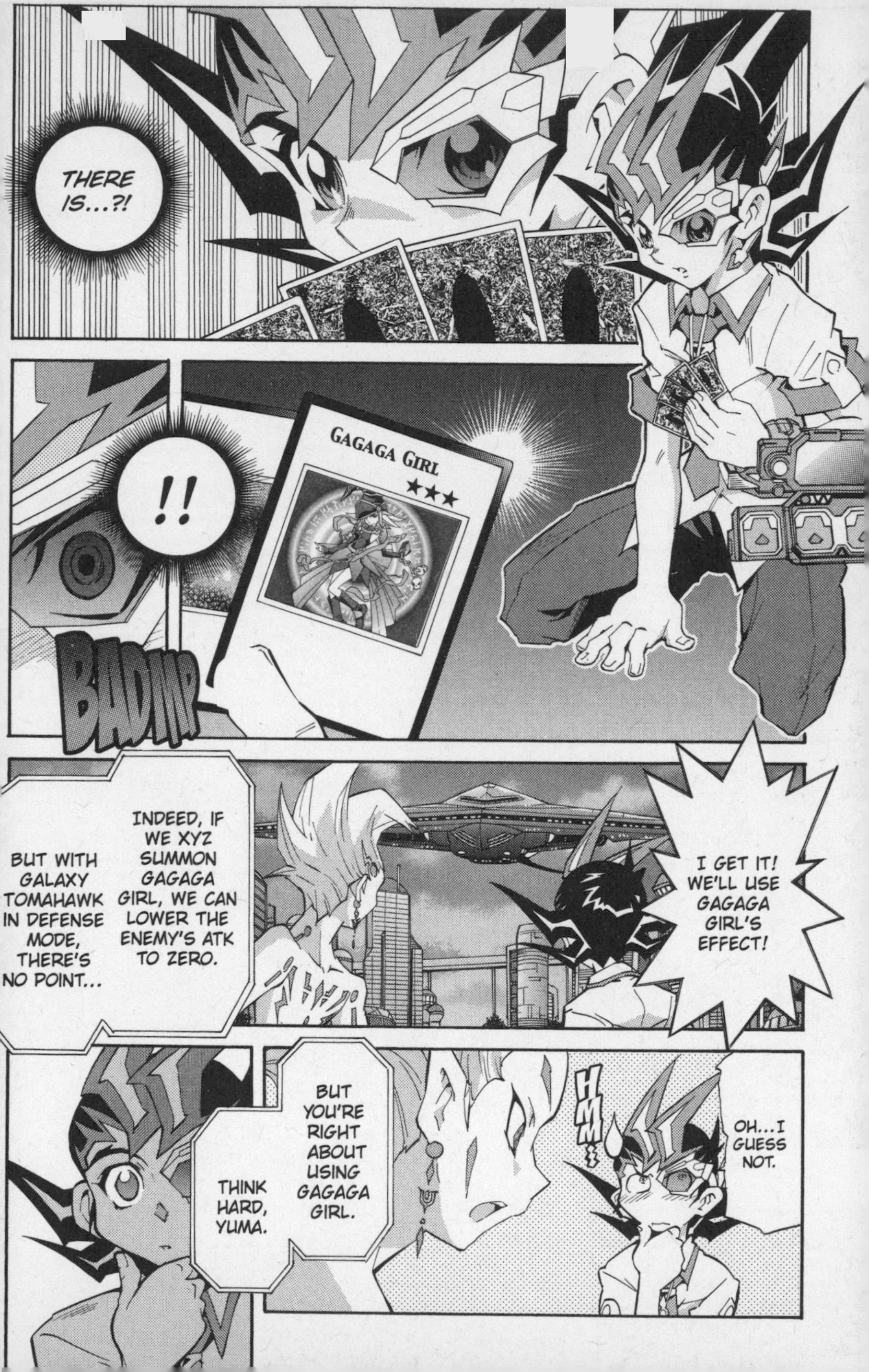
THERE IS...?!
GAGAGA GIRL
!!
BADMP
I GET IT! WE'LL USE GAGAGA GIRL'S EFFECT!
INDEED, IF WE XYZ SUMMON GAGAGA GIRL, WE CAN LOWER THE ENEMY'S ATK TO ZERO.
BUT WITH GALAXY TOMAHAWK IN DEFENSE MODE, THERE'S NO POINT...
OH...I GUESS NOT.
HMM
BUT YOU'RE RIGHT ABOUT USING GAGAGA GIRL.
THINK HARD, YUMA.

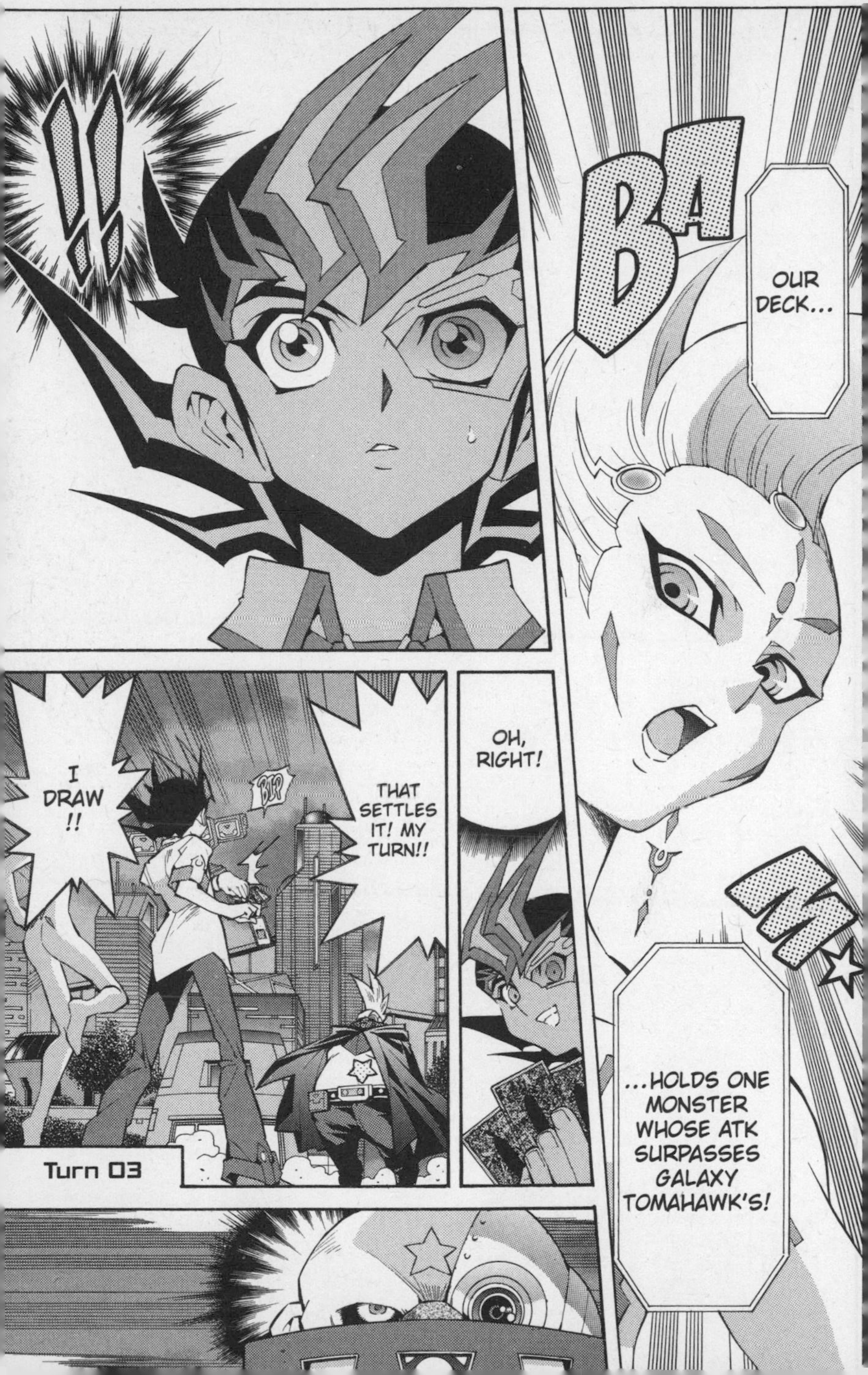
BA
OUR DECK...
M☆
...HOLDS ONE MONSTER WHOSE ATK SURPASSES GALAXY TOMAHAWK'S!
!!
OH, RIGHT!
THAT SETTLES IT! MY TURN!!
I DRAW!!
Turn 03

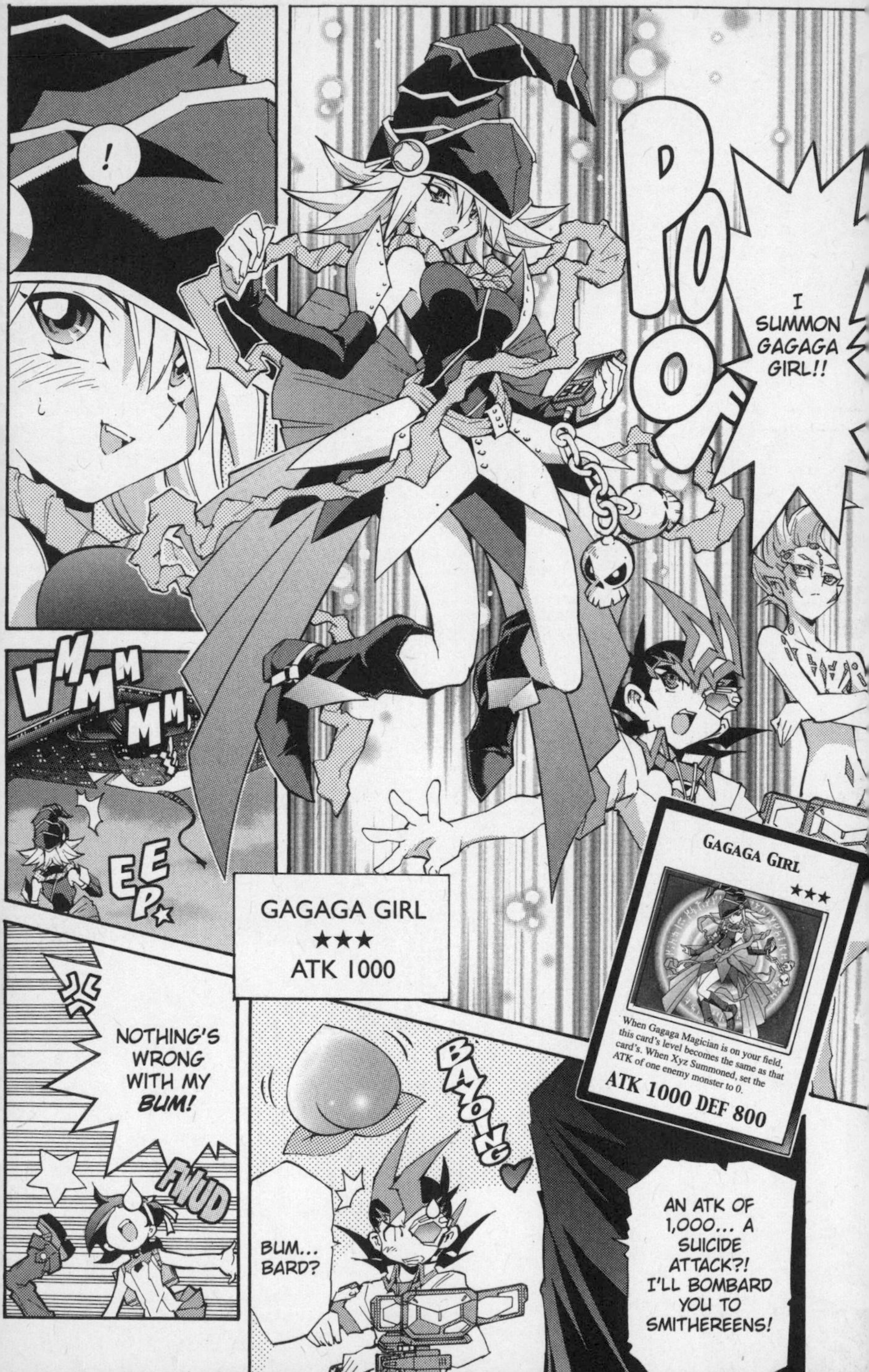
POOF
I SUMMON GAGAGA GIRL!!
GAGAGA GIRL
★★★
ATK 1000
GAGAGA GIRL
★★★
When Gagaga Magician is on your field, this card's level becomes the same as that card's. When Xyz Summoned, set the ATK of one enemy monster to 0.
ATK 1000 DEF 800
!
VMMMMMM
EEP
AN ATK OF 1,000... A SUICIDE ATTACK?! I'LL BOMBARD YOU TO SMITHEREENS!
BAOING
BUM... BARD?
NOTHING'S WRONG WITH MY *BUM!*
FWUD

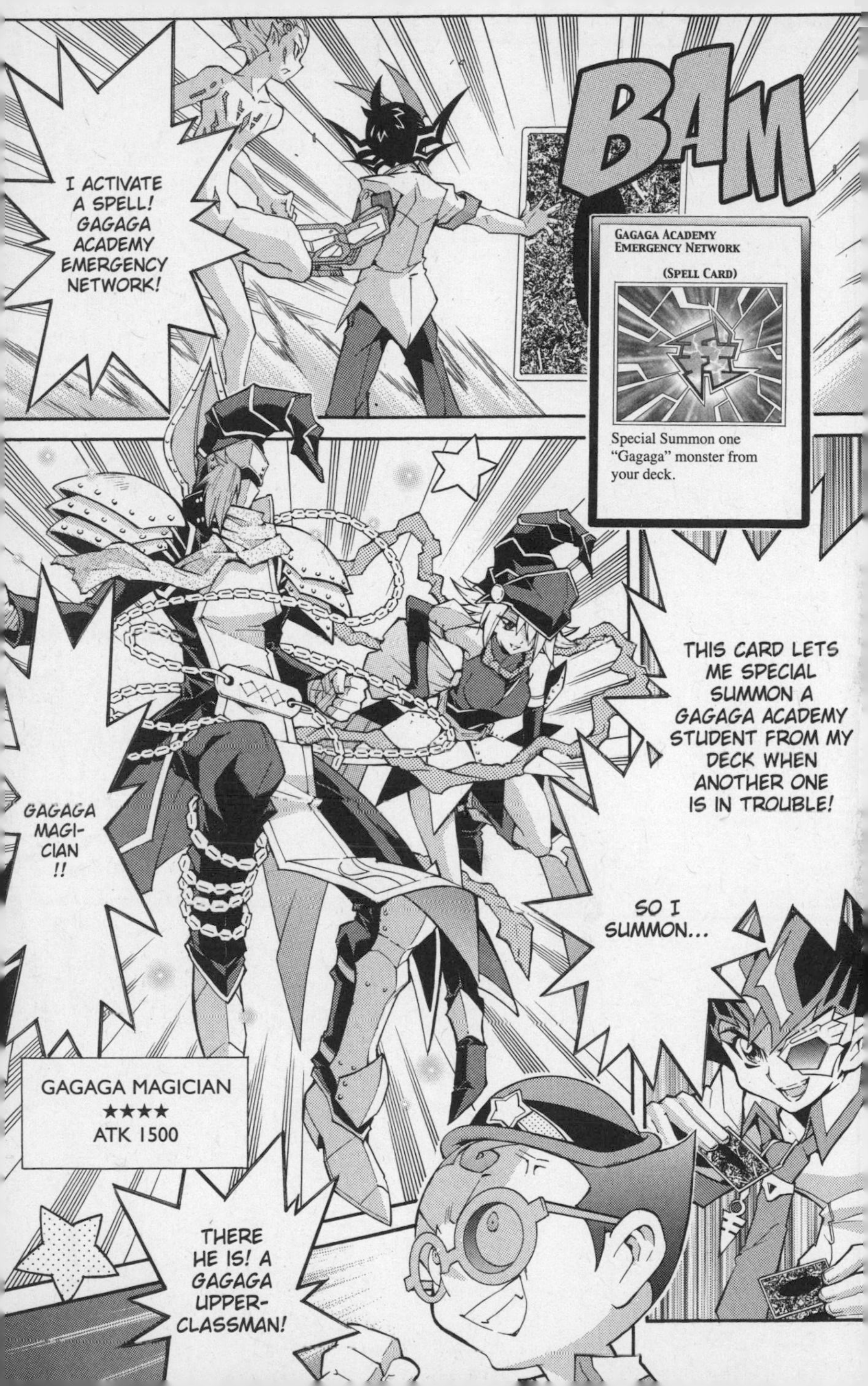
BAM
I ACTIVATE A SPELL! GAGAGA ACADEMY EMERGENCY NETWORK!
GAGAGA ACADEMY EMERGENCY NETWORK
(SPELL CARD)
Special Summon one "Gagaga" monster from your deck.
THIS CARD LETS ME SPECIAL SUMMON A GAGAGA ACADEMY STUDENT FROM MY DECK WHEN ANOTHER ONE IS IN TROUBLE!
SO I SUMMON...
GAGAGA MAGI-CIAN!!
GAGAGA MAGICIAN
★★★★
ATK 1500
THERE HE IS! A GAGAGA UPPER-CLASSMAN!

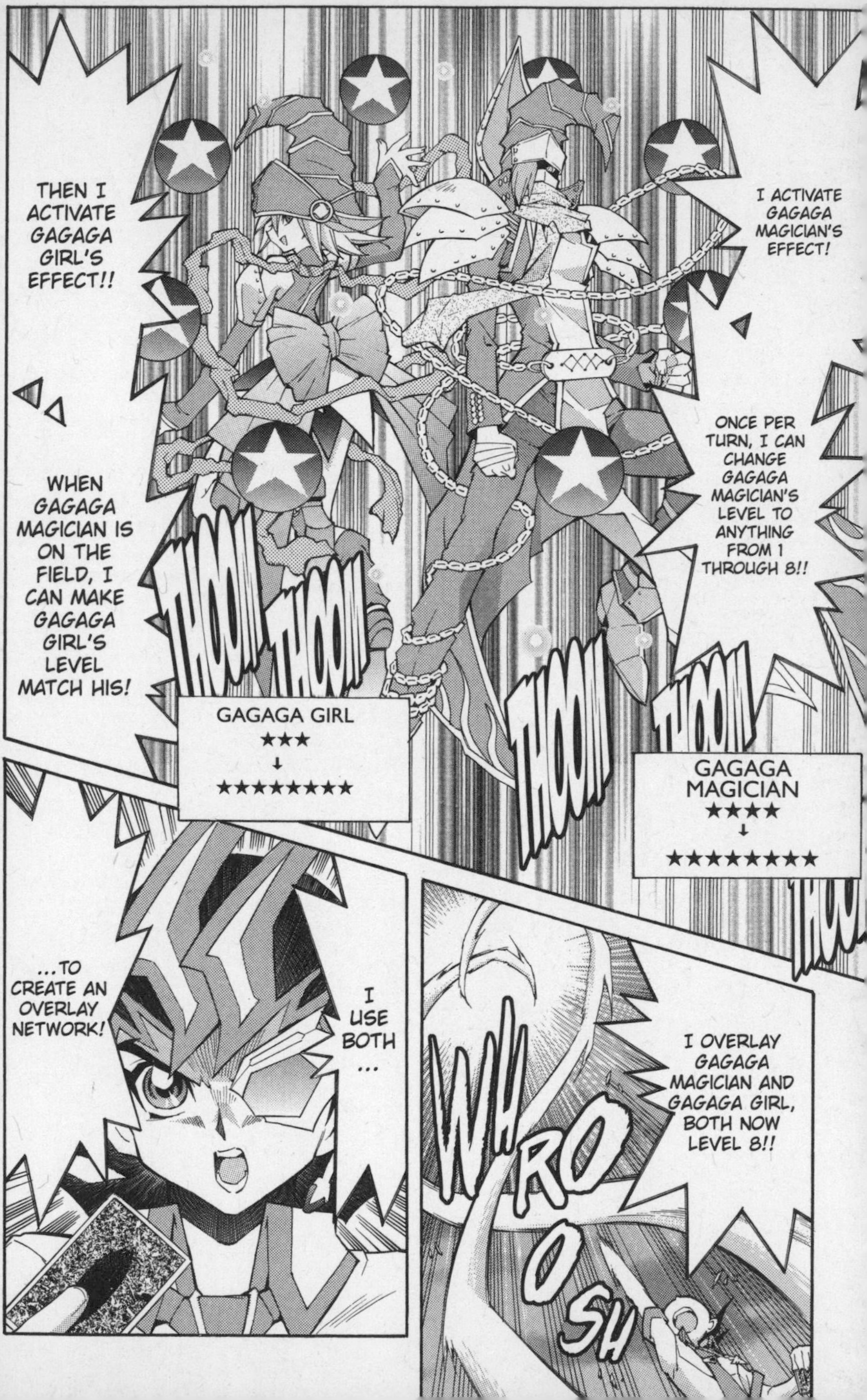
I ACTIVATE GAGAGA MAGICIAN'S EFFECT!
ONCE PER TURN, I CAN CHANGE GAGAGA MAGICIAN'S LEVEL TO ANYTHING FROM 1 THROUGH 8!!
THEN I ACTIVATE GAGAGA GIRL'S EFFECT!!
WHEN GAGAGA MAGICIAN IS ON THE FIELD, I CAN MAKE GAGAGA GIRL'S LEVEL MATCH HIS!
THOOM
THOOM
THOOM
THOOM
GAGAGA MAGICIAN ★★★★ ↓ ★★★★★★★★
GAGAGA GIRL ★★★ ↓ ★★★★★★★★
I OVERLAY GAGAGA MAGICIAN AND GAGAGA GIRL, BOTH NOW LEVEL 8!!
WHROOOSH
I USE BOTH ...
...TO CREATE AN OVERLAY NETWORK!

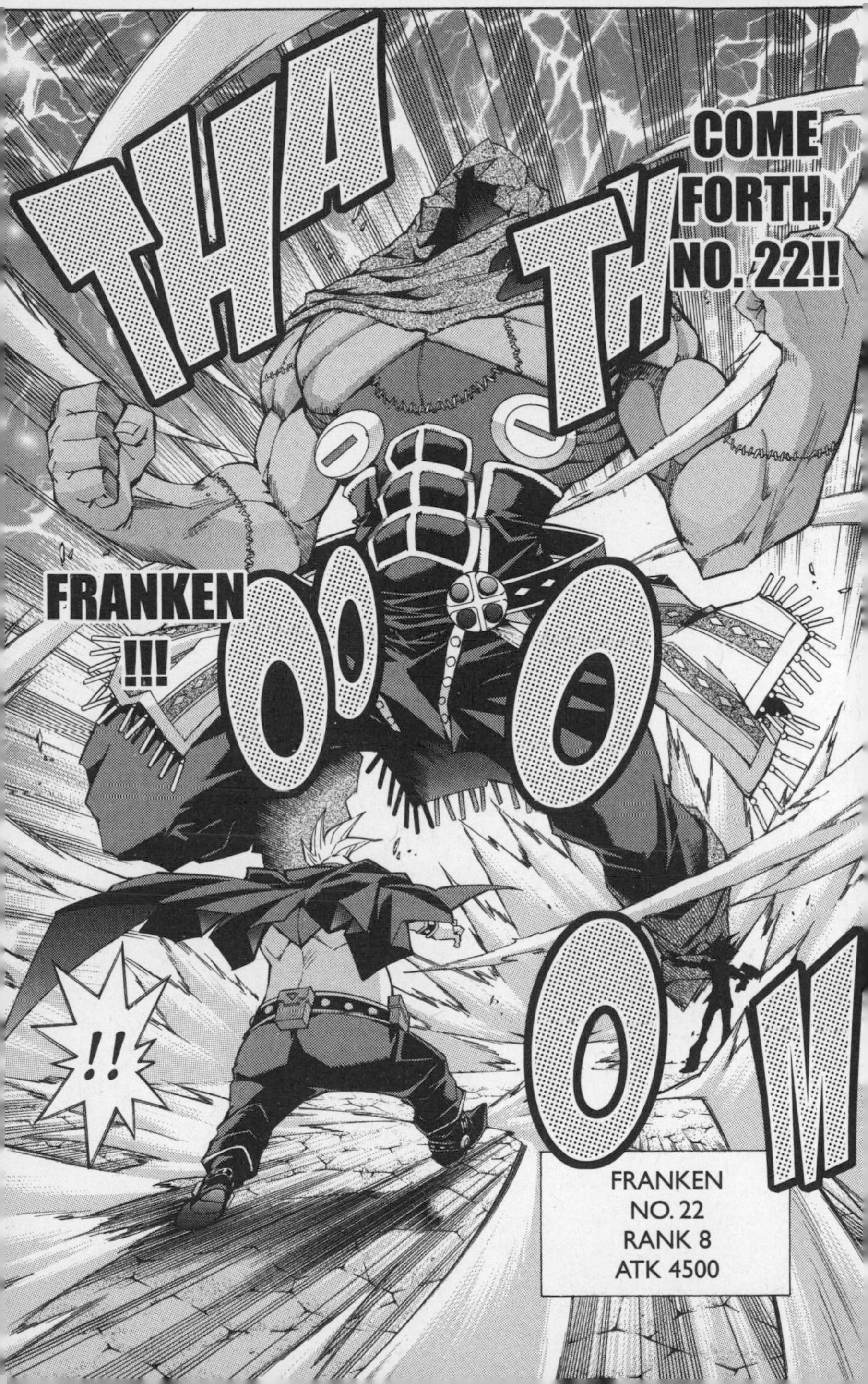
COME FORTH, NO. 22!!
THA
TH
OOO
OM
FRANKEN !!!
!!
FRANKEN
NO. 22
RANK 8
ATK 4500

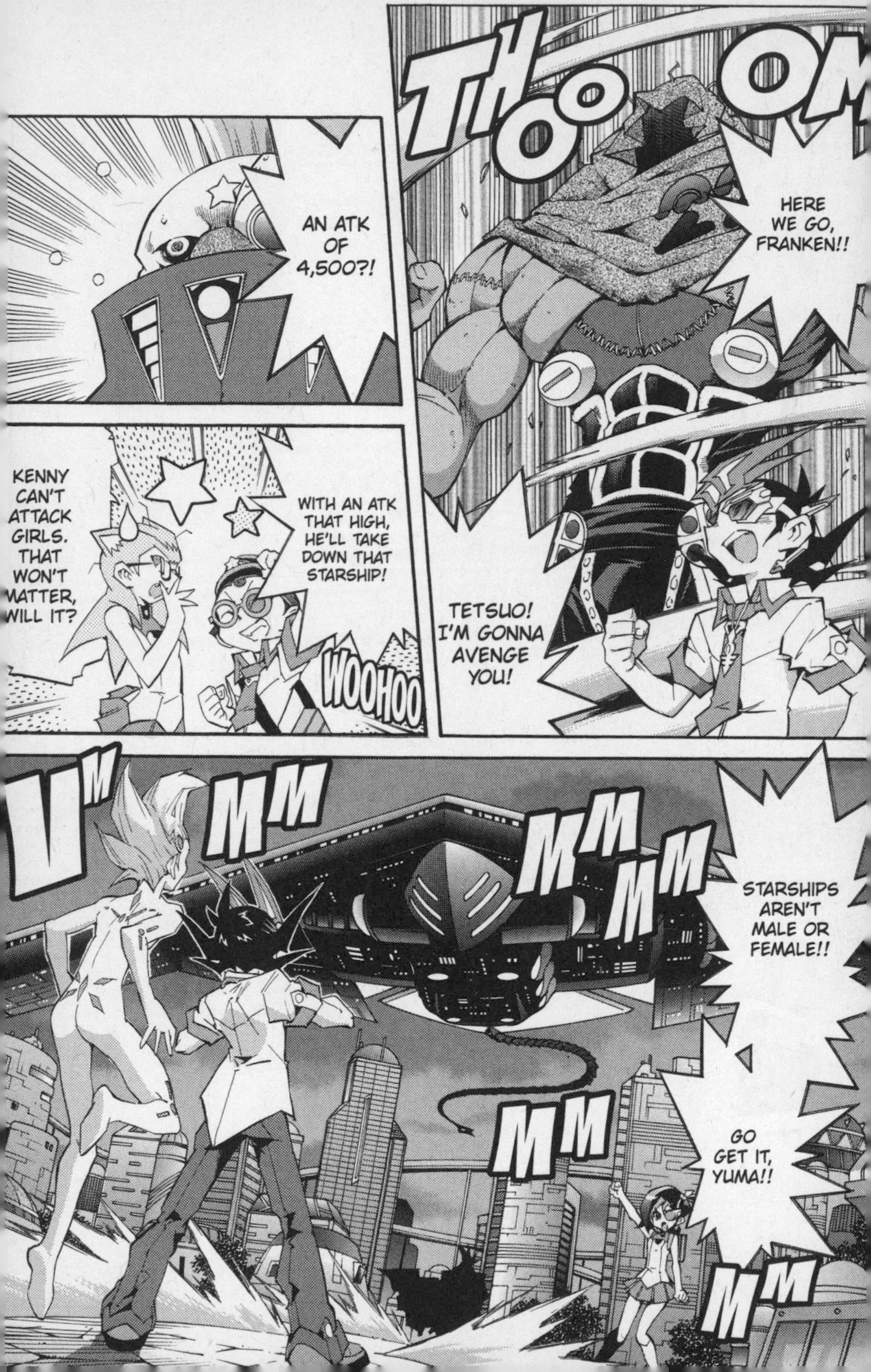
THOOOM
HERE WE GO, FRANKEN!!
TETSUO! I'M GONNA AVENGE YOU!
AN ATK OF 4,500?!
WITH AN ATK THAT HIGH, HE'LL TAKE DOWN THAT STARSHIP!
KENNY CAN'T ATTACK GIRLS. THAT WON'T MATTER, WILL IT?
WOOHOO
STARSHIPS AREN'T MALE OR FEMALE!!
VMMMMMMMMMMM
GO GET IT, YUMA!!

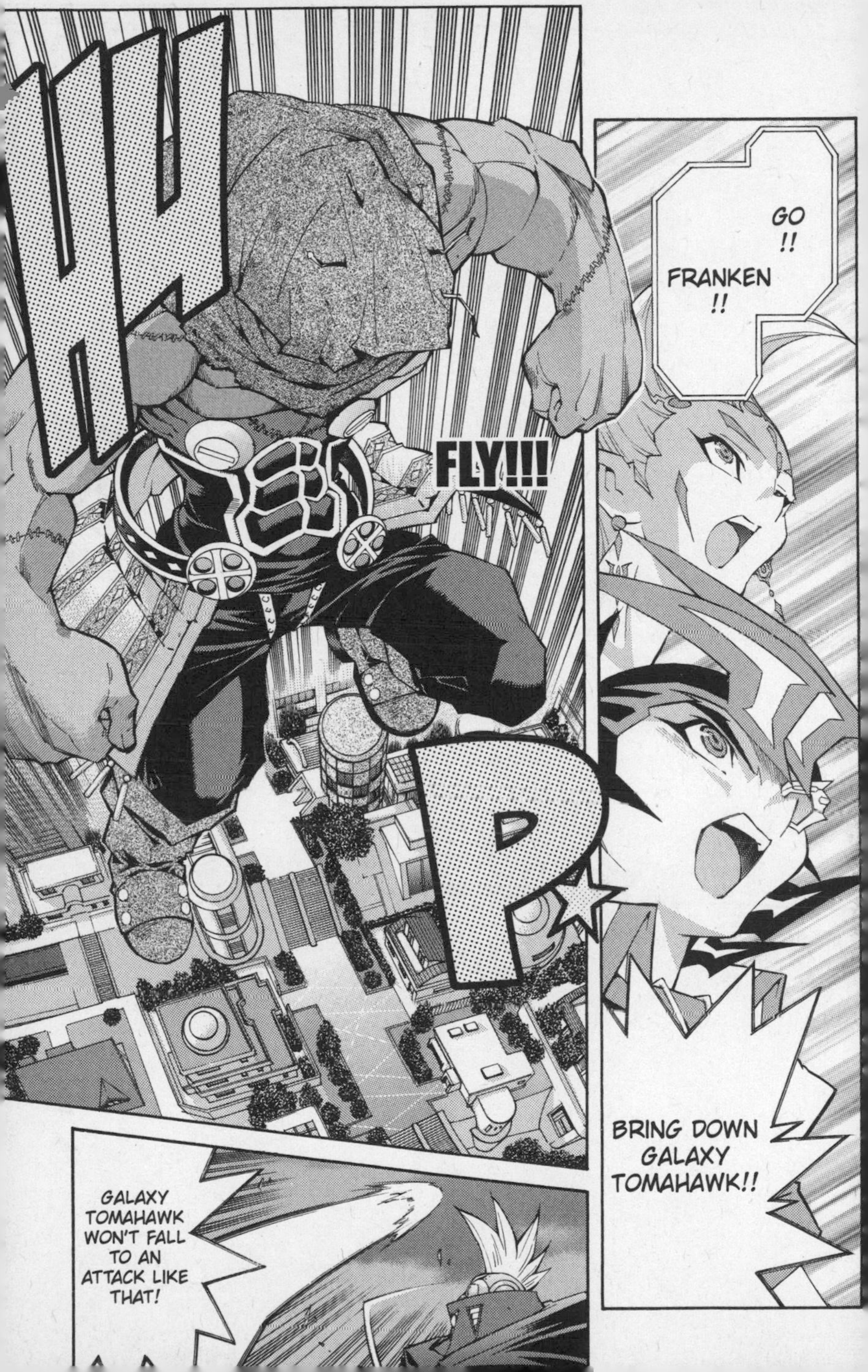
GO !! FRANKEN !!
BRING DOWN GALAXY TOMAHAWK!!
WH
P
FLY!!!
GALAXY TOMAHAWK WON'T FALL TO AN ATTACK LIKE THAT!

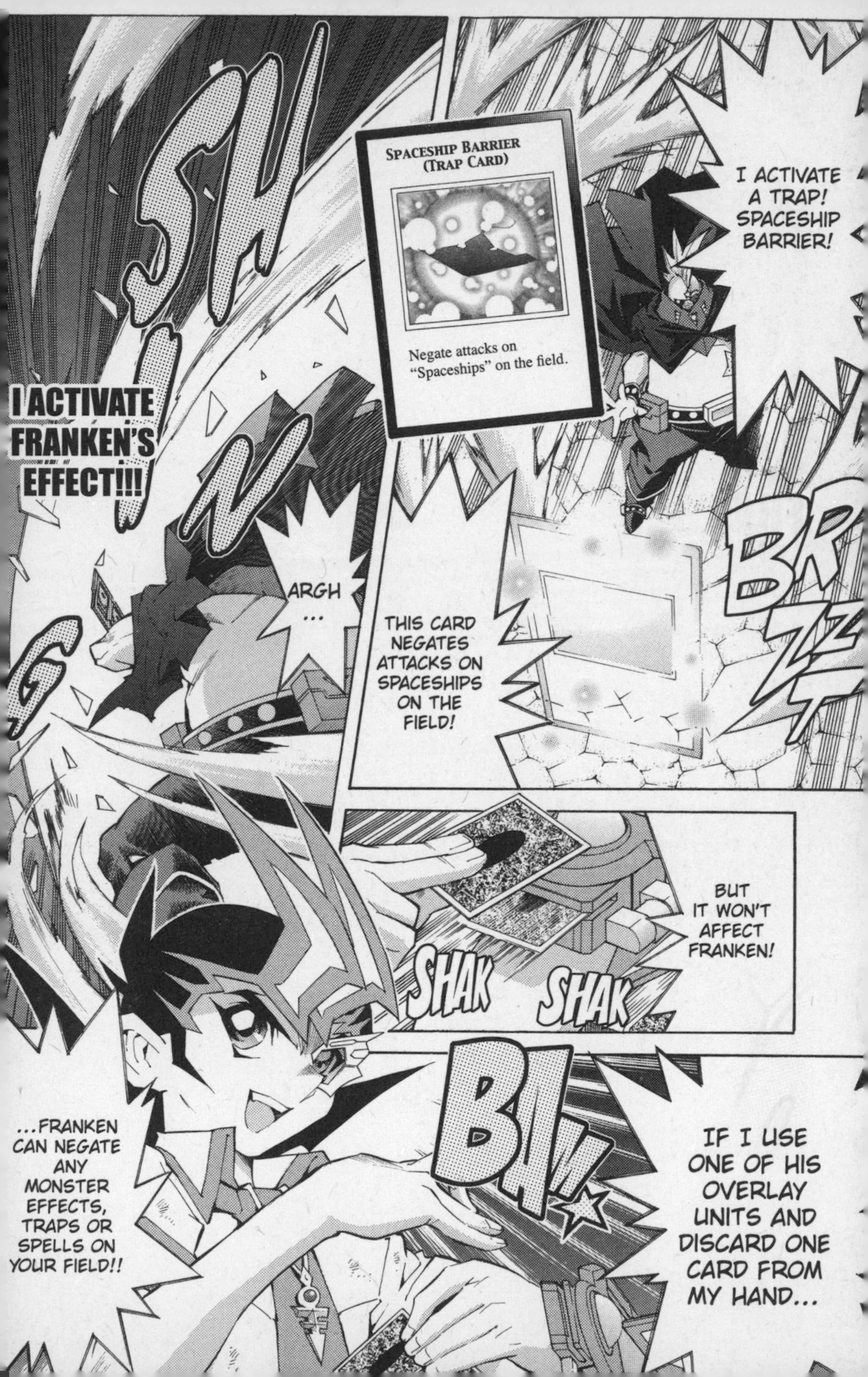
I ACTIVATE A TRAP! SPACESHIP BARRIER!
SPACESHIP BARRIER (TRAP CARD)
Negate attacks on "Spaceships" on the field.
BRZZT
THIS CARD NEGATES ATTACKS ON SPACESHIPS ON THE FIELD!
BUT IT WON'T AFFECT FRANKEN!
SHAK
SHAK
SHIN
I ACTIVATE FRANKEN'S EFFECT!!!
ARGH...
G
IF I USE ONE OF HIS OVERLAY UNITS AND DISCARD ONE CARD FROM MY HAND...
BA!!
...FRANKEN CAN NEGATE ANY MONSTER EFFECTS, TRAPS OR SPELLS ON YOUR FIELD!!

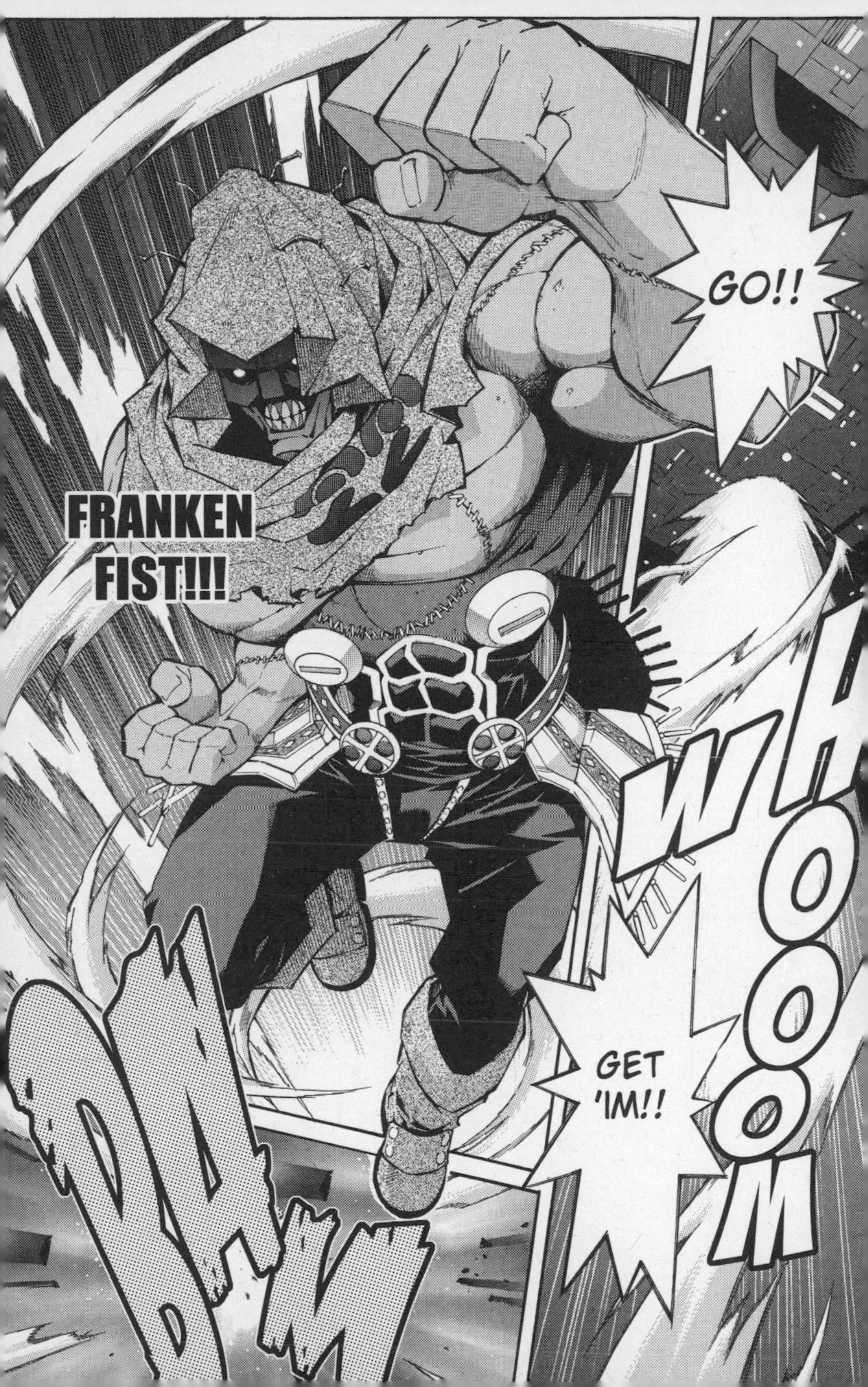
GO!!
FRANKEN FIST!!!
WHOOOM
GET 'IM!!
BAM

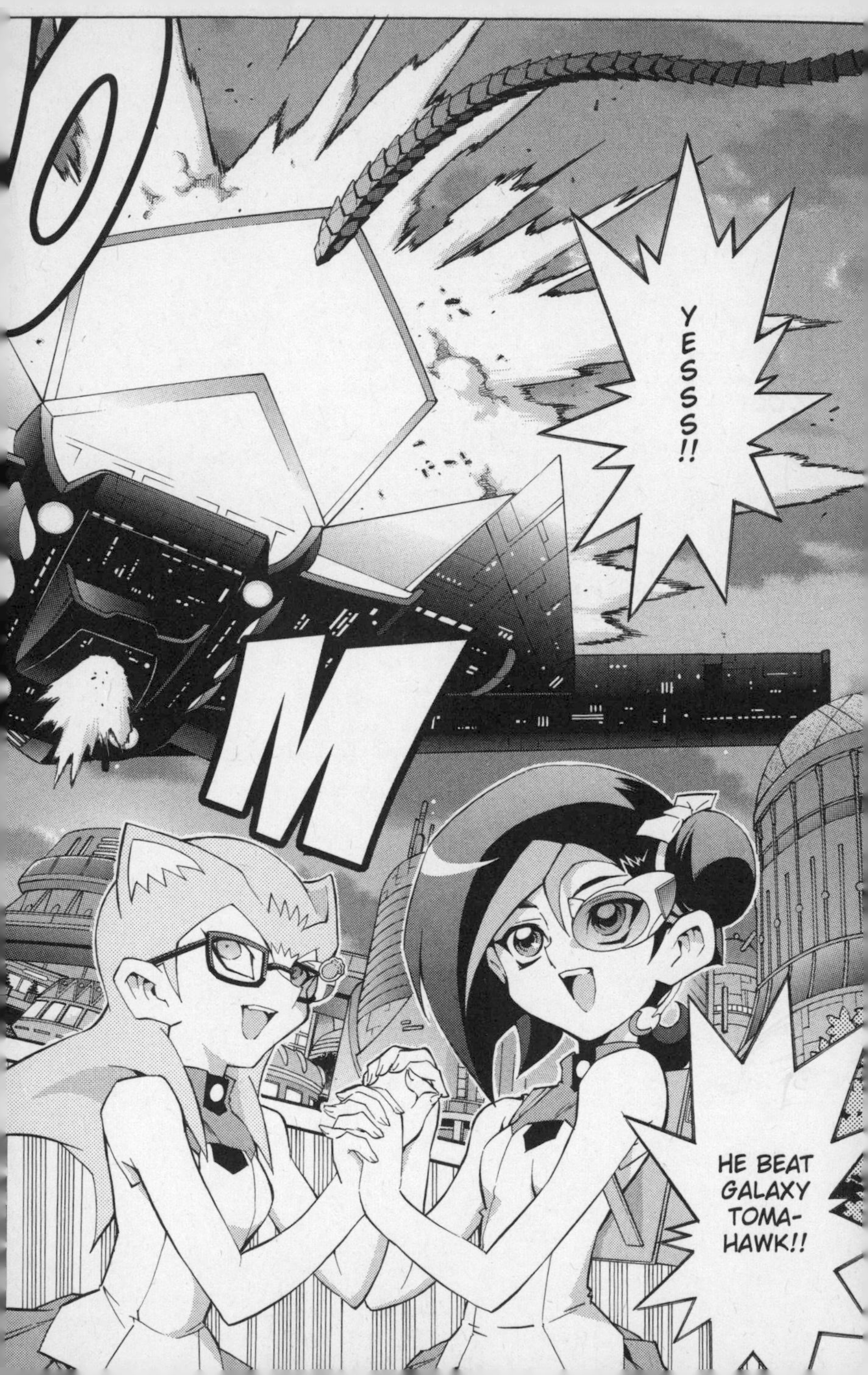
YESSS!!
M
HE BEAT GALAXY TOMA-HAWK!!

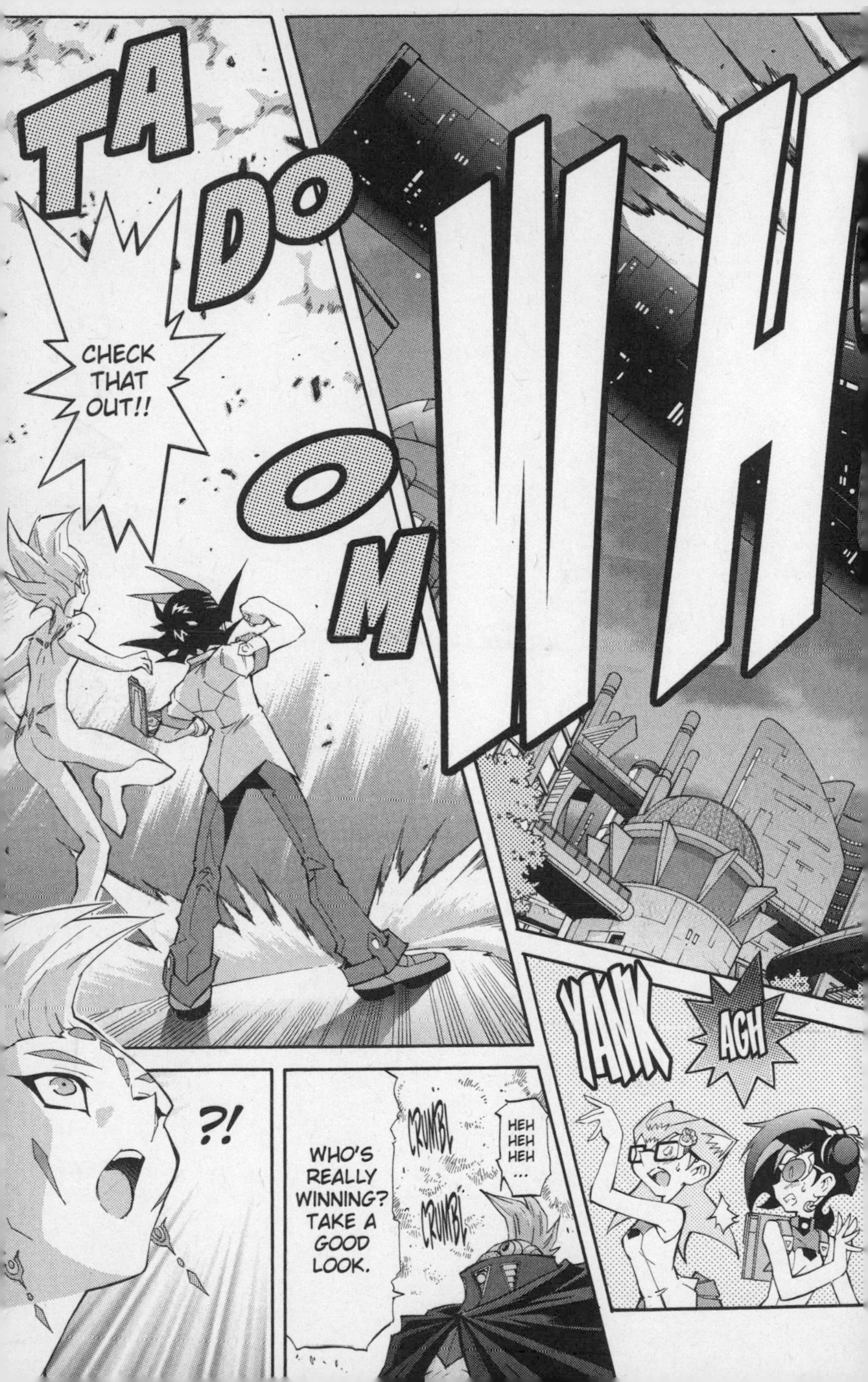
TA DO O M
CHECK THAT OUT!!
YANK
AGH
HEH HEH HEH ...
CRUMBL
CRUMBL
WHO'S REALLY WINNING? TAKE A GOOD LOOK.
?!

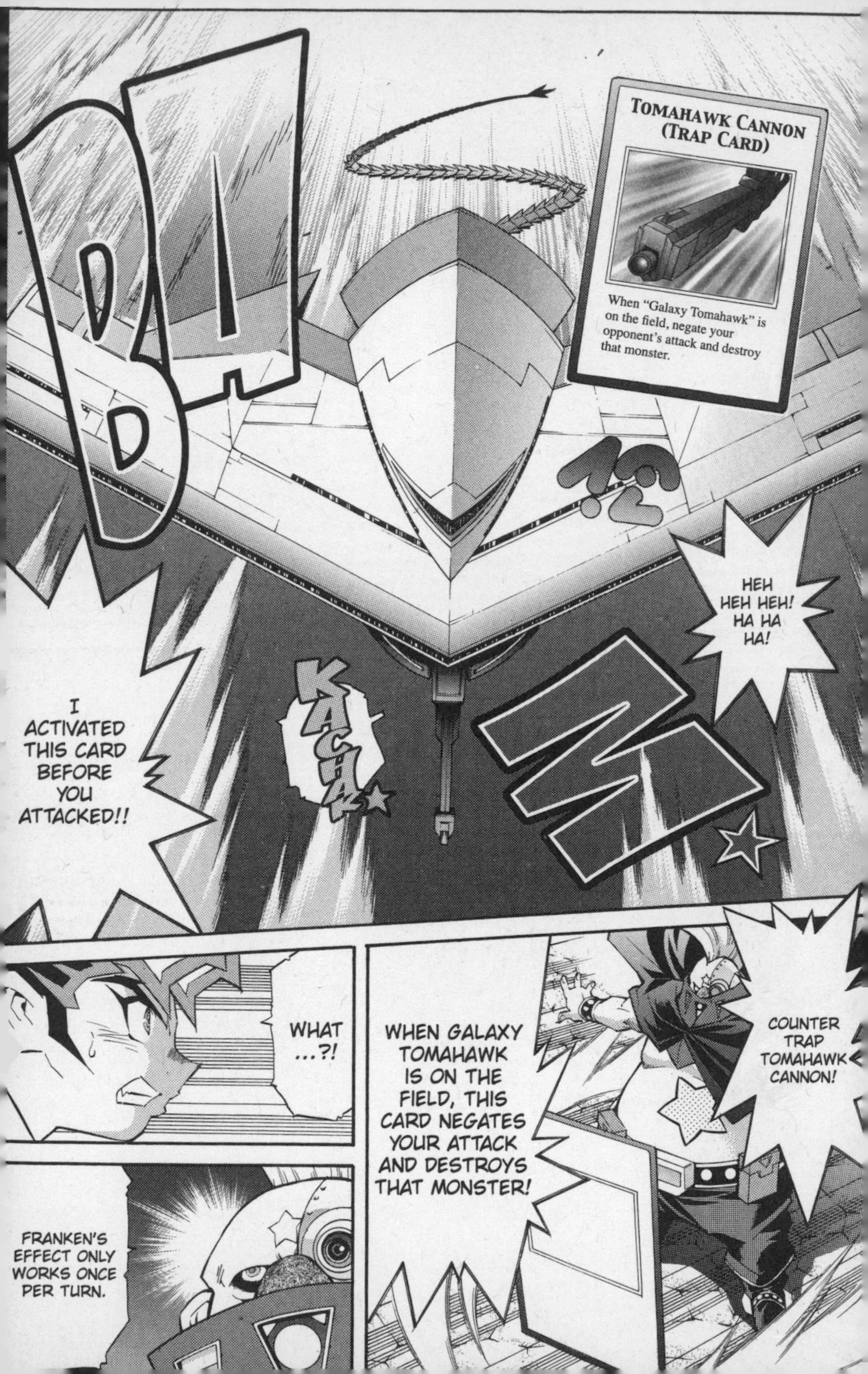
TOMAHAWK CANNON (TRAP CARD)
When "Galaxy Tomahawk" is on the field, negate your opponent's attack and destroy that monster.
HEH HEH HEH! HA HA HA!
I ACTIVATED THIS CARD BEFORE YOU ATTACKED!!
COUNTER TRAP TOMAHAWK CANNON!
WHEN GALAXY TOMAHAWK IS ON THE FIELD, THIS CARD NEGATES YOUR ATTACK AND DESTROYS THAT MONSTER!
WHAT ...?!
FRANKEN'S EFFECT ONLY WORKS ONCE PER TURN.

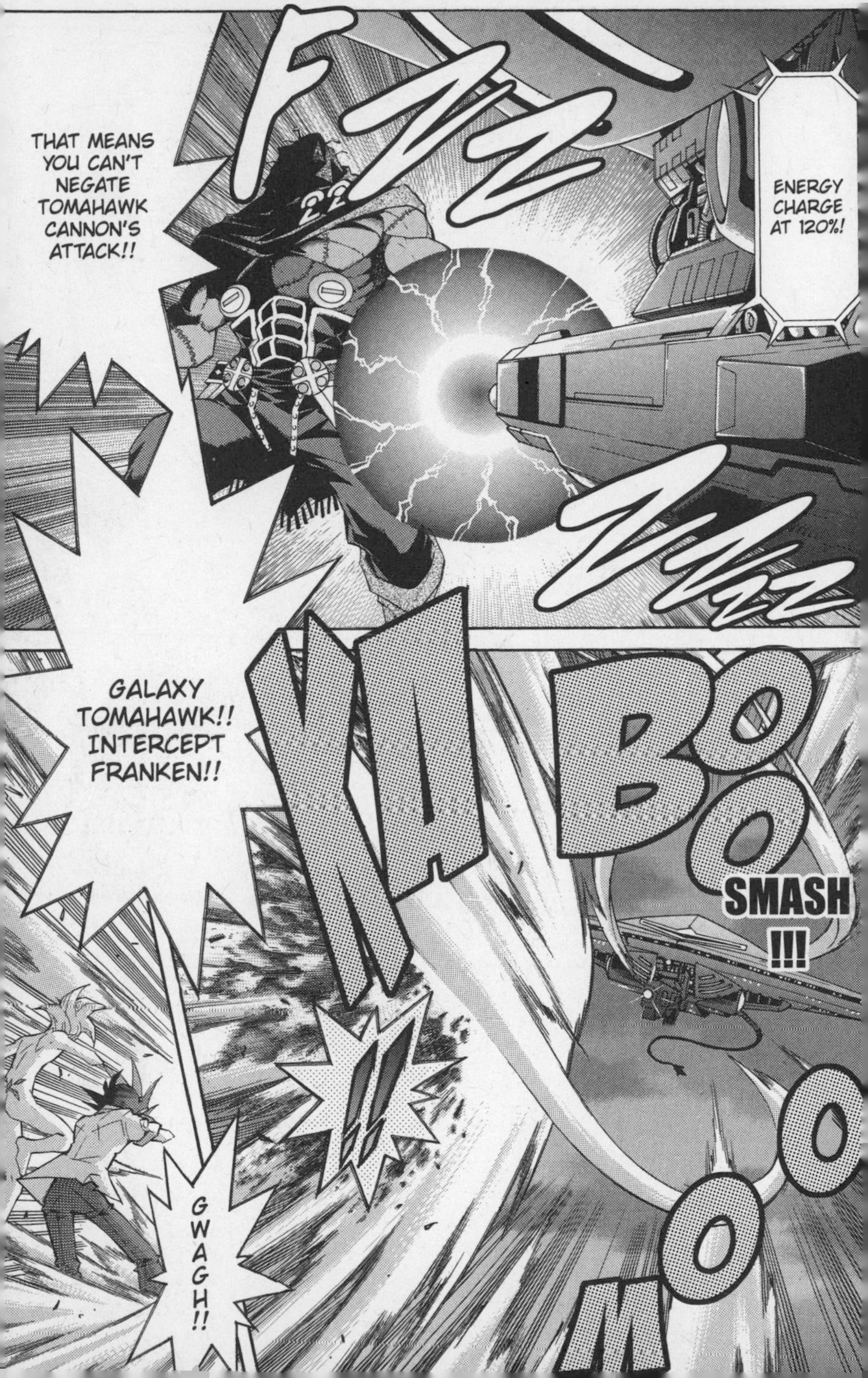
ENERGY CHARGE AT 120%!
THAT MEANS YOU CAN'T NEGATE TOMAHAWK CANNON'S ATTACK!!
KA
BOOOOOM
SMASH!!!
GALAXY TOMAHAWK!! INTERCEPT FRANKEN!!
!!
GWAGH!!

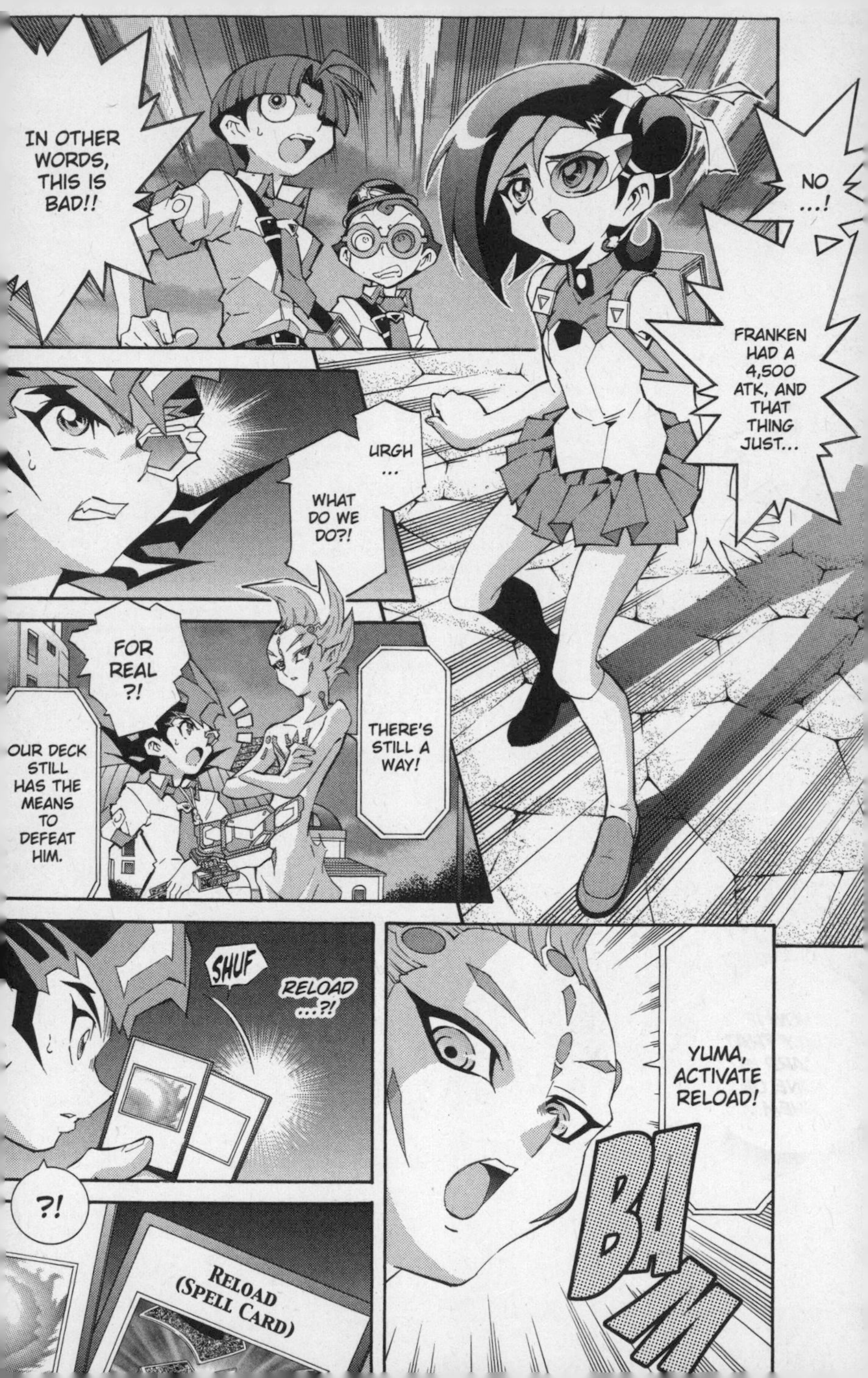
NO ...!
FRANKEN HAD A 4,500 ATK, AND THAT THING JUST...
IN OTHER WORDS, THIS IS BAD!!
URGH ...
WHAT DO WE DO?!
THERE'S STILL A WAY!
FOR REAL ?!
OUR DECK STILL HAS THE MEANS TO DEFEAT HIM.
YUMA, ACTIVATE RELOAD!
BAMM
SHUF
RELOAD ...?!
?!
RELOAD (SPELL CARD)

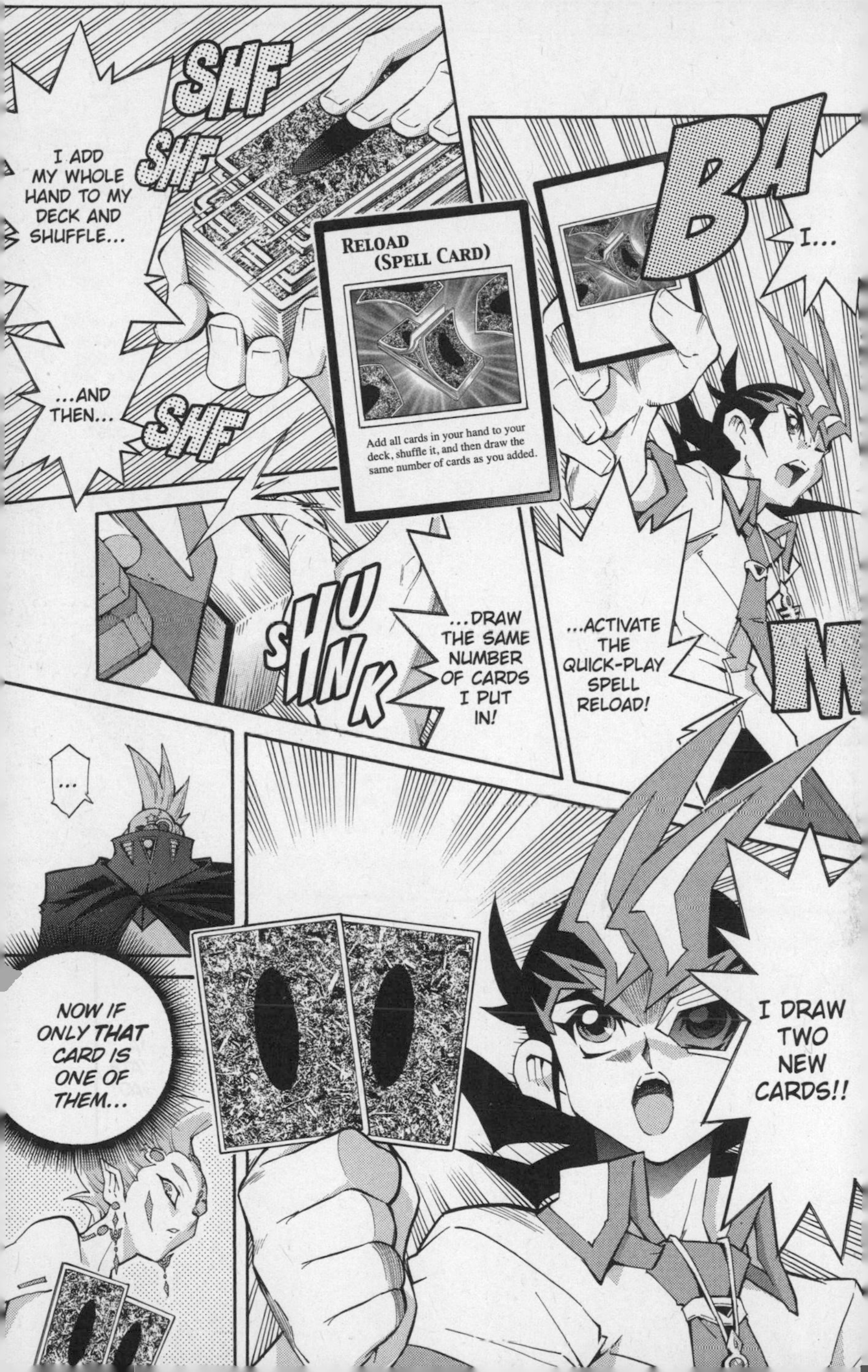
BA
I...
M
...ACTIVATE THE QUICK-PLAY SPELL RELOAD!
RELOAD (SPELL CARD)
Add all cards in your hand to your deck, shuffle it, and then draw the same number of cards as you added.
SHF
SHF
I ADD MY WHOLE HAND TO MY DECK AND SHUFFLE...
...AND THEN...
SHF
...DRAW THE SAME NUMBER OF CARDS I PUT IN!
SHUNK
I DRAW TWO NEW CARDS!!
...
NOW IF ONLY THAT CARD IS ONE OF THEM...

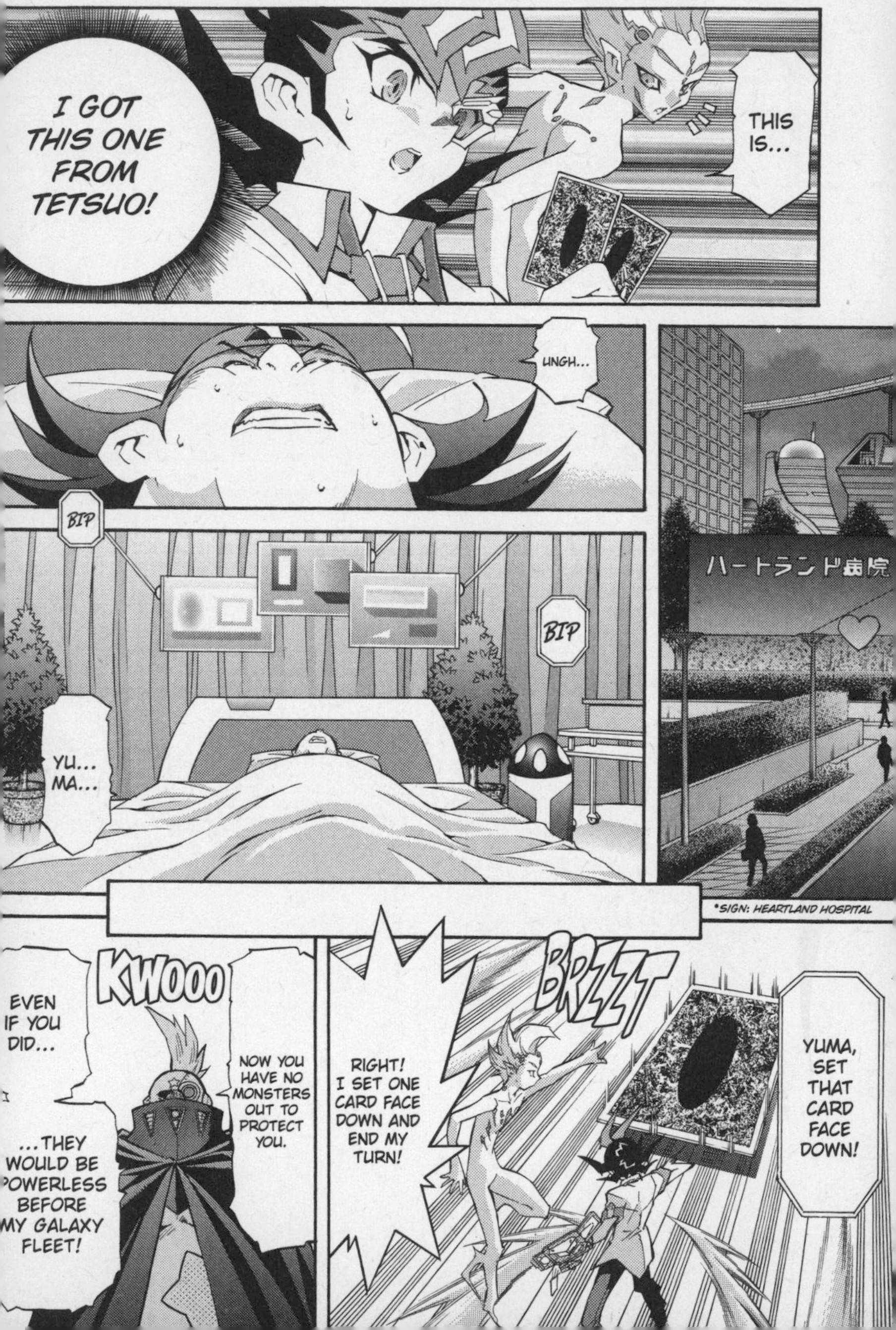
THIS IS...
I GOT THIS ONE FROM TETSUO!
ハートランド病院
*SIGN: HEARTLAND HOSPITAL
UNGH...
BIP
BIP
YU... MA...
YUMA, SET THAT CARD FACE DOWN!
BRZZT
RIGHT! I SET ONE CARD FACE DOWN AND END MY TURN!
NOW YOU HAVE NO MONSTERS OUT TO PROTECT YOU.
KWOOO
EVEN IF YOU DID...
...THEY WOULD BE POWERLESS BEFORE MY GALAXY FLEET!

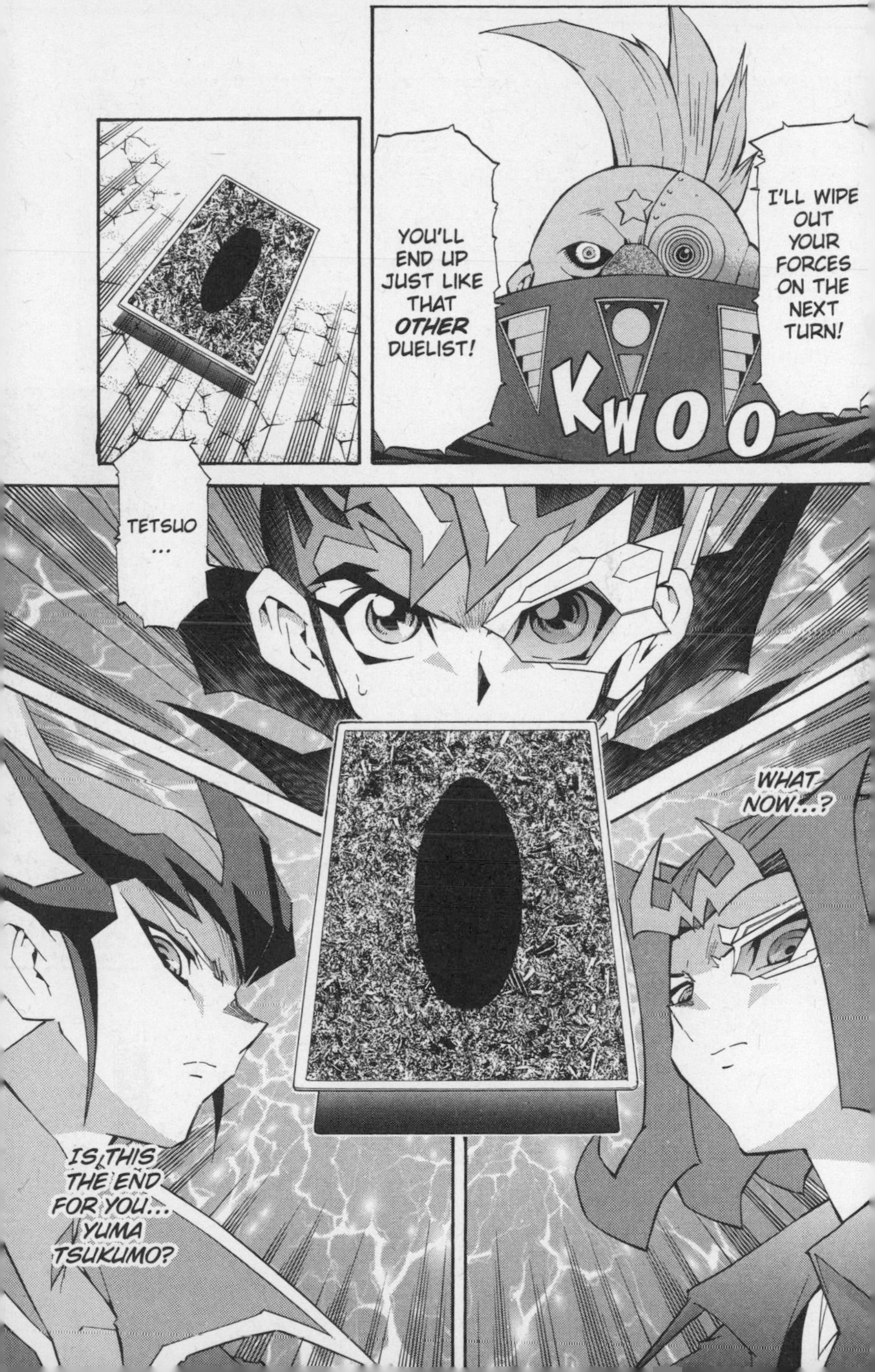
I'LL WIPE OUT YOUR FORCES ON THE NEXT TURN!
YOU'LL END UP JUST LIKE THAT *OTHER* DUELIST!
KWOO
TETSUO ...
WHAT NOW...?
IS THIS THE END FOR YOU... YUMA TSUKUMO?

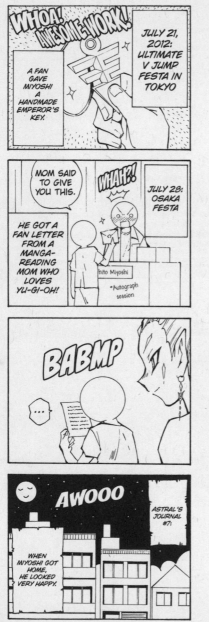

ASTRAL'S JOURNAL
#7

JULY 21, 2012: ULTIMATE V JUMP FESTA IN TOKYO
WHOA! AWESOME WORK!
A FAN GAVE MIYOSHI A HANDMADE EMPEROR'S KEY.
JULY 28: OSAKA FESTA
WHAH?!
MOM SAID TO GIVE YOU THIS.
HE GOT A FAN LETTER FROM A MANGA-READING MOM WHO LOVES YU-GI-OH!
hito Miyoshi
*Autograph session
BABMP
...
ASTRAL'S JOURNAL #7:
AWOOO
WHEN MIYOSHI GOT HOME, HE LOOKED VERY HAPPY.

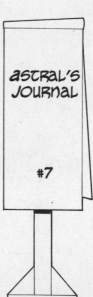

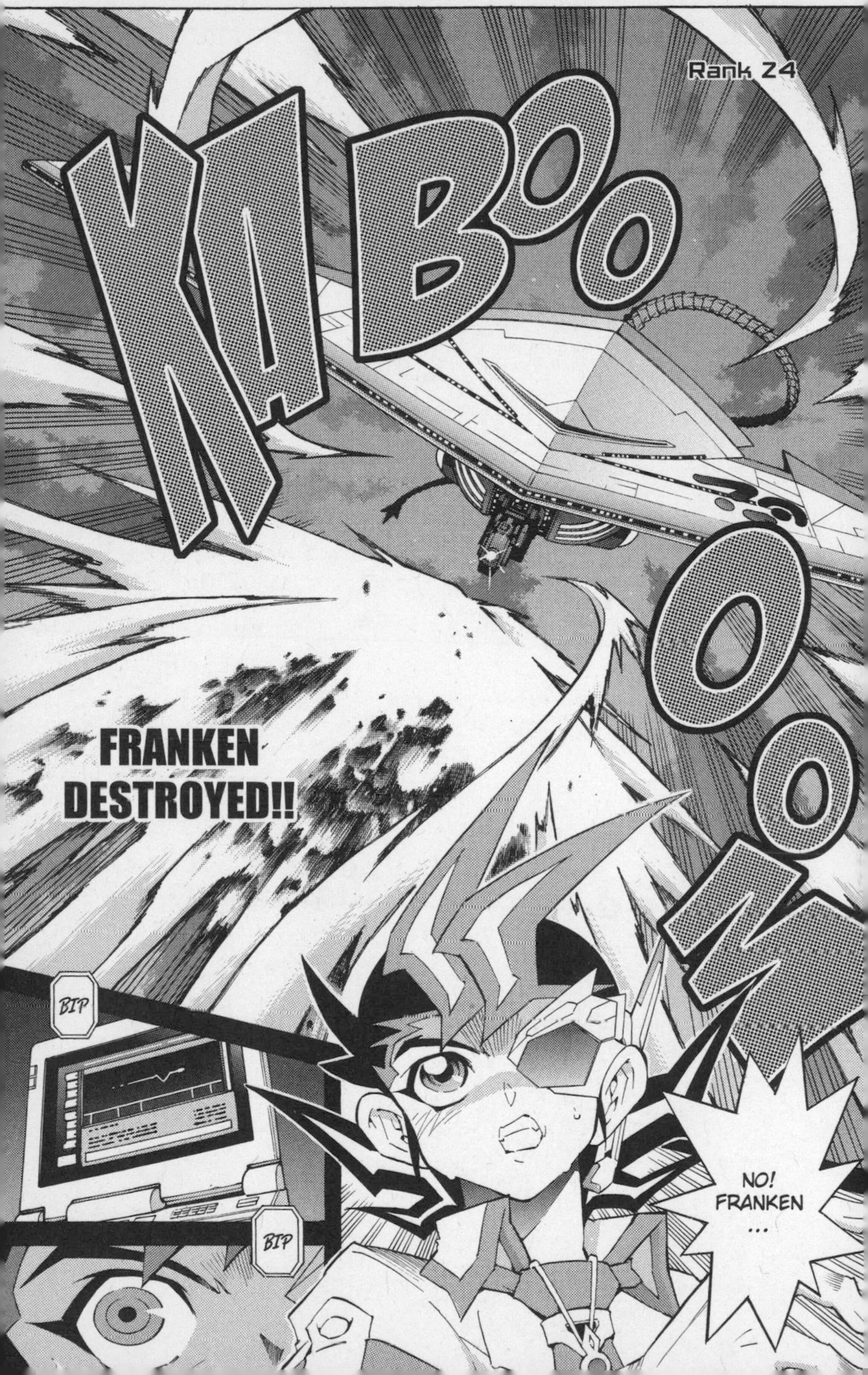
KABOOOOM
FRANKEN DESTROYED!!
NO! FRANKEN ...
BIP
BIP

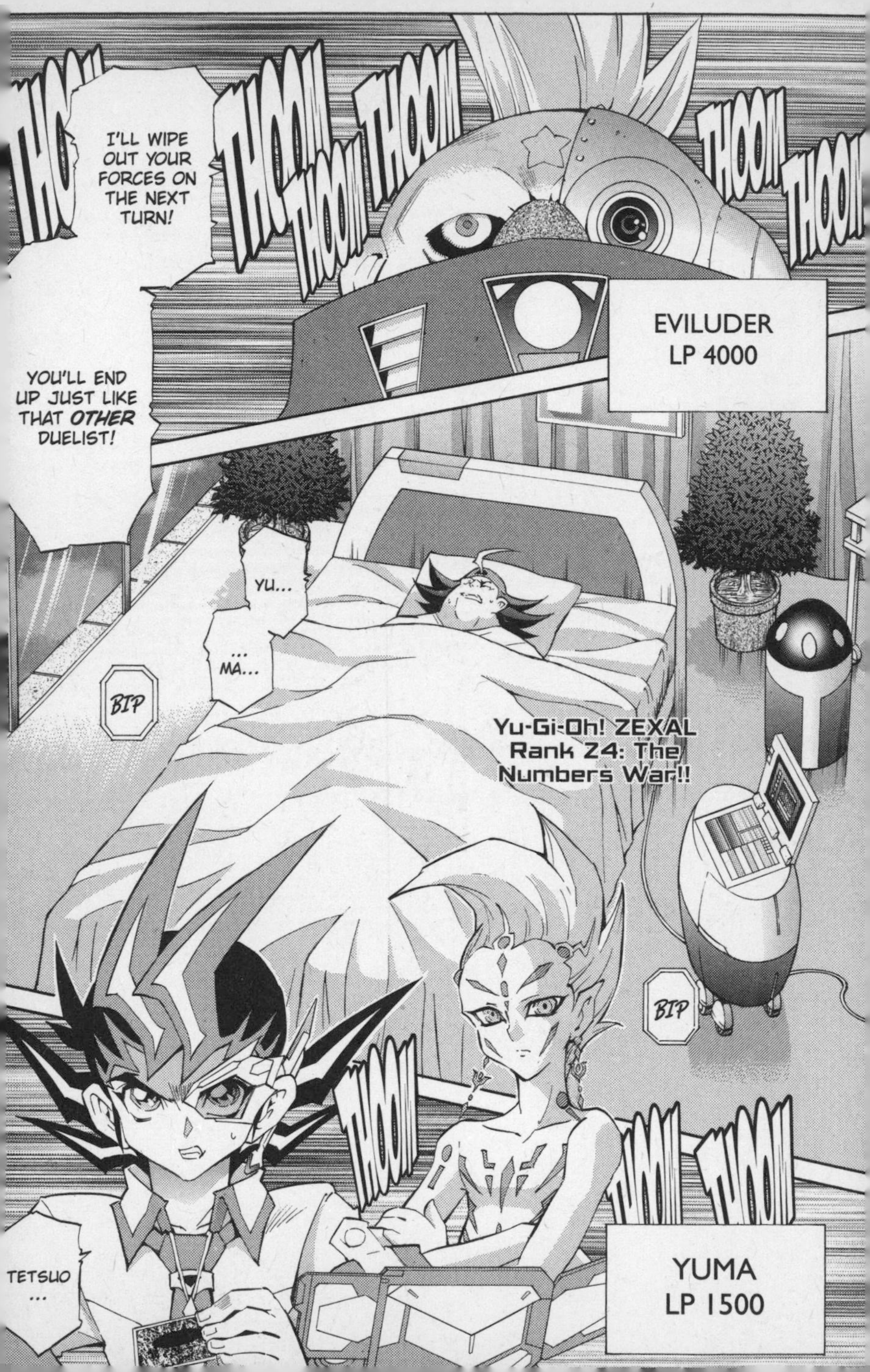
THOOM THOOM
EVILUDER
LP 4000
THOOM THOOM THOOM
I'LL WIPE OUT YOUR FORCES ON THE NEXT TURN!
YOU'LL END UP JUST LIKE THAT *OTHER* DUELIST!
Yu-Gi-Oh! ZEXAL
Rank 24: The Numbers War!!
BIP
YU...
...MA...
BIP
THOOM THOOM THOOM
YUMA
LP 1500
TETSUO ...

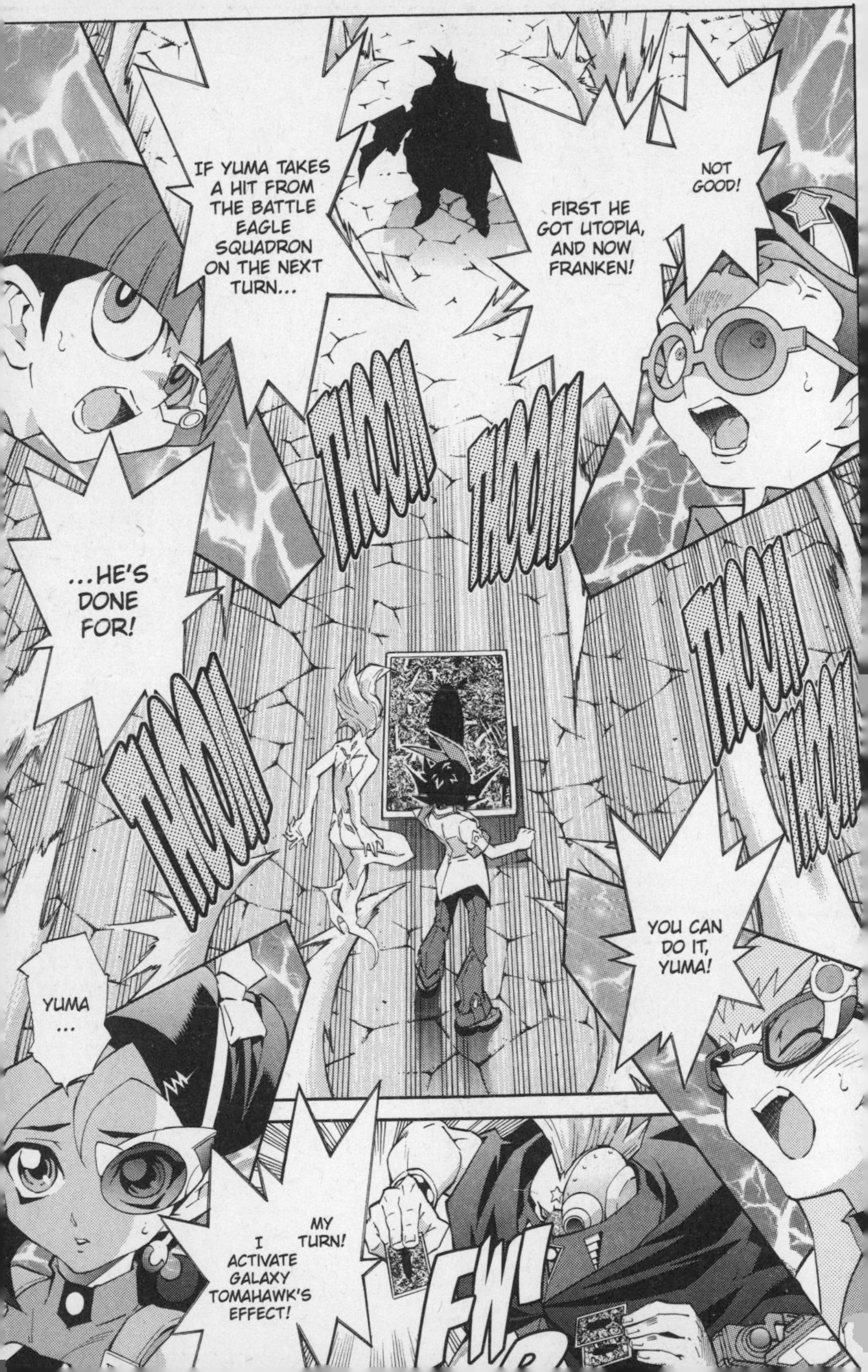
NOT GOOD!
FIRST HE GOT UTOPIA, AND NOW FRANKEN!
IF YUMA TAKES A HIT FROM THE BATTLE EAGLE SQUADRON ON THE NEXT TURN...
THOOM
THOOM
THOOM
THOOM
...HE'S DONE FOR!
THOOM
YOU CAN DO IT, YUMA!
YUMA ...
MY TURN!
I ACTIVATE GALAXY TOMAHAWK'S EFFECT!

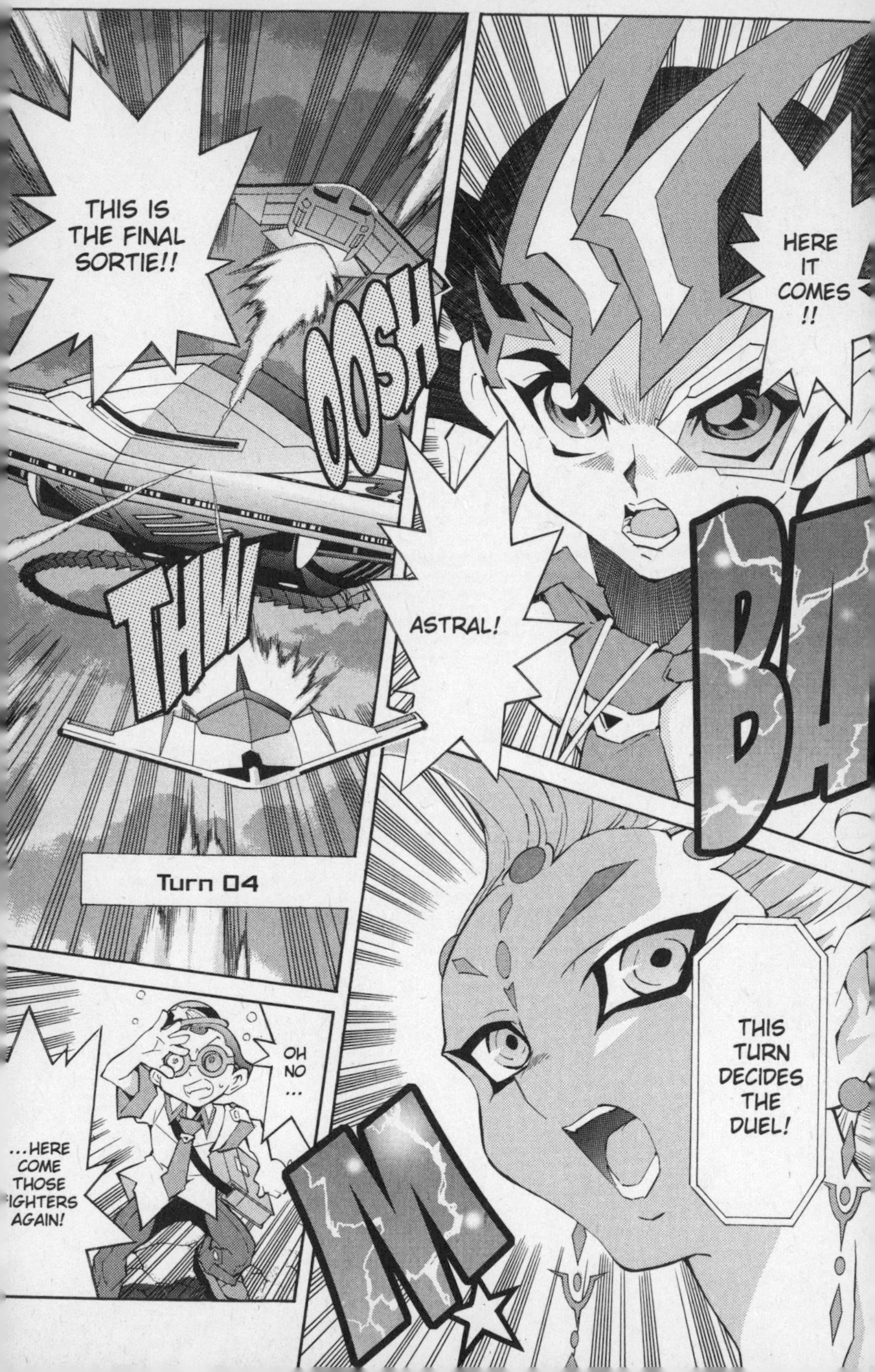
HERE IT COMES!!
ASTRAL!
THIS IS THE FINAL SORTIE!!
OOSH
THW
BA
THIS TURN DECIDES THE DUEL!
M
Turn 04
OH NO ...
...HERE COME THOSE FIGHTERS AGAIN!

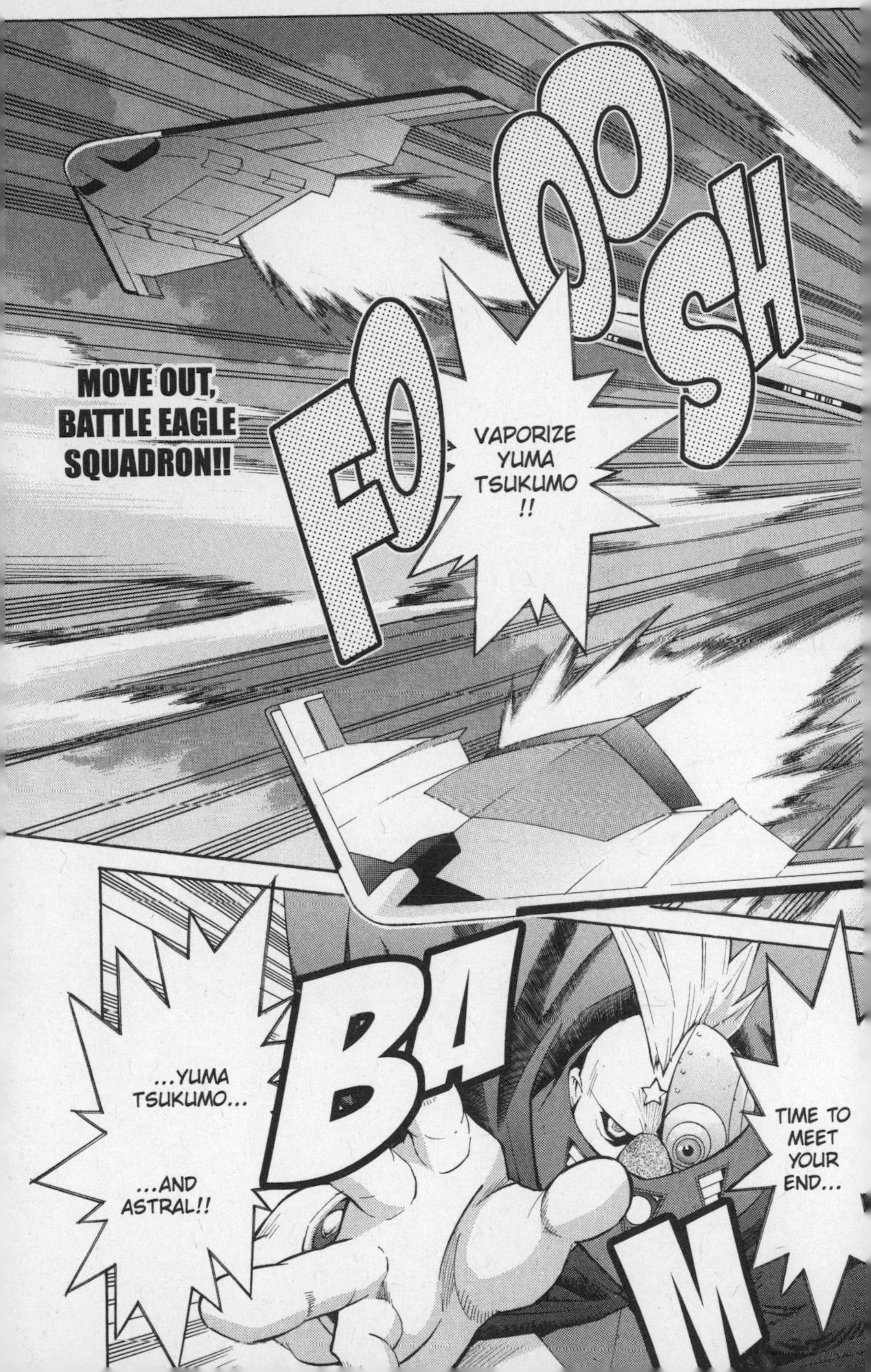
FOOOOSH
VAPORIZE YUMA TSUKUMO!!
MOVE OUT, BATTLE EAGLE SQUADRON!!
TIME TO MEET YOUR END...
BAM
...YUMA TSUKUMO...
...AND ASTRAL!!

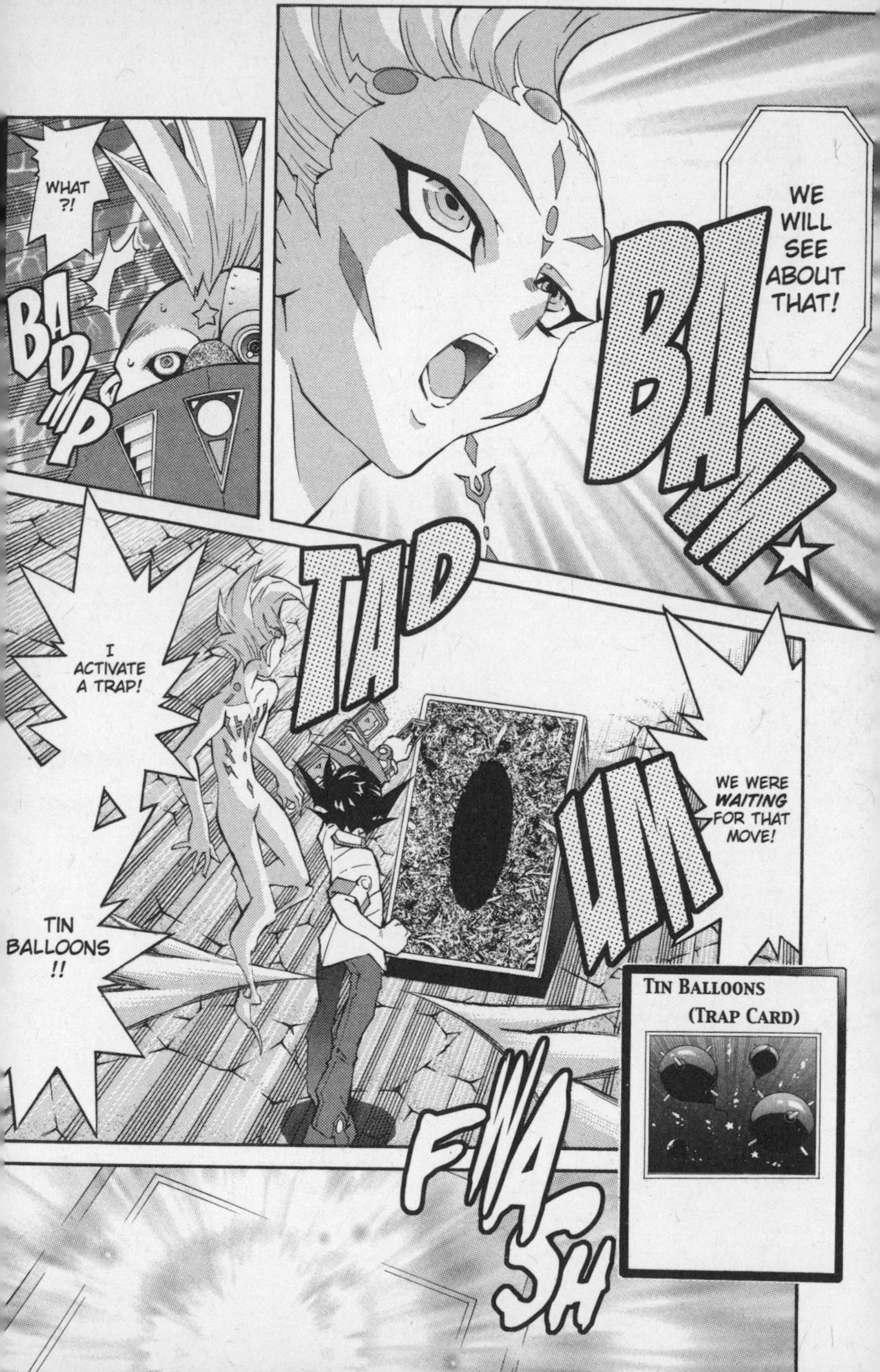
WE WILL SEE ABOUT THAT!
BAM
WHAT ?!
BADMP
TAD
WUM
WE WERE WAITING FOR THAT MOVE!
I ACTIVATE A TRAP!
TIN BALLOONS !!
TIN BALLOONS
(TRAP CARD)
FWASH

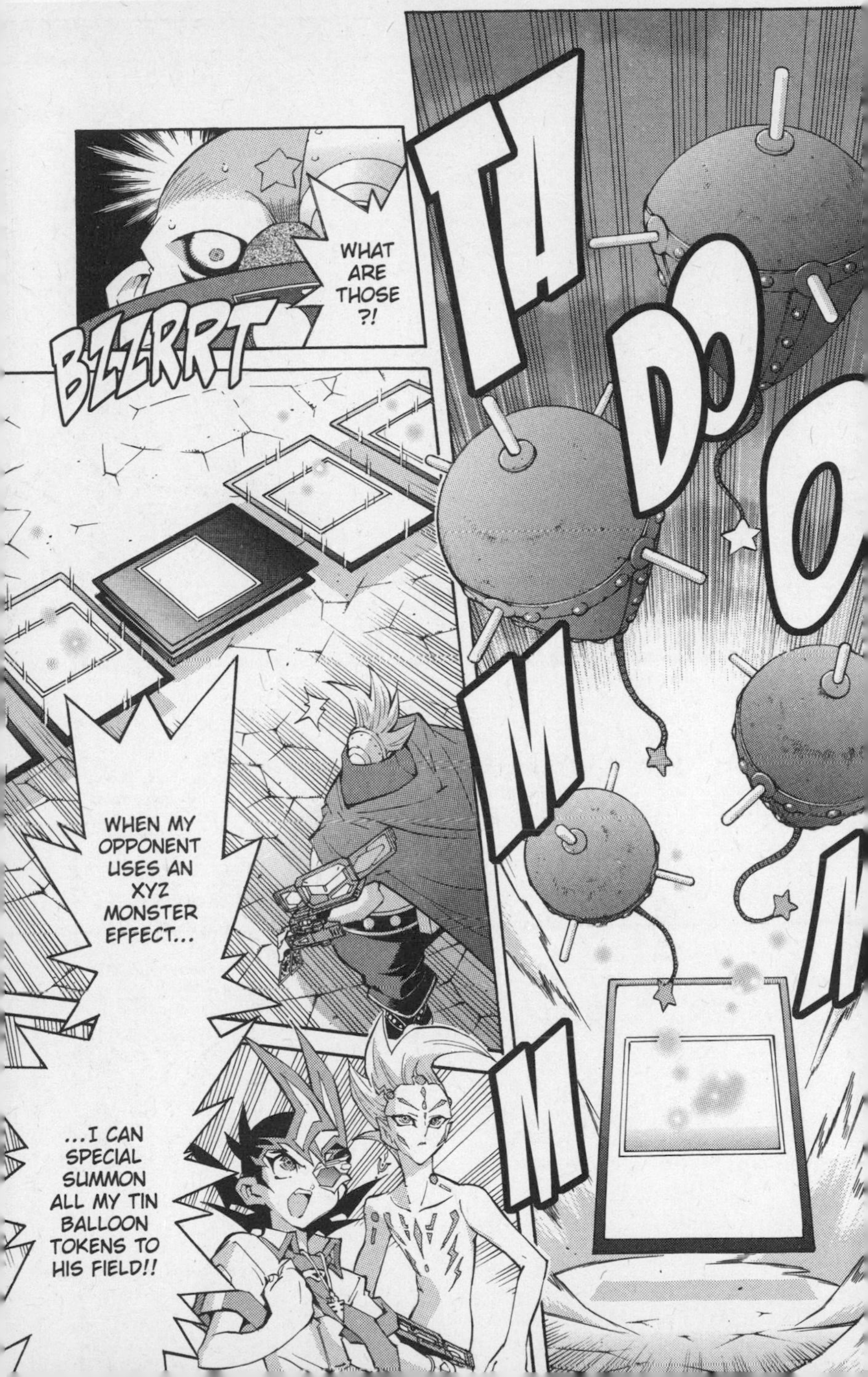
TADOOMMM
BZZRRT
WHAT ARE THOSE ?!
WHEN MY OPPONENT USES AN XYZ MONSTER EFFECT...
...I CAN SPECIAL SUMMON ALL MY TIN BALLOON TOKENS TO HIS FIELD!!

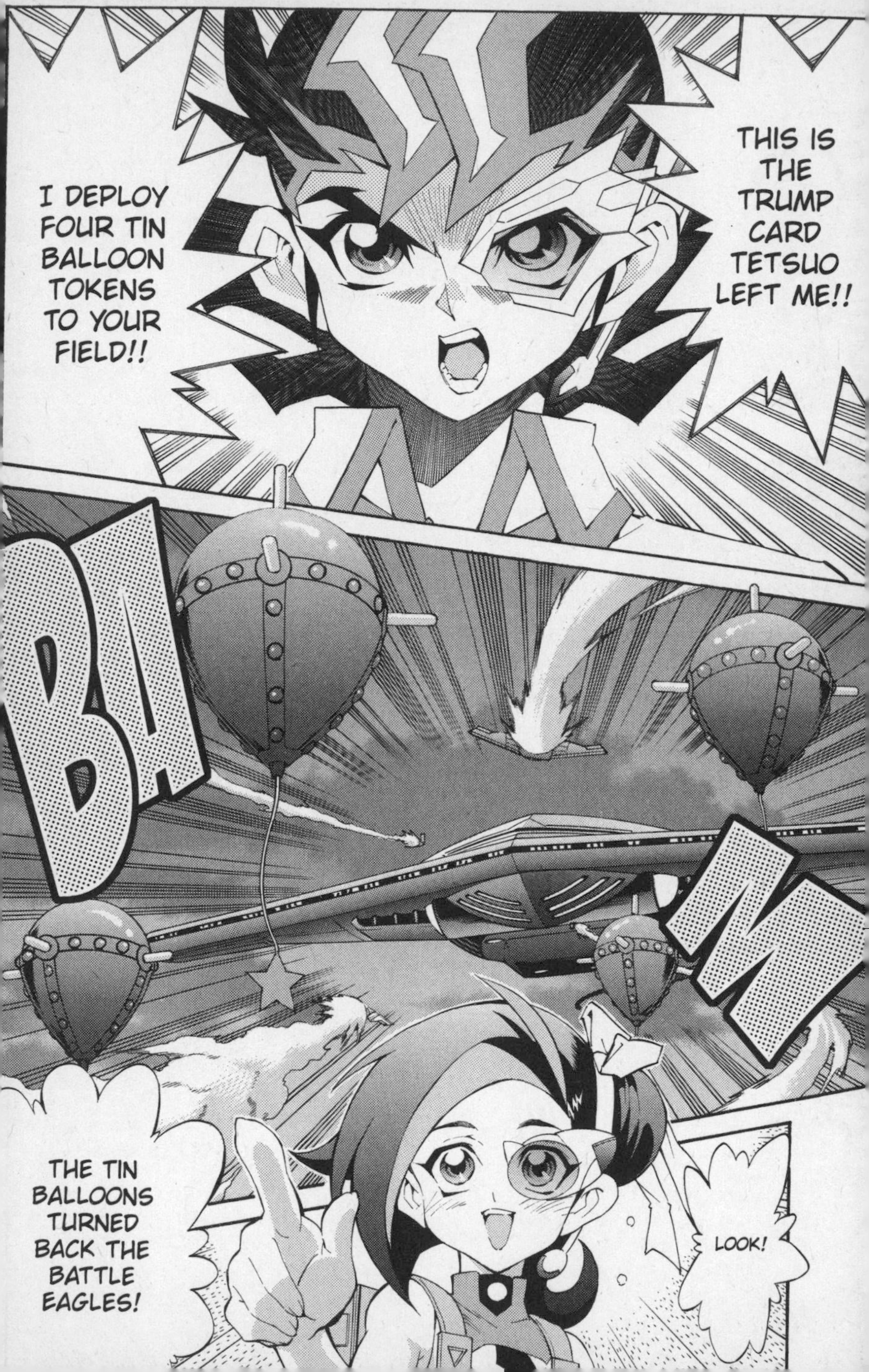
THIS IS THE TRUMP CARD TETSUO LEFT ME!!
I DEPLOY FOUR TIN BALLOON TOKENS TO YOUR FIELD!!
BAM
LOOK!
THE TIN BALLOONS TURNED BACK THE BATTLE EAGLES!

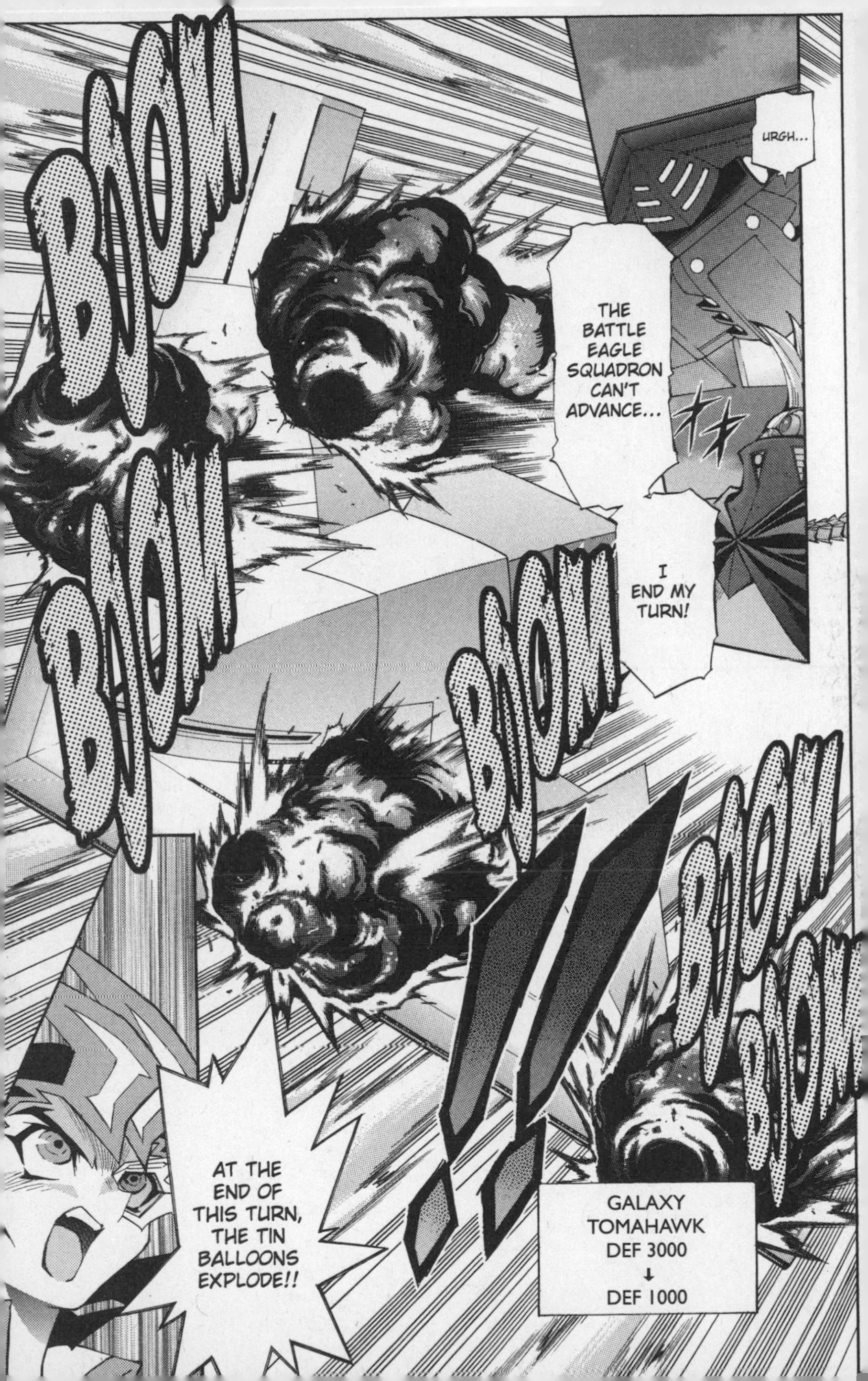
URGH...
THE BATTLE EAGLE SQUADRON CAN'T ADVANCE...
I END MY TURN!
BOOM
BOOM
BOOM
BOOM
BOOM
BOOM
GALAXY TOMAHAWK DEF 3000 ↓ DEF 1000
AT THE END OF THIS TURN, THE TIN BALLOONS EXPLODE!!

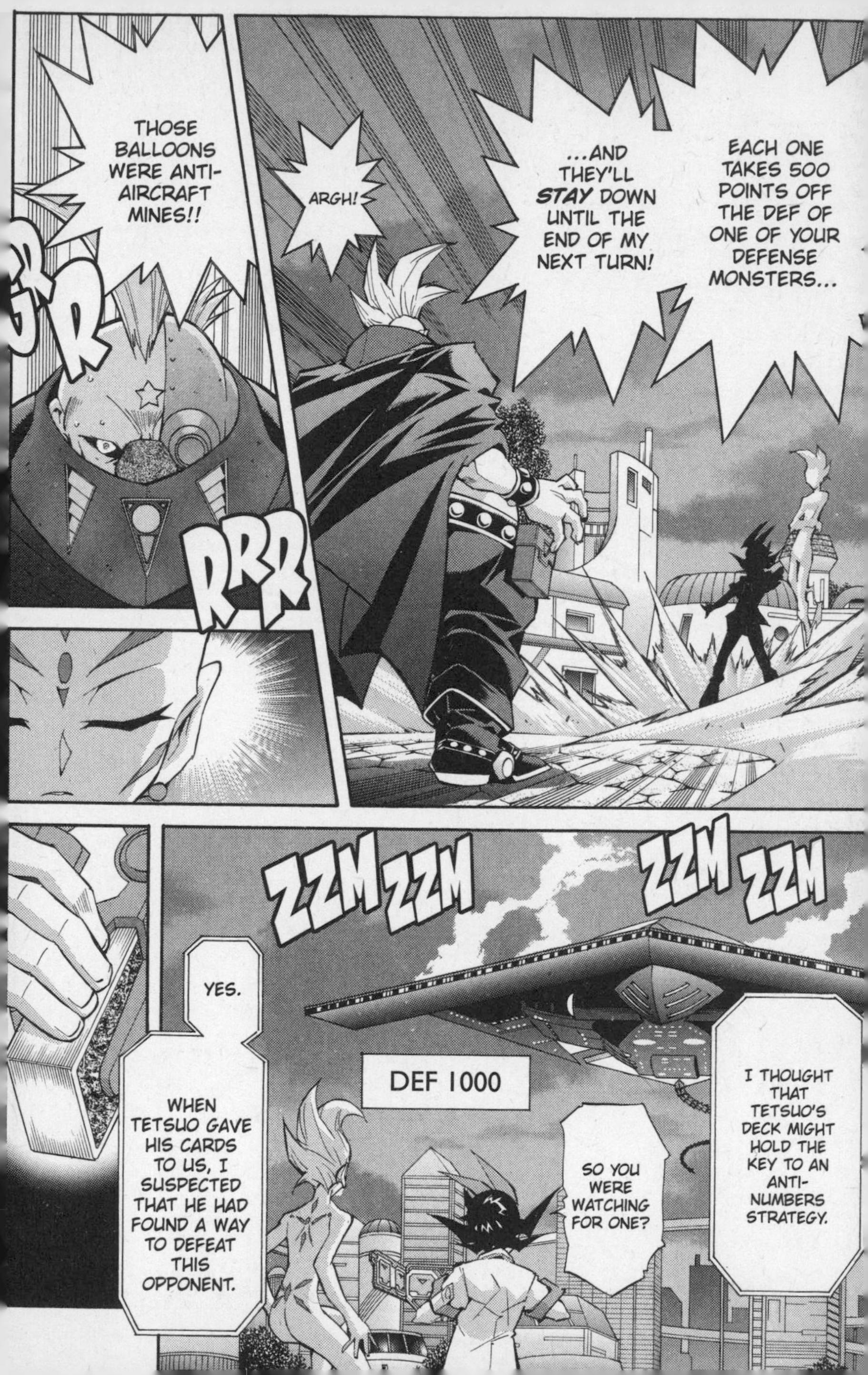
EACH ONE TAKES 500 POINTS OFF THE DEF OF ONE OF YOUR DEFENSE MONSTERS...
...AND THEY'LL STAY DOWN UNTIL THE END OF MY NEXT TURN!
ARGH!
THOSE BALLOONS WERE ANTI-AIRCRAFT MINES!!
GRR
RRR
ZZM ZZM
ZZM ZZM
DEF 1000
I THOUGHT THAT TETSUO'S DECK MIGHT HOLD THE KEY TO AN ANTI-NUMBERS STRATEGY.
SO YOU WERE WATCHING FOR ONE?
YES.
WHEN TETSUO GAVE HIS CARDS TO US, I SUSPECTED THAT HE HAD FOUND A WAY TO DEFEAT THIS OPPONENT.

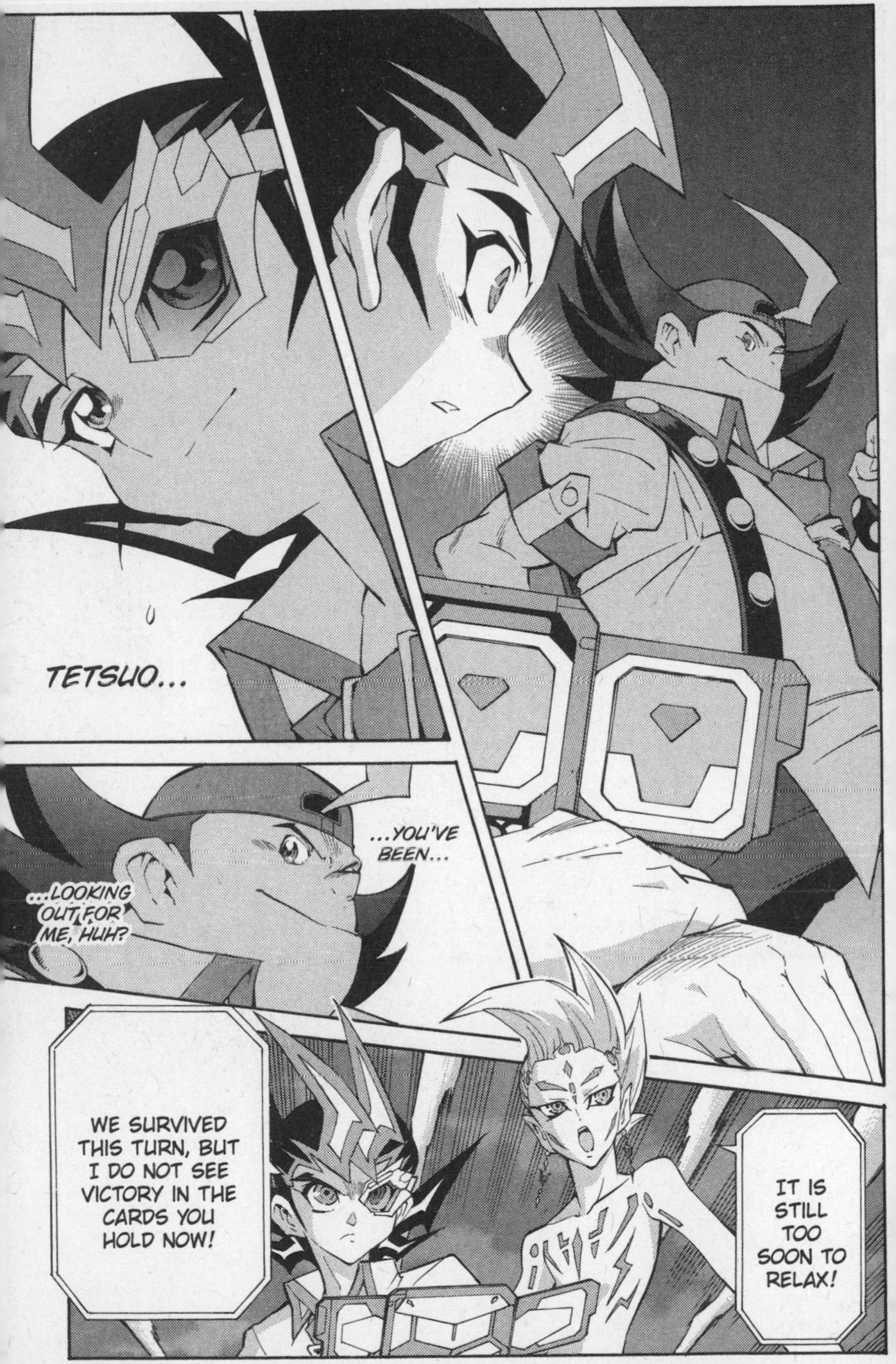
TETSUO...
...YOU'VE BEEN...
...LOOKING OUT FOR ME, HUH?
WE SURVIVED THIS TURN, BUT I DO NOT SEE VICTORY IN THE CARDS YOU HOLD NOW!
IT IS STILL TOO SOON TO RELAX!

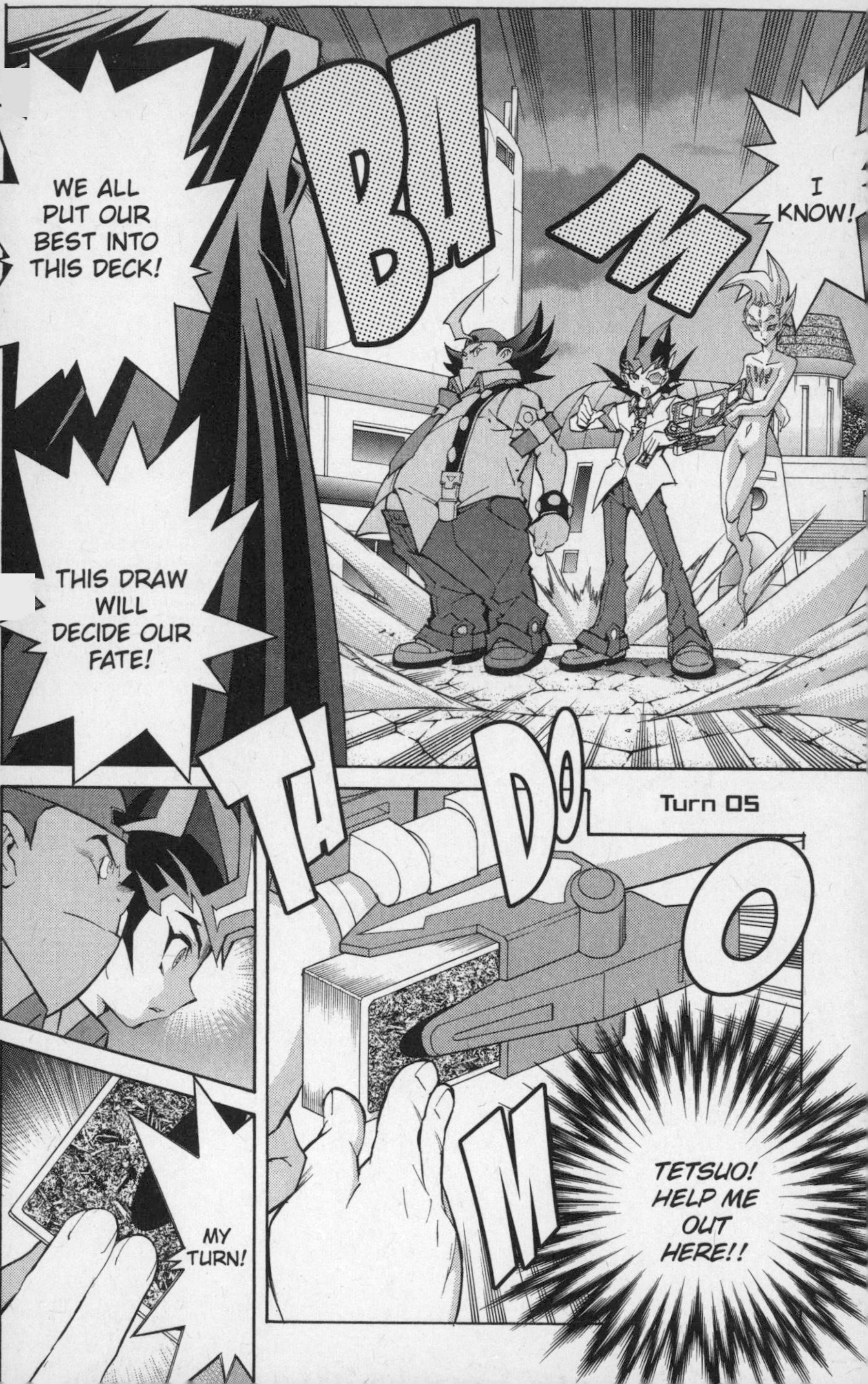
I KNOW!
BAM
WE ALL PUT OUR BEST INTO THIS DECK!
THIS DRAW WILL DECIDE OUR FATE!
Turn 05
TETSUO! HELP ME OUT HERE!!
MY TURN!

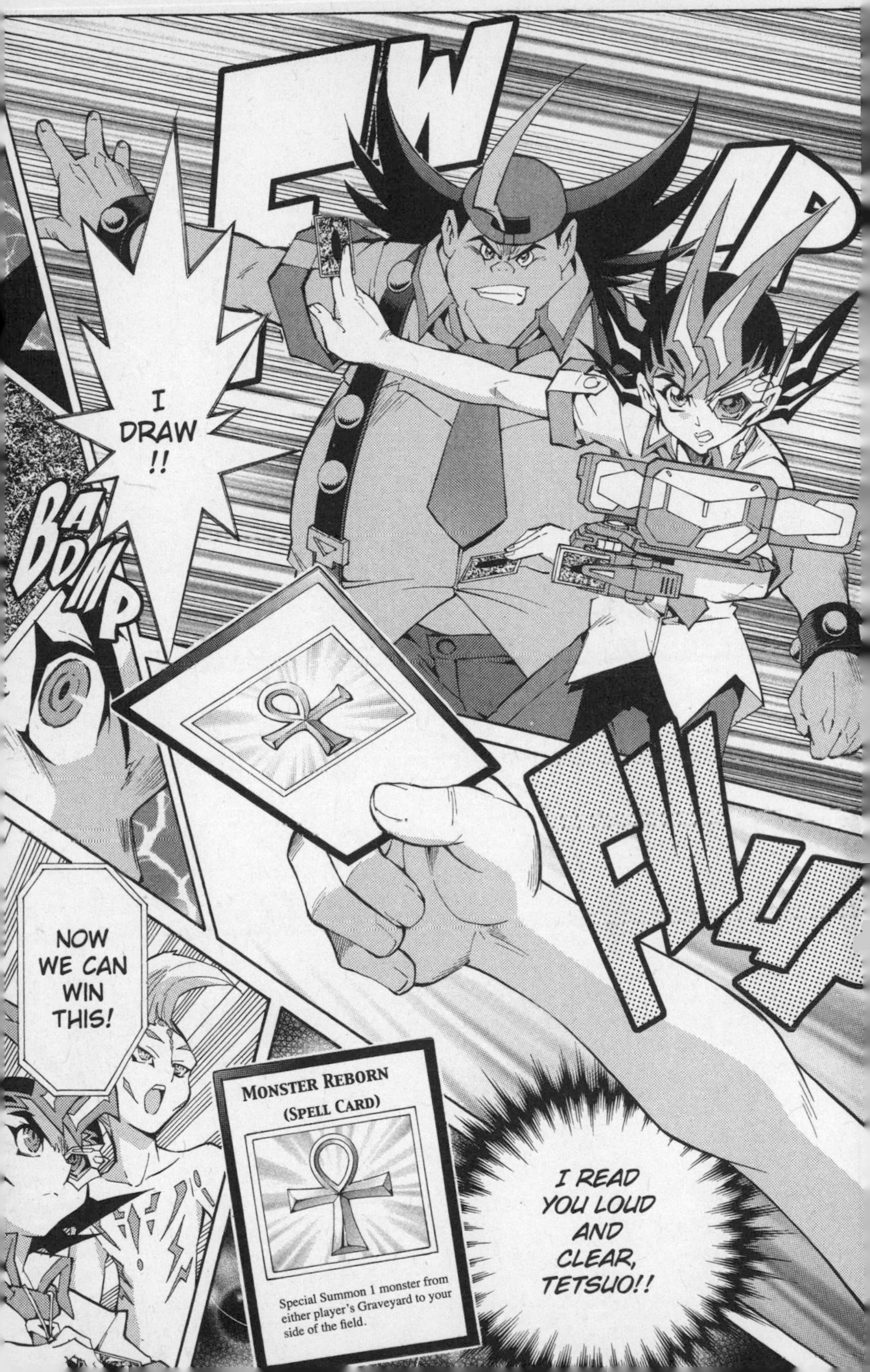
I DRAW!!
I READ YOU LOUD AND CLEAR, TETSUO!!
MONSTER REBORN
(SPELL CARD)
Special Summon 1 monster from either player's Graveyard to your side of the field.
NOW WE CAN WIN THIS!

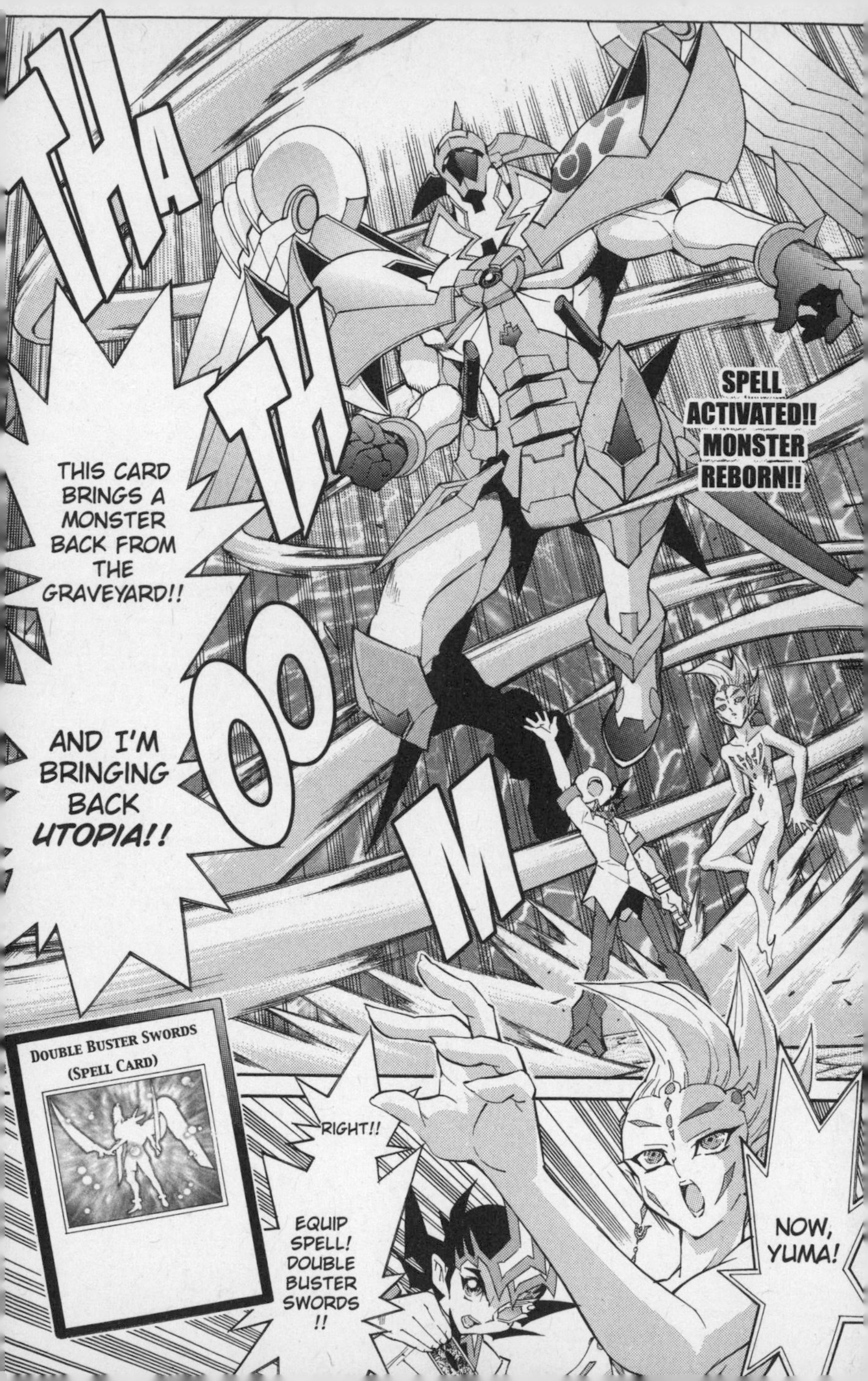
THATHOOM
SPELL ACTIVATED!! MONSTER REBORN!!
THIS CARD BRINGS A MONSTER BACK FROM THE GRAVEYARD!!
AND I'M BRINGING BACK UTOPIA!!
NOW, YUMA!
RIGHT!!
EQUIP SPELL! DOUBLE BUSTER SWORDS!!
DOUBLE BUSTER SWORDS
(SPELL CARD)

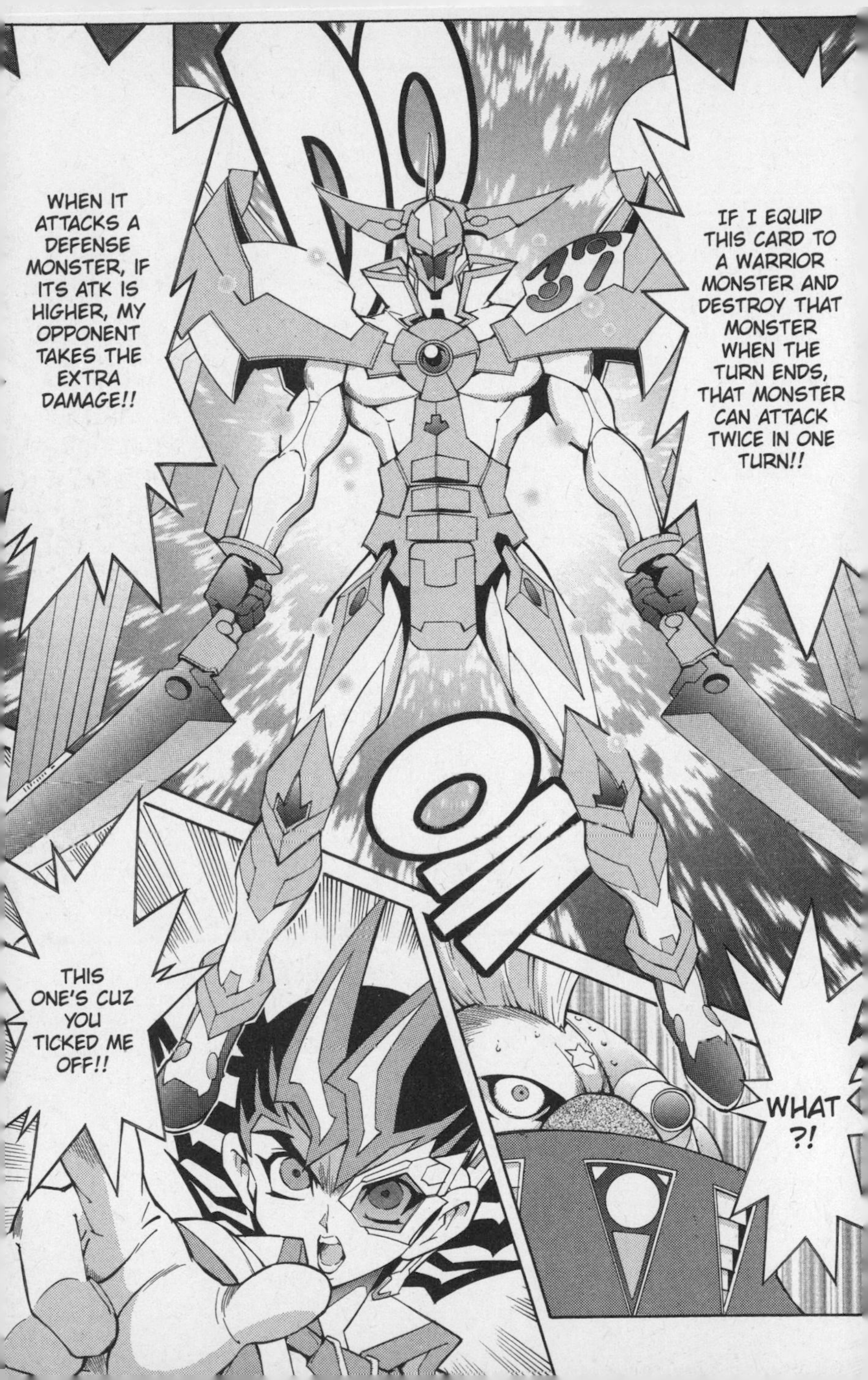
IF I EQUIP THIS CARD TO A WARRIOR MONSTER AND DESTROY THAT MONSTER WHEN THE TURN ENDS, THAT MONSTER CAN ATTACK TWICE IN ONE TURN!!
WHEN IT ATTACKS A DEFENSE MONSTER, IF ITS ATK IS HIGHER, MY OPPONENT TAKES THE EXTRA DAMAGE!!
WHAT ?!
THIS ONE'S CUZ YOU TICKED ME OFF!!

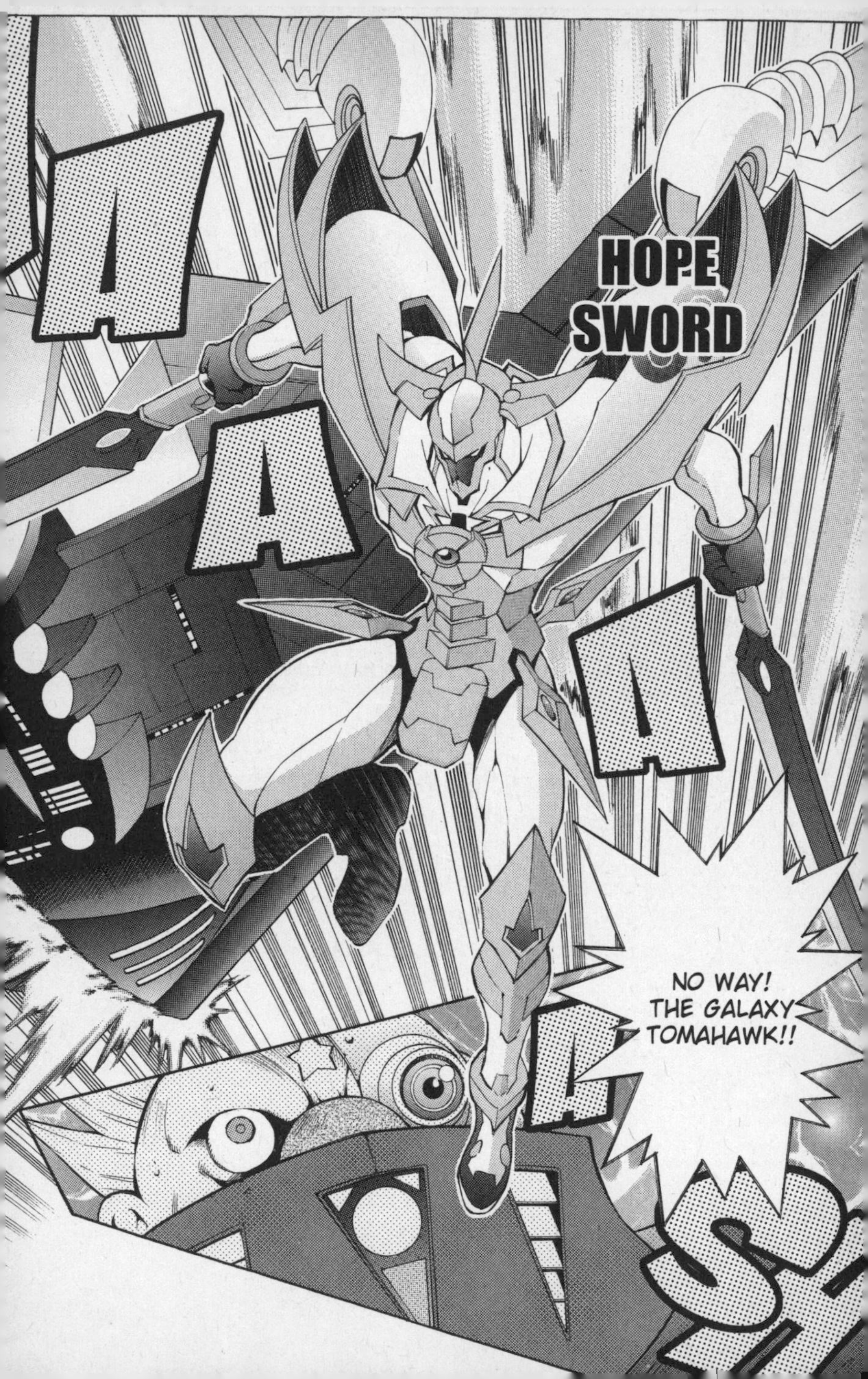
HOPE SWORD
NO WAY! THE GALAXY TOMAHAWK!!

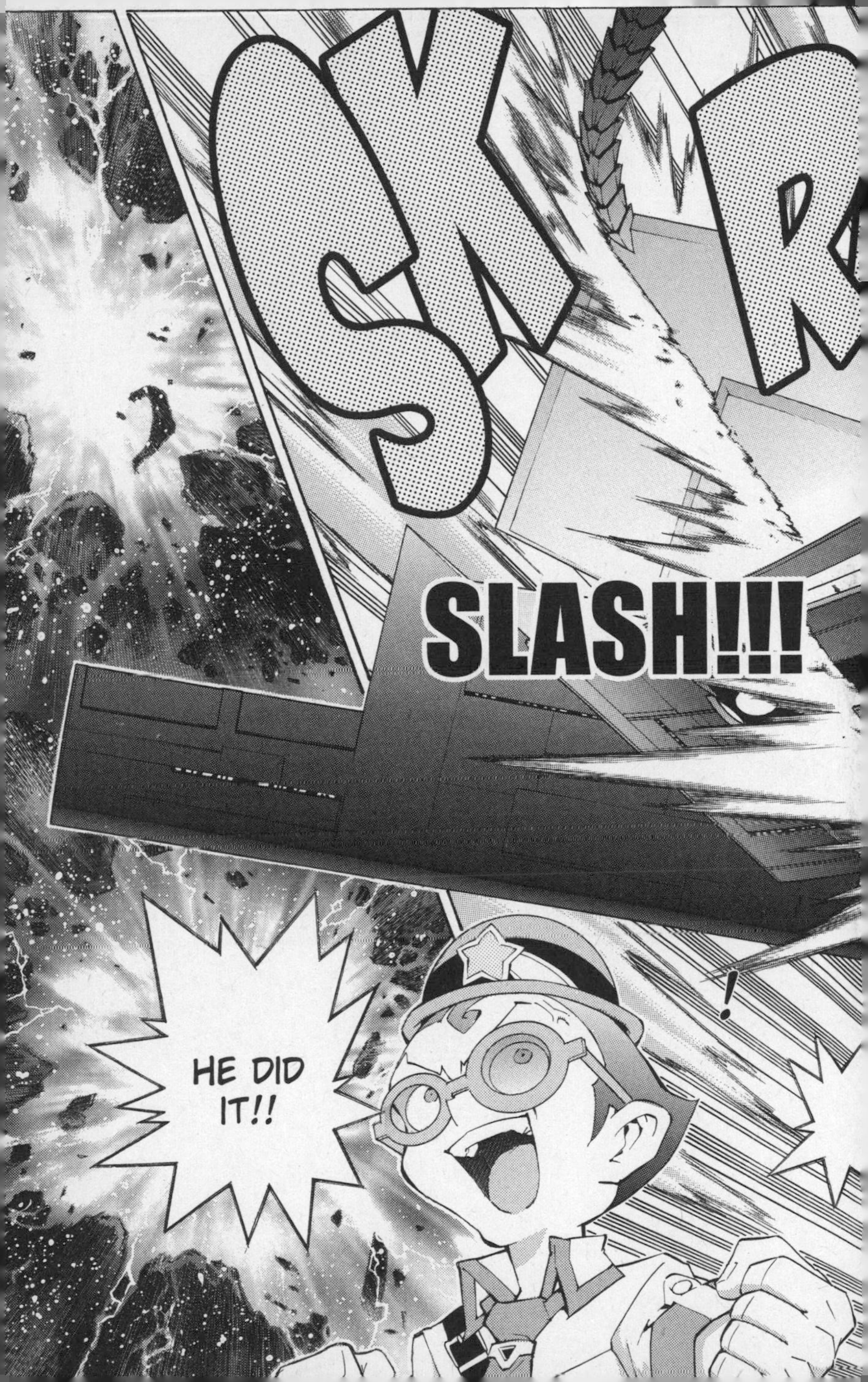
SLASH!!!
!
HE DID IT!!

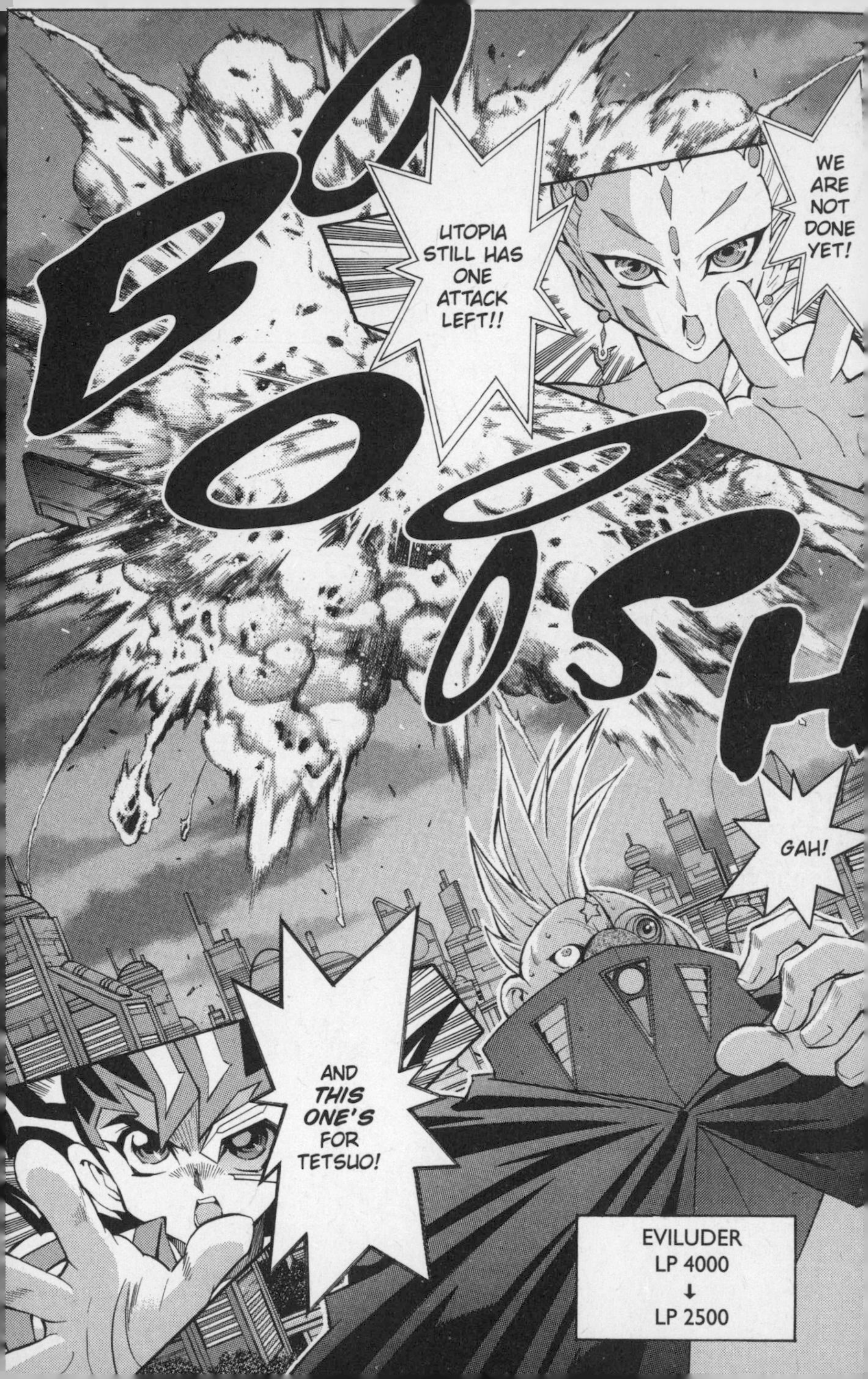
WE ARE NOT DONE YET!
UTOPIA STILL HAS ONE ATTACK LEFT!!
BOOOOSH
GAH!
AND *THIS ONE'S* FOR TETSUO!
EVILUDER LP 4000 ↓ LP 2500

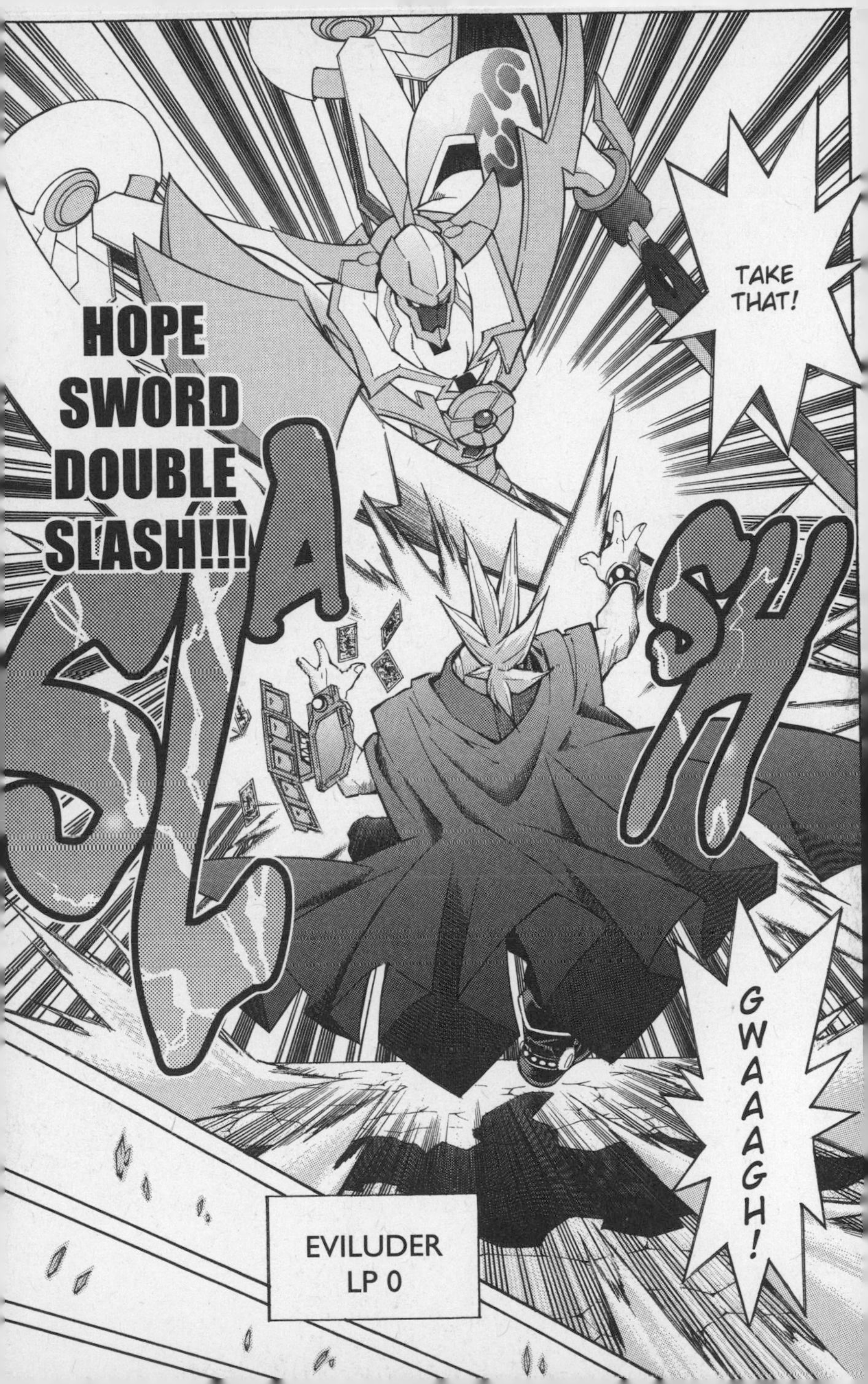
TAKE THAT!
HOPE SWORD DOUBLE SLASH!!!
SLASH
GWAAAAGH!
EVILUDER LP 0

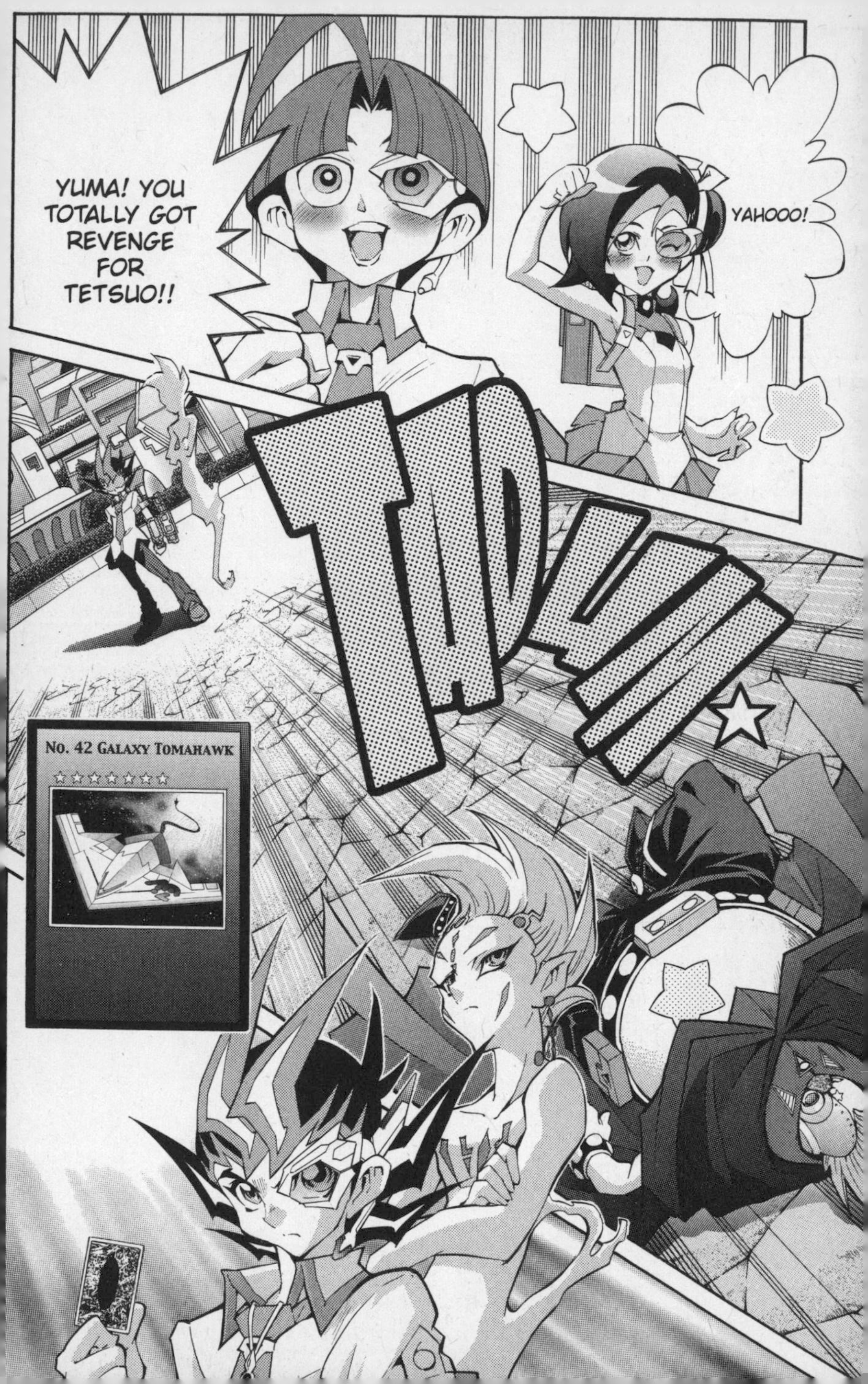
YAHOOO!
YUMA! YOU TOTALLY GOT REVENGE FOR TETSUO!!
No. 42 Galaxy Tomahawk

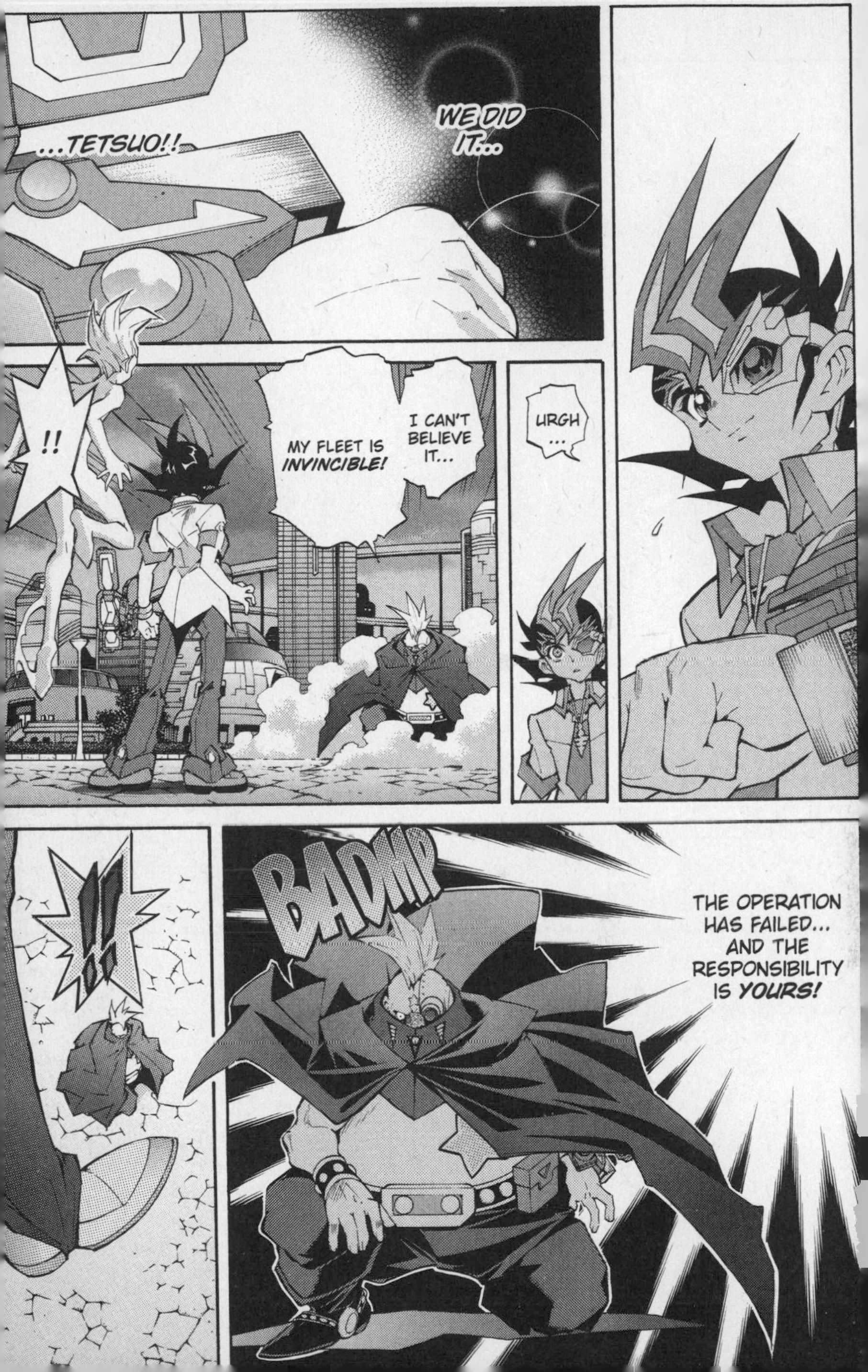
WE DID IT...
...TETSUO!!
URGH...
I CAN'T BELIEVE IT...
MY FLEET IS *INVINCIBLE!*
!!
BADOMP
THE OPERATION HAS FAILED... AND THE RESPONSIBILITY IS *YOURS!*
!!

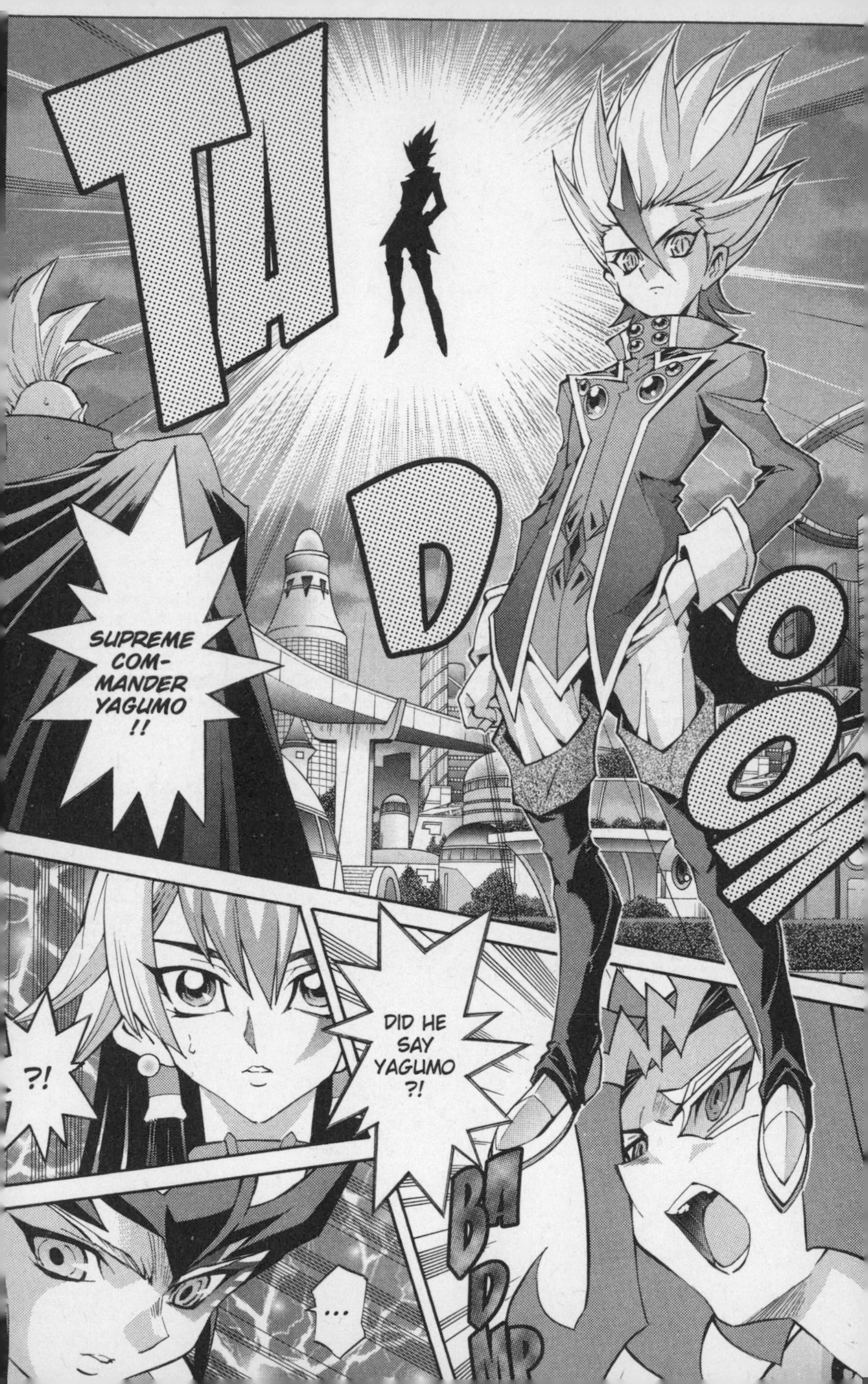
TA
D
OOM
SUPREME COM-MANDER YAGUMO !!
BA
D
UMP
DID HE SAY YAGUMO ?!
?!
...

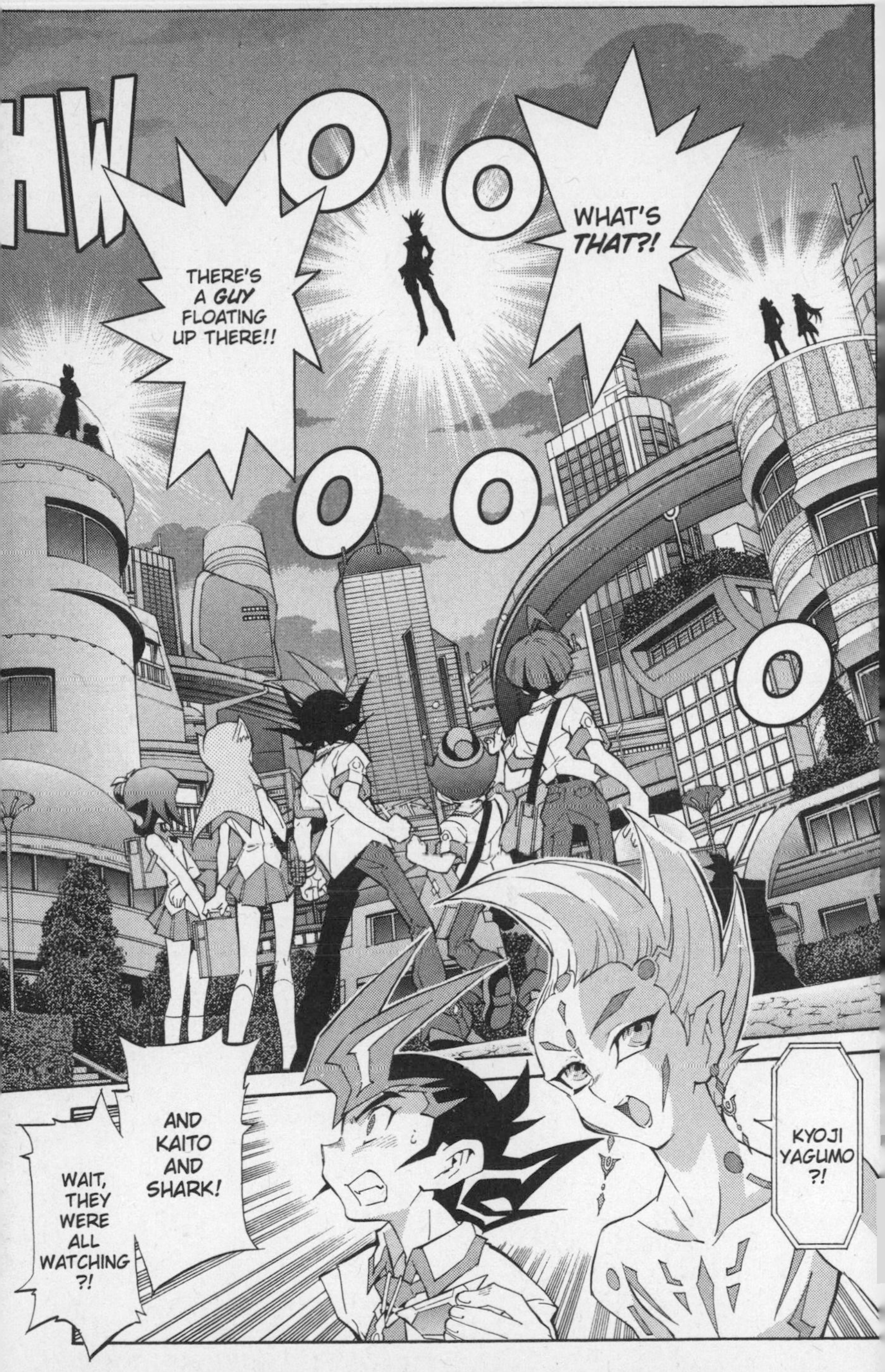
HWOOOOO
WHAT'S THAT?!
THERE'S A GUY FLOATING UP THERE!!
KYOJI YAGUMO ?!
AND KAITO AND SHARK!
WAIT, THEY WERE ALL WATCHING ?!

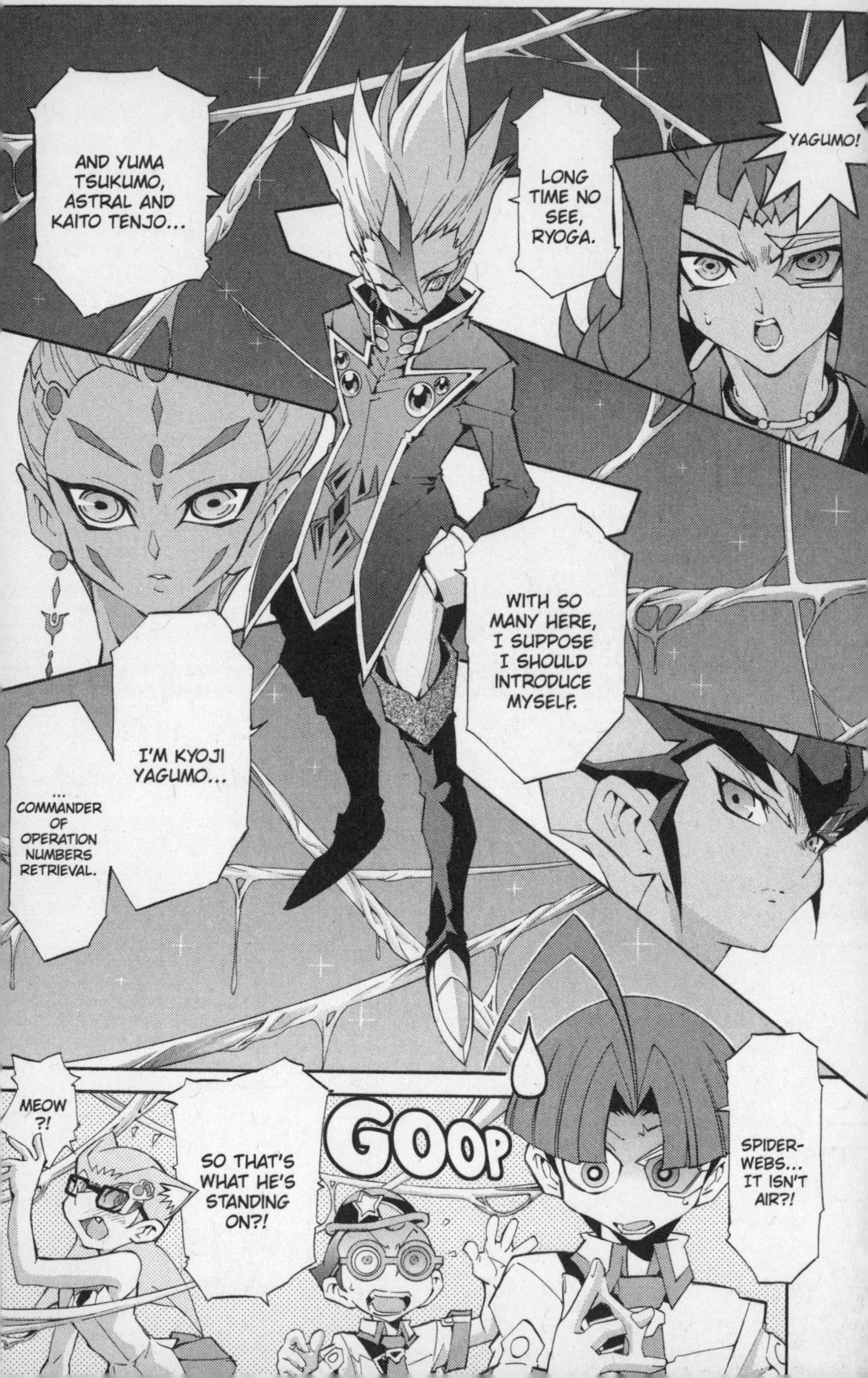
YAGUMO!
LONG TIME NO SEE, RYOGA.
AND YUMA TSUKUMO, ASTRAL AND KAITO TENJO...
WITH SO MANY HERE, I SUPPOSE I SHOULD INTRODUCE MYSELF.
I'M KYOJI YAGUMO...
... COMMANDER OF OPERATION NUMBERS RETRIEVAL.
SPIDER-WEBS... IT ISN'T AIR?!
GOOP
SO THAT'S WHAT HE'S STANDING ON?!
MEOW ?!

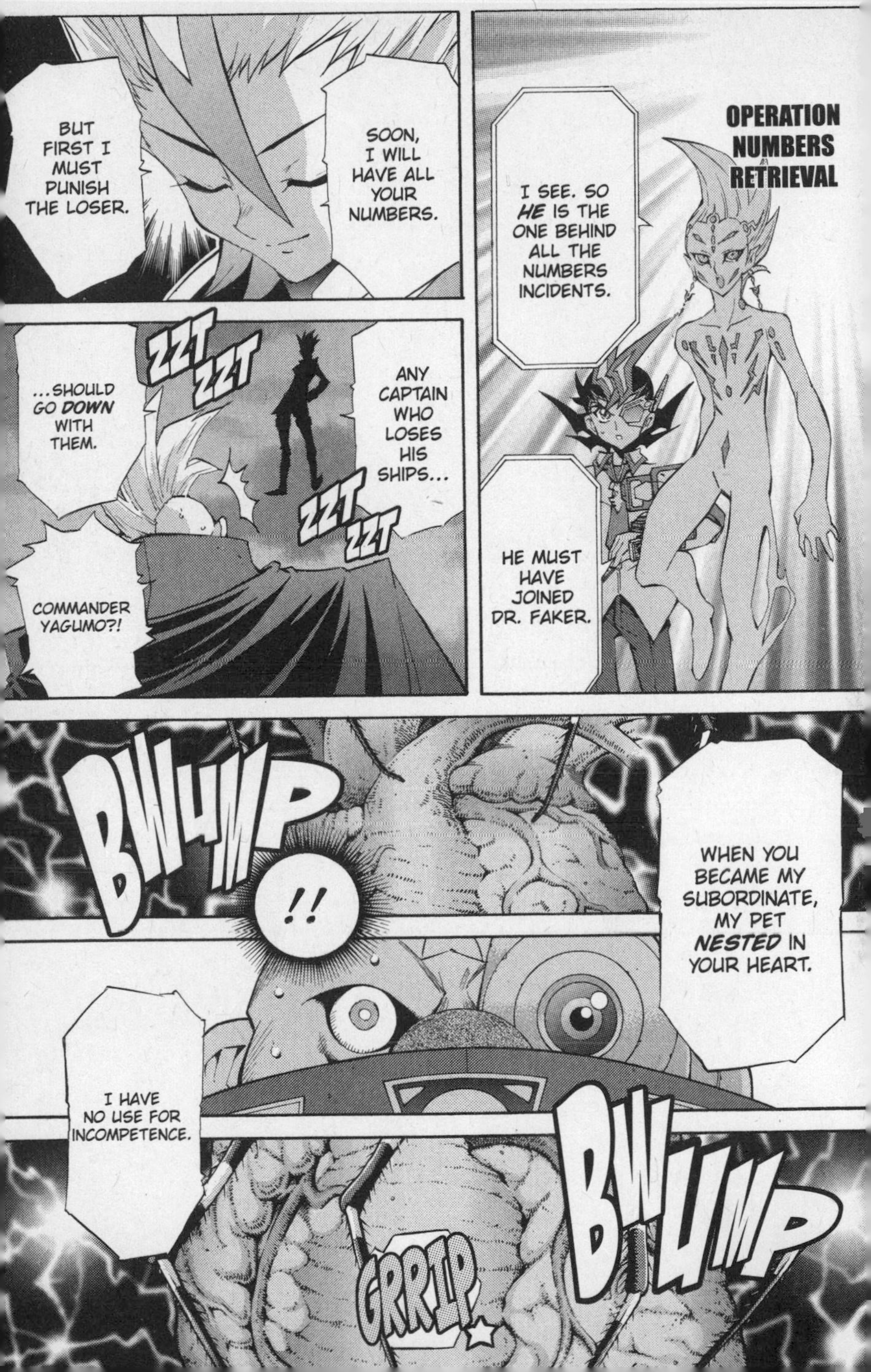
OPERATION NUMBERS RETRIEVAL
I SEE. SO HE IS THE ONE BEHIND ALL THE NUMBERS INCIDENTS.
HE MUST HAVE JOINED DR. FAKER.
SOON, I WILL HAVE ALL YOUR NUMBERS.
BUT FIRST I MUST PUNISH THE LOSER.
ANY CAPTAIN WHO LOSES HIS SHIPS...
ZZT ZZT
ZZT ZZT
...SHOULD GO DOWN WITH THEM.
COMMANDER YAGUMO?!
WHEN YOU BECAME MY SUBORDINATE, MY PET NESTED IN YOUR HEART.
BWUMP
!!
I HAVE NO USE FOR INCOMPETENCE.
BWUMP
GRRIP

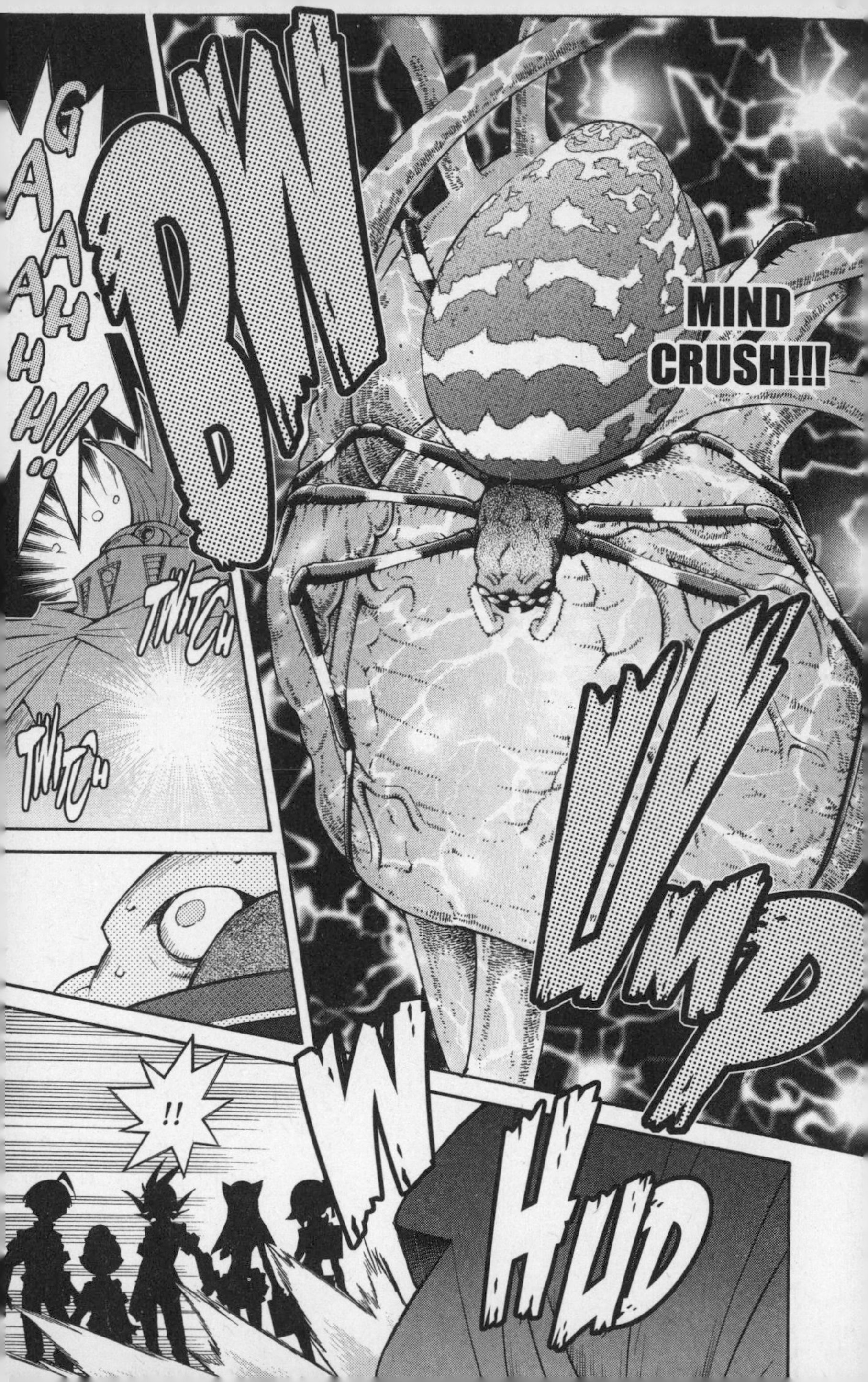
MIND CRUSH!!!
GAAAHHH!!..
TWITCH
TWITCH
!!

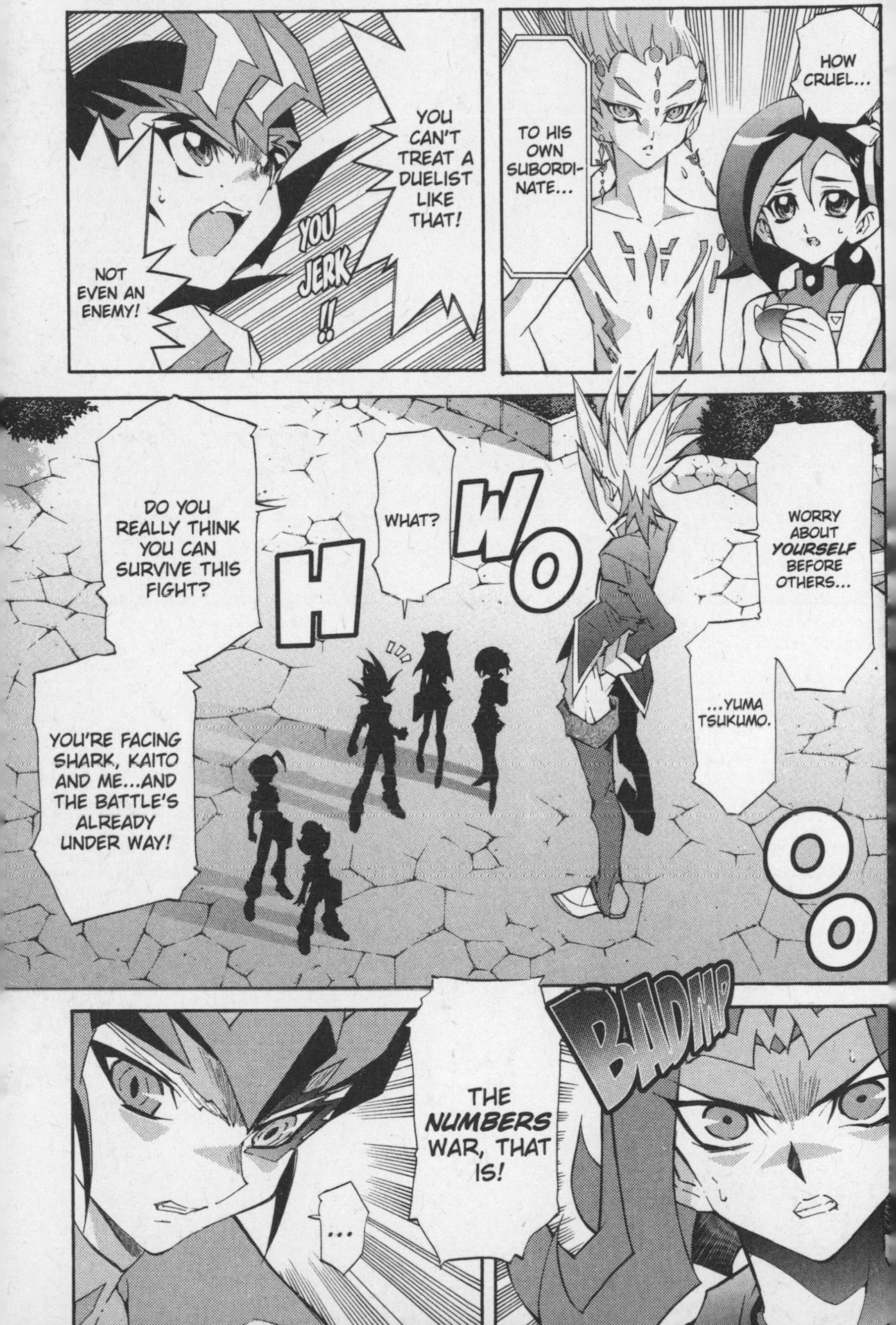
HOW CRUEL...
TO HIS OWN SUBORDINATE...
YOU CAN'T TREAT A DUELIST LIKE THAT!
YOU JERK!!
NOT EVEN AN ENEMY!
WORRY ABOUT *YOURSELF* BEFORE OTHERS...
...YUMA TSUKUMO.
HWOOO
WHAT?
DO YOU REALLY THINK YOU CAN SURVIVE THIS FIGHT?
YOU'RE FACING SHARK, KAITO AND ME...AND THE BATTLE'S ALREADY UNDER WAY!
BADMP
THE *NUMBERS* WAR, THAT IS!
...

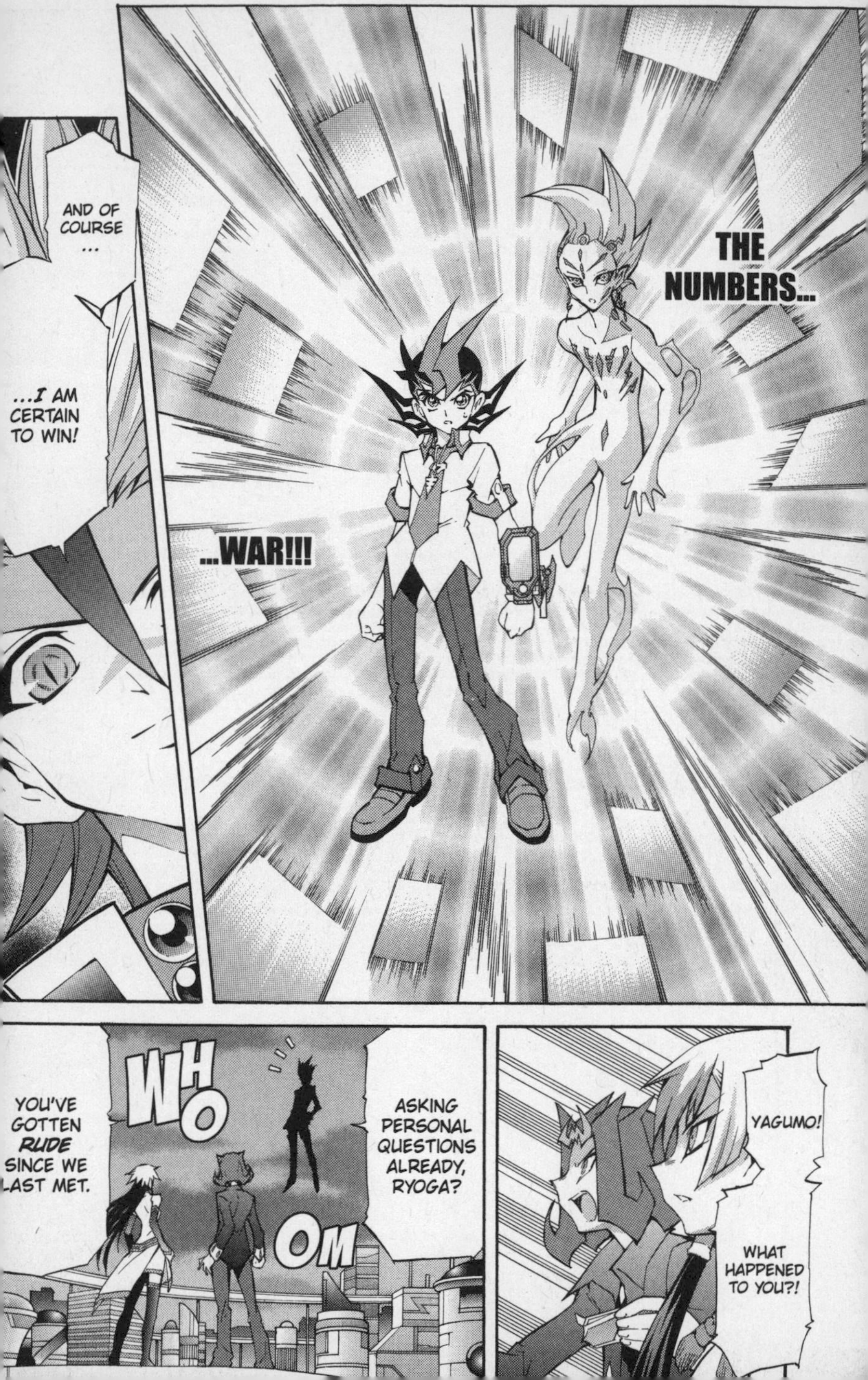
THE NUMBERS...
...WAR!!!
AND OF COURSE ...
...I AM CERTAIN TO WIN!
YAGUMO!
WHAT HAPPENED TO YOU?!
WHOOM
ASKING PERSONAL QUESTIONS ALREADY, RYOGA?
YOU'VE GOTTEN *RUDE* SINCE WE LAST MET.

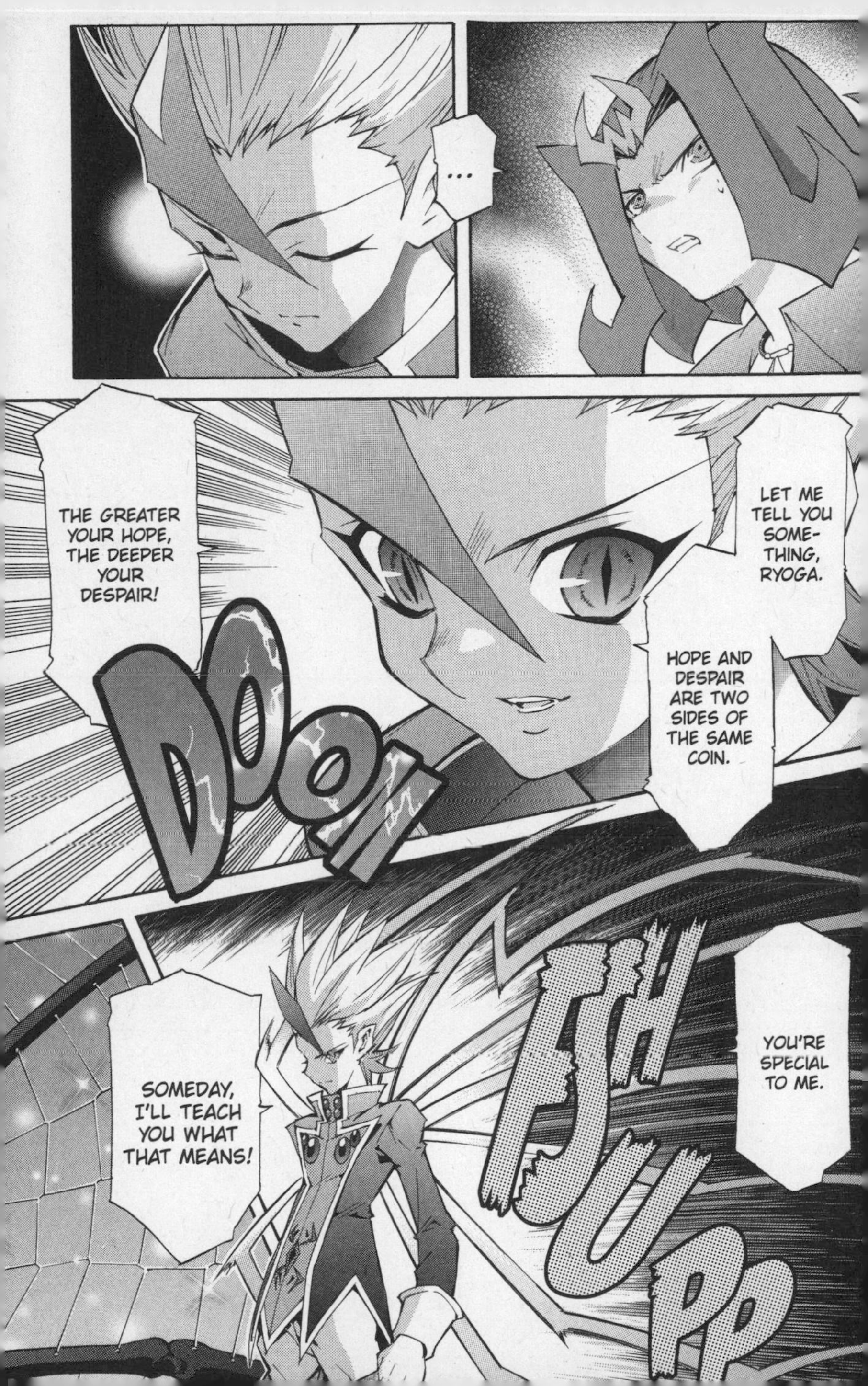
...
LET ME TELL YOU SOMETHING, RYOGA.
HOPE AND DESPAIR ARE TWO SIDES OF THE SAME COIN.
THE GREATER YOUR HOPE, THE DEEPER YOUR DESPAIR!
YOU'RE SPECIAL TO ME.
FSHUPP
SOMEDAY, I'LL TEACH YOU WHAT THAT MEANS!

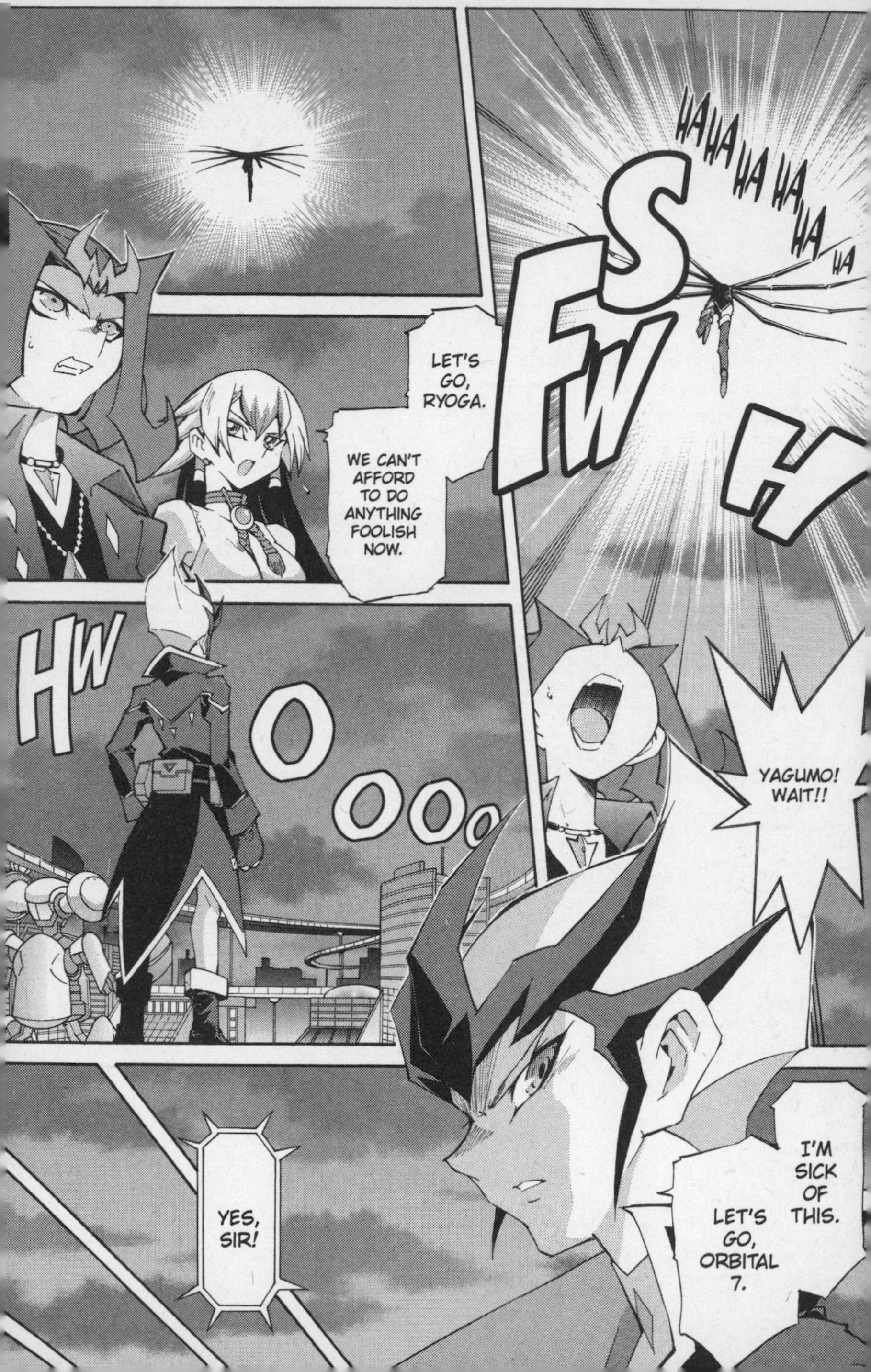
HAHAHAHAHAHAHA
FWSH
LET'S GO, RYOGA.
WE CAN'T AFFORD TO DO ANYTHING FOOLISH NOW.
YAGUMO! WAIT!!
HWOOOO
I'M SICK OF THIS.
LET'S GO, ORBITAL 7.
YES, SIR!

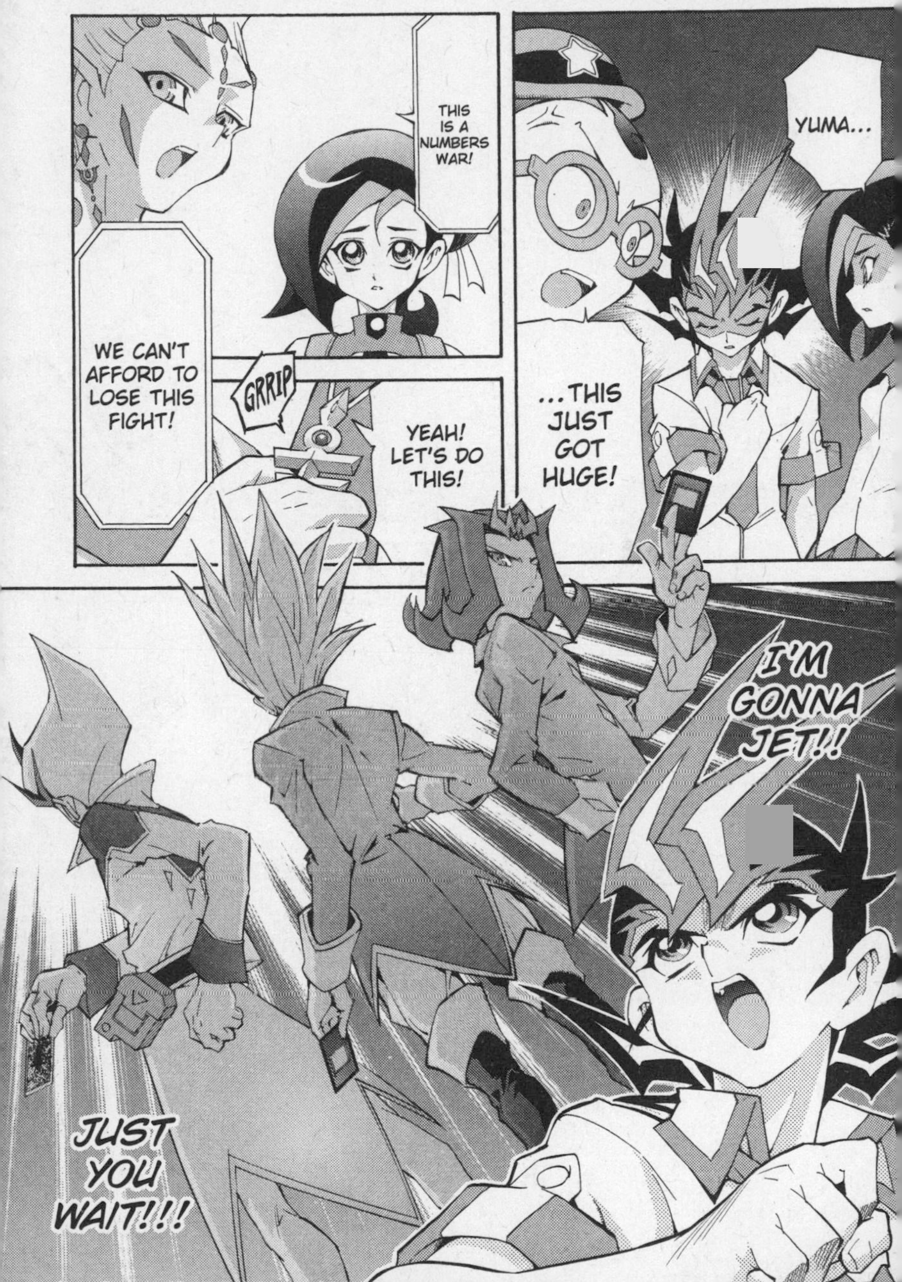
YUMA...
...THIS JUST GOT HUGE!
THIS IS A NUMBERS WAR!
WE CAN'T AFFORD TO LOSE THIS FIGHT!
GRRIP
YEAH! LET'S DO THIS!
I'M GONNA JET!!
JUST YOU WAIT!!!
YU-GI-OH! ZEXAL -VOLUME 4- THE END

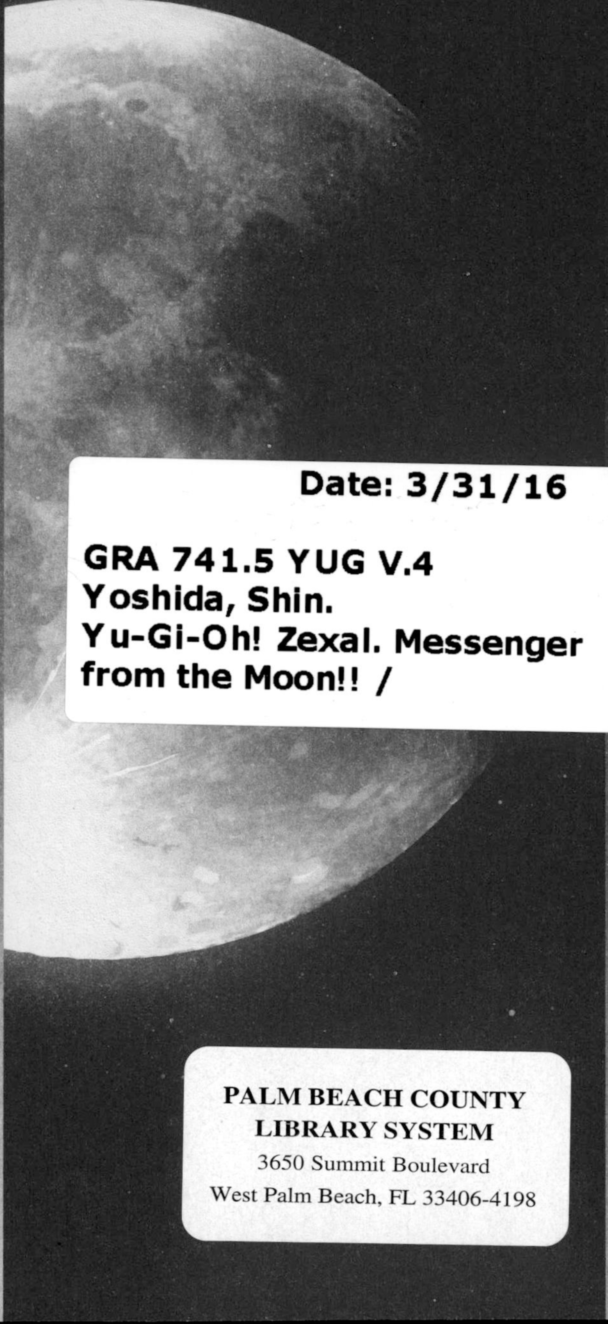

STAFF
KAZUO OCHIAI

TOSHIAKI KATO

MASAHIRO MIURA

FUMITAKA
MURAYAMA

COLORING
TORU SHIMIZU
(COVER)

STUDIO TAC -
TAKUMI YOKOOKA

EDITOR
DAISUKE TERASHI

SUPPORT
GALLOP

YOU ARE READING IN THE WRONG DIRECTION!!

**Whoops!
Guess what?**
You're starting at
the wrong end
of the comic!

...It's true! In keeping with the original Japanese format, *Yu-Gi-Oh! ZEXAL* is meant to be read from right to left, starting in the upper-right corner.

Unlike English, which is read from left to right, Japanese is read from right to left, meaning that action, sound effects and word-balloon order are completely reversed... something which can make readers unfamiliar with Japanese feel pretty backwards themselves. For this reason, manga or Japanese comics published in the U.S. in English have sometimes been published "flopped"—that is, printed in exact reverse order, as though seen from the other side of a mirror.

By flopping pages, U.S. publishers can avoid confusing readers, but the compromise is not without its downside. For one thing, a character in a flopped manga series who once wore in the original Japanese version a T-shirt emblazoned with "M A Y" (as in "the merry month of") now wears one which reads "Y A M"! Additionally, many manga creators in Japan are themselves unhappy with the process, as some feel the mirror-imaging of their art alters their original intentions.

We are proud to bring you Shin Yoshida and Naohito Miyoshi's *Yu-Gi-Oh! ZEXAL* in the original unflopped format. For now, though, turn to the other side of the book and let the duel begin...!

—Editor